Styling Shanghai

Styling Shanghai

Edited by
Christopher Breward and
Juliette MacDonald

BLOOMSBURY VISUAL ARTS
LONDON • NEW YORK • OXFORD • NEW DELHI • SYDNEY

BLOOMSBURY VISUAL ARTS
Bloomsbury Publishing Plc
50 Bedford Square, London, WC1B 3DP, UK
1385 Broadway, New York, NY 10018, USA

BLOOMSBURY, BLOOMSBURY VISUAL ARTS and the Diana logo are trademarks of Bloomsbury Publishing Plc

First published in Great Britain 2020

Cover design by Sharon Mah
Cover image © Adam Katz/Trunk Archive

A catalogue record for this book is available from the British Library.

A catalog record for this book is available from the Library of Congress.

ISBN: HB: 978-1-3500-5114-0
PB: 978-1-3500-5113-3
ePDF: 978-1-3500-5116-4
eBook: 978-1-3500-5115-7

Typeset by RefineCatch Limited, Bungay, Suffolk
Printed and bound in India

To find out more about our authors and books visit www.bloomsbury.com and sign up for our newsletters.

Contents

Illustrations

Figures

Plates

Tables

Notes on Contributors

Djurdja Bartlett is Reader in Histories and Cultures of Fashion at the London College of Fashion, University of the Arts London, where she directs the Transnational Fashion Hub. She is author of *FashionEast: The Spectre That Haunted Socialism* (2010), editor of the volume on East Europe, Russia and the Caucasus in the *Berg Encyclopedia of World Dress and Fashion* (2010) and co-editor of *Fashion Media: Past and Present* (Bloomsbury, 2013). Her new monograph *European Fashion Histories: Style, Society and Politics* (Bloomsbury, 2020) has been funded by an Arts and Humanities Research Council Fellowship grant. She is also editor of the book *Fashion and Politics* (2019).

Anthony Bednall is Acting Director of Manchester Fashion Institute, Manchester Metropolitan University. He works on the relationship between fashion, art, culture and society, was a regular judge at China International Fashion Week and has written articles for newspapers and journals including *China Textiles*, *China Apparel* and *China Fashion Weekly*.

Christopher Breward is Director of Collection and Research at the National Galleries of Scotland and Professorial Fellow at Edinburgh College of Art, University of Edinburgh. He has published widely on the histories of fashion, urban life and masculine style.

Anja Aronowsky Cronberg is the founder and editor of *Vestoj*, a platform for critical thinking in fashion which focuses on the intersection of appearance and themes such as failure, time, power and magic. The *Vestoj Journal* and Salons are produced under the partial patronage of London College of Fashion, where she also works as a Senior Research Fellow in Fashion Theory and Practice. She is currently researching all forms of capital for *Vestoj*'s forthcoming issue, as well as an oral history account of the role of fame in the rise of designer Virgil Abloh.

Antonia Finnane is Honorary Professor in the School of Historical Studies, University of Melbourne, having recently retired from her substantive position there. A specialist in Chinese history, she is the author of *Changing Clothes in China: Fashion, History, Nation* (2007) among other works. She is currently writing a book on clothing production during the Mao years.

Zhong Hong is Professor and Director of International Cooperation at Donghua University in Shanghai. His academic interests include historical and cultural studies related to textile design. He held a number of research and teaching posts at other Chinese and British universities in earlier decades, including Tsinghua University Academy of Art and Design and Durham University.

Yan Lanlan is a lecturer at the School of Fashion Engineering, Shanghai University of Engineering Science. Her research focuses on costume history, fashion culture and clothing social psychology.

Juliette MacDonald is a Senior Lecturer at Edinburgh College of Art, University of Edinburgh and International Dean at Shanghai International College of Fashion and Innovation, Donghua University. She publishes on historical and contemporary craft and design with a particular emphasis on issues of cultural identity and nationalism, consumerism, craft and design theory and practice, and loves Argentine Tango.

Agnès Rocamora is Professor of Social and Cultural Studies at the University of the Arts London. She is the author of *Fashioning the City: Paris, Fashion and the Media* and has published widely on fashion. She is a co-editor of *Thinking Through Fashion: A Guide to Key Theorists*, *The Handbook of Fashion Studies* and *Fashion Media: Past and Present*. She is also a co-founder and co-editor of the *International Journal of Fashion Studies* and is currently working on a book on the influencer economy (with Marco Pedroni).

Bian Xiangyang is Professor at the Fashion & Art Design Institute, Donghua University, President of the Shanghai Museum of Textile & Costume, Vice President of the China Fashion Association and Director of the Shanghai Promotion Center for City of Fashion. His research interests include fashion and textile history and theories, fashion brands and fashion industry, and fashion culture and fashion cities.

Chia-Ling Yang is Senior Lecturer in History of Art at the University of Edinburgh. She works on Chinese painting and cross-cultural exchanges between East and West in the modern era.

Liu Yu is Professor at the Fashion & Art Design Institute, Donghua University, where she is a leading scholar in the field of fashion history and culture. Her research focuses on the history of women's costumes and aesthetics, as well as fashion media and communication. She is the author of *Zhongguo Qipao Wen Hua Shi (The History of the Chinese Qipao)*. Her most recent project is a comparative study of female dress in China and the West.

Acknowledgements

The editors and authors of *Styling Shanghai* are grateful to the Chinese Ministry of Education, Donghua University, Shanghai College of Fashion, Edinburgh College of Art at the University of Edinburgh and London College of Fashion for their support of this publication. Travel, accommodation, research, copyright, editorial and translation costs were supported by an academic collaboration grant from the Chinese Ministry of Education, funding from the International Office of Donghua University, the Research and Knowledge Exchange Office at Edinburgh College of Art and, in the case of Christopher Breward's work and the cover image, the award of a Rita Bolland Fellowship at the Research Center for Material Culture at the Museum Volkenkunde in Leiden during 2016/17. We are particularly indebted to the translation skills of Li-Heng Hsu, the patience and expertise of Frances Arnold and Yvonne Thouroude at Bloomsbury, the incisive comments of our anonymous peer reviewers, and the local intelligence of our student guides in Shanghai, Ruan Yanwen and Tian Zhiwei. Also to Helen Liu (Liu Chunhong) at Donghua University for initiating the project, Frances Corner for her support to LCF colleagues, Chen Cuijue at Shanghai International College of Fashion and Innovation for her time on managing the financial and logistical details, and Jaine Heggie at the National Galleries of Scotland for her support on technical and communication issues. Most importantly, we note here the contribution of all contributors and their collaborators in Shanghai, whose collegial and convivial enthusiasm for the project made for a highly rewarding experience over almost five years in one of the most exciting cities in the world.

1

Introduction

Christopher Breward

Among the many tourist guides to contemporary Shanghai, the handout provided by the cocktail bar and restaurant M on the Bund to trend-hungry travellers in the 2010s provides perhaps the most telling snapshot of entertainment in a city that has become a byword for fashionable pleasures. Its punchy listings of museums, warehouse art galleries, cinemas and concert halls, bookshops, markets, malls and designer stores, restaurants, bars, luxury hotels, spas and parks is both sharply contemporary and worldly in its snappy international-English idioms, but also rooted in a longer history of local tradition and global connection that places Shanghai within its own mythic narratives.[1]

Such is the speed of change within the city, that M's guide is liberally punctuated with website links and advice to seek updated information, yet also holds on to descriptions of outlets for 'old stuff', the 'junk' and material textures that describe a 'classic' Shanghai lexicon of the early twentieth century.[2] It is nevertheless a good source for the new visitor, particularly the new visitor from Australasia, Europe or North America, hungry to taste both sides. From Pudong airport in, the choice of transit between twenty-first-century high-speed Maglev, crowded subway or traffic-choked motorway sets up the contradictions. But once inside the city, which is surprisingly navigable to the novice, time, speed and space conflate and open up, offering an urban experience that is immediately intriguing to those with an interest in the interlinked histories of fashion and cities.

This book, rather like M's guide aims at navigating past and present versions of fashion culture in Shanghai's stimulating environment. In doing so it builds on an extensive literature concerning Shanghai's development as an entrepôt linking China to the world and its localized narratives of consumption, pleasure and creative production, and a more recent interest in tracing networks of fashion cities within the context of global (rather than Eurocentric) histories. Its interests are firmly located in the varied perspectives of a cross-disciplinary and international collective of authors whose objects of focus cohere within the fabric of the city itself, a site we have been privileged to meet, research and discourse in at regular moments over the past five years.

Three Hundred Years of Change

So far as Shanghai is concerned, its story as a cosmopolitan centre for exchange is a unique one, whose circumstances define the distinct characteristics of its fashion cultures and style of presentation in the present. Complex territorial, political and social pressures have come to play varyingly upon the shape and personality of the city, attracting a significant scholarly interest from social, economic and urban historians. For the purposes of this study, a brief summary of growth and flux provides the broader context in which succeeding chapters should be placed.

Emerging as a fishing village at the mouth of the Yangzi river in the Song dynasty, by the mid-seventeenth century with the arrival of the East India Company and other European commercial interests in China, Shanghai had diversified to trade in textiles and tea, though its own interests and that of China at large were increasingly drawn into the damaging opium trade, which by 1839 had forced the first opium war and resulted ten years later in the ceding of Hong Kong to Great Britain and the complete opening up of Shanghai to international trade under the Treaty of Nanjing. Shanghai's location at the cross-point of trading routes between Japan and the West, and into the heartlands of China proved highly attractive to European nations, Russia and the United States. Following intercession by the latter through the 1844 Treaty of Wangxia, the city became subject to the principle of extra-territoriality, which meant that foreigners resident in Shanghai and the other treaty ports were subject to their own national laws, rather than those of China, enjoying an unprecedented level of freedom and establishing a strong expatriate culture within the city's zoned international districts or concessions.[3]

On these principles Shanghai began to grow as a polyglot, but highly demarcated conglomeration of nationalities and industries, marked by the distinctive architectural forms of banks, warehouses, mansions and pleasure palaces centred along the banks of the river. Behind the fine colonial facades an ever-expanding hinterland of slum dwellings housed the thousands of Chinese, escaping from rural poverty and servicing the needs of foreigners.[4] Corruption, inequality and the desire for change resulted in a succession of violent rebellions, which eventually forced Chinese refugees into the Western enclaves, increasing competition for land and fuelling a real estate boom that still marks the city's ethos today. By 1870 Shanghai's Chinese population had exceeded 70,000. In this crowded context the city began to re-fashion itself as a modern metropolis, introducing department stores, tarmacked roads, gas lighting, and by the early twentieth century electricity and trams.[5]

Modernity grasped Shanghai with a power equal to the transformations taking place in Paris, New York, Vienna and London, but the geo-politics of location and history determined that such changes took on distinctively cosmopolitan and commercialized characteristics in the Yangzi Delta. The rapid opening up and modernization of Japan over the previous half-century exerted an inevitable pressure, with the investment of Japanese companies hastening heavy industrialization across the city. This was challenged by the dual influences of a strong tradition of scholarship and progressive thought among the Chinese professional classes. Technological and bureaucratic advancements thus went hand in hand with provocative and revolutionary thinking about the nature of power and an acute understanding of inherited cultures.[6] Rapid change and the social inequalities it brought in its tow inspired political activism, and Shanghai's buzzing streets and salons gave birth first to the nationalist movement of Sun Yat-sen and then in 1921 to the Chinese Communist Party.

Through the 1910s, 1920s and early 1930s Shanghai witnessed both the violent political turmoil of nationalist versus communist struggle, the burgeoning confidence of a local literary and philosophical tradition, and the parallel decadence of expatriate culture. In the latter case, and so far as stereotypical understandings of fashion history go, this was the golden era of Shanghai's reputation as a glamorous and corrupting city of creativity, style and pleasure, known as the 'Paris of the East'.[7] In the concessions, dance halls, cinemas, restaurants and brothels boomed, and while foreign emigres were free to come and go at their leisure, the majority of the local Chinese population were banned from the elegant parks and could only find their place in servile roles of labour or sexual exploitation. Meanwhile, the Nationalist government of Chiang Kai-shek became embroiled in civil war with resurgent communist agitators alongside increased aggression from Japan, who in 1937 cut off Shanghai's river trade with inland China, precipitating industrial decline and the flight of foreign investors from the city.

A decade later, by the rise of Mao Zedong, luminous Shanghai had been reduced to a grey shadow. Its former materialism, metropolitanism, amorality and sophistication symbolized all that the Communist Party sought to eradicate and, in a bid to reclaim its political influence and atone, the city's communist fathers were doubly fanatical in their adherence to the new puritanism. It was no coincidence that Mao chose to launch the Cultural Revolution from the city in

1966. But it was also in this most fluxive and entrepreneurial of cities that the counter-revolution emerged in the 1990s. Under the policies of one-party capitalism promoted by Deng Xiaoping, Shanghai became an autonomous municipality and a 'Special Economic Zone' in which the virtues of trade, development and individualism were encouraged rather than suppressed.[8]

In the twenty-first century Shanghai has changed beyond recognition. Its turn as host of the 2010 World Expo initiated a rash of infrastructure projects, expanding Pudong airport and linking it with the Maglev train and five new subway lines. Inward investment has seen the population double to over 21 million people, attracted by new financial and service industries, expanded manufacturing (not least in fashion and textiles), and served by inner-city and suburban real estate developments and enhanced educational, leisure and cultural facilities. Museums, galleries, shopping malls and restored urban heritage have also brought Chinese and international tourists back to a city that seems to have re-discovered its cosmopolitan past.[9]

Rapid expansion has not come without a significant cost. In common with many other global cities, London and New York among them, the gulf between super-rich and poor has widened, the density of urban living has become oppressive, pollution has increased to unsustainable levels and political and financial corruption rather than meritocratic values appear to drive and taint innovation.[10] But this is the story of urban development the world over, and in Shanghai's case, the rise of China as a political and industrial superpower provides for compelling future scenarios. The usual story of inevitable decline, doesn't quite fit here.[11] One might argue that the concerns of fashion are peripheral to this dramatic three-century narrative, but seen through the spectrum of 'style', a term familiar to the Shanghainese lexicon, the transition of a fishing village to a trading port, to an experiment for cosmopolitan internationalism, to an industrial powerhouse, to a political fulcrum, to a super-city, is a process made material and comprehensible through the clothes of its actors. As the chapters of this book demonstrate bodies and clothes are at the heart, not the periphery of those changes.

Shanghai in the World of Fashion

In an earlier collaboration on the meanings of fashion in the global city, my colleague David Gilbert opened the introduction to our edited collection of essays *Fashion's World Cities* with some reflections on the emergence of Shanghai and Chinese fashion more generally into contemporary debates concerning global flows around fashion. He cited the millennial pledge of Shanghai's mayor, Xu Kuangdi to build the city into the 'world's sixth fashion centre, alongside London, Paris, New York, Milan and Tokyo' and the fashion-focused discussions that supported the siting of the World Expo in the city in 2010. But he also noted the faltering attempts to establish international fashion shows in Shanghai in the intervening period and the deeply ingrained prejudices of an international fashion community refusing to see China as anything other than a convenient source of cheap manufacturing and Western brand-obsessed consumers or an undercutting rival to luxury producers. In the end this disconnect lead us to conclude that Shanghai's status as an aspirant world fashion city set it apart. David's introduction concluded with the observation that 'for all the efforts that its planners and politicians are taking to make Shanghai fit the mould of the fashion world city, this is the place where that mould is likely to be broken'.[12]

More than a decade later, following profound political, economic and technological change across the world, that prediction still holds fairly true. While Shanghai's local fashion culture remains (as several chapters in this book argue) a vibrant and distinctive one, its values and textures are increasingly shared with mega-cities across the globe. Its intense sense of hyper-modernity produced through its hybrid cultural practices has also become almost a self-fulfilling prophecy, demarcating and pushing, as authors including Meng Yue and Alexander Des Forges have argued, at the city's limits as a stable concept.[13]

At the same time, the certainties and characteristics that once defined the 'classic' world fashion cities of Paris, London, New York, Milan and Tokyo (a flexible manufacturing base, availability of specialist local production skills, proximity to respected fashion education institutes, developed media and promotional industries, a heritage of elite fashion production and consumption, and connections to other cultural industries including contemporary art or film) now seem quaintly twentieth century in their references. In a world where intensive gentrification has set cities like Paris, London or New York well out of reach of the very workers and aspirant fashion designers who guaranteed their status, and when the flattening power of social media bloggers, online business, instantaneous gratification and a collapsed understanding of copyright have rendered redundant the ideas of a fashion elite or ordered, top-down, seasonal promotion, the very term 'fashion city' has become an anachronism.

In this context perhaps Shanghai has nothing to prove in its claims to international fashion relevance? It is what it is, 'many-sided ... unique among the cities of the world ... almost indescribable', as Jeffrey Wasserstorm attests in an interesting article on its contemporary energy and complex relationship to academic practices of comparison.[14] And yet it is surprising how rarely its unique take on style has captured the attention of writers on fashion. While scholars including Antonia Finnane, Wessie Ling, Simona Segre Reinach, Valerie Steele and Wu Juanjuan have produced substantive works on the broader history and culture of fashionable dress in China and institutions from the V&A, London to the Costume Institute at the Metropolitan Museum of Art, New York have hosted major exhibitions on the same theme, China's first fashion city has not, as yet, received discrete attention as a fashion phenomenon in its own right.[15]

Situating Shanghai Style

In positioning a range of chapters and approaches that combine accounts of historical fashion change in Shanghai over time, focused case studies and perspectives informed by social history, art and design history, sociology, biography and the broader profession of style journalism, this collection shares an interest, then, in accounting for the distinctiveness of Shanghai as a fashion capital and the ways in which its hybrid cultures have produced concepts and forms of fashion that capitalize on the city's 'foreign' status, within and beyond China, and its openness to innovative patterns of fashion production, representation and consumption. It aims to put Shanghai style back on the map.

A particular feature of the collection is its genesis as a collaborative project between academic institutions in Shanghai, London and Edinburgh, funded by the Chinese Ministry of Education, and intended to foster international research collaboration and new understandings of Shanghai's reputation as a global centre for fashion education, production and promotion. Chapters developed over a three-year period of archival and field study, and in a context of mutual critique and discussion between Chinese, European and Australian authors. The arising cultural, methodological and historiographical challenges of working across disciplinary, political and geographical boundaries became part of the experience, and the book retains the multi-vocal flavour of a project and a city that seeks to celebrate sartorial and scholarly diversity. Whilst at times the object-focused, precise delineation of successive style changes important to our Shanghai-based colleagues seemed at odds with the contextual interests of European scholarship in the humanities and social sciences, the complementary textures of both traditions offer a kaleidoscopic perspective only possible when viewed through a city such as Shanghai. We have, then, deliberately retained the distinctive address and approach of Chinese and European academic writing styles, a reminder of the city's partitioned, concessionary past.

The collection focuses on the twentieth and twenty-first centuries, constructing a history of Shanghai's fashion cultures that starts in the early Republican period, during a moment of industrial consolidation and political reform, tracing the ways in which Shanghai's openness to international influences informed an exciting engagement with concepts of modernity, hybridity and modernization. It considers the ways in which Shanghai's pre-eminence as a city of fashion was challenged during the mid-twentieth century and traces the resurgence of the city's status as a style capital following the reforms of the late 1980s and 1990s.

Zhong Hong's chapter opens the book with a historical perspective on textile designs, produced in Shanghai and shaped by the clashes of cultural and political forces during the twentieth century. The purpose of his study is to show the key factors that made Shanghai the most important centre in China for fashion ideas and products through a period of radical social and economic change, and to illustrate how the visual vocabulary of fashion and textiles were influenced by industrial innovations, political ideologies and imported aesthetic values. The angle of the analysis is focused on the textile designers who produced the patterns and images on textiles (especially printed textiles), and considers the training they received, the professional resources and technological conditions they worked with, and the cultural and political environment they were confined within.

Generations of Shanghai textile designers were trained in art and technical colleges to meet the demands of a changing population of consumers. From the early factory-based training systems where students were tutored by European designers, to the emergence of Surface Pattern Design courses set up by Chinese artists returning from visits to Europe, America and Japan, systems of art education became increasingly sophisticated. For example, Lei Guiyuan who went from Shanghai to Paris in the early years of the twentieth century, brought back a fresh perspective to established textile design circles, and also wrote a number of important books on design that formed the foundation for Chinese design education in succeeding years. Similarly key textile technologists such as Chen Weiji were trained at Leeds University in the United Kingdom (where a significant collection of Chinese patterned textiles contributed by staff and students has been kept), and brought back to Shanghai new models for the textile curriculum in the 1930s, establishing a modernized education and research basis for the textile and clothing industries in China during the Republican period.

As several chapters in the book attest, people in China were regularly subject to changing dress codes after the regime changes of the early twentieth century. This continued after 1949, when the new political force of communism was in firm control of the state and Maoist norms dominated all forms and contents of visual presentations in society, including textile design. A greater influence from the Soviet Union was evident in the 1950s, and the political restrictions and propaganda values of visual imagery were pushed to an extreme during the Cultural Revolution. However, designers did find limited room to stretch their creativity and skills in designing products targeted for export markets, or to meet foreign tastes. Dress design was covered in textile design courses before the early 1980s when fashion design eventually split from textile design departments in Chinese art academies, and fashion education in China has expanded dramatically ever since.

As Zhong's chapter demonstrates, Shanghai has risen, sometimes in the face of serious barriers, to become the most important city for the creation of Chinese textiles and fashion in the modern era, with a far-reaching influence in terms of productivity, style and knowledge. Although there were periods when a top-down push led to the mass relocation of production lines with expertise from Shanghai to other parts of the country, or as in more recent years when all textile printing mills have moved to the peripheral areas in the region, the city has remained a powerhouse for fashion trends and a hub for design creativity, nurtured in part by the underlying presence of cloth in Shanghai's DNA.

Moving from cloth to clothing, Liu Yu's chapter demonstrates how, against a background of rising Western feminism and the Chinese 'New Culture Movement', a new kind of women's wear called "Wenming Xin Zhuang" (Civilized Costume) appeared in Shanghai during the early twentieth century. This simple look came to dominate conceptions of style for modern and progressive womanhood for a short but decisive period in the history of Chinese fashion. The characteristics of this new style, which radically reconstructed the traditional image of Chinese femininity, were a short blouse and matching long skirt. The look abandoned complicated decoration and luxury embroidery and introduced a completely fresh concept, representing new knowledge and a new society. On the other hand, as Liu argues, under the design idea of changing old patterns into new dress types through simplification, the style still reserved a sense of traditional charm, so that the new look was also called 'making the past serve the present'.

Compared with the other, more familiar, new style of '*qipao*' which succeeded and overshadowed it, 'Civilized Costume' enjoyed a relatively short period of popularity, and was accepted by fewer people, but it still represents an important innovation and its history as a fashion trend that affected women's lives in a crucial period of modernization cannot be neglected. The question of why it was substituted by the *qipao* is worth pursuing, for the light it throws on a deeper understanding of women's clothing concepts and life conditions at that time, and the nature of Shanghai as an emerging centre for progressive sartorial trends.

'Civilized Costume' marked the beginning of a revolution in traditional Chinese female styles. It preceded and created the conditions necessary for the emergence of *qipao* and its subsequent rise to popularity. Because 'Civilized Costume' did not remain the consistent vanguard and vogue, it was eventually replaced by *qipao* and was unable to represent the new style of women's clothes in the Republic of China. However, it reflected the open-mindedness of society in the Republic of China (particularly in Shanghai) as well as encouraging women's hybrid pursuit of basic and fashionable Western clothing styles, based on the maintenance of key Chinese traditions.

For Bian Xiangyang and Yan Lanlan, Shanghai was the undisputed fashion centre of China during the period of the Republic and, like 'Civilized Costume', the appearance of *qipao* was the outcome of a meeting of Western and Chinese cultures. It functioned both as fashionable women's wear, but also as an icon of the Shanghai Modern movement, becoming a model for Chinese costume culture and fashion, and also attracting the world's attention. Their chapter's assertions are made on the basis of the principles of Chinese historical method, and the social psychology of clothing and iconology, and draw on many primary materials in Shanghai's archives and collections including newspapers, magazines, painted and photographed images and sartorial objects.

The goal of the chapter is to analyse and discuss the original time, place and consumer context for the introduction of *qipao* fashion; to compile a chronicle of *qipao* fashion from 1925 to 1941; to summarize the initial style and wear combinations of *qipao*; and to analyse the broader social psychology of *qipao* fashion in Shanghai. It draws some tentative conclusions. Firstly, *qipao* as a form of 'one-piece' dress was not inherited directly from the robe of the Banner Style. It was a new fashion in the 1920s, which combined the elements of the long vest called *qipao* Majia, Wenming Xin Zhuang (see Liu Yu's complementary chapter) and Western dress. Secondly, the period from 1925 to 1941 was *qipao*'s golden age during which *qipao*'s style changed very fast and frequently. The chapter thus collates a detailed chronicle of *qipao*'s style year by year, including the features of the *qipao* fashion trend, the typical habits and appearance of *qipao* dressing, and the variety of *qipao* images available to consumers. Thirdly, as the 'Paris of the East', Shanghai fashion culture was deeply influenced by Western clothing, which created a Westernized 'Shanghai style'. Many forms of traditional dress absorbed Western styles and *qipao* was the most typical fashion of this type. Fourthly, the acceptance of *qipao* was mainly due to its unique aesthetic character, the ease of its production and consumption as well as the circumstances of the social background of that time. Indeed, it became the daily wear of many Chinese women after 1927, barely five years from its initial introduction.

Using modernity as the contextual lens, Juliette MacDonald's chapter reflects on the relationship between popular dance practices, urban leisure spaces, fashion and fashionability in Shanghai in the early decades of the twentieth century. By the 1920s popular dance and dance halls were providing an exciting spectacle within the city and making an important contribution to the entertainment culture in this era. *The North China Herald* highlights this growth of interest in an article from 1919 which commented on the 'veritable [dance] craze' that had gripped Shanghai. Asia scholar Andrew Field has produced detailed work on the night culture of the city in works such as *Shanghai's Dancing World: Cabaret Culture and Urban Politics, 1919–1954* and *Shanghai Nightscapes: The Nocturnal Biography of a Global Metropolis, 1912–2012*. However, the role of fashion within this context has not received such in-depth coverage. The close relationship between fashion, dance and the burgeoning film industry of Shanghai was central to the construction of the cult of wealth, glamour and beauty, and dance halls were the ideal spaces for film stars and other celebrities to gather to promote themselves and their fashionability. This creation of innovative consumer-based transcultural forms represents a vibrant conversation between Orientalism and Occidentalism which the chapter explores and develops.

Drawing on descriptions of Shanghai's dance scene in the 1920s by writers such as Zhou Shoujuan whose short stories were published in the popular newspaper *Shanghai Huaboa* and other articles and newspaper items from the period, as well as personal diary accounts from ex-patriot residents and visitors to the city, Juliette maps some of the principal associations between dance, fashion and pleasure. In a city known for its 'exotic' decadence (and one only need look at the many names given to signal Shanghai's place in the collective fantasy of the exotic: 'Paris of the East', 'Sin City', the 'wickedest city in the world'), this reading of Shanghai offers a fascinating perspective on a persistent trope of the city's enduring style identity.

Djurdja Bartlett's chapter is dedicated to the sartorial choices of Soong Ching-ling and Soong May-ling, who were born into an influential and affluent Shanghai family in 1893 and 1898, respectively. Their father Charlie Soong made his wealth in printing and banking. Socially progressive and American-educated himself, he had sent his daughters to study in America at the turn of the century. Following their returns, Soong Ching-ling and Soong May-ling became involved in the social and political life of their homeland, which was changing rapidly from a backward, feudal country into a modern state.

Soong Ching-ling and Soong May-ling took an active part in shaping and promoting the very different narratives of modern China, both through their marriages to the two politically most powerful men in the Chinese interwar period, and through their own politically motivated activities, stretching up to the end of their lives in 1981 and 2003, respectively. Soong Ching-ling married the first President of the Republic of China, Sun Yat-sen, and Soong May-ling his ideological enemy, Chiang Kai-shek. Accordingly, both sisters turned into celebrated figures in the ideologically opposing camps of modern Chinese history.

Additionally, numerous media accounts and a number of biographies, published both in China and in the West in the last couple of decades, as well as some more recent lavish biographical feature films, have contributed to their mythical status in mainland China and the West (Soong Ching-ling), and in Taiwan and the West (Soong May-ling). In academia, on the other hand, both their political activities and their sartorial choices have been considered mostly as part of wider historical analyses.

While Djurdja's chapter feeds on existing biographical, political, cultural and historical fashion research, it also focuses on the relationship between the sisters' respective political beliefs and their respective styles of dress, in order to explore the notions of cosmopolitanism, national identity, gender, femininity and the modern Chinese family in the interwar period and beyond. Moreover, a careful analysis of the original Chinese and Western visual sources not only contextualizes the differences in the sisters' looks within their different ideological positions but offers new readings of the notions of Orient and Occident within the framework of this topic.

Raised in an environment that offered the best of both the East and the West, both Soong Ching-ling and Soong May-ling were at home with the world, while remaining Chinese. Yet, their cosmopolitan practices sheltered different national identities, and this initial difference informed their respective concepts of dress, gender and femininity. While Soong May-ling famously said, 'My face is the only Chinese thing about me', she skilfully played with the West's expectations of the Orient, by almost exclusively wearing brightly coloured *qipao*, and seducing the West with her very traditional femininity. In contrast, Soong Ching-ling declared that the 1912 Chinese revolution was the most important date in world history of the twentieth century, but proved her internationalist credentials by easily slipping between an elegant black *qipao* and Western-style dresses throughout her life.

The chapter also addresses some important similarities between the sisters. By taking an active role in their husbands' professional careers, they played a very important part in the formation of a new type of the Chinese family during the Republican period. Moreover, both Soong Ching-ling and Soong May-ling moved from being equal partners in their marriages to pursuing their own political careers by the time of the interwar period and beyond, and so presented two very different but equally modern faces of China to the world. In these connections, tensions and contradictions the Soong sisters emerge as personifications of the hybrid and contradictory nature of Shanghai itself.

In common with other authors in *Styling Shanghai*, Chia-Ling Yang asserts that the radical shift in Chinese dressing especially after the defeat in the Sino-Japanese War (1894–5) shows a relationship between dress and the country's determination for modernization. Although Western cultures had had a visible presence in everyday life in the international settlements such as Shanghai since 1843, it was as part of this post-war reaction that Chinese learned society came to realize that the old ways should be abolished, including clothing that transcended cultural inertia, and that traditionalism should be reconsidered in their search for modernity. This increasing demand for new clothing styles as 'image signifiers' of a modernized nation was fuelled by both women and men.

As a series of articles published in Shanghai in 1911 noted, changing cloth was a crucial matter for creating a new national identity; polarity of opinion and social attitudes were subsequently focused on commenting on institutional official uniform, students' wear, and on creating a new look for professional women and men in the city. The new fashionable ways of life were firmly established and evidenced by the late 1920s with the popular media publishing photographs of celebrities and glamorous designs to suggest metropolitan styles of living. Nonetheless, debates on 'What should the Chinese wear?' and 'Where is the "Chineseness" in its global construction?' continued from the Republican era to the communist regime, and such confusion and pliancy has also been brought to consideration of sartorial discourse in China today.

The study focuses on pictorial magazines and newspapers, taking the graphic artist, fashion illustrator and designer Zhang Guangyu (1900–1965) and others who followed as key examples. Such figures regularly contributed their fashion designs, cartoons, comments and photographs of fashionably dressed women in the daily news media. Through a series of case studies, the chapter's aim is to investigate how Shanghai painters, without receiving any formal training in fashion or dress-making, turned to become influential fashion designers, and how they incorporated inspirations from various sources. It also discusses the development of fashion and the cultural dimension in Shanghai in relation to its image-makers and media as part of the modernist movement. Crucially, Chia-Ling argues for a broader perception of modernist aesthetics traditionally limited to movements in literature, music, theatre and mainstream painting by higher institutions of artists or intellectuals, recognizing this as connecting to the extended domain of human sensitivity and public interest, as part of the history and changing fabric of economy and everyday life in Shanghai before 1949.

At a fundamental level the chapter asks: who has the insight to consider the 'look' of the Chinese? Why has a hybridity of Eastern and Western styled clothing been designed for and suggested to a mass public? And why should the trends of fashion illustration be considered as a modernist aesthetic linked to vernacular forms of modernism? The fluidity and diversity of arising styles, which have varied dramatically by class, region and gender, suggest that this history of indigenous Shanghai fashion illustrators in popular pictorials from the late 1910s to the 1930s offers a complementary perspective to current scholarship, adding a new art historical element to our understanding of the history of everyday life in Shanghai in this pivotal period.

Georg Lukács fondly imagined that socialism would enable a society to recover from the cultural devastation inflicted by capitalism and reconnect with an authentic, pre-capitalist culture. This scenario was patently not realized in communist China, where the principle of 'breaking with the past' was only slightly qualified by a nationalist atavism. In Shanghai a strong cultural identity had emerged in the course of capitalist development and urban growth over the preceding century. The most obvious outcome of the imposition of socialism here was cultural loss, manifest not least in the textiles and apparel sector. Tailors, key contributors to the fabrication of Shanghai's modern look in the Republican era, left Shanghai in droves in 1949, establishing themselves in Hong Kong and Taiwan where they became the tailors of choice for mainland émigrés and international tourists. In the subdued political and economic climate of 1950s Shanghai, those who remained had to lend themselves not to rediscovering a pre-capitalist culture but to creating a post-capitalist one. Antonia Finnane's chapter draws on this sense of loss and flux and explores the process whereby industry participants and political players sought to align themselves with the socialist project, while old clothing dealers, street hawkers and dissident dressmakers or consumers produced a counter-narrative of covert dandyism and 'deviant dress'. In it she argues that despite the homogenization of material culture under communist rule, Shanghai maintained its cultural distinctiveness, managing to remain a byword for style even under a regime that was at best ambivalent about fashion.

Similarly, Anthony Bednall's complementary chapter shows how, against the context of a century or more of economic, social and political developments in China, fashion or clothing has acted as a representational and symbolic illustration of a culture trying to clarify its own existential questions. Its urban populations, with Shanghai being the most vibrant, have negotiated unparalleled turmoil and seismic societal and economic change, which contributed to individual and collective dress styles and represented the birth and rebirth of a series of distinctive cultural and sartorial codes.

Shanghai's continuation as a consumer city with its multinational imperial heritage was always going to be ideologically at odds post-1949, when the city was 'liberated' by the forces of the New Republic. With mature light and textile industries already existing and a well-conceived infrastructure, Shanghai should have been ideally located to support the new regime's first five-year plan of industrialization and the move to a totalitarian narrative of self-reliance. This did not initially transpire as the new government focused away from the city ports in a policy of Soviet-designed mechanization. As a producer of commodities such as shoes, textiles and garments (and although considered a centre for innovation), Shanghai's commerce and its working population would inevitably be dramatically affected by central policy, evident in the tragic consequences of the Great Leap Forward, earlier poor cotton crop harvests and the general failure to build and grow textile production in a sustainable manner.

With severe shortages in resources and ration coupons for all textile products including lengths of sewing thread, clothing was not particularly high on the social or political agenda in the early years of the 1960s. All across China garments were referred to as 'new for three years, old for three years, fixed for another three years' and the propaganda of frugality became a common message. As early as October 1957, the Shanghai Cultural Department in conjunction with the Shanghai Textile Company produced a pattern-cutting book showing practical examples of how to re-work and re-model existing garments. The book entitled *New Clothes from Old Clothes* set the tone of the times in its introductory statement: 'Lessening resources and raw materials, significant volumes of historic pre-worn and waste garments and inefficient and ineffective ways to recycle garments and fabrics on a commercial scale.'

There was a brief respite from severe hardship in 1964–6, when production increased and the party leaders took a more pragmatic and somewhat commercial approach to the overarching communist philosophies. Rationing was relaxed and urban areas such as Shanghai started producing and trading in greater volumes adding to the choices available in fabrics and products. While recovery developed, crisis ensued, as the Red Army of young people under the direction of Chairman Mao instigated the Cultural Revolution in 1966. If there was already a proliferation of a homogenized visual code for the population it was violently reinforced, as handmade and surplus military uniforms for all genders became de rigueur.

Shanghai and its population through both dystopian and normative scenarios, like other cities across the country, already had an appetite to associate and stylistically align with cultural heroes, but from 1966 not doing so was often life threatening. Anthony's chapter thus reveals the personal narratives and contextual references which illustrate how ordinary individuals in Shanghai managed to procure and adapt clothing for themselves and their families in this volatile era; it records how they responded to the expectations of visual codes and identifies how these were often modified and personalized, with a view to recognizing that individuality, no matter how discreet, managed to find a role even in the harshest of conditions.

Despite these deprivations and beyond its association either with the constructed 'exotic' femininity of *qipao* or asexual uniformity of Cultural Revolution era dressing, Shanghai has also developed a distinct reputation for the craft skills associated with traditional menswear, particularly suits and shirts. It also enjoys a cultural heritage informed by a number of masculine stereotypes, many of them carrying strong sartorial associations (artists and the literati at the turn of the twentieth century, film stars and colonials in the 1920s and 1930s, celebrities, fashion leaders, taste makers and models in the 1990s and early 2000s).

My own chapter on the Shanghai dandy analyses these three categories, considering the material context of menswear design and production in the historical and contemporary city, the narratives and cultural representations attending the question of masculine fashionability in Shanghai through the twentieth century, and the playing out of local and global influences in their dissemination via the contemporary fashion media (the global style magazines produced for a Chinese and Asian market that are ubiquitous on Shanghai's twenty-first-century news-stands).

There is a limited, but growing secondary literature on tailoring industries and styles in Shanghai, masculinities and sexuality in China, on screen studies in relation to Shanghai-based male stars, and on the business of fashion magazines and masculine consumption. The chapter draws on all of these, producing a portrait of the Shanghai dandy rooted in the city and distinct from his European and American counterparts, but also intimately connected to shared histories and hybrid influences.

Throughout the 1990s Shanghai experienced an unprecedented programme of urban renewal, economic restructuring and growth that fuelled the consuming practices of both men and women. The city shifted from a manufacturing economy to one focused on finance, real estate and the service sector. This urban and economic shift was reflected in the restructuring of the spatial organization of the city, with skyscrapers, avenues and newly constructed roads central to its reshaping and globalization. Agnès Rocamora's chapter looks at the role of one particular type of urban formation in the redefinition of the city: the luxury shopping mall. Indeed, in the 1990s and following China's post-Cultural Revolution opening to the West as well as the Party-state's adoption of a socialist market economy, the city saw the emergence and rapid proliferation of luxury shopping malls. Multi-storey buildings hosting international brands such as Fendi, Chanel, Louis Vuitton or Coach are recurring sights in the city. Plaza 66, CITIC and Westgate Mall (known as the Golden Triangle of luxury malls) are only a few among the still rising list of luxury shopping malls.

The chapter reflects on the role of such malls in building the definition of Shanghai as a fashion city in the context both of the city's geography of fashion spaces such as department stores, concept stores, international fashion chains and independent fashion stores, and of China as the third largest luxury market in the world in 2015, after the US and Japan. Besides critically engaging with texts from the fields of Chinese studies, luxury studies, fashion studies, studies in consumer culture and urban studies, it also draws on ethnographic work conducted across the city and its luxury shopping malls in 2015 and 2016. It particularly focuses on three shopping malls, all located at a walking distance on the Nanjing Lu – Kerry; Réel; Plaza 66 – to ask: what roles do luxury shopping malls have in the definition of Shanghai and its ambition to be a 'world-class city'? What do they say about Shanghai and its recent development? And how do they participate in China's urban development and its recent embrace of neo-liberalism, consumerism and globalization? Interrogating the malls' spatial formation and surroundings, as well as the system of signs and the material culture they host and anchor in the centre of Shanghai, Agnes contributes to understandings of the significance of urban spaces and locales in the making of a fashion city, as well as to debates on contemporary consumer culture in China.

Finally, Anja Aronowsky Cronberg reflects on the words of Didier Grumbach, one-time president of the Chambre Syndicale de la Haute Couture in Paris, who made the statement that 'there will never be a Chinese fashion industry' during a 2013 interview with the author. His comment appears emblematic of the way many opinion leaders in the mainstream fashion industry view recent attempts by Chinese designers to establish themselves in Europe and America. In Anja's chapter, informed by her experience as a journalist, she examines this attitude, dominant in part perhaps due to a lingering 'Orientalist' attitude and because there is a lot at stake for an industry in Europe and the United States that still relies on China for cheap production, as well as consumption of Western luxury fashion on a grand scale.

The few Chinese fashion designers who are creating a name for themselves in the West are predominately educated abroad, or have strong family ties in the market they are established in. The best-known Chinese designers of recent decades are in fact Chinese-American (New York-based Mary Ping, Anna Sui, Jade Lai and Alexander Wang being good examples), and typically produce their garments in China (often in family-run factories), but show their collections in New York. Newer internationally recognized Shanghai-based designers such as Masha Ma, Ziggy Chen and Uma Wang have all studied in the West (typically at Central Saint Martins in London), and use their time abroad to institute connections that aid their subsequent presence at one of the four main Western fashion capitals (New York, Milan, London or New York).

Though a domestic fashion scene and industry is beginning to take shape in China, as evidenced by the establishment of fashion weeks, showrooms and stores in Beijing, Shanghai and several second- and third-tier cities, for many the ambition is still to become successful in the West: the number of Chinese designers who have a presence during the Paris, London, Milan and New York fashion weeks is growing with every season, though many appear to be struggling to acquire prominent slots during the calendar as well as sufficient attention from Western press and buyers.

It has become apparent in recent work on fashion and China that Paris is the most desirable fashion city for Chinese designers to be present in, and Shanghai the Chinese city with the most vibrant fashion scene. Anja's study thus focuses on the experiences and words of Shanghai-based designers who either already have a presence during Paris fashion week, or who aim to do so in the future. Her chapter examines where contemporary Chinese fashion design sits in the world in terms of distinctiveness and reputation, how young Chinese designers regard the Western-dominated fashion industry, and how this fashion system sees them in return. By talking to both opinion leaders in the Western and Chinese fashion industries and to Chinese designers who work abroad as well as those who have elected to stay in China about what a successful career constitutes to them, and whether making it abroad is still considered an important part of this, Anja discovers a privileged insight into the current condition of Chinese fashion, and anticipates where it is headed in the immediate future. Once more, Shanghai style finds itself positioned as a barometer, measuring the contrasting pressures exerted between old and new, East and West.

Conclusion

Styling Shanghai thus constructs a complex history of the city's fashion cultures, starting in the Republican period, during a moment of political reform and industrial consolidation, marking a period of disruption and catastrophic change in the middle years of the twentieth century and ending in the twenty-first century as Shanghai emerges from three decades of rapid development and enters into a new relationship with the world. Throughout all of this, as the chapters in this book variously demonstrate, the textures and surfaces of its vestimentary character, informed by hybrid influences and the forces of modernity, have produced a distinctive sartorial imprint that deserves recognition alongside those more familiar centres of fashion production in Europe and North America.

In 1934 H.J. Letherbridge opened his travel guide to Shanghai with a fanfare: 'Shanghai, sixth city of the World! Shanghai, The Paris of the East! Shanghai, the New York of the West! Shanghai the most cosmopolitan city in the world, the fishing village on a mudflat which almost literally overnight became a great metropolis.'[16] M on the Bund could not have put it better in 2018. In compiling this guide to the layered histories of style in the city over a century and a half we hope we have come some way towards providing a sense of its endless fascinations and contradictions, and setting up some questions for further research.

Notes

1 http://www.m-restaurantgroup.com/glam/wp-content/uploads/sites/4/2016/07/Sep2016_MShanghaiGuide.pdf.

2 H.J. Letherbridge, *All About Shanghai: A Standard Guidebook* (Shanghai: Shanghai University Press, 1934).

3 G. Lanning and S. Couling, *The History of Shanghai: Part I* (Shanghai: Kelly & Walsh, 1921); Linda Cooke Johnson, *Shanghai: From Market Town to Treaty Port 1074–1858* (Stanford, CA: Stanford University Press, 1995).

4 Hanchao Lu, *Beyond the Neon Lights: Everyday Shanghai in the Early Twentieth Century* (Berkeley, CA: University of California Press, 1999).

5 Wen-hsin Yeh, *Shanghai Splendour: Economic Sentiments and the Making of Modern China, 1843–1949* (Berkley, CA: University of California Press, 2007), Sherman Cochran (ed.), *Inventing Nanjing Road: Commercial Culture in Shanghai, 1900–1945* (Ithaca, NY: Cornell University East Asia Program, 2000).

6 Leo Ou-fan Lee, *Shanghai Modern: The Flowering of a New Urban Culture in China, 1930–1945* (Cambridge, MA: Harvard University Press, 1999).

7 Catherine Vance Yeh, *Shanghai Love: Courtesans, Intellectuals, and Entertainment Culture, 1850–1910* (Seattle, WA: University of Washington Press, 2006).

8 Christopher Howe (ed.), *Shanghai: Revolution and Development in an Asian Metropolis* (Cambridge: Cambridge University Press, 1981).

9 Marie-Claire Bergere, *Shanghai: China's Gateway to Modernity* (Stanford, CA: Stanford University Press, 2009).

10 Jeffrey N. Wasserstrom, *Global Shanghai, 1850–2010: A History in Fragments* (London: Routledge, 2009).

11 Stella Dong, *Shanghai: The Rise and Fall of a Decadent City* (New York: HarperCollins, 2000).

12 David Gilbert, 'From Paris to Shanghai: The Changing Geographies of Fashion's World Cities' in Christopher Breward and David Gilbert (eds), *Fashion's World Cities* (Oxford: Berg, 2006), 3–32.

13 Meng Yue, *Shanghai and the Edges of Empires* (Minneapolis, MN: University of Minnesota Press, 2006); Alexander Des Forges, *Mediasphere Shanghai: The Aesthetics of Cultural Production* (Honolulu, HA: University of Hawaii Press, 2007).

14 Jeffrey N. Wasserstrom, 'Is Global Shanghai "Good to Think"? Thoughts on Comparative History and Post-Socialist Cities', *Journal of World History*, Vol. 18, No. 2 (June 2007), 199–234.

15 Andrew Bolton (ed.), *China: Through the Looking Glass* (New Haven, CT: Yale University Press, 2015); Antonia Finnane, *Changing Clothing in China* (New York: Columbia University Press, 2008); Wessie Ling and Simona Segre-Reinach (eds), *Fashion in Multiple Chinas: Chinese Styles in the Transglobal Landscape* (London: I.B. Tauris, 2018); Valerie Steele and John Major, *China Chic: East Meets West* (New Haven, CT: Yale University Press, 1999); Wu Juanjuan, *Chinese Fashion: From Mao to Now* (Oxford: Berg, 2009); Zhang Hongxing and Lauren Parker (eds), *China Design Now* (London: V&A Publications, 2008).

16 Letherbridge, *All About Shanghai*, 1.

2

A Century of Chinese Printed Textiles in Shanghai

Zhong Hong

Introduction

The purpose of this chapter is to illustrate the key factors that made Shanghai such an important centre in China for textile designs and fashionable styles through diverse historic periods, and to explain how the visual vocabulary of fashion and textiles were shaped by technical innovations, political ideologies, and both inherited and imported aesthetic values. The angle of the analysis focuses on the textile designers who produced the patterns and images on printed textiles, considering such aspects as the training they received, the professional resources and technological conditions they worked with, and the cultural and political environment they were confined within.

Limiting the scope of discussions to printed textiles, out of the wide range of textiles produced in China, is based on the consideration that for ordinary people printed textiles are the most common and affordable patterned fabrics for clothing, with the most diverse ranges of motifs and sensitive in responding to the changes of social and political currents. In comparison to printed textiles, for instance, woven textiles like silk brocades produced in the same periods were often limited to centuries-old traditional Chinese patterns, too expensive for everyday domestic consumption, and often aimed at foreign currencies, while machine-knitted textiles were also produced with a very limited range of simple patterns because of the technical restrictions of the time.

The developments of designing and manufacturing printed textiles are reviewed in two historical time frames: the first sixty years during which modern technologies and design education were introduced to China, and the later forty years from the moment the communist government took power in the mainland that saw the textile industries and education systems evolving under the tight control of a centralized political regime.

In addition to consulting existing references and archive materials related to the topic, this chapter includes some reflections on my own personal experience, as a designer for printed textiles in a factory relocated from Shanghai and later as a design college teacher connected to some eminent designers at Shanghai textile printing mills during the 1970s and 1980s.

Industrial Revolution in Shanghai

There is a long history and rich tradition of textile production in China and in particular the Yangzi River delta where Shanghai is located. Traditional printing methods of applying coloured patterns to fabrics were mainly executed by hand using stencils and woodblocks, practised for centuries in small and private workshops and mills, such as the well-known cottage industries based in Songjiang, a town on the outskirts of Shanghai.

By the late nineteenth century, however, foreign powers, in particular the British, the French and the Japanese, had built factories in Shanghai and, under the name of the Joint Shanghai Municipal Council, had a practical monopoly over the city's services, from electricity and water to public transport.[1] At the same time, textile imports from European countries, especially from Britain where well-developed technology in textile industries helped to bring down the cost of manufacturing, became dominant in the Chinese market and accelerated the decline of domestic handicraft industries in the urban and rural areas of Shanghai and Yangzi River delta, with the production of cotton textiles hit hardest. This grave economic situation spurred reformers within the Qing imperial government to modernize industries more quickly, leading to the establishment of regional railways as well as a range of machine-powered manufacturing industries.

The key figure in promoting the transformation of Chinese national industries was Li Hongzhang (1823–1901), a top politician and diplomat of the Qing court, best known in the West for his pro-modern stance and importance as a negotiator. In 1878, a former Sichuan governor, Peng Rucong (彭汝琮 (前四川候补道), wrote to Li, the then Beiyang trade minister (*Beiyang tongshang dachen*), with a proposal of establishing a Shanghai Bureau of Machine-Woven Textiles (*Shanghai jiqi zhibu jü*). This plan was much appreciated by Li and granted immediate approval. At the end of 1889, this national government-sponsored manufacturing plant opened, though with a modest start to production lines with 530 machine-powered looms and 35,000 spindles.[2] This could be seen as a significant turning point from the old handicraft industries to machine-powered textile industries in China and, as a result, Shanghai became the birthplace of the modern Chinese textile industries.

It is worth noting that, from 1889, there was a continuing transformation process in Shanghai, as well as in China at large, of converting foreign enterprises into nationalized ones in the decades prior to 1949, and then converting privately owned firms into state enterprises in the 1950s. In 1913, an early year in the newly established Republic of China, for instance, the output of foreign-owned textile businesses still accounted for 70 per cent of the total of Shanghai cotton textile production.[3] During the first twenty years of the Republican era, the national textile industry in Shanghai developed steadily with many new plants built by native Chinese entrepreneurs. It was also during the same period that Japanese companies made a big push to set up their factories in Shanghai, to fill the vacuum left by shrinking European investments. However, 1945 saw a dramatic ending of the expanding Japanese presence with the Chinese victory in the Second Sino-Japanese war and the Republican government took over all Japanese textile enterprises in the city.

Printing is the process of applying one or more colours to fabric in definitely designed patterns. With the introduction of machine-printing technology, there was a huge leap in terms of richness in design and quality of colours of domestically produced textiles in Shanghai at the start of the twentieth century. From then on Chinese printed textiles moved from simple stencil or block prints with a limited colour range to multi-coloured machine-prints with sophisticated patterns and techniques. Two main types of machine printing were used in Shanghai's textile printing mills for decades: copper-roller printing machines were widely used, especially for cotton textiles, from the 1920s to the 1980s, while screen-printing machines were more favoured for silks. After printing, all the fabrics underwent a further finishing process to achieve the expected colour shades and fastness. And the printing mills went the extra length to convince their customers of the unrivalled quality of their new fabrics.

In 1919 a local business Qinyingzhai started operating new machine-printing facilities in a mill in the North Chengdu Road of Shanghai, printing silk fabrics with new designs to meet market needs. In 1925, Lunchang Printing Mill, which was originally set up by the French but had changed hands by that time to British ownership of the Manchester-based company CPA (the Calico Printers' Association Ltd), installed the first production line of roller printing, with full facilities of copper-cylinder engraving and a technical team from Great Britain.[4]

Figure 2.1 Roller printing machine with engraved copper cylinders in operation at the British-owned Lunchang Printing Mill, Shanghai, 1920s. © Shanghai Textile Museum, Shanghai.

By 1934, a total of thirty-eight cotton-printing mills were in operation in Shanghai and with the highest concentration of both technical expertise and designers in China, a guild of textile printers was formed in the city.

The technology revolution in the textile industries had a profound influence on people's aesthetic values and awareness of fashion. The high-speed production lines for weaving and printing in Shanghai brought down prices and made a rich variety of textiles available and affordable to domestic consumers. The unique openness of this port city, known for the foreign technology and cultures brought in by expat communities and entrepreneurs, helped to establish Shanghai as a prime location for finding fashionable goods and a source of inspirations for novel designs and styles for people from near and far regions in China throughout the turbulent decades of the twentieth century.

Early Design Studios for Printed Textiles in Shanghai

Although patterned textiles, printed, woven or embroidered, were produced in China for centuries, professional designers and design studios for the domestic textile industry only appeared in the early twentieth century in Shanghai. There were two main tracks of developing textile design into a modern profession, in terms of both operational concepts and human resources, which included apprentices' training in the factories and college courses offered in newly formed art and design schools.

The early design studios in the textile firms had to recruit local artists to be trained in-house by designers from overseas. For example, Lunchang Printing Mill first hired a well-known local artist in 1925 to cope with the demands of their newly installed roller-printing line. But then in 1931 the firm invested a lot more to recruit French designer Madam Ellen to train selected Shanghai artists in the following years. From this studio several trainees, most notably Zhang Zhiyu (1913–2000), later became leading designers in the textile trades.[5] In contrast to the rather open-minded approaches to local designer training at European-owned firms, the Japanese firms in Shanghai adopted very protective measures to their designs, brought in their native design teams from Japan and kept the designs top secret, away from the local Chinese staff.

The 1920s and 1930s saw the rapid expansion of textile printing factories in Shanghai, especially the ones set up by local businessmen and by Japanese firms, among them the Japanese-owned No. 2 Cotton Processing Factory, considered as the 'largest printing mill in the Far East'. After the taking over of Japanese factories in Shanghai after the war in 1945, the then Nationalist government formed the China Textile Development Corporation (*Zhongguo fangzhi jianshe gongsi*), and appointed UK-trained Chen Weiji to head the printing operation and Zhang Zhiyu to head a new design studio supplying patterns for the printing mills within this group.[6] This corporation was renamed in 1952 as the Shanghai Eastern China

Bureau for Textiles (*Shanghai Huadong fangguanjü*), and with its design studio gathered some of the best-known designers for printed textiles in China.

The appointing of apprentices at in-house design studios was retained as a traditional approach in the textile industries for over a century in Shanghai, and has proved to be a convenient and effective way of training local artistic talents to produce traditional or trend-aware patterns to keep the factory printing machines running. There were not many hurdles for the Chinese artists to translate their brush painting skill into surface design patterns for fabrics, especially for those who practised the traditional flower-and-bird painting which is remarkably close and transferable to textile design in terms of subject matter and technical application of lines and colours. The main obstacles that prevented some local artists from moving to or staying in this design profession during the early twentieth century were mainly social and psychological ones. During the long history of imperial China, applied art or decorative art have always been looked down upon as the creation of skilled but anonymous craftsmen and inferior to literati art such as scholar-officials' painting or calligraphy, which were regarded as gentlemen's art and superior in their cultural status. Also, much of the work in the early in-house design studios was copying and adapting foreign designs to meet the clients' orders and safeguard the profits, so there was very limited freedom for artistic innovation or risk taking for artists turned designers.

The other track of fostering designers for the textile industries was through college education, which was only first introduced into Shanghai in the 1920s but has gradually grown into the mainstream in later decades. The Western model of art and design education was not an option in formal education in imperial China and the teaching of subjects such as perspective, life drawing and painting were offered in workshops by a small number of churches and private tutors. One of the early modern art schools was, however, set up in 1912 in Shanghai by a group of rebelling artists and students who broke away from traditional training. The Shanghai Academy of Painting, later renamed as Shanghai School of Fine Art, with Pattern Design added as a major in 1925, became a pioneering training centre for many well-known Chinese artists and designers in the first half of twentieth century, before it was moved and merged with other art institutions in 1952.[7] In comparison with the apprentice-trained designers in printing mills, the college graduates lacked technical and operational experience on the factory floor but were overall better prepared with formal education in design and artistic concepts (in theoretical, historical and professional matters) and skills (in drawing, space and rendering), and, once settled in the design studios, they often took the key professional roles in the long run.

Privately funded and government sponsored students who went overseas to study also played an important role in bringing in modern technology as well as new design concepts and systems of education. Art students who went to Paris and Tokyo in particular and came back to China to set up new schools and courses were pioneers in changing the landscape of art and design education in China. Likewise, the technology students, privately funded by wealthy parents, usually textile entrepreneurs, or with government scholarships, went to Britain to study at well-established textile centres such as the Departments of Textile Industries and Colour Chemistry at the University of Leeds. Once they completed their studies abroad, some came back to Shanghai and Beijing, some joined universities or colleges to train local textile specialists while others joined their family businesses implementing the modern technology into production lines there. They often invited their European teachers over as well to help in establishing the academic base for local industries. Some interesting exchanges of textile design aesthetics were revealed when I studied the records of the Clothworkers' collection of Chinese textiles at the University of Leeds. Some of the pieces, such as dresses and tapestries and samples of patterned textiles, were donated to the university by the successive Chinese students who studied there. Plate 1, showing a carefully adapted version of a popular Chinese New Year print as a design for roller-printed cotton fabrics, is among the pieces brought back from Shanghai by Professor Aldred Barker, author of *An Introduction to the Study of Textile Design* (1903), who, after his retirement from Leeds, was invited by his former Chinese students to teach at the Textile School of Shanghai Chiao-tung University (Shanghai Jiao Tong University) in the 1930s.[8]

Similarly key textile technologists such as Chen Weiji (1902–84), who was best known for his books on the history of Chinese textiles and his principal role in the Shanghai textile industries, were trained at Leeds University, and brought back new models of the textile curriculum, connecting science and design, in the 1930s, establishing a modern education and research foundation for the textile and clothing industries in China during the Republican period.[9]

Shanghai in the 1930s and 1940s saw the unprecedented flourishing of emerging art schools, artistic associations and the publication of art and lifestyle periodicals. From the early factory-based training systems where students were tutored by European designers, to the appearance of Surface Pattern Design courses set up by Chinese artists returned from their studies in Japan, Europe and America, systems of art and design education in China became increasingly sophisticated in the Republican period.

Symbolism played an important role in Chinese textile design through these unsettling decades, and textile designs were often viewed as status symbols and fashion statements. There was a long tradition in Chinese society that patterns on clothing were used to reflect the wearers' social status, from the imperial court systems to the designs of the present day chosen by political and business elites. The surface patterns on clothing and other fashion materials were often manipulated, subtly or intensely, to reflect wearers' visual identities or as personal statements about attitudes, tastes or wealth, in a rapidly changing society. Shanghai as an emerging modern city in the early twentieth century had flourished during the Republican era in terms of its economic capacity as well as its stylistic influence. The restrictions on dress codes and decorative motifs were gone with the overthrow of the last imperial court. And before the new set of restrictions on dress codes and motifs enforced after 1949, people in Shanghai enjoyed experimenting with various forms of literature, art, dress and decorative styles.

New printing technology (especially the engraved copper-roller printing) in textile mills together with the rising desire for new styles fundamentally changed the landscape of the Chinese textile industries. Styles of textile design were dominated by imported aesthetic expressions, such as the influences of Art Nouveau and Art Deco in the 1920s and 1930s, the Soviet influence in the 1950s, and the propaganda protocols of the 1960s and early 1970s. There are still a good variety of resources available for studying modern Chinese textile designs, with printed textiles in particular. In addition to the surviving clothing and textiles in museums and collectors' hands, old photos of the elder generations' special occasions are still treasured by numerous Shanghai families, and fashionable patterns on printed fabrics were meticulously depicted in many Shanghai calendar posters of the first half of the twentieth century. Printing thus played an important supporting role in the development of Shanghai fashion.

Leading Educators of Chinese Textile Designers

There were two major camps of scholars and designers that shaped the course of developing textile design education in China: the students who returned from studying in Japan and those who returned from studying in Europe, notably in France. Among them the most influential figures for twentieth-century Chinese textile design are Chen Zhifo (1896–1962), who brought from Japan the modern textile design terminology and practice, and Lei Guiyuan (1906–89), who established the theoretical framework of Chinese pattern design that was rooted in the ancient tradition but interpreted through Western concepts and methodology. In other words, while Chen had a pioneer role in introducing surface pattern as a design discipline as well as the professional practice in textile design in the early decades of the twentieth century, Lei became the key figure in establishing textile design as an academic discipline in Chinese higher education and creating new approaches in training textile designers in the mid-twentieth century.

There were strong drives for opening up in the late Qing period and early Republican period, pushed by reformers in government and business circles. Droves of Chinese students of increasing numbers left Shanghai ports each year in the early twentieth century on their voyages to the foreign cities of the modern world to learn science and the arts. 'Go to Japan or France?' This was a big question facing Chinese students with plans to study art and design overseas, though most of them could not afford to enrol as full-time students but rather intended to undertake part-time study while working in their new destinations. There were even more options for those who lived or arrived in Shanghai, the most open city in China at the time, under great influence from both directions, Japan in the East and Europe in the West, and with large expat concessions in the centre of the city's cultural life.

Paris, in particular, was long regarded as the capital of the art world among Chinese artistic circles, and France a land for artistic and stylistic inspiration dreamt of by many. However, there were also good reasons to study in Japan, according to documents circulated by the government at the time, such as cost savings with the huge differences in travel expenses; ease of travel because of the short distance; ease of learning the language because of the similarities in writing; and, perhaps most important of all, the Japanese had already digested a vast amount of Western literature and absorbed the essences of Western learning (so there you could 'get twice the result with half the effort' as the old Chinese saying went).[10] The statistics show that during the period 1905 to 1937 about 600 Chinese students studied at twenty art schools in Tokyo and other Japanese cities, with the majority studying fine art and the rest studying in architecture and design disciplines.[11] There was also a similarly large number of Chinese students who studied art and design in Paris and other French cities, with Lyon favoured by many of the textile students. However, the waves of study-in-Japan drew to an abrupt end in 1937 when the war broke out. France then became the undisputed prime destination for Chinese art students.

Chen Zhifo was an early pioneer in surface pattern design in China, he published his first textbook on this subject in 1917 when he was teaching at the textile department of a technical college in Hangzhou, even before his trip to Tokyo in 1918 to study design.[12] After returning home, he had been engaged in the teaching of surface pattern design for a long time, and went on to write a number of books on this subject, such as *Image Handbook*, *Pattern Design ABC* and *Pattern Construction Methods*. These texts made great contributions to the systematic study of patterns as a design discipline in China. It is worth noting that many of the basic terms used in the modern-day Chinese language are originated from Japanese: such as design (*sheji*), textile design (*ranzhi sheji*), pattern (*tu'an*) and motif (*wenyang*), all thanks to the efforts by Chen Zhifo and his contemporaries who studied in Japan a century ago.

Another important role Chen Zhifo played in the history book of Chinese textile design was that after returning from Tokyo in 1923, he set up a pattern design studio called Shangmei Studio in Shanghai, one of the earliest of such independent privately run design studios in China, to provide professional design services for the industries, especially the textile printing firms.[13] His experimental efforts in blending Western or Japanese styles with Chinese elements, such as embedding Buddhist, Taoist and Confucian visual elements with a modern twist, are evident in the surviving samples of his designs, most of which are now in a museum converted from his old residence at Cixi, near Shanghai. For example, in Figure 2.2 (left), lotus pods, a Buddhist motif, were depicted with exotic flower motifs, while in Figure 2.2 (right) whirling clouds and air, the Taoist motif of *yunqi*, were drawn in a Paisley pattern framework, to meet perhaps the fashion tastes of the time. Chen's studio also became a hot incubator in Shanghai for young designers who wanted to enter into the textile design profession and needed his guidance.

Chen spent most of his time in design education in the 1930s and 1940s, and during the war he was appointed as the Principal of the National Academy of Fine Art, which had a design faculty. After 1949, however, Chen gradually shifted his energies from teaching to painting, and became one of the most celebrated flower-and-bird painters of the modern era.

Another eminent educator and designer, Lei Guiyuan, who went to France in 1929 to study textile design brought back a fresh perspective on surface patterns to art and design schools in China, and also wrote a number of important books on design that contributed to the foundation for Chinese design education in succeeding years.[14] His writing and design works injected fresh air into the centuries-old patterning formulas of colours and forms. Lei Guiyuan had gained a lot of working experience in Parisian studios and factories, and was heavily influenced by French designers, such as Raoul Dufy the Fauvist painter turned textile designer whose style was popular at the time, with very free (even naïve) brushwork and fresh non-traditional colours. His early design works, some of which can be seen at his family home, which is also now a museum, in Songjiang

Figure 2.2 Details of textile designs by Chen Zhifo, at Shangmei Studio, Shanghai, mid-1920s. Ink and watercolour on paper. © Chen Xiufan and Li Youguang.

district, Shanghai, showed a very relaxed manner in his designs, unrestrained and unsophisticated (Figure 2.3).

On his return from France in 1931, Lei enthusiastically participated in the activities of the design circles at Shanghai and Hangzhou, and played a founding role in setting up the first Chinese designers association, Shanghai Association of Industrial and Commercial Artists (*Shanghai gongshangye meishujia xiehui*), in 1935.[15]

Lei designed a wide range of surface patterns from textiles and wallpapers to porcelains and logos. But most of his time after 1949 was devoted to design education, especially as a professor and vice-principal at the Central Academy of Art and Design (CAAD) from its inauguration in 1956 to his last years. Although he had already reached his retiring age when I was studying Textile Design at the CAAD in the late 1970s, he was still actively involved in teaching and academic work. The curriculum and course design of CAAD were profoundly embedded

Figure 2.3 Details of pattern designs by Lei Guiyuan in 1940s. Gouache and watercolour on paper. © Tsinghua University Academy of Art and Design.

with his philosophy, concepts and methodology in the study of the structure and forms of Chinese design. His books, such as *Exploring the Methods in Chinese Patterns* (*Zhongguo tu'an zuofa chutan*), have been reprinted numerous times and are still widely used in design schools and by textile designers today.

Designers' Training and Practice in the People's Republic of China

After the Chinese capital moved back to the north in 1949, the communist central government tightened its grip on all cities and industrial centres, ensuring the absolute power, politically and culturally, stayed within this 'northern capital' (Beijing), not the southern capital (Nanjing) of the former Nationalist government, or the economic powerhouse of Shanghai.

Institutions in Beijing with their names starting as 'Central' had their superiority, in terms of financial and human resources, in the new hierarchical system over the provincial ones. This applied to art and design institutions as well. For instance, after several years of drastic reconstructions nationwide, the central government made the decision to set up a new design institution to play a leading role in responding to the increasing demands of industries for well-designed products. Under this scheme, some well-established academics in design were selected from a number of major art colleges in the country, including Lei Guiyuan and a number of his colleagues from Hangzhou Art Academy, and were relocated, willingly or unwillingly, with their families to Beijing in 1953 to set up this central design institution known as CAAD. With its distinctive logo symbolizing 'Wearing, Eating, Living, Transportation' (*yi shi zhu xing*), textile design was the first faculty set up and running at CAAD in 1956.[16] Some 1200 km away in Shanghai, however, there was a very different situation as the city endured double-sided losses with its design education and industrial facilities. Relocations of schools and factories under the centralized government planning resulted in a drain of precious expertise and facilities from the city.

Soon after 1949 there was a nationwide reorganization of academic departments, colleges and universities. In 1952 the last art institution in Shanghai's higher education sector, the Shanghai College of Fine Art, was moved away and merged into the East China College of Fine Art in Wuxi, and left a huge vacuum of art and design education in such a mega city with great industries, a dire situation mourned by many locals but not by the planners at central offices in the north. Without much hope of getting adequate supplies of design graduates, the Shanghai textile industries

Figure 2.4 Design motifs for textile designers: new courses at Central Academy of Art and Design: (above) students holding a large fabric banner during the rehearsal for 1 May celebrations, 1957; (below) teachers collecting local patterns during their trip to the North West regions, 1961. © Tsinghua University Academy of Art and Design.

adapted a variety of approaches to fill the talent gap such as the old-style apprentice training, retraining fine art graduates to be designers and attracting graduates from far-away institutions. These measures proved to be so effective that, during the following decades, not only were their own design studios well supported, but they also helped to train hundreds of textile designers for other provinces.[17]

The links between Shanghai industries and textile design programmes in higher education elsewhere were not all cut off in the decades after 1949, but rather evolved into different forms. Connections between Shanghai as the industrial base and Beijing as the academic centre were maintained in the form of retraining factory-grown designers in tailor-made short courses in the academic environment while group internships at Shanghai factories were embedded in the textile design curriculum of art and design schools elsewhere. I retain lots of fond memories of such regular internship trips between Beijing and Shanghai, first as a student and later as a teacher leading large groups of students to Shanghai printing factories in the late 1970s and 1980s.

Relocations in the industry network, on the other hand, also resulted in a drain of expertise and production facilities from the Shanghai textile industries. Factory relocation in the late 1950s and early 1960s had a profound impact on the city where the modern Chinese textile industries started. Some Shanghai textile printing firms were relocated, under the master plans drawn by the central government, to other small cities and towns of underdeveloped regions for the purpose of technology transfer and stimulating the development of local industries. Well-established Shanghai printing firms relocated away in the late 1950s including Meiguang (to Hefei, Anhui province), Jiouru (to Nanchang, Jiangxi province) and Tianyi (to Wuhan, Hubei province).[18] On the surface, this massive movement indeed diluted the high concentration of textile technical and design expertise in Shanghai. In the long run, however, it sowed the seeds of a Shanghai spirit in the vast regions of China, resulting in an expansion of Shanghai's influence to a much bigger network of textile industries, particularly with many key positions in the provincial industries taken by Shanghainese experts who kept their unbroken links, professionally and emotionally, and a pride in their native city on the east coast.

One of the big provincial benefactors was Xiangtan Weaving and Printing Corporation (XWPC), with its printing factory formed with two Shanghai printing mills, Guangxin and Nanhua, relocated from Shanghai to the small city of Xiangtan, Hunan province, in 1957. Before it was eventually broken up four decades later, XWPC was one of the largest state enterprises in Hunan province, with over 11,000 staff workers.[19] I worked as a trainee designer at XWPC for over three years in the latter half of 1970s, where I experienced first-hand working with many Shanghai *shifu* (technical masters in engraving, printing, finishing, etc.) and *laoshi* (tutors or senior designers in the factory studio). Most of them shared a unique reputation for their meticulous attitude and professionalism in a time when professionalism was under vicious attack from radical movements.

Factories, especially the ones located in smaller cities, benefitted from the state allocation (*fenpei*) system for graduates from higher education, in which the graduates had to go and work in the towns and factories not according to their own choices but according to the distribution for the nationwide industrial network. Many design graduates even though they had dreamed of starting their professional careers in big cities like Shanghai often ended up with allocated posts at unheard-of places.

Design Studio Practice

In the following three decades after 1949, in-house design studios set up by the state-owned enterprises became the norm in the Chinese textile industries, with freelance designers or private design practices all becoming things of the past. To work as a textile designer meant that you had to follow routine practices inside or outside of the studio, according to the official guidelines of the time. Standard practices required in the printing design studios included: life drawing and painting to get fresh visual images and inspirations; field investigations to learn the preferences of the consumers; and engaging in design related events in the highly centralized industrial system, such as attending the twice-a-year pattern ordering trade fairs.

Designers had to show their designs (originals on paper or fabric samples) regularly at two very different types of venues to test the market needs: one was the twice-a-year trade fairs, usually held at big cities with a substantial textile industry network, in which designers and sales representatives were able to detect the directions of the market according to the orders they received from different regions; the other was the places where the textiles ended up, for which designers did regular feedback trips to targeted areas to talk with the end-users of their designs. One important factor for having designers present at trade fairs was that the regional buyers could talk directly to the designers to have available designs modified or to have the forthcoming season's designs specified according to their regional needs. It was a common scene at national pattern-ordering fairs that the stands presenting Shanghai designers' collections became star attractions, not only for the regional buyers to get hold of the desired goods but also for the designers from other provinces to catch some ideas for fashionable patterns, colour schemes and design techniques.[20]

Regular organized study trips, typically twice a year to do drawing and paintings away from factory studios, were the favourite routine, a privilege at the time enjoyed by most textile designers, thanks to the Western art-training concepts brought back by those who had studied in Europe and was later reinforced by the Soviet advisors in the early 1950s. These trips were usually the best chance to get

Figure 2.5 Hearing feedback from the villagers – obligatory fieldwork for textile designers, early 1970s. © Ling Liu, private collection.

away from the politics at work and get closer to nature, for inspiration to be used in designs for the next season. Such trips were often combined with field investigations into local consumer behaviour, to get first-hand knowledge of what they liked and disliked in terms of fabric colours and motifs.

On the design tools and materials side, gouache was the most widely used medium for designing patterns on paper for printed textiles. Gouache, better known as 'poster colour' (*guanggaose*) in China, as most political or commercial posters of the time were painted with gouache, is opaque, easy to mix with water and effective in creating layers of fine details. However, there were tools associated with particular types of textile design. For example, airbrush, working with an air-compressing pump, was most commonly used for large quilt-cover designs featuring almost photographic depictions of flowers and scenes. In addition to designing patterns, designers had to use their artistic skills to serve the propaganda purposes of various political campaigns, painting party posters, leaders' portraits or on-the-wall caricatures, for instance.

Textile Design under Political Impact

There were waves of political movements in China every few years after 1949, with the ten-year Cultural Revolution (1966–76) as the climax of them all, which severely shook and disrupted the industries as well as the education systems. In hindsight it might be difficult for people, especially younger generations, today to comprehend the absurdity of such movements but for most people who lived at those times the choices they faced were stark: you either followed the tides or you would be crushed mercilessly.

In an atrocious resemblance to the 'Great Leap' movement ten years earlier, in which machines and tools were destroyed for overblown reports of iron production, the Cultural Revolution caused massive destruction to the textile industries in China. Take the example in 1969 when, driven by the ultra-left propaganda, a brand new 'one-step printing procedure' was introduced into Shanghai printing factories, in which a series of finishing treatments such as singeing and mercerizing were eliminated to speed up the production speed. This was hailed by the party media as a revolution in printing to beat the 'creeping conservatism'. But as a result, equipment and finishing lines were dismantled and destroyed, the quality of textile products suffered terribly and the economic losses were huge.[21]

People in China have often been subject to changing dress codes after regime changes. This was also the situation after 1949 when the new political establishment's political norms dominated forms and contents of all visual presentations in the society, including clothing and textile designs. There was a big influence from the Soviet Union in the early 1950s, which was diminished when the relationship of the two countries went sour. But the political restrictions and propaganda values of visual imagery were pushed to the extreme during the Cultural Revolution. The palette for people's dress in public was very limited in those years, usually grey, blue and military green. Vibrant colour schemes were only adapted without much controversy for private usage such as personal accessories, underwear or quilt covers.[22] Motifs in design were even more sensitive issues as symbolism was always playing an important part in Chinese decorative art. The censorship for unacceptable motifs in those years was pushed further by the extreme political correctness. Any hint or even imaginative connection to politically unfitting messages in design works might result in serious trouble for the designer and the producer. Designs often needed therefore to be carefully checked by designers themselves or vetted by someone above in the studio or the working unit prior to going to production.

Fortunately, designers found a space to stretch their creativity and imagination, in the product ranges targeted for export markets, or designing fabrics (especially printed silks) to meet foreign tastes.[23] Patterns for export were listed as an exceptional category, separated from designs for domestic consumption, and for which foreign fashion and design information were allowed to be used for references. This was an area where some designers enjoyed seemingly endless possibilities, as if picking wild flowers in an open field well beyond the monitored domestic walls. Although occasionally sample designs provided with orders from overseas might touch the official red lines for prohibited images, the relevant offices usually were much more relaxed towards designs for export textiles aiming for higher foreign currency returns. Some good samples of foreign designs were regularly compiled by Shanghai designers as reference catalogues and circulated in the wider textile industrial networks. At a time when even the Impressionists' art was not allowed to be published, such internal circulation of visual references, such as the *New Patterns* (*Xinhuase*) compiled and distributed by the Shanghai Silk Import & Export Company, proved very valuable stimulants to enrich designers' work at many provincial factories.[24]

One of the most popular types of printed textiles of the time was the large floral designs for quilt covers (*dahua beimian*), usually with bright colours and large auspicious motifs such as flowers, birds or landscapes in large scale compositions (or 'large repeats' in printing design term). This type of design was originally developed from traditional celebrative patterns by Zhang Zhiyu and his colleagues at the design studio of Shanghai Eastern China Bureau for Textiles in early 1950s, but gradually gained its popularity in the vast Chinese rural areas, from the north-east provinces to the south-west mountain regions.[25] Although the primary use of such patterned textiles was for bedding, they were also used by many people for clothing with strong cultural flavours. It is worth remembering that, before the more recent urbanization in China, most printed textiles for domestic consumption went to the population in the countryside, for whom the bright and cheerful colours brought much needed visual delight to those living in harsh and plain environments.

There were also specified categories reserved for quilt cover designs at the trade fairs and production lines, and because of the complexity in design and multi-rollers preparing processes, quilt cover designs were usually assigned to the most experienced designers and engraving technicians in a printing factory.

Figure 2.6 A senior designer demonstrating quilt-cover design techniques to a trainee designer at an in-house studio for printed textiles, early 1970s. © Ling Liu, private collection.

Originally many traditional auspicious motifs were used in such designs targeting rural markets, such as phoenix, cranes, peacocks and pheasants with peony, magnolia, or plum blossom. In the 1960s and 1970s, however, more radical revolutionary images went into quilt cover designs, ranging from Mao's books and propaganda slogans to electric cable towers and atomic bomb mushroom clouds. Anything went with the political winds in a state planned economy. And revolutionary motifs became the new auspicious motifs in Mao's era, offering peace of mind in the midst of political hassles. (See Plate 2.)

The New Life of the Shanghai Textile Industries in the Post-Cultural Revolution Era

The ending of the Cultural Revolution, following the death of Mao, enabled Chinese people to breathe fresh air with hope, and provided new opportunities for the textile industries.

For over three decades after 1949, ordinary people in Shanghai and other cities were living with limited basic commodities, including textiles, soap bars or cooking oil, and were totally out of reach from any luxury goods. In 1984, the thirty-year-old rationing system came to its end. All kinds of vouchers for purchasing textiles were abolished and the industries began to face the increasing pressure of changing demands and supplies.[26] With supplies growing more abundant, the prospect of surviving in a new market-oriented economy became particularly severe for state-owned textile firms. By then the Shanghai textile industries were already suffering from 'aging disease', with old, often unsafe factory buildings built in the 1920s or 1930s, out-dated equipment and old-fashioned products that lacked consumer appeal.[27]

Reform was badly needed and then it came on an unprecedented scale. In the following decades all major textile printing factories in Shanghai were either closed down or moved out of the city to the peripheral regions in the city's efforts to reduce pollution in water and air, and in service of the transformation of those city centre spaces into office buildings, art parks or shopping malls.[28] Yet, in historical perspective, the textile industries have remained an important pillar of the economy of Shanghai. Until the early 1990s, textile products accounted for a quarter of the value of total exports from Shanghai, and the textile sector employed a half-million workforce.[29] Shanghai as the centre of textile design and production has also made a far-reaching impact on design studios and printing factories in other parts of China.

For textile designers working in this opening-up and reforming era, fashion trends in the domestic and international markets also became increasingly important. For collecting and sharing such information with the industries, the first society for colour trends for the silk industry was set up in 1982 in Shanghai.[30] Three years later the China Society for Colour Trends was also formed to embrace other products, including printed cotton textiles for instance, to provide comprehensive forecasting services. Fashion also became the buzzword in higher education after the Cultural Revolution. Clothing design was a small part of the textile design curriculum in Chinese design schools up to the early 1980s when fashion design appeared as an independent discipline in higher education, split from textile design faculties. Since then the number of schools offering fashion education in China has expanded many fold, not only in big cities like Shanghai or Beijing, but also in many provincial cities, while textile design faculties have kept shrinking.

In comparison to the transformation process in textile industries in earlier decades of the twentieth century, a reverse tide emerged from the 1980s when state-owned firms were broken up one by one, closed or converted into private business, and foreign capital moved in again to set up joint ventures or new branches of established Western brands. That perhaps also signified a full circle of life for the evolving textile industries in Shanghai. A hundred years after the humble start of a national industrial revolution, 1989 saw more dramatic changes taking place in centres of political gravity around the world. In Shanghai, however, while industrial reforms were gathering pace, few still remembered the birth of this modern textile industry a century earlier, as Li Hongzhang had long been turned into a collaborator with Western powers in school history books. In Beijing, the death of the founder of modern Chinese design education, Lei Guiyuan, was almost unreported, as all media attention was on the historic events happening in the streets of the city centre. The world moved on, and so did Shanghai and China.

Notes

1 Yao Yuan, '"Collaborative Policy" and the Creation of Joint Shanghai Municipal Council "合作政策" 与上海公共租界的诞生', *Problems in the Teaching of History*, 4 (2015): 102–6.

2 Wang Shengyun, 'On the Rise and Historical Role of the Modern Textile Industry in China 论中国近代纺织工业的兴起及其历史作用', *Journal of Wuhan University of Science and Engineering* 2 (2002): 85–6.

3 Wang Shiwei, '*150 Years of Shanghai Textile Industries – Chronicle of Events 1861–2010*上海纺织工业一百五十年1861–2010年大事记' (Beijing: China Textile Press, 2014), 5.

4 Jin Yancao, 'The Development and Change of Printing Designs in Shanghai, 上海印染图案的发展与变化', *Chinese Textile Art*, 1 (1994): 7.

5 Shanghai City Local Chronicle Office, http://www.shtong.gov.cn/node2/node2245/node73148/node73151/node73201/node73233/userobject1ai87027.html (accessed October 2016).

6 Lia Xia, 'A Brief Introduction to the Archives of Old Shanghai Textile Enterprises 旧上海纺织企业档案简介', *Shanghai Archives* 2 (1992): 53.

7 Shanghai Municipal Archives and Liu Haisu Art Museum, *Meizhuan 1952* 美专一九五二, (Beijing: Zhongxi Press, 2016).

8 Michael Hann, 'Dragons, Unicorns and Phoenixes – Origin and Continuity of Technique and Motif', University of Leeds, 2004, 2.

9 Yang Dongliang, 'A Concise History of Chinese Printing and Dying Industries in the Modern Time 我国近代印染业发展简史', *Printing* 12 (2008): 50.

10 Yin Zhenji, 'Exhortation to Study and the Climax of Studying in Japan in Modern China 《劝学篇》与中国近代留日高潮', *Journal of Japanese Language Study and Research* 2 (2011): 119–215.

11 Hua Tianxue, 'Artists Studied in Japan and the Reform of Chinese Painting 留日画家与中国画改良', *Art Observation* 9 (17): 134.

12 Xia Yanjing, 'Analysing the Records of Shangmei Design Studio of Chen Zhifo 陈之佛创办"尚美图案馆"史料解读', *Journal of Nanjing University of the Arts* 2, (2006): 167–73.

13 Ibid., 160.

14 Jia Jingsheng, Guo Qiuhui and Zhang Jingsheng, *1906–1989 Lei Guiyuan's Collection* 雷圭元作品集 (Shandong: Shandong Art Publishing House, 2016), 215.

15 Ibid., 216.

16 Yang Chengying and Lin Wenxia, *Lei Guiyuan on Pattern Design Art* 雷圭元论图案艺术, (Shanghai: Shanghai Culture Publisher, 2016), 280.

17 Zhu Dan, 'The Research into Shanghai Designers of Printed Textiles of Mid-20th Century (1949–1979) 20 世纪中期 (1949–1979)上海印染设计师群体研究', MA thesis (Nanjing University of the Arts, 2012), 17–25.

18 Xie Zhongqiang, 'Studying the Relocation of Shanghai Factories during the 50s of 20th Century, 20 世纪50年代上海工厂内迁研究', *Researches in Chinese Economic History*, 3 (2013), 88–99.

19 Guo Jian, 'State Own and Private Run: New Approaches in Transforming Operation Systems 国有私营：企业转换经营机制的新举措', *Enterprise Dynamics* 6 (1993): 52.

20 Dan, 'The Research into Shanghai Designers', 25.

21 Shanghai City Local Chronicle Office, http://www.shtong.gov.cn/Newsite/node2/node2245/node4483/node56675/index.html (accessed September 2016).

22 Gong Jianpei, 'Rethinking of Passionate Fashion – Analyzing the Colour Phenomenon of the Cultural Revolution Period 对激情时尚的再思考 – 文革时期色彩现象解读', *Chinese Fashion: Beijing*, 11 (2004): 20.

23 Yancao, 'The Development and Change of Printing Designs in Shanghai', 14–18.

24 Jianpei, 'Rethinking of Passionate Fashion', 52.

25 Yancao, 'The Development and Change of Printing Designs in Shanghai', 13.

26 Lv Chuanyou, 'The Directions of Reform of State Enterprices – on the Current Situation and Way out of Shanghai's Printing and Dying Industries 国企改革路在何方 – 谈上海印染行业的现状和出路', *Printing Technology* 3 (2002): 43.

27 Wang Demao, 'Retrospect and Outlook of Shanghai Dyeing and Printing Industry 上海印染行业的回顾与展望', *Dyeing & Finishing Technology* 5 (2000): 1–7.

28 Shiwei, *150 Years of Shanghai Textile Industries*, 19.

29 Ibid., 18–19.

30 Wu Yong, 'China Silk Colour Trends Society Inaugurated in Shanghai 中国丝绸流行色协会在上海成立', *Journal of Textile Research*, 6 (1982), 59.

3

Wenming Xinzhuang (Civilized Costume)

Liu Yu

Introduction

In 1911 China entered into the Republican period which heralded an era of great historical and social change for Chinese people. The revolution represented a profound ideological enlightenment movement with a deeply rooted concept of democracy and republicanism. In the late Qing dynasty (1840–1912), especially after the Sino-Japanese War (1894–5), Western ideas were introduced into China and influenced the younger generation.

In the early years of the Republic of China, with the development of publications such as *La Jeuness* and the promotion of the Vernacular Movement (which promoted democracy and science and criticized traditional Chinese culture), the thought of freedom and resistance against tradition was a popular concept for many students and citizens. The new cultural movement advocated democracy and science, inspiring and influencing the enthusiasm of Chinese people for saving the nation from the ideological, political and cultural fields, especially Chinese students. These two ideas fundamentally laid the ideological and intellectual foundation for the May Fourth Movement which began in Beijing on 4 May 1919.

Whilst these events were unfolding people's costume similarly reflected unprecedented and revolutionary changes, especially in relation to women's clothing. These frequent changes that continued through the 1920s mainly had stylistic, formal and symbolic emphasis: from decoration to comfort, from luxury to fashion and from the embodiment of identity to the manifestation of individuality. That is to say, these frequent changes could be understood as the beginning of the modernization of Chinese women's wardrobes. When talking about this beginning, most scholars regard the *qipao* worn by women in the Republican period as typical and representative of radical change. They have suggested that the *qipao* was the pioneer of sartorial modernization. However, as this chapter will suggest, there was one important mode of dressing that appeared before *qipao* in this period of women's dress reform. It liberated women from the traditional complicated and extravagant clothing of previous centuries and had a name to match the revolutionary characteristics of the time, namely *wenming xinzhuang* (civilized costume).

Wenming xinzhuang was a novel variety of popular dress among specific groups of Chinese women in the early Republican period. The civilized costume was opposed to luxury and extravagant styles while promoting plain, simple and comfortable attire. The clothes were made in plain colours, and classical decorations such as traditional binding and embroidery were removed making the general appearance simple and elegant. The new form of dressing comprised a short blouse, with short arc shaped vents on both sides, flared sleeves that were worn just over the elbows and a long black calf-length skirt replaced the longer instep-length of preceding modes. The style was worn with minimal accessories such as hairpins and rings. Because of these stylistic changes, civilized costume gave rise to the more open display of the female body as well as an unprecedented freedom of movement. This new kind of comfortable women's wear was closely associated with the image of the New Woman in the early Republican period: women who studied abroad or in domestic missionary schools, and who were often considered as intellectuals. The clothing also reflected the anti-feudal and anti-pedantry social morality prevalent at that time. It took less than twenty years for civilized costume to be created, become popular and almost fade away, and its peak time of popularity only lasted for a few years in that period. Because of its relatively short period of popularity scholars have tended to pay less attention to civilized costume and have focused on the *qipao*. But what is undeniable is that the creation and the popularity of civilized costume deeply influenced Chinese society at that time. Its appearance was one of the symbols of the Chinese woman's release from feudal manners and laid the foundation for a sartorial and ideological revolution.

The Emergence of *Wenming Xinzhuang*

The Revolution of 1911 overthrew the rule of the Qing Dynasty and abolished the feudal clothing hierarchy as well as the tedious clothing decrees and regulations. The era of judging identity and class by discernible clothes and accessories finally came to an end, which caused a great and profound change for the understanding and use of Chinese traditional garments. At that time, the new government formulated the first *Regulation on Clothing* (*Fuzhi tiaoli*) for the Republic of China. In the *Regulation on Clothing* published by the Senate in July 1912, clothes were divided into three categories, namely Western formal clothes, official's costume and casual clothes. Formal clothes reflected the modes of the central government at that time in China, while official's costume, which was made of Chinese material such as silk, and cotton, had much in common with more general Western styles. Casual clothes still followed traditional Chinese garments in style but also incorporated some adaptations like the calf-length hem for ease of wearing boots. Boots to match formal clothes and official's costume were made of leather, while boots to match casual clothes were made of leather and brocade. The rules of women's wear were even simpler (with fewer restrictions and regulations). The newly established Republic of China also needed rules to unify official clothing. Adopting Western styles was a common trend among many countries all over the world. However, adopting Western style was not easy to promote on account of long-standing Chinese traditions, so traditional robes were temporarily permitted alongside the new formal clothes.[1] Thus traditional Chinese clothes and new Western clothes were adopted at the same time and were all vigorously promoted by government.

Under these social circumstances *wenming xinzhuang* combined traditional Chinese dress with elements of Western clothing. The new style was first advocated by female students and intellectual women in Beijing and Shanghai and then extended its appeal to ordinary women.

In the article *Shishang pinglun gaizhuang* (General Survey of the Fashion Criticism), the author details women's fashion wear in the Beijing area in the early 1920s. The article recorded, 'women's clothing in the early Republic of China was either inherited from the previous imperial dress or imitated western style, but the most popular is still the upper top under dress or upper shirt under pants'.[2] Young women wear *aoqun* (coat-and-skirt), which is called *wenming xinzhuang*. 'But compared with Shanghai, where western clothing is all the rage, women in Beijing still adhere to the traditional dress code.'[3] The fashionable centre Shanghai was still a vibrant port away from the political centre. So it had more freedom to experiment with new ideas from the East and the West.

This experimentation is noted by the popular Shanghai-based author Eileen Chang who described a female student's clothes in *Wusi yishi* (Stale Mates – A Short Story Set in the Time When True Love Came to China; a novel published in 1957, describing the love stories of youths after the Revolution of 1911): 'A black silk skirt which is tied high to the waist, a violet-blue lined undercoat with tightened waist, flared sleeves and rippled edge, as well as a white silk scarf on the neck.'[4]

Wenming xinzhuang thus offered a general image of modern dressing and was very different from traditional forms Though constructed in two pieces, it was different from the traditional *yishang* (a typical clothing style consisting of an upper garment called *yi*, which was also known as tops, and a lower garment

Figure 3.1 Painting displayed in the Paris Exhibition in 1928, by Fang Junbi (1898–1986), an artist who studied in France. The woman in the painting wears the new-style female clothing, namely *wenming xinzhuang* (civilized costume), which was popular in the early Republican period. It was the typical dress of the New Woman, with simple design, plain colour and fresh style. This painting was published in *Young Companion* (no. 29, pp. 6) in Shanghai in August 1928.

called *shang*, which was also known as bottoms and could be either skirt or trousers). With its very simple design, which was also very convenient and comfortable for people to wear, the clothing was considered enlightened hence the name *wenming xinzhuang*.

The Style and Development of *Wenming Xinzhuang*

As stated, the origins of *wenming xinzhuang* can be traced back to the early years of the Republic of China and it faded out gradually in the early 1930s. These twenty years of development can be divided into three main stages. The first stage is from the Revolution of 1911 to the time leading up to the May Fourth Movement (1919). The second stage is from 1919 to 1925, from the May Fourth Movement to the emergence of the reformative *qipao*, and was the prosperous stage of the civilized costume. The third stage is from 1925 to about 1930, from developing simultaneously with *qipao* to its eventual decline.

The blouse and matching skirt was the basic clothing mode of traditional Han women in China, reflected in the civilized costume, especially at the beginning of its development, where the basic style was clearly inherited from the ancient form, although the details began to change. As previously noted the enlightened qualities of *wenming xinzhuang* were reflected in the radical reduction of decoration. The blouse was usually cyan and blue. The long skirt was deeply coloured, mostly in black. There were no complicated ornaments, and binding and embroidery of traditional female clothes was rejected, the only trimming being a narrow binding on the hem.

In design terms the general silhouette was slim, using straight lines, which de-emphasized the body's curves. The blouse usually had a standing collar and was rather long in shape. Its hemline was generally cut below the hips and even could reach the knees. The side vents were rectangular. The sleeves were short and wrists were left visible. The characteristic of the collar was rather obvious. It was high-standing, reaching four or five *cun* (a *cun* equals a third of a decimetre), and developed into *yuanbaoling* (a style of collar in the shape of the traditional Chinese shoe-shaped ingots). This unique shape was extremely popular in the years after 1911 and became one of the main features of civilized costume in this stage.

Building on this design, there were some changes of form in the middle of the 1910s. The skirt was reformed from *baizhequn* (a skirt that has all-round small pleats) into a dark long skirt with large pleats. Later, the length became shorter and revealed the bare calves of the wearer. The blouse also saw reformations, such as a lower collar and the emergence of arc shaped vents on both sides. Moreover, civilized costume was made of new textiles (such as cotton and wool, rather than the traditional fabrics of brocade and silk). The waist was slightly tightened to display the fitted silhouette. Simple narrow laces decorated the neckline, sleeve ends and vents.

The May Fourth Movement of 1919 was a revolutionary moment of anti-imperialism and anti-feudalism. It marked the great beginning of the new democratic revolution and brought various new ideological trends into China. It also had an obvious impact on women's clothes. Appropriate political thoughts, social environment and cultural concepts promoted modernity and, according to the records, female students who attended the May Fourth Movement wore short light-blue blouses with rounded hemlines and long black dress, matching white stockings and black cloth shoes. The general image was simple and elegant. From that time, the civilized costume, led by female students, were widely popularized and developed.

The style was thought of as more convenient, fresh and free. The simplicity and plainness reflecting the female students' spiritual state of pursuing simplicity

Figure 3.2 Female students in the early Republican period. The 'blouse matching skirt' style abandons traditional complicated ornaments, adopting white blouse, deep-colour long skirt with rectangular vents on both sides. Photo from *Funü zazhi* (no. 3, vol. 1, 1915).

and natural status. Whilst the clothes were plain and almost without decoration in the early period, luxuriant fabrics were adopted in the later period. During and after the May Fourth Movement, however, the main change in women's clothes was the length. Blouses and skirts tended to be shorter. This trend satisfied the demands of society at that time. According to the records, because 'the short blouse was better than the gown in both spirit and hygiene. It was very convenient for working . . .'[5] The blouse became shorter, transforming from long and tight at the beginning to more latterly being short and loose. The shape of the hemline developed from right-angles into semicircles. The sleeve was shorter and of elbow-length, it became wider from the armhole to the sleeve end and was named *daodaxiu* (inversed big sleeves). The 'blouse matching trousers' style was popular among women in the early 1920s. At that time, whether with trousers or long skirt to match, the blouse became shorter. The hemline was below the calf at the beginning of the period but later turned so short that it was just below the knees. In 1925, the skirt was of calf-length. The shorter blouse and the symbolic

Figure 3.3 An advertisement published in *Shenbao* on 9 May 1920. The clothing of the two women on the left is typical. The woman seated in the middle wears a plain blouse and matching middle-length black skirt, which is the typical style of the civilized costume. The style of the clothes worn by the woman standing on the left is the 'blouse matching pants' style, which is a transformation of the civilized costume. The blouse retains the flare sleeves and the side vents, while changing the long skirt into pants. The pants are of calf-length, bravely revealing the calf.

daodaxiu were the two characteristics of the civilized costume in the prosperous stage, and became a key representation of a bold and new fashion. Eileen Chang described the style in *Gengyi ji* (Chronicle of Changing Clothes or Chinese Life and Fashion): 'the fashionable clothing shows naivety, briskness and joy unprecedentedly. The "flared sleeves" flutter, baring the beautiful wrist. The waist of short blouse is extremely tight.'[6] The short blouse with tightened waist outlined the waist curve of women. Meanwhile, the hemline was short and arc-shaped, displaying the curve of women's hips. *Daodaxiu* displayed the wrist as well as the forearm. The shorter long skirt or trousers bared women's calves. This undisguised way of displaying the body was rare in the history of China, and was also considered very bold and avant-garde.

The emergence of the reformed *qipao* after 1925 made *qipao* the most popular dress of Chinese women in the Republic of China. At that time *qipao* was a new style of clothing and just beginning to rise in popularity. Civilized costume had been available for more than ten years and in this last stage the style incorporated a more luxurious and nostalgic trend, emphasizing decoration in the so-called '*Shanghaizhuang*' (Shanghai-style clothes). Women began to pursue more decoration and tended to use rich and traditional fabrics like silk and brocade. Civilized costume now incorporated complicated decorations like embedding, binding and embroidery and were no longer characterized by plain colours.

Many changes of details emerged, especially during the heyday of *Shanghaizhuang*. As Ling Boyuan wrote in *Funü fuzhuang zhi jingguo* (Development of Women's Fashion):

> Most women chose to wear *Shanghaizhuang* in early 1925. *Shanghaizhuang* had an oblong blouse with round vents. The standing collar was named as '*doujiaoling*' (a style of collar shaped like string bean). The sleeves were of wrist length while the pants were loose and long enough to reach the instep. Most clothes were coloured, few were in plain colour. Women wearing *Shanghaizhuang* displayed their waist curves and showed their charm. Therefore, this style became extremely popular at that time.[7]

After the Revolution of 1911, civilized costume, which was initially adopted by female students, became widely popularized because of its simple, plain and fresh style. Its emergence was also affected by the Western feminist movement and the influential New Culture Movement (1915 to 1923) in China. The development of this new style reached its peak during the May Fourth Movement. It was considered a symbol of the acceptance of the new knowledge and new civilization, reflecting Chinese women's new ideology and new

Figure 3.4 Photo of Zhang Zhiyun (1904–?), a movie actress in Shanghai. The brocade blouse has flared sleeves and tightened waist, while the exaggeratedly arcuate hemline emphasizes the waist and hips. Multiple trimmings are decorated at sleeve ends, hemline and both sides. The hemline of the long skirt has wide tassels as decoration. Photo from *Beiyang huabao* (Pei-yang Pictorial News, no. 36, 1926, p. 3).

awareness. It was also the embodiment of women's gradually maturing ideology of liberation.

In style, detail, design, aesthetics and other aspects, civilized costume showed respect to tradition as well as the absorption of Western style, thus reaching a balance. It obeyed the aesthetic rules of traditional clothes and catered to the aesthetic trend of international mainstream fashion, and was thus a perfect combination of Chinese and the Western styles.

The Inheritance of Traditional Chinese and Western Clothing Styles

As previously noted, civilized costume also originated from traditional *yishang* which continued to be worn until the Republican period. In July 1912 (the first year of the Republic), the Senate published rules with clear guidelines requiring that women's dress remained in the '*aoqun*' style of the late Qing Dynasty:

> The upper garment is knee-length. It has collar, front opening, and vents on the right, left and back hemline, with brocading ornaments on the whole bodice. The matched skirt has *qunmen* [which is also called *mamian* in Chinese, namely skirt panel, the flat surface with no pleat] at the front and the back. The right and the left sides are pleated, with ribbon on the top hem.[8]

It can be seen that even though it was named as new, civilized costume followed tradition and did not break the established rules of the 'blouse matching skirt' style which had been obeyed by Han women for thousands of years. In other words, it still followed the traditional basic form of Han women's wear.

Wusi yishi, the novel written by Eileen Chang, tells of love stories of youths in 1924. The description of two women's dress styles at the beginning largely represents women's image at that time:

> Miss Chou's vivacity is admired by others. People think she could represent the New Woman. However, Miss Fan has a peaceful beauty. She sits there with a smile and seldom talks. Her oval face is narrow and slightly pointed. Her long fringe keeps abreast of her eyebrows. She combs her hair and makes it into two buns, on the right and left. She wears a little make-up, a black silk skirt which is tied high to the waist, a violet-blue lined undercoat with flared sleeves and rippled edge, as well as a white silk scarf on the neck. She has no decoration, except for the golden watch on her wrist and the golden fountain pen at her bosom.[9]

The violet-blue undercoat and the matching black long skirt worn by Miss Fan are typical of civilized costume, which has a 'peaceful beauty'.[10] Therefore, though civilized costume was new and deeply influenced by Western clothing styles in the early Republican period, people still thought it maintained an oriental elegance and followed the rules of traditional Chinese aesthetics.

From a Chinese perspective, Westerners lay emphasis on artistic forms of clothing, and also attach more importance to the natural structure of the human body. They think that physical beauty is full of aesthetic value, just like all the beautiful things in nature. This concept of clothing, based on nature and the human body, was (so far as Chinese accounts were concerned) adopted throughout the Western history of clothing development. During the New Culture Movement in China, people embraced literature, respecting human nature and humanism as the primary tasks in the cultural and artistic field. Fashion followed suit.

Though there were not many breakthroughs in the style of civilized costume, the changes of design and details were significant. In the initial stage, civilized costume adopted a relatively tight and straight silhouette, while changing the loose-fitting style of Han women's dressing in the Qing Dynasty. After the May Fourth Movement, the design of civilized costume was more revolutionary. In general, changes occurred in two aspects. One was the shortening of blouse, skirt and sleeves. The shortening of these three vertical lines reformed the visual effect of civilized costume completely. That is to say, it displayed more of the female body. The other was the emergence of curves. On the one hand, it adopted cutting technology to tighten the waist and display the curves of bust, waist and hips. On the other hand, the shape of the vents on both sides of the blouse transformed from straight lines into curves. This change directly led to the partial display of female hip curves. *Nüzi fuzhuang de gailiang* (Improvement on Women's Fashion) was an article published in the *Funü zazhi* (The Ladies' Journal), a significant journal during the Republican period:

> Women's clothes in our country have always emphasized straight silhouettes and were different from those in the west, which focused on female figures. For this reason, our female clothes were neat when packed, but so loose when worn that they swayed behind and could not keep the wearer warm. Small clothing constricts the body tightly and impedes the flow of blood, which disobeys hygiene. Therefore, the reformers need to consider the factors above . . .[11]

As can be seen from this, reformation of 'curving' on civilized costume after the 1920s echoed the voice of society. In this article, detailed illustrations of the 'curving' reformation was shown. It intuitively displayed the reformation of women's garments, ranging from technique to skill, from silhouette to detail, from inner conception to outer image.

In Chinese traditional clothing vocabulary, ornament of clothes ranks first. Ornament is important because it reflects people's identities, status, wealth and so on. In the vocabulary of early Western clothing, the decorative function of clothes was also thought to be most important, particularly in their symbolism of class identity and status. But by the early twentieth century this concept changed. Male and female clothing witnessed a revolution of less decoration and more function successively. Civilized costume was obviously influenced by this

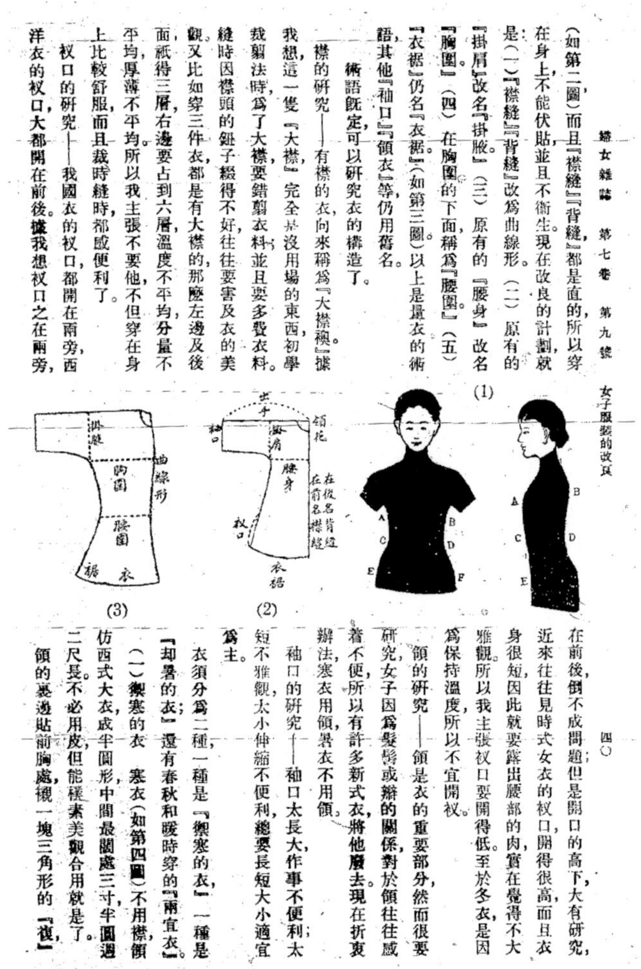

婦女雜誌　第七卷　第九號　女子服裝的改良　四〇

(如第二圖，)而且『襟縫』『背縫』都是直的，所以穿在身上，不能伏貼，並且不衛生。現在改良的計劃，就是：(一)『襟縫』『背縫』改爲曲線形。(二)原有的『掛肩』改名『掛腋』。(三)原有的『腰身』改名『胸圍』。(四)在胸圍的下面，稱爲『腰圍』。(五)『衣裾』仍名『衣裾』。(如第三圖。)以上是量衣的術語，其他『袖口』『領衣』等，仍用舊名。

術語既定，可以研究衣的構造了。

襟的研究——有襟的衣，向來稱爲『大襟褂』。據我想，這一隻『大襟』完全是沒用場的東西，初學裁翦法時，爲了大襟，要錯翦衣料；並且要多費衣料。縫時因襟頭的鈕子綴得不好，往往要害及衣的美觀。又比如穿三件衣，都是有大襟的，那麽左邊及後面，祇得三層，右邊要占到六層，溫度不平均，分量不平均，厚薄不平均。所以我主張不要他，不但穿在身上比較舒服，而且裁時縫時，都感便利了。

衩口的研究——我國衣的衩口，都開在兩旁，西洋衣的衩口，大都開在前後。據我想衩口之在兩旁，在前後，倒不成問題；但是關口的高下，大有研究，近來往往見時式女衣的衩口，開得很高，而且衣身很短，因此就要露出腰部的肉，實在覺得不大雅觀。所以我主張衩口要開得低。至於冬衣，是因爲保持溫度，所以不宜開衩。

(1)　(2)　(3)

領的研究——領是衣的重要部分，然而很要研究，女子因爲髮髻或辮的關係，對於領往往感着不便，所以有許多新式衣，將他廢去。現在折衷辦法，寒衣用領，暑衣不用領。

袖口的研究——袖口太長大，作事不便利；太短不雅觀，太小伸縮不便利，總要長短大小適宜爲主。

衣須分爲二種，一種是『禦寒的衣，』一種是『卻暑的衣；』還有春秋和暖時穿的『兩宜衣』。

(一)禦寒的衣　寒衣(如第四圖)不用襟，領仿西式大衣，或半圓形，中間最闊處三寸，半圓週二尺長。不必用皮，但能樸素美觀合用就是了。領的裏邊貼前胸處，襯一塊三角形的『複，』

Figure 3.5 Article entitled *Nüzi fuzhuang de gailiang* written by Zhuang Kaibo (act. 1910–20s) in *Funü zazhi* (no. 9, vol. 7, 1921, pp. 39–44). It not only puts forward the main reform orientation of traditional female clothes, but also describes the specific methods and details of the reformation.

new Western concept and many changes were made with regard to the simplifying of fabric, surface decorations and other aspects as well as following the no make-up and no hairpin or earrings standard, reflecting the modern concept of function rather than decoration. Thus it can be seen that civilized costume was a representation of the New Woman's lifestyle in the Republic of China.

In 1920, Hu Huaichen (1886–1938) published an article entitled *Nüzi dangchu zhuangshi* (Women Should Abolish Fashion) in the *Fuzü zazhi*, which was the

Figure 3.6 Still from the movie shot by Shanghai Lang Hua Film Company called *Hongxian zhizhan* (The War of Anti-Yuan Shikai). Female medical workers in the 1920s were the representatives of the New Women who had education and a career. They were also pioneers who stepped out of their homes and into society. The uniform worn by the three nurses in the still is in the style of the civilized costume, which has a short blouse with a standing collar, side opening and flared sleeves matched by a below-knee-length skirt. The clothes are all in white, the common colour for a nurse's uniform, and have red-cross patterns on the side of the flared sleeves, hat and medical bag. This still was published in *Young Companion* (no. 27, 1928).

most influential magazine in the early Republican period. He emphasized his belief that decorations represented a 'wasting of resource and time, insanitation, spoiling natural beauty, causing disrespect from others . . . The decorations should be abolished completely.'[12] He also reminded women of the benefits of keeping clean and neat as well as favouring natural beauty in order to avoid looking unkempt without ornamentation from gorgeous clothes. As civilized costume removed complicated ornamentation like floral embroidery, binding, embedding and swirling, it also diminished in size and weight at the same time. Moreover, comfort and functional qualities were intensified. This new kind of dressing was lighter and more convenient to wear, and thus popular among the New Women.

Civilized Costume and *Qipao*

As previously noted when the representative forms of women's clothes in the Republican period are considered, the *qipao* is usually the main focus of

Table 3.1 The characteristics of civilized costume and *qipao*, 1911–30

Time		1911–19	1919–25	1925–30
Characteristics	Civilized costume	Traditional design: *yuanbaoling*, long blouse matching long skirt.	Flared-sleeved short blouse, below-knee-length skirt, few decorations and fabric in plain colour. The style was delicate and simple.	Short blouse with matching long skirt. Gorgeous fabric appeared, while decorations started to be emphasized.
	Qipao	As the inheritance of gown in the Qing Dynasty, its sleeves were narrower and the hem almost reached the instep. By discarding complexity and pursuing simplicity, fabric and decorations were simpler than that in the Qing Dynasty.	Named as '*nuanpao*' (a dress with straight bodice, loose waist, wide cuffs and long length).	It was known as reformative *qipao* and went through the periods of vest *qipao* and flared-sleeved *qipao* successively.

attention. However, civilized costume and the *qipao* developed simultaneously and have a close relationship which is worth exploring.

During the period from 1911 to 1919, both of the two styles were considered to be traditional, although the civilized costume was simpler and plainer. In the years from 1919 to 1925, namely after the May Fourth Movement, civilized costume witnessed unprecedented development, promoting a delicate modern style and it became the representative clothes of the new lifestyle, gaining more popularity than the loose *qipao*. Hu Lancheng (1906–81), a famous scholar in the Republican period, described women's fashion in *Shanhe suiyue* (China through Time).

> Woman in Shanghai and Hangzhou in the early Republic period wore *qipao* with narrow sleeves and diamonds of crystal glass embedded at opening and sleeve-ends. They had delicate eyebrows and bright eyes. Powders on the face were like frost in deep autumn, with anxiety in glow. In the era of the May Fourth Movement, women's wear was reformed to a short blouse and matching long skirt. The blouse was azure, while the long skirt was black. Women seldom wore makeup and were in their natural status.[13]

It was, therefore, not *qipao* but civilized costume with the short blouse and long skirt that was accepted as the vogue in the era of the May Fourth Movement (1919–1925). The traditional *qipao* began to change and rise in popularity from 1925 to the early 1930s. Again it was students who wore the reformative *qipao*, thus leading to the rise of the modern Shanghai-style *qipao* although other women soon followed the students' style and the once old-fashioned *qipao* eventually became the vogue not only with Shanghai women but throughout China. The *Fuzhi tiaoli* (Regulation on Clothing) of the Republic of China, which was promulgated by the Republic government in April 1929, stipulated two female clothing styles. One was short blouse with matching skirt. The other one was long *qipao*.[14] Though both of them were permitted by the government, civilized costume became less popular in the later period, and gradually faded from the fashion stage.

The geneses of both civilized costume and *qipao* can be attributed to female students' willingness to experiment. These female students broke away from the bondage of 'an unaccomplished woman is a virtuous woman' as the Chinese proverb says, which was a traditional concept in China for thousands of years. Studying at school was a revolution, not only of knowledge, but also of conception and ideology. Female students in the Republican period were advocates and practitioners of new ideological trends and a new lifestyle. The article entitled *Nüxuesheng fuzhuang wenti* (The Problem with Female Students' Clothing), was written by Jiang Yuanlin (1899–1987) and was published in the *Funü zazhi* (No. 4, Vol. 10, 1924). It mentioned that 'speaking of the current clothes in China, both male and female clothes have the necessity of reformation. But I think the reformation of female clothes is more urgent, because women's wear is more irrational and more insanitary than that of men.'[15] From this, it could be seen that people in that society had many veiled criticisms of women's wear and thought it should be reformed. The article also said that 'female students are the leaders among women, and they have the obligation to be the pioneers. So the reformation should be led by female students.'[16] Civilized costume and *qipao* were typical cases of clothing reformation in the early Republican period. Moreover, they were also important representations of female students' achievement in challenging old social customs.

Both the civilized costume and *qipao* originated from the metropolis. Civilized costume originated from Beijing and Shanghai, while *qipao* originated from Shanghai. Beijing and Shanghai were the most important cities in modern China. One was the centre of politics and culture, the other one was the centre of business and fashion. As the gathering places for people who had the most pioneering thoughts in the Republican period, these two cities had the most open conceptions. They were the places where novelties were more easily created. And the two cities were also the places that blended various cultures and civilizations. Especially after being opened as a commercial port in 1843, Shanghai had been the 'paradise for adventurers' to Westerners for more than a century. With the establishment of the concessions and its growing status as a business centre, Shanghai saw rapid development in foreign trends. Because of its special geographical location, social environment and commercial function, Shanghai attracted lots of Western immigrants as well as frequent exchanges between China and other eastern countries. By the early twentieth century, it had become the largest commercial port for foreign trade in China, possessing the social conditions and material basis for becoming China's fashion centre. Eventually, Shanghai developed into the financial, economic and trade centre, and was also the largest commercial city, port and international metropolis in modern China. The general environment in the metropolis was unique and showed an inclusive attitude towards innovation and new ideologies, which in turn made a major contribution to the formation of women's new image.

Civilized costume and *qipao* each exhibited both Western and Chinese influences. Either of them can be characterized as reformative clothes. But the reformation did not thoroughly deny traditional tastes. It was based on those traditions, blended into new fashions and eventually creating a new image that combines traditional elements with voguish styles. Civilized costume completely inherited the *yishang* style from traditional Chinese Han female dressing. The reformations were mainly in the details of style, colour and tailoring techniques as well as incorporating the simple and functional features of Western garments. Civilized costume retained the silhouette and some details of Chinese clothes. However, the reformation of *qipao* combined the general style of Manchu men's and women's robes with the simplicity and shortness of Western clothes. Though *qipao* was different from traditional Han women's wear in silhouette, it retained Chinese details and styles. In general, both of these two styles catered to the distinguishing features of Chinese women like tenderness and conservatism and reflected the New Woman's pursuit of Western styles in the new era.

In the development process, civilized costume and *qipao* shared certain rapid reformations in styles. Meanwhile, their other aspects like details and tailoring techniques were reformed gradually. In other words, they both had different typical styles in different stages of development. Accordingly, a relatively specific period should be defined when comparing these two styles. In this chapter, the comparison is aimed at exploring why civilized costume, despite its undeniable popularity in the 1920s, declined and ultimately faded from the historical stage. Therefore, the third development stage of civilized costume was important. It was defined as the specific stage to compare the styles, which was from 1925 to the early 1930s. In this period civilized costume and *qipao* were popular simultaneously for several years.

Despite the similarities of their general forms, there are significant differences between civilized costume and *qipao*: the one-piece robe and the two-piece clothing were quite different. If we consider civilized costume as an inheritance from traditional female garments, *qipao* thoroughly overthrew the Han women's

Figure 3.7 Photo of two noblewomen in Tianjin. The caption is *Jinmen guibin* (Honoured Guests in Tianjin). In this photo, the wife of Sun Chuanfang (1885–1935) wears a flared-sleeved blouse matching a dark ankle-length skirt, which shows the typical style of the civilized costume, while the wife of Lu Xiangting's (1880–1948) wears a straight *qipao* with wide sleeves. Published in Pei-yang Pictorial News (no. 168, 1928).

traditional way of dressing. The one-piece style of *qipao* is the typical traditional clothing style of Han men and minorities in northern China. In general, *qipao* represents the overturning of traditional modes, while civilized costume was an inheritance of classical styles.

From the perspective of style and detail, both similarities and differences have been found between them. After 1925, civilized costume came into the third and final stage of its development. Its typical characteristics were that the bodice became short and tight, the waist was tightened and the figure was emphasized intentionally. Moreover, the skirt became longer. Most were at calf-length, some even reached the ankle. Reformative *qipao*, appeared in around 1925, and successively went through different stages of popular styles, like the vest *qipao* and the flared-sleeved *qipao*, in the late 1920s. The style of *qipao* became more fitted while the length was shorter. Seen from the point of view of fabrics, colour and patterns, a new style named *Shanghaizhuang* appeared during the popularity of civilized costume. *Shanghaizhuang* had gorgeous and exquisite fabrics, adopting traditional multi-coloured brocade as fabric rather than plain new fabrics. Traditional ornamental skills like embedding, binding and embroidery started to appear and obviously showed a pursuit of luxury as well as a nostalgic look. However, the general style of *qipao* was plain and simple. It had a loose silhouette and long length, with the hem reaching the ankle. The bodice was loose-fitting with a wide hem, and the waist was slightly tightened in the later period. The sleeves were wide and flared. The fabrics were plain and delicate, with simple trimmings as decoration rather than complicated traditional ornaments like embedding, binding and embroidery. Thus it can be seen that, though named as 'civilized costume', it adopted a trend of receding to the past. It became similar to traditional clothes in style, and initial characteristics like no decoration and no accessories were gradually weakened. However, the reformative *qipao* featured simplicity, ease and no decoration, and became the representative of the modern new style.

The initial emergence of both civilized costume and *qipao* derived from the urban intellectual woman's pursuits of new life and new image, which were also a resistance to the conservatism, banality and complexity of traditional clothing styles. They both were representative of fashionable clothing in the new era. But civilized costume lacked a driving force. In the later period, it even had a trend of returning to tradition in aspects such as style, design, fabric, decoration and colour. However, the reformative *qipao*, which developed later, persevered with its reformation, remained Chinese in its details and followed the Western trends in style, tailoring technique and aestheticism. It kept a good balance between tradition and modernity, inheritance and development. For this reason, *qipao* became a fashionable way of dressing as well as the most popular daily wear of women in the Republic of China.

Conclusion

Civilized costume and *qipao* are two significant inventions of Chinese women's clothes in the Republican period. Seen from their origins, they are reformations of traditional clothes as well as reflections of women's pursuits of a new life and a new image. But they were very different in their development processes. In the late 1920s, these two styles existed simultaneously, while civilized costume was completely replaced by *qipao* and faded out after the 1930s. *Qipao* developed into the primary form of women's wear in the Republican period and has subsequently had profound impacts to this day.

The different development processes of these two styles can be expressed in the following ways. First, the fundamental processes of design and dressing. Civilized costume was typically designed in a traditional two-piece mode of Chinese clothing practice (Han Chinese). Though it was transformed in aspects like details, tailoring techniques and decorations, it was still in a basic traditional mode. Whereas the one-piece *qipao* was anti-traditional since its basic form differed from the traditional style of Han women's clothes. The one-piece mode of the *qipao* was in accordance with the styles of the minorities' robes and Han men's garments, thus immediately endowing it with features of being new, novel and bold in its appearance. Moreover, it is worth mentioning that the one-piece mode was also the typical style of Western women's gowns. Therefore, *qipao* was still similar to Western female clothing in image and style which again emphasized it as anti-traditional in its Western outlook.

And then they were caused by different reformations of details. In the late 1920s, for example, the waist of the blouse was much tighter in civilized costume. The form of curve was adopted in tailoring techniques to make the clothes fit the body better. This reformation in details was obviously influenced by the concepts of Western clothes. They displayed the body's curve instead of covering it up. However, the trends of Western styles were also changed at that time. They were no longer in the classical 'X' style, but in the straight 'H' one, which was popular through the whole 1920s. The H-shaped silhouette was named as 'Tubular Look'. It abandoned the extreme emphasizing of the curves of breast, waist and hips in traditional Western clothing, and pursued a straight silhouette without waistline, producing a boyish flat figure. That is to say, civilized costume was not focused on the dynamics of mainstream fashion trends. On the contrary, the reformative *qipao* in the middle and later 1920s kept in step with the Western straight silhouette that ignored body curves in the 1920s and displayed a similar 'pipe-like' silhouette. The high consistency with Western mainstream vogues made *qipao* seem more fashionable and modern.

Lastly, both civilized costume and *qipao* originated from innovations derived from tradition. But civilized costume lacked a driving force in its later development and even returned to a traditional emphasis. *Qipao*, however, kept moving forward and pursuing new changes while retaining certain traditional elements. In the general social environment of the era, fashion, convenience, Westernization and elegance were the keywords of female clothing. Intellectual women and urban youth were leaders of fashion trends. Therefore, the way *qipao* blended innovations with traditions was more able to meet the needs of the era.

Whilst it is true that, as the new style of women's clothing in the Republican period, *qipao* was more successful than civilized costume in terms of widespread popularity over a longer time, what is undeniable is that civilized costume was the vanguard of *qipao*. It played an exemplary role and exerted a linking function in the development of the modernization of women's clothing in China. Without the innovation of civilized costume, there would be no reformative *qipao* or even the revolution of Chinese women's clothes that started in the Republican period.

Notes

1 Senate of the Republic of China, *Fuzhi tiaolI* 服制条例 (Regulation on Clothing), 1912.

2 Jiarui Li, *Beiping fengsu leizheng* 北平风俗类正 (The Folk Custom of Beiping [Beijing]) (Shanghai: Photocopy of Shanghai literature and art press, 1985).

3 JinLing Xie, 'Qingmo Minchu Beijing fushi bianhua yanjiu 清末民初北京服飾變化研究' (Study on the Development of Fashion in Beijing from Late Qing to Early Republican Era) (China Academic Journal Electronic Publishing House, 2007).

4 Eileen Chang, '*Wusi yishi*', *Chang Ailing mingzuo xinshang* 张爱玲名作欣赏 (Famous Works of Eileen Chang) (Beijing: China Peace Publishing House, 1996).

5 Senate of the Republic of China, *Fuzhi tiaoli* 服制条例 (Regulation on Clothing), 1912.

6 Xie, 'Qingmo Minchu Beijing fushi bianhua yanjiu'.

7 Chang, '*Wusi yishi*'.

8 Senate of the Republic of China, *Fuzhi tiaoli*, 1912.

9 Chang, '*Wusi yishi*'.

10 Ibid.

11 Kaibo Zhuang, 'Nüzi fuzhuang de gailiang 女子服装的改良' (Improvement on Women's Fashion), *Funü zazhi* 妇女杂志 (The Ladies' Journal), vol. 7 (1921): no. 9.

12 Lancheng Hu, *Shanhe suiyue* 山河岁月 (China through Time) (Nanning: Guangxi People's Publishing House, 2006).

13 Ibid.

14 Senate of the Republic of China, *Fuzhi tiaoli*.

15 Yuanlin Jiang, 'Nüxuesheng de fuzhuang wenti 女学生的服装问题' (Female Students' Clothing Problem), *Funü zazhi* 妇女杂志 (The Ladies' Journal), vol. 4 (1924): no. 10.

16 Ibid.

4

Shanghai *Qipao*, 1925–49

Bian Xiangyang and Yan Lanlan

Definitions

The *qipao* can be defined as a one-piece dress, distinguished by the following elements: an upright opening or mandarin standing collar, Chinese-style 'frog' fastenings fashioned from the same material as the dress itself, the skirt slit on either side, sometimes as high as the thigh; the sleeves continuous with the shoulder of the dress (*tongxiu*) rather than inset, and a two-dimensional structure and cut. Although from some points of view, the female robes of the Banner style (*qizhuang*) in the Qing dynasty (1644–1912) and the *qipao* in the early Republican period are similar to each other and easy to confuse, the *qipao* is in fact regarded as a distinct kind of Chinese women's clothing from the 1920s onwards.[1]

Origins

The original period of *qipao* fashion is often identified as the 1920s, but the exact year of its emergence has not been isolated in past scholarship. Zheng Yimei (郑逸梅) affirmed that women wore short jackets in the Qing dynasty, and that people did not begin wearing *qipao* until the early Republican period.[2] Both Zhou Xibao (周锡保)[3] and Eileen Chang (Zhang Ailing, 1920–95)[4] thought that *qipao* emerged in China after 1921, and Zhou inferred from illustrated magazines or newspapers produced in 1923 that the number of Shanghai women wearing *qipao* was still very small at that time. In fact, given the sensitivity at that time of the Shanghai press to social phenomena, any innovative fashion style would be paid great attention if it was popular. However, it is difficult to find any information about *qipao* in newspapers like *Shenbao* (Shanghai Daily) before March 1925. Only evident in many sources from that year, it can be inferred that *qipao* appeared by the middle of 1925.[5] *Qipao* fashion was also recorded in 1925 in Beijing, once the capital city of China in the Qing Dynasty.[6] As a result, it is quite reasonable to take the year 1925 as the original period of *qipao* fashion.

The geographical origin of *qipao* would presumably be either Shanghai or Beijing, as in both Chinese fashion was deeply affected by the new design. The literal meaning of *qipao* seems to relate with Manchu: *Qi* people (*Qiren*) means Manchu people, and both *Qi* people (*Qiren*) and *qipao* use the same character *qi*. Suggestively, the number of Manchu people in Beijing was much higher than in Shanghai. In Beijing, some Manchu women wore Banner Style clothes (*qizhuang*).[7] *Qipao* fashion began in 1925 in both Beijing and Shanghai, but as a new kind of fashionable style, *qipao* was quite different from the robe style of Banner Style and was instead very similar to Western dress in the way it was worn. Shanghai, as the only fashion centre in China since the late Qing dynasty, was the first place to encounter Western fashion styles. The city had the feature of pursuing

Figure 4.1 Chinese students went to study in the United States, 25 October 1925, in the magazine *Eastern Times Photo Supplement* (*Tuhua shibao*). Student in *qipao* marked by the oval. Courtesy of The Shanghai Library.

modernity, which in Chinese is called modern (*shimao*).[8] Thus it is understandable why Tu Shipin (act. 1940s) asserted in 1948 that: '*Qipao* first became popular in Shanghai and then gradually succeeded in other places.'[9] Xu Dishan (1894–1941) suggested the same as early as 1935.[10]

It seems that the first consumers of *qipao* fashion were female students in Shanghai. As the leading women in that time, female students ensured the popularity of certain fashions and also incorporated new things from the West. Therefore, Shanghai female students were most probably the pioneering group for wearing *qipao*.[11] For example in the magazine *Eastern Times Photo Supplement* (*Tuhua shibao*) in 1925, in a photograph titled as 'Chinese students went to study in the United States', one can see a female student wearing *qipao* (Figure 4.1).[12]

A Chronicle of *Qipao* Fashion 1925–49

From the 1920s to the 1940s, the *qipao* was very popular in Shanghai, being the main trend in Shanghai women's fashion. *Qipao* changed very quickly, with a variety of styles developing in Shanghai during the Republican period, making it the golden age of *qipao*. In 1940, the magazine *The Young Companion* (*Liangyou*) published an article named 'The Melody of *Qipao*' (*Qipao de xuanlü*), which reviewed the classic styles of *qipao* from the years 1926 to 1938, with illustrations (Figure 4.2).[13] Some photographs used in this article even identified the users, which could mean they better reflect the typical *qipao* style during the periods that *qipao* was popular.

The length of *qipao* was the most important marker and weathervane of *qipao* fashion's changes. The styles of collar, sleeves and opening, the length of slits, the level of waistline and its decorations changed in accordance with the total length. Among different communities of women during the Republican period, *qipao* fashion could be different. Outside of 'The Melody of *Qipao*', literary and pictorial references in the press to the *qipao* furnish a wealth of information. By synthesizing different materials, we can investigate the changing fashion of *qipao* in different periods. This approach is in keeping with the anthropologist Alfred Kroeber who carried out an in-depth review of American fashion, particularly changes in waistlines and lengths of sleeves in the early decades of the twentieth century.[14]

From 1925 to 1926 was the initial period of *qipao* fashion, with it worn only by a few daring modernizing women. Its silhouette was a loose, inverted

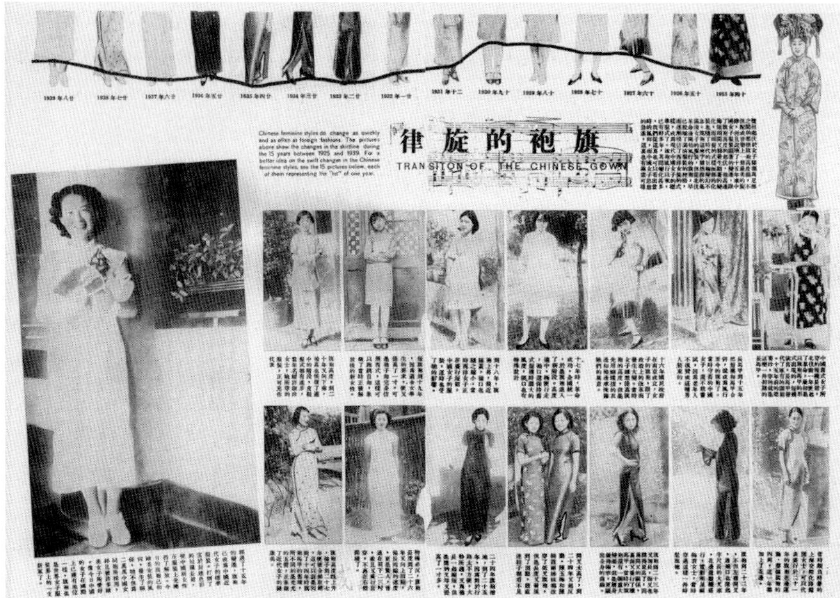

Figure 4.2 'The Melody of *Qipao*', 1940, in the magazine *The Young Companion*. Courtesy of The Shanghai Library.

ladder-type shape, with the waistline invisible. The hemline was just to the ankles, although some were above the ankles, leaving exposed shoes. Normally, the sleeves were wide and a trumpet shape, called 'inversed big sleeves' (*daodaxiu*), with a length just to the elbow. At that time, clothes with big sleeves were very popular.[15] This kind of sleeve was also a symbol of the 1920s, and was mainly matched with flat heeled leather shoes (Figure 4.2). Girls from bourgeois families wore luxuriant styles of *qipao* with gorgeous patterns, whereas female students and less well-off women wore simple styles of *qipao*. The fabric patterns included plain colour, as well as geometric and striped designs.

In 1927, the hemline rose, with the shortest hemline in the middle of the calf. The silhouette was still an inverted ladder-type shape. The article 'The Melody of *Qipao*' suggests that 'The government was based in Nanjing. Women's *qipao* was changed dramatically by the political revolution. Women wanted to shorten the hemline, but they tried to use the butterfly pleats (broad flounces) to hide their real purpose.'[16] The third image of Figure 4.2 shows these 'butterfly pleats', or wide lace in the cuff and hemline. In the front of a *qipao*'s fabric, there were few gorgeous patterns, but the variety and pattern were more abundant.

In 1928, the hemline rose, just covering the knees. The sleeves were short and broad. The article 'The Melody of *Qipao*' asserted that: 'The revolution is successful. All China was unified. Therefore, *qipao* enters upon a new stage. The height of the hemline is medium, very convenient for walking. The cuff continues to be as wide as previous short gowns. The neckline also has special designs.'[17] *Qipao*'s style continued to be simple and elegant in 1928.

At that time, the short skirt was very popular in Western fashion. In 1929, influenced by the Western fashion, the hemline of *qipao* rose again, to being nearly at the knees. To echo the shorter hemline, the cuffs narrowed and the sleeves were shortened to the elbow. Meanwhile, the height of heels rose. The government issued new dress regulations in 1929; as the short *qipao* was very popular, the longer *qipao* became formal dress and the colour that was most esteemed was blue. While the short *qipao* was considered plain and simple, wide laces decorated the edges of the long *qipao*, gradually replacing the panels and bindings.[18]

The 1930s was the brightest period for Shanghai *qipao*. *Qipao* began to be waisted and the curve of women's bodies was revealed. Furthermore, the hemline changed from high to low and *qipao* was at its longest, to the ground, in 1935. Subsequently, it gradually rose. The collar and slits also lengthened, from low to high, and from high to low again. The styles of sleeves alternately changed to short sleeves, long sleeves and non-sleeves. The decorations also varied and changed.

In 1930, the hemline of the *qipao* worn by Shanghai students was at the knees, making it the shortest *qipao* fashion. It also had long sleeves decorated with Western cuffs, and the height of collar was middling, with the silhouette coming to fit the body. This style was simple, convenient and popular for a while. Short *qipao* were worn by students and fashionable women, but long *qipao* were also worn by young women for formal occasions, and by middle-aged and elderly women in daily life.

In 1931, the hemline went down, below the calf, and the slits were at the knees. The sleeves of the dress went long to the elbow, with the cuffs moderate in size. The style of hair and shoes all followed Western fashion. Celebrities played a leading role of fashion, with their dress becoming popular within one or two years. In summer this year, the most fashionable appearance was the flaxen *qipao* matched with underskirt, the face applied with white powder, rosy cheeks and red lips, a perm and silk stockings, capped with high-heeled leather shoes.[19] By contrast, students and intellectuals still preferred the simpler *qipao* style.

In 1932, the hemline of *qipao* continued to extend, now to the ankle. Lace decoration of *qipao* was fashionable, with the collar called 'little shoe-shaped gold ingot' (*xiaoyuanbao*). Looking like small shoe-shaped ingots, the *xiaoyuanbao* was comparatively high. Furthermore, the sleeves were short, ending above the elbows and tending to be fitted. It was popular to use various decorative laces on the collar, as well as openings, the sleeves, slits and hemline. For these, both Western laces and Chinese facings were used. In comparison, in the magazine *La Petite Woman's Magazine* (*Linglong*), it can be seen that students' and intellectuals' dresses were still simple and some of them continued to wear short *qipao*.

The following years saw the *qipao* continue to lengthen. By 1933, the hemline of *qipao* had extended to cover the ankle. Young women seem to have preferred to wear waisted *qipao*. The long and wide sleeves with big slits were popular. For convenience, women rolled up their sleeves and fixed them by buttons. The standing collar rose, and the two side slits were cut to above the knee. 'The Melody of *Qipao*' wrote: 'Not only the left front has slits, but also the cuffs have half foot length slits. The laces are still very popular.'[20] Of course, this kind of exaggerated sleeve only appeared on a few modern leaders' *qipao*. Most *qipao* had common and fitting sleeves. The fashion etiquette in this year was carefully described: 'The stiff collar is so high that if you want to look back, you must turn your whole body. And *qipao* is so long that when you get in the car, you must lift it. The high-heel shoes, you must wear very carefully.'[21]

In 1934, the hemline of *qipao* continued to lengthen, below the ankle, the collar becoming higher, the sleeves shortening and becoming very fitted. The waist was very narrow to show women's body curves. The slits were cut to higher than the hip, so the waistcoat (*majia*) could be worn as an inner layer with *qipao*. The print patterns were very various; stripes, checks and broken floral patterns were very popular, especially in student and intellectual groups. In 1935, the length was at its most extreme, almost to the ground. This resulted in the dress being called the 'sweeping *qipao*' (*tuodi qipao*), when even the shoes were hidden (see the *qipao* photograph of 1935 in Figure 4.2). The slits of *qipao* in 1934 seem to have been thought too high, and were much shortened in 1935 by about five to six *cun* (寸: one-third of a decimetre).

In 1936, because wearers had some difficulty moving, the length of *qipao*'s body was shortened, just to the feet. A high collar was still popular, yet the sleeves were shortened, while the length of the slits increased four or five centimetres. The waist was tightened to be fitted. In 1937, the hemline rose with the pull-on style with the horizontal opening recalling character-one-openings (*yizijin*) or character-eight-openings (*bazijin*) in traditional waistcoats (*majia*) and forming a new fashion for *qipao*. In this mode, the sleeves were very short and looked like shoulder knots. The waist was tight, again showing off women's body curve, and the slits were to the calf.

From 1938 to 1941, due to the Second Sino-Japanese War, business in Shanghai was 'island[ed]'; as a result, *qipao* became simple and practical, with its fashion changing slowly. Although *qipao* in this period kept the typical style of its golden age, for contemporary writers they apparently expressed the influence of the war.

Thus, in 1938, *qipao* continued to be shortened and the ankles were exposed. A sleeveless *qipao* became fashionable, exposing both arms completely. It returned to the past *qipao* waistcoat fashion of 1925, so to speak. The difference was the bare arms, symbolizing women's healthy beauty in modern times. Because of the war, people tried to wear old clothes, rather than making new clothes, while even the new clothes were simple and coarse. Convenient, simple and beautiful was the new standard of *qipao* fashion. Some articles introduced how to cut old long *qipao* to short *qipao* to cope with material scarcity during the war.[22] In 1939, the height of the standing collar reduced to the normal height. The shoulder part of the sleeve was wider. Most women wore the mid-calf-length *qipao* to move more conveniently.

The major difference in *qipao* fashion of 1940 from 1939 was the return of sleeves. They featured simple decorated fabric with solid colour bases, and stripes or checks were popular. Later, there was a state of slight change. In 1941, *qipao* almost stayed the same as it was in 1940.

From 1942 to 1949, after Japan captured Shanghai in 1941, the main feature of *qipao* was simple and practical. *Qipao* fashion changed less. After the Sino-Japanese War, Shanghai *qipao* was influenced by Hollywood movie stars' fashion, and the tight waist was popular in a short time. Then, during the Civil War until 1949 (in which year the People's Republic of China was established), the style of *qipao* basically remained unchanged.

Given this history of change and adaption, the picture in the article 'The Melody of *Qipao*' in 1940 is not clear enough. Indeed, some typical styles appeared inexactly. Therefore, by synthesizing all kinds of materials, predominantly from images in newspapers and periodicals, the fashionable styles and hemline change of *qipao* from 1925 to 1941 are presented in Figure 4.3.[23]

Through these changes, the material of *qipao* was mainly cotton, silk and ramie. Both Chinese traditional textiles and Western fabrics could be used. Poplin, satin, damask, velvet and satin brocade were common. Woollen fabrics were also used. Light textiles like gauze and sheer silk were fashionable for a while. The traditional patterns tended to be simple, and some Western patterns were popular. Striped or checked fabrics, solid coloured fabrics and printed fabrics were in fashion from the 1930s.

Figure 4.3 The fashionable styles and hemline change of *qipao* in Shanghai from 1925 to 1941. Courtesy of Zhang Qi Li Linzhen.

The Mix and Match of *Qipao*

For the study of fashion history, the mixing and matching of some clothes can better reveal the condition of dress and the most fashionable image than studying a single piece of clothing during a period. Shanghai women's images also included make-up and social etiquette. The following section will discuss how women in the Republican period wore and matched *qipao*, as the key aspect of *qipao* fashion. *Qipao*'s combination with other clothing, hairstyles, shoes, stockings and other accessories helped *qipao* express various styles, as well as the social condition, dressing images and modern fashion of Shanghai women from the 1920s to the 1940s.

The Matching of *Qipao* with Corresponding Clothes

During the Republican period, items that were matched with *qipao* mainly included capes and shawls, Western-style overcoats, sweaters, vests and so on. The style of capes matching with *qipao* varied. Sometimes they were above-knee-length or even ankle-length, fastened or buttoned at the front, single- or double-layered in cotton or leather. Images and feelings of woman wearing *qipao* matched with capes or shawls were also different. The capes were steady and demure; while the shawls were elegant and sophisticated. Meanwhile, sometimes the matching with *qipao* in both styles was used to present a woman's particular identity. Indeed, they were adopted mainly by fashionable women such as movie stars and social celebrities. Figure A in Table 4.1 shows a *qipao* matched with a cape, as worn by the movie star Hu Die (1908–89) in 1933.[24]

The combination of *qipao* with corresponding Western-style overcoats was very popular for the modern female in Shanghai. They could include short overcoats, coats and parkas, which were often elegant. *Qipao* matching with such overcoats reflected a chic interjection of Western fashion. The matching of *qipao* with Western-style overcoat was also the characteristic of the 'peculiar style' that made *qipao* a member of the international clothing family.[25] *Qipao* matching with Western-style short overcoat modelled a steady and generous image, while with Western-style overcoat and parka it presented a fashionable and elegant image. This matching was not only worn by modern women, such as movie stars and celebrities, but also by women from well-known families, and also by ordinary women, including intellectuals, office clerks and students. Figure B in Table 4.1 shows female students wearing *qipao* matched with Western-style overcoats.[26]

Sweaters matched with *qipao* mainly included knitted sweaters, braiding sweaters and crotchet sweaters. As the book 'Complication Committee of the Recordation of Shanghai Women' (*Shanghai funüzhi bianzhuan weiyuanhui*) explains, 'in the Republic period 1930s, the woollen sweaters, imported from foreign countries, were worn over *qipao* or shirts by Shanghai movie stars. They were mainly front-opening style.'[27] To meet the functional needs of keeping warm, women usually wrapped the *qipao* with a crotchet sweater in early spring and autumn, or with sweaters or wool clothing in autumn and winter. In addition, it also provided more choices for the appearance of *qipao* by matching it with these sweaters. Figure C in Table 4.1 shows *qipao* worn with sweaters.[28] The combination of *qipao* with sweaters was quite popular in Shanghai at that time.

Table 4.1 Table of *qipao* matching with clothes . Images courtesy of The Shanghai Library.

Matching Clothes	Images	People and Time
Capes and Shawls		Figure A: Hu Die wore *qipao* matching with a cape, 1933
Western-style Overcoats		Figure B: female students Zheng Qianru (the first left), Chen Shanzhen (the second right) and Su Huiying (the first right) wore *qipao* matching with Western-style overcoats, 1934
Sweaters		Figure C: Shanghai musician Madam Fang Yu (1903–2002) (right) and writer Madam Su Mei wore *qipao* matching with sweaters, 1929
Vests		Figure D: Man Ying wore *qipao* matching with a vest, 1937

The styles of vests matched with *qipao* were mainly front-opening styles, while some were pullovers. When matched with *qipao*, these front-opening style vests were usually unfastened, producing a natural and innocent look (Table 4.1, Figure D).[29] Female students and some fashionable women such as office clerks, social celebrities and movie stars were fond of it.

The Matching of *Qipao* with Hairstyles

During the Republican period, there were two main types of hairstyles, straight hair and curled hair, which were matched with the *qipao* in Shanghai. Short straight hair, commonly up to ear length, was the most fashionable mode to match with *qipao*, rather than traditional plait or chignon. The matching of *qipao* with short straight hair was an outcome of the women's liberation movement and the impact of fashion from Western countries. It could express both an innocent, simple image of girlhood or the capable and experienced image of a mature woman. In the late 1920s, a wide group adopted it, including the most fashionable movie stars, students and female intellectuals. In Figure E of Table 4.2, the film star Li Minghui (1909–2003) in 1926 wore short straight hair with her *qipao*.[30]

Curled hair was an outcome of perm technology which spread to Shanghai from the United States and Europe and became fashionable. Figure F in Table 4.2 shows the actress Lin Huilü in a performance at Fudan University in 1933, when

Table 4.2 Table of *qipao* matching with hairstyles

Matching Hair-styles	Images	People and Time
Straight Hair		Figure E: film star Li Minghui had short straight hair to combine with *qipao* in 1926
Curly Hair		Figure F: actress Lin Huilü wore *qipao* with short curly hair, 1933

she combined a *qipao* with short curled hair.[31] The matching of *qipao* with short and medium-length curled hair presented a charming or elegant image according to different styles of *qipao*. In the 1930s the matching of *qipao* with curled hair was very popular. Modern women including movie stars, social celebrities and some female students who were fashion-conscious were fond of the new mode, while ordinary women preferred neat, more generous and lasting ones.

The Matching of *Qipao* with Footwear

As a one-piece dress, *qipao* was rarely matched with trousers. Therefore, footwear including stockings and shoes able to suit the *qipao* were more important. At that time, shoes, matched with *qipao*, included leather shoes and cloth shoes. Meanwhile, high-heeled leather shoes were more popular to match *qipao*, and few of them were flats. The style of high-heeled shoes were similar to and synchronous with Western styles, but were also more classic in style. Wearing these shoes, women were taller and perceived in eroticized terms when they were walking. Therefore, high-heeled shoes made a woman appear more enchanting in a *qipao* according to contemporary norms. This image was mature and elegant, and fitted the contemporary pursuit of Western aesthetic standards. This matching was popular with social celebrities, movie stars and other modern

Table 4.3 Table of *qipao* matching with footwear

Matching Footwear	Images	People and Time
Stockings and Shoes		Figure G: Ge Luxi wore *qipao* matching with heeled leather shoes and dark silk stockings, 1930
Stockings and Shoes		Figure H: Shen Wenying wore *qipao* matching with black cloth shoes, 1930

pioneer groups. In Figure G of Table 4.3, Ge Luxi wears a *qipao* with heeled leather shoes.[32]

Western-style stockings were worn in lieu of trousers, forming the dominant leg covering. This was also influenced by Western fashion. Garters were very popular with fashionable women, emphasizing the silhouette of women's legs, where silk stockings were especially visible through the high slits of *qipao*. An appropriate pair of stockings ensured an enchanting image for women, matching progressive Western aesthetics for women at that time. As shown in Figure G, Miss Ge wore *qipao* with dark translucent silk stockings. In contrast, ordinary women were more likely to choose light colours or incarnadine stockings. Figure H in Table 4.3 shows Shen Wenying wore *qipao* with black cloth shoes. She was the Sports Director of both Shanghai High School and Minli Female Middle School.[33]

The Matching of *Qipao* with Accessories

The accessories matched with *qipao* during the Republican period were numerous, with the main examples including ornaments for the neck and head. Usually they were chosen according to the styles and mode of *qipao*, as well as personal taste preferences and the occasion of use. They emphasized both the figure and the harmonious appearance of a woman, reflecting the tradition of fine urban dressing.

Neck ornaments and accessories worn with *qipao* were mainly fitted to the neck, including mufflers, silk scarves and necklaces. The matching of *qipao* with silk scarves or mufflers presented an image of women which was capable, sophisticated, or gentle and delicate. The necklaces matched with *qipao*, mostly worn outside of the *qipao*, were not only aspects of dressing appropriately but also formed symbols of the wearers' identities. For example, Shanghai actress Miss Yang Naimei (1904–60) wore translucent short-sleeved *qipao* matched with a thicker light-coloured beaded necklace (Table 4.4, Figure I).[34] In contrast, ordinary females liked to wear simple neck ornaments such as scarves, while more fashionable groups of people preferred a diverse choice of neck ornaments.

Other accessories matched with *qipao* included watches, earrings and other small items of jewellery. Watches not only held practical functions, but also presented the wearers' identities and status, as watches were very expensive at that time. With earrings, it was necessary to take facial form and the style of *qipao* into consideration when choosing them. Figure J in Table 4.4 shows Shanghai social celebrity Sun Qifang used spindling eardrops to match with her *qipao*. The

Table 4.4 Table of *qipao* matching with accessories

Matching Accessories	**Images**	**People and Time**
Neck Ornaments		Figure I: Yang Naimei wore short-sleeved *qipao* matching with a necklace, 1927
Head Ornaments		Figure J: Shanghai social celebrity Sun Qifang wore *qipao* matching with earrings, 1938
Other Accessories		Figure K: Li Xiaqing wore *qipao* matching with a leather bag, 1936
		Figure L: Jiang Hailian wore *qipao* matching with glasses, 1937

eardrops not only ornamented her rounded face, but also created an enchanting look matched with her *qipao*.[35] Certain fashionable groups preferred to use different kinds of head ornaments, while more ordinary women chose simpler and more socially appropriate styles. Alternatively, they might dispense with all these kinds of accessories.

The other accessories matched with *qipao* included bags, glasses, rings, decorative flowers, fans, and umbrellas, among others. These were used by different groups of women and their specific use mainly depended on the overall appearance, aesthetic and practical needs of a given person. For example, the left picture of Figure K of Table 4.4 features Shanghai female aviator Li Xiaqing (1912–98) matching her *qipao* with a leather bag. Miss Li's dress models the image of a successful woman, capable and experienced, stable and dignified.[36] Also present is Shanghai social celebrity Jiang Hailian, wearing a sleeveless *qipao* with exquisite glasses. Her look is both delicate and elegant (Figure L).[37]

Social Psychological Analysis of the Origin of *Qipao* Fashion

Any style that wants to become fashionable must be in accordance with public aesthetics, consumers' economic abilities and the atmosphere of a given community. At its beginning, *qipao* fashion was an integration of characteristics of Chinese style with Western dress. Some reasons can be given to explain *qipao*'s popularity all over China: first, the power of fashion was very strong which went beyond people's imagination; second, people at that moment were yearning for aspects of Western civilization, including its clothing; third, the basis of dress customs and traditional apparel manufacturing; and fourth, the social backgrounds of the Northern Expedition in China (the First Revolutionary Civil War from 1924 to 1927).

Aesthetically, *qipao* fashion was considered by some people to be the same as Western fashion, focused on displaying physical beauty.[38] In fact, *qipao* fashion materialized the subconscious of Chinese traditional aesthetics, yet it also formed a new fashion aesthetic melding Chinese characteristics with the spirit of the times. The *qipao* at its early stage was still in a traditional planar structure. With plain cut sleeves (*tongxiu*), the *qipao* emphasized the sloping shoulders that were thought beautiful in Chinese traditional views. With two side slits, the integrated impression of legs could be imagined. *Qipao* was cut out properly for chest and hip, but without horizontal divisions nor darts in the waist. The dress was not too close-fitting at the waist, though margins were constricted by cut. Despite the smooth outline of *qipao*, the breast was not as prominent as that of Western dress, the Easterners' flat upper arms were ignored and the curve of the fine waist could be emphasized. This kind of *qipao* not only fitted women with traditionally understood graceful figures, but also made many plump women look slimmer. Even with a slight abdomen, a woman in *qipao* would be optimal plump (*futai*) – a positive description for noble and slightly overweight women in the Chinese tradition. For this reason, *qipao* was thought suitable for most Chinese women whether young or aged.

Not only did Chinese women like *qipao*, but also Chinese men enjoyed women wearing *qipao*. More conservative people accepted *qipao* because it was emblematic of Chinese clothing with its traditional aesthetic features. Moreover, combined with some characteristics of Western clothing, *qipao* was in accordance with an enlightened ethos. Progressive society welcomed *qipao* for it visualized China meeting the West; the *qipao* followed Western fashions yet had a meaningful Chinese name. Furthermore, the dressed-up behaviour pattern of *qipao*, containing both Chinese and Western merits, also expressed the various different aesthetic preferences for social groups in China at that time.

Qipao was popular also because it was easy to manufacture. Its structure in early times was simple and like traditional clothing. Its concise shape and decoration were compatible with various fabrics, and its cutting and sewing were convenient for different individuals. People could go to street cloth-stalls or ask tailors to come home to make *qipao* according to their own figure. If someone had not enough money, she could make it by herself or ask other people for help. The fashion stores often made and sold Western-style garments at that time, having just one or two counters that accepted orders of *qipao* for those women who were not satisfied with busy tailors' practices or reluctant to make it by themselves. Without professional designers, Chinese women with good fashion traditions, especially fashionable women in Shanghai, still unconsciously materialized their ideas of fashion with the tailors' help. Thus, the guises of *qipao* looked similar, but it had a variety of details and decorations, which further promoted the *qipao* fashion presenting many different personalities at that time.

The social background of the 1920s provided a good opportunity for the popularity of *qipao* fashion. As a style of the modernizing woman, *qipao* was admitted and commended during the Northern Expedition and the women's liberation movement.[39, 40] Throughout society, textile mills and fashion stores especially facilitated the development of *qipao* fashion for the benefit of business. The access to fashion, especially in cities, accelerated *qipao* entering into ordinary people's daily life. After 1927, *qipao* fashion gradually spread from the city to the small towns and rural districts.[41, 42] By the 1930s, *qipao* had replaced the Chinese traditional dress mode combining a jacket with skirt, and became the main category of clothing for Chinese women.

Conclusion

Female students in Shanghai pioneered the wearing of *qipao* in 1925. Due to its aesthetic character, production, consumption as well as the social background of wearers at that time, *qipao* was widely accepted and became quite popular from 1927. Meanwhile, the period from 1925 to 1941 became known as the golden age of *qipao* fashion, as it was very popular in Shanghai and formed the dominant women's fashion trend. During these years, the styles of *qipao* changed very fast and frequently. The hemline was the most important style determinant of a *qipao*. The styles of collar, sleeves and opening, the length of slits, the level of waistline and its decorations changed in accordance with the length of hemline. From 1942 to 1949, the style of *qipao* kept the style of its golden age, almost remaining unchanged. However, the mixing and matching of *qipao* with other clothes, different hairstyles, footwear and varied accessories better revealed the condition of *qipao* and aligned with shifting fashionable images. All of these changes in style and dressing, social psychology and context, synthetically produced *qipao* fashion as the leading trend during the Republican period in Shanghai and ensured an afterlife beyond that still reverberates today.

Notes

1 Bian Xiangyang 卞向阳. (2003), 'Origin of Qipao Fashion in Early Republic Period', *Journal of Donghua University* (English edition), 20(4): 21–26.

2 Zheng Yimei 郑逸梅. (1946), 'Fuyu zhi bianqian 服御之变迁' (The Changing of Costume and Equipage), *Fangranzhi gongcheng* 纺染织工程 *(Textile and Dyeing Engineering)*, 4: 5.

3 Zhou Xibao 周锡保. (1984), *Zhongguo gudai fushishi* 中国古代服饰史 *(A History of Ancient Chinese Apparel and Accessories)*, Beijing: China Theatre Press, 534.

4 Eileen Chang 张爱玲. (1943), 'Gengyiji 更衣记' (Chronicle of Changing Clothes), *Gujin* 古今, 36.

5 Lu Lijun 陆立钧. (2008), *Minguo shiqi Shanghai baokan zhongde fushi xinxi yanjiu* 民国时期上海报刊中的服饰信息研究 (Study on the Information Related with Fashion in Newspapers and Magazines Published in Shanghai during Republic Period), Donghua University, 45.

6 Jing Ru 菁如. (1934), 'Beiping funü fuzhuang de yanbian ji xianzhuan 北平妇女服装的演变及其现状' (The Evolution and Actuality of Women's Fashion in Beijing), *Dagongbao* 大公报 (Ta-Kung-Pao) (天津 TIENTSIN), 10 January.

7 Xiao Boqing 肖伯清. (1996), *Jiujing renwu yu fengqing* 旧京人物与风情 (The Personages, Culture and Customs in Old Beijing), Beijing: Yanshan Press, 224.

8 Bian Xiangyang 卞向阳. (1997), 'Shanghai's Fashion during the Late Qing Dynasty Period', *Journal of China Textile University* (English edition), 14(3): 55–56.

9 Tu Shipin 屠诗聘. (1948), *Shanghaishi daguan* 上海市大观 (The Grand Sight of Shanghai), Shanghai: Zhongguo tushu zazhi gongsi 中国图书杂志公司 (China Books and Magazines Company), volume two, 19–21.

10 Xu Dishan 许地山. (1935), *Jin sanbainianlai zhongguo di nüzhuang (xia, xüwu)* 近三百年来中国底女装 (下，续五) ('The Chinese Women's Wear of the Past 300 Years, the second part'), *Dagongbao* 大公报 (Ta Kung Pao), 22, June.

11 Jiang Changlin 姜长麟. (1924), 'Nüxuesheng de fuzhuang wenti 女学生的服装问题' (Female Students' Clothing Problem), *Funü zazhi* 妇女杂志 *(The Ladies' Journal),* 10 (4): 694.

12 Photo. (1925.10.25), *Tuhua shibao* 图画时报 (The Illustrated Eastern Times).

13 'Qipao de xuanl ü旗袍的旋律' (The Melody of *Qipao*). (1940), *Liangyou* 良友 (The Young Companion), 150: 63.

14 Alfred Kroeber. (1919), 'On the Principle of Order in Civilization as Exemplified by Changes in Fashion', American Anthropologist, 21 (3): 235–63.

15 Qu Daoyuan 瞿道援. (1926), 'Liuxing daxiu zhi tuice 流行大袖之推测' (The Speculation about Large Sleeves Fashion), *Liangyou* 良友 (The Young Companion), 5: 19.

16 'Qipao de xuanlü 旗袍的旋律' (The Melody of *Qipao*). (1940), *Liangyou* 良友 (The Young Companion), 150: 63. The original Chinese text is '国民政府在南京成立, 女子的旗袍, 跟了政治上的革命而发生大变。当时的女子虽想提高旗袍的高度, 但是先用蝴蝶褶的衣边和袖边来掩饰她们的真意。'

17 'Qipao de xuanlü 旗袍的旋律' (The Melody of *Qipao*). (1940), *Liangyou* 良友 (The Young Companion), 150: 63. The original Chinese text is '革命成功，全国统一，于是旗袍进入了新阶段。高度适中，极便行走，袖口还保持旧式短袄时阔大的风度，领口也有特殊设计。'

18 'Qipao de xuanlü 旗袍的旋律' (The Melody of *Qipao*). (1940), *Liangyou* 良友 (The Young Companion), 150: 63.

19 Hao Wen 浩文. (1931), 'Cong shidai shuodao zhuangshi 从时代说到装饰' (Discussing Ornament from Era), *Shidai huabao* 时代画报 (The Modern Miscellany, February), 2(3): 19–20.

20 'Qipao de xuanlü', 150: 64. The original Chinese text is '不但左襟开衩，连袖口也开起半尺长的大衩来，花边还在盛行。'

21 Wei 薇. (1933), Modeng funü de zhuangshi 摩登妇女的装饰 ('The Ornament of Modern Women'), *Linglong* 玲珑 (La Petite Woman's Magazine), 110: 1593. The original Chinese text is '那高高的硬领，若要回顾，就要全身旋转，还有长长的旗袍，上车时必须提起来。高跟皮鞋，走起来要特别小心。'

22 Yu Zhenxiong 余振雄. (1938), 'Jiechang chengduan de duanqipao 截长成短的短旗袍' (The Short *Qipao* Cut from Long *Qipao*), *Shengbao fukan* 申报复刊 (*Shengbao Newspapers, resume publication*), 10, October.

23 Lu Lijun 陆立钧. (2008), *Minguo shiqi Shanghai baokan zhongde fushi xinxi yanjiu* 民国时期上海报刊中的服饰信息研究 (Study on the Information Related with Fashion in Newspapers and Magazines Published in Shanghai during Republic Period), Donghua University, 91.

24 Shengbao xinwen sheyingshe 申报新闻摄影社 (*Shenbao* Newspapers Photo Service). (1933), 'Shizhuang biaoyan 时装表演' (Fashion Show), *Liangyou* 良友 (The Young Companion), 82: 24.

25 Bao Mingxin 包铭新. (2000). 'Ershi shiji shangbanye de Haipai qipao 20 世纪上半叶的海派旗袍' (Shanghai *Qipao* during the First Half of the 20th Century). *Zhuangshi* 装饰 (Decoration), 97(5): 11–12.

26 Photo by Gao Liutang 高柳堂. (1934), 'Shitai shangzhi meiren tu 石台上之美人图' (Beauties on the Stone Platform), *Linglong* 玲珑 (La Petite Woman's Magazine), 132: 419.

27 Shanghai funüzhi bianzhuan weiyuanhui 上海妇女志编纂委员会 (Complication Committee of the Recordation of Shanghai Women) ed. (2000), *Shanghai funüzhi* 上海妇女志 (The Recordation of Shanghai Women), Shanghai: Shanghai Academy of Social Sciences Press, 560.

28 Huang Jingwan 黄警顽. (1929), 'Funü zhi ye 妇女之页' (The Pages of Women), *Liangyou* 良友 (The Young Companion), 37: 24.

29 Photo by Xi Xingqun 席兴羣. (1937), *Linglong* 玲珑 (La Petite Woman's Magazine), 271: 262.

30 *Fengmian* 封面 (The Cover Page). (1926), *Liangyou* 良友 (The Young Companion), 3: 27.

31 Xuehong 雪鸿. (1933), 'Dianying yu xiju 电影与戏剧' (Movies and Theatre), *Liangyou* 良友 (The Young Companion), 73: 33.

32 Photo of Ge Luxi (1930), *Liangyou* 良友 (The Young Companion), 52: 31

33 Photo by Xu Yanying 徐雁影. (1931), *Linglong* 玲珑 (La Petite Woman's Magazine), 5: 150.

34 'Zhongguo dianyingjie xianjin nüyanyuan zhi yiban 中国电影界先进女演员之一班' (A Class of the Advanced Actresses in Chinese Film Industry). (1927), *Liangyou* 良友 (The Young Companion), 22: 20.

35 Gong Botang 龚伯堂. (1936), 'Kong decheng zhi hunli 孔德成之婚礼' (The Wedding of Mr. Kung Techeng), *Liangyou* 良友 (The Young Companion), 123: 19.

36 Guojishe 国际社 (International Community). (1936), 'Guonei lingshi 国内零拾' (The Scrappy Materials in China), *Liangyou* 良友 (The Young Companion), 118: 8.

37 'Wumei zhi mu, miaoling zhi nü 妩媚之母 妙龄之女' (Charming Mother and Young Lady). (1937), *Liangyou* 良友 (The Young Companion), 126: 18.

38 Valerie Steele. (1999), *China Chic: East Meets West*, New Haven, CT: Yale University Press, 45–48.

39 Jing Ru 菁如. (1934), 'Beiping funü fuzhuang de yanbian ji xianzhuan 北平妇女服装的演变及其现状' (The Evolution and Actuality of Women's Fashion in Beijing), *Dagongbao* 大公报 (Ta-Kung-Pao) (天津 TIENTSIN), 10 January.

40 Shipin, *Shanghaishi daguan*.

41 Ibid.

42 Xu Dishan 许地山. (1935), 'Jin sanbainian lai zhongguo di nüzhuang (Xia, xüwu) 近三百年来中国底女装 (下，续五) ('The Chinese Women's Wear of the Past 300 Years, the second part'), *Dagongbao* 大公报 (Ta-Kung-Pao), 22 June.

5

'Through the Maloo to the City'

Fashion, Decadence and Dance Culture in Shanghai in the Early Twentieth Century

Juliette MacDonald

Dry, muddy, wet or gritty,
He took to dancing all the way
Through the Maloo to the City.
You do not often get the chance
Of seeing bullion brokers dance
From their abode
In Gordon Road
Down the Maloo to the City.[1]

Urban Exoticism and Modernity in Shanghai

Between the 1910s and 1930s Shanghai was one of the most exciting cities in Asia. Its rapid economic growth, cultural freedom and diversity tempted industrialists, entrepreneurs and adventurers from across the world, as well as from other parts of China, all keen to find a way to benefit from the opportunities afforded by its cosmopolitanism. The journalist J.O.P. Bland commented on Shanghai's increasingly wealthy position and the degree of luxury to be experienced in Shanghai which in his opinion was unequalled by New York or Buenos Aires. 'No Croesus of America, North or South, can ever hope to attain to the comfortable heights and depths that Shanghai takes for granted.'[2] Alongside the pursuit of wealth was a desire to engage with the perceived exoticism of the city. The International Settlement and French Concession provided spaces which were not quite European nor were they Chinese; strange and yet familiar, they facilitated a freedom for all the visitors to the city to engage with new experiences associated with a modern city. This liminality allowed for the construction of an imagined Shanghai, one that was seductive, opulent, exotic and glamorous. As a result, Shanghai, alongside Paris and Berlin, was a place where abandoned decadence was permitted to flourish with transgression and excessive self-indulgence being synonymous with the reputation of the city. One only need look at the many names given to this city – 'Paris of the East', 'Sin City', 'wickedest city in the world' – to understand its place in this collective fantasy of the exotic. With the focus on enjoying life and leisure time it is of little surprise that dancing and the spaces and fashions associated with dance were central to life in Shanghai. Using modernity as the contextual lens this chapter will reflect on the relationship between Argentine tango, other popular dance practices, fashionable leisure spaces and clothing fashions for dance in Shanghai.

Tango arrived in Shanghai in 1913 and remained a popular dance form throughout the Republican era (1912–49). It is, then, intriguing to view tango and social dancing in general from a Shanghai perspective: as Andrew Field in his comprehensive account of Shanghai's night-life from 1919 to 1954 has discussed, the urban dance world of Shanghai was a place of fantasy and spectacle and simultaneously functioned as an intersection between urban politics and culture.[3]

The tango emerged in Buenos Aires in the late nineteenth century where, as was the case in Shanghai a few years later, the mix of cultures brought together by modernization, urbanization and immigration gave rise to racial and class conflicts. Tango was considered scandalous, cosmopolitan and fascinating, and it was these elements that fed both European and Eastern imaginations, leading critics and participants to think of the dance as an exciting and exotic opportunity to indulge in decadence in terms of how one behaved, what one wore and what one might consume:

> Dress was important in establishing the symbolic frontiers between tango's authenticity and modernity. Moreover in 1913 one could feel that almost everything in France was related to tango: tea-tango, champagne-tango, chocolate-tango, dinner-tango and exhibition-tango (Zalko 1998: 72). The tango-colour, an intense orange, was popular in the making of women clothes. A popular drink, the mixing of beer and grenadine, that even today is possible to get in Paris was called tango.[4]

Since Shanghai was a cultural and economic entrepôt where the exotic was celebrated, it is perhaps of little surprise that the tango was initially introduced to Shanghai in the same year it arrived in Paris and London, and was the first of the new dance forms to infiltrate the more formal ballroom-style dancing found in the national balls which had been the central event on the Shanghai social calendar around the turn of the century. It quickly became established as a popular dance, and by 1914 the *thé dansant* or tango tea was a permanent fixture in the Astor Hotel whose popular ballroom was sumptuously decorated with mirrors running the length of the room and white murals highlighted with gold set against a polished oak floor, which the *North China Herald* deemed in 'beautiful condition for dancing'.[5] Given the dance's strong, contemporary association with a colonialist exotic, an exploration of the impact of the arrival of tango, and other new dances, in a city also known for exotic decadence promises a useful reading.

Shanghai: City as Decadent Spectacle

The Nanjing Road, the site of the bullion broker's dance in the verse quoted at the start of this chapter, received its name from Shanghai Municipal Council in 1865 and was given primary status as the main street in Shanghai, being referred to in Chinese as *Damalu* (the Great Road). Furnished with gas lamps, electricity and running water by the 1880s, it was by the twentieth century firmly established as the fashionable, commercial centre of Shanghai. Alongside the change in physical landscape came changes in the cultural landscape, with Chinese and Western-owned magazine and book shops, silk and textile shops and cinemas sitting alongside new department stores stocking brands imported from Western Europe, North America and Japan. This reflected the development of Shanghai as a modern metropolis with business entrepreneurs, publishers and artists working towards the creation and acceptance of a modern consumer lifestyle and culture in keeping with Shanghai's burgeoning economic prosperity: 'In the Republican period, mass market publications, department stores, and radio broadcasts promoted the consumption of luxury commodities through advertisements that glorified the "Shanghai style" (*Haipai*) as refined, dashing, cosmopolitan and, above all "modern."'[6]

By the 1920s, with the growth of consumerism, hotel restaurants, dance halls and cafés became popular spaces to relax, whilst the pursuit of the latest fashions in interior design and clothing was an essential element in the modernizing process within the city. The Nanjing Road Department stores also provided entertainment for their customers ranging from roof gardens and cafés to theatres and ballrooms. These new flamboyant spaces which blurred public and private settings were not just about shopping and entertainment. They provided an exciting visual experience reflecting values of change and progress whilst also encouraging the city's inhabitants, and its visitors, to think of the landscape as modern and cosmopolitan. What these entertainment spaces had in common was the attempt to create a sense of luxury and escape for their customers, and the size and focus on the ballrooms in all of these spaces underlines the central position of dance in the social life of Shanghai.

The Ritz café built in 1921 was, according to the *North China Herald*, inspired by Monte Carlo and the Jockey Club in Buenos Aires, and 150 Chinese artisans created the wood and brass work interior to 'add a new elegance and luxury to the fascinations of the fox trot'.[7] The 15 by 15 metre ballroom which was the main feature of the café was 'a handsomely designed structure in oak and Italian marble, with a beautifully painted ceiling, and dome of cathedral glass to shed its mellow light upon the dancers below'.[8] The Hôtel de France was also being constructed at this time with fluted Doric columns on the facade and was furnished throughout in Louis XVI style. A French chef was in charge of the kitchen and the centre-piece of the hotel was a dance hall with sufficient floor space to accommodate one hundred and fifty couples.[9] In 1922 the Astor Hotel enlarged and upgraded its ballroom to one of opulent luxury. The Spanish architect of the refurbishment, Abelardo Lafuente, created a space that provided the dancers with an exotic and striking experience combining images drawn from classical Greek and Roman mythology with the technological advancements of the time. The *North China Herald* reports that the light-blue walls of the ballroom were adorned with

> maidens and sylphs dancing in the open spaces, ... surmounted by the plaster reliefs for the indirect lighting system suspended from the ceiling, while high on the marble pillars beautifully cast female figures appear to support the roof. [The orchestra was accommodated in a peacock shell and] five primary colours [were] used for still effects throughout the variegated bedecked panels of features [with a] revolving cylinder hidden adding hundreds of shades of light that blended and dissolved over the whole giving the appearance of running waves of rainbow hues.[10]

It is perhaps of little surprise that attendees at the opening were reported as being unable to find words to describe the combination of colours and lights.

Domestic properties belonging to the Shanghai elite also boasted large ballrooms. Sir Elly Kadoorie, a merchant banker and avid fan of the tango, was known for his generous hospitality at his home, Marble Hall (built 1918), on what was then Bubbling Well Road (now Yan'an xi lu), where his 24 metre by

15 metre ballroom boasted an ornate 20 metre high ceiling and eight chandeliers comprising 3,600 coloured light bulbs which could change the room's lighting scheme from red to pink to blue.[11] In 1923 the Hong Kong and Shanghai Hotel syndicate (which included the Kadoorie family as shareholders) purchased a ten-acre (four hectares) private estate on Bubbling Well Road and commissioned Lafuente to create the thirty-two suite Majestic Hotel. According to the advertising leaflet for the Majestic, it was 'designed as a residence for those who desire the best of everything'.[12]

The ballroom was vast (the largest in Shanghai at the time) and again drew on a broad range of classical-style decoration. The seating was placed around the edge of the dance floor under a low ceiling held aloft by marble Corinthian columns; the orchestra were positioned under a Byzantine-style dome decorated with murals and with Graeco-Roman statues in niches on either side. In the centre of the dance space was a fountain complete with four cherubs splashing in the pool of water. Outside in the garden, ethereal spaces were created for dancing in the height of summer. Wallis Simpson recalled dancing in this garden in a sunken courtyard under a bower of flowers lit with coloured lanterns, and she reflected on the ability of the Majestic's garden ballroom to transport its dancers to another, other-worldly, place: 'It was here . . . that I first heard Vincent Youman's *Tea for Two*, and the combination of that melody, the moonlight, the perfume of jasmine, not to mention the Shangri-la illusion of the courtyard, made me feel that I had really entered the Celestial Kingdom.'[13]

In the 1910s and early 1920s social dancing venues had largely catered for the foreigners living in the city and elite Chinese. By the late 1920s, however, 'dance madness' had spread to the wider Chinese population in Shanghai, and cabarets, restaurants and hotels appeared on Nanjing Road and nearby streets. Comparable with Parisian cabarets and nightclubs the extravagant decor for these venues played with oriental and occidental forms of exoticism to transport their patrons to other worlds with imagery drawn from Chinese mythology and fantasy as well as from contemporary clubs in Paris and Berlin. Venues such as the Black Cat Cabaret, Palace of the Moon and Peach Blossom Palace quickly established themselves as part of Shanghai's entertainment world. As Liu, in *Wujuan guilai* (Exhausted after Dance) reports, 'Anybody who has not set foot in a cabaret cannot be considered fashionable'.[14]

Of the three hundred or so dance venues open in the 1930s in Shanghai, the Paramount Dance Hall was the best known. Designed by Chinese architect Yang Ximiu (S.J. Young, 1899–1978) it was completed in 1933. The name 'Dance Hall' is somewhat misleading and its Chinese name of *Bai le men*, which translates as 'place of a hundred pleasures' was perhaps more fitting since there were two large dance floors, various bars and lounges as well as banquet halls for its patrons to enjoy. Yang's aim was to create a leisure space which would surpass any other ballroom in Shanghai, in ambience and style.[15]

To achieve this Yang designed the three-level Art Deco style building on an L-shaped plan with a tower positioned where the two projections met forming the main entrance on the corner of Jessfield and Yuyuan Roads. The lower outer walls were covered with orange and brown glazed tiles and a black terrazzo course; the simple geometric lines of the facade that accompanied the vertical strip windows recalled New York's iconic buildings from the 1920s such as the Empire State or Chrysler Building. By choosing to use Art Deco as the style, Yang brought a particular message to the streets of Shanghai, as Lee notes: 'The Art Deco artifice also conveyed a new urban lifestyle: the image of men and women living in a glittering world of fashionable clothes and fancy furniture was to Chinese eyes, very much part of its exotic allure.'[16]

The eight-metre tower of the Paramount comprises cylindrical spheres which decrease in size, placed on top of one another and ending in a gleaming spire. Whilst lacking the height of an American-style skyscraper the overall impression from the street was that of an impressive, thrusting and self-confident building. At night vertical neon lights, which ran alongside the windows, guaranteed the building could be seen from miles away and ensured that the tower functioned as a beacon; calling dancers to enter under the lit canopy and through the doors and giving the customers the sense that they were leaving their daily life behind and entering into an exotic and glittering fashionable world.

The entire three-storey building was constructed around a steel skeleton using reinforced concrete. This allowed the architect to create a spectacular 36 metre long and 18 metre wide first-floor main ballroom without the need for supporting columns. On a practical note this meant there was more space for dancing and in terms of visual impact it provided onlookers with an impressive unobstructed view of the vast dance floor, the decoration, the orchestra and the crowd of dancers. The dance floor followed the fashion of the period, set on cantilevered springs to absorb the shock of the impact of dancers' feet on the floor and encourage them to dance long into the night. The dance floor was oval in shape to accommodate the necessity in partner dancing, perhaps especially in tango the so called 'walking dance', to progress in the same direction and therefore in a continuous circuit. At the far end of the space a curtained stage surrounded with gilded figures of dancers provided the orchestral platform and the entire space was illuminated with long strips of lights, again highlighting the modernity of the entire design.

On the second floor the dance floor was designed as a mezzanine overlooking the main floor space and was equally innovative, made of glass and lit with 50,000 lights that could rotate through red, violet, blue, yellow and white, and fill the floor with vibrant colour. An American visitor to Shanghai, Ruth Day, commented in her memoirs about her experience of dancing on this floor: 'On the balcony over the entrance, there was another dance floor, but made of glass with electric lights under it, which made me feel as if I were dancing on eggs'.[17] Madame Wellington Koo recalled the parties given at the Paramount and compared it to Les Ambassadeurs in Paris. She also commented on the cosmopolitan atmosphere: 'The Paramount food was exquisite, its White Russian cabaret excellent and the medley of Chinese and every imaginable variety of foreigner made it glamorously cosmopolitan.'[18] In an online article published in 2016, a ninety-one-year-old dancer, who at the time of the interview still wore thin-soled leather shoes to dance in the local park (similar to the shoes he used to wear when he went dancing as a young man), recalled his dancing years at the Paramount: 'Before, at the Paramount, my favorite dances were the waltz and tango. I would go dance once or twice every week, and dance through the night on weekends. I kept up this habit for 16 years.'[19]

The architectural language of the Paramount reflects Shanghai's commitment to its modern image through the pursuit of luxury and leisure. The Art Deco aesthetic and incorporation of the skyscraper-style tower and use of neon lighting clearly demonstrated Chinese ability to create a dance space which could equal those designed by Western architects in the city. The fluid internal spaces of private and public where Chinese and Western dancers intermingled represented some blurring of boundaries of social mores as well as giving an opportunity for patrons to enjoy and engage with the new excitement offered by the developing modernity of the city.

These examples provide a brief insight into the role and importance of the ballroom and dance hall's visual imagery and spatial dynamics. The architectural advancements enabled larger spaces to be created; the use of blazing neon signs, brilliant exterior lights, coloured lighting indoors and the lavish incorporation of silver, and chrome, stainless steel, glass and mirror, all called the fashionable to take their places on the dance floor. Together these elements created novel places of excitement and escape where many echelons of Shanghai society might share the dance floor. Walking into a newly created ballroom or dance hall one could forget about the hardship of daily routine and imagine a new more glamorous, albeit temporary, identity for oneself as a yet-to-be discovered film star or fashion icon. There was the thrill of the possibility of rubbing shoulders with celebrities, aristocracy or well-placed socialites who were regulars at these venues, any of whom might influence a serendipitous turn of your fortune. Furthermore, as Farrer and Field note, drawing from the findings of historian William McNeill: 'nightlife spaces in large anonymous cities are a modern way of "keeping together in time," a ritual urbanites create for themselves in order to experience the imagined community of the city at play.'[20] Shanghai was a city which valued the opportunity to play, and the leisure spaces of the city went to great lengths to encourage and facilitate the projection of individual and communal desires for escape from everyday life and its limitations, and to shape the lifestyle of its inhabitants and visitors

Dance, Fashion and Diversity

In *On Dance Fashion and Fashionable Dances,* Adelheid Rasche comments on the strong relationship between fashion and dance in the 1920s suggesting that they were at the core of the metropolitan zeitgeist in the fast-growing city of Berlin.[21] It was no different in Shanghai. Having created the magnificent ballrooms, cafés and dance halls as backdrops for dancing in Shanghai it was, of course, imperative that conspicuous personal expression through fashion matched the luxurious backdrops of the new urban buildings in the city. Dancers needed to appear in suitably fashionable attire to ensure that they were in vogue with the new modern and glamorous environments. The American journalist Elsie Cormick, who regularly wrote for the *North China Herald*, provides wry accounts of ex-pat life in Shanghai and highlights the reach of fashion and the central place of dancing in everyday life within the city, observing that the newcomers could easily be recognized on the dance floor by their old-fashioned clothing and inability to dance the latest popular dances: 'one never fails to see the married couple verging on middle age, who are having their first taste of the Shanghai atmosphere. They generally wear the evening clothes of several years ago and they jog through the dance in a way which proves that their last appearance in a ballroom was contemporary with the schottische.'[22]

In the 1910s the fashion industry in Paris, London and New York was influenced by the tango as the dance grew in popularity in the dance halls and ballrooms of these cities.[23] There are accounts of tango being danced in Paris as early as 1907 and it is thought that the dance arrived in France via Marseille where Argentinian sailors would dance with local girls from whence it made its way to Paris. We may note with interest that Marseille was one of the ports for ships crossing between Europe and Shanghai so whilst tango's formal arrival was in the elite ballrooms of Shanghai around 1913 it is possible that it was danced in less formal places before that, brought by sailors and travellers crossing between the two continents. What is of no doubt, however, is that as tango became popular in society it exerted a powerful cultural force, influencing changes in fashion and styles of social interaction, not just in Paris but in other fashionable, cosmopolitan cities in Europe and the USA as well. Irene Castle, the popular dancer of the early decades of the twentieth century, discusses the power that dance had over the fashion industry in her book on modern styles of dance. She comments on the rise in the popularity of soft crepes de Chine, chiffon and soft and supple taffetas in dress design where traditional material such as velvet was too heavy to cope with the faster moves of the dance and tended to wrap itself around the legs of the dancer: 'Perhaps the designers and the manufacturers will not admit that the dance is responsible for the vogue of these fabrics. But we all know that the demand makes the supply, and the demand of the women who dance is, "Give me something soft and light." '[24]

Tango required couples to dance cheek to cheek in a close embrace. It was this close contact that was such a striking contrast with the style and form of other popular dances of the time and was the reason why the dance was deemed to be so outrageous. Couples were also required to extend their legs in an exaggerated walking stride and fashion magazines were quick to note the impact the dance had on women's posture and the way they walked, on and off the dance floor. *Femina* magazine in 1913 commented: 'For the moment, at least, a wave of suppleness has come down on our fashions and lifestyle: the Orientalizing look has thrown its undulating veil on feminine shoulders . . . and women "walk the tango." '[25]

The dance duo Irene and Vernon Castle had a huge impact on the dance culture of the 1910s and 1920s. They were instrumental in popularizing and endorsing new dance forms for social consumption, such as the tango and foxtrot; they challenged conventions of the time by working and touring with a band of African-American musicians; and they were credited with having invented the concept of the tea dance. Irene also became a trendsetter and an icon of contemporary style advising women regarding what was suitable and appropriate to wear for dancing. In the foreword to their book *Modern Dancing*, the Castles comment that part of the intention of the text was to show that dancing, when correctly performed, was 'neither vulgar nor immodest, but, on the contrary, the personification of refinement, grace, and modesty'.[26] Photographs of the elegant gowns worn on stage and on screen by Irene Castle appeared in

Vogue and *Harper's Bazaar*, and her light dresses, which were ideal for dancing and were known as 'Castle frocks', were copied by women who were keen to embrace the latest dance fashion styles. Irene's dresses were so popular that dressmakers would take note whenever new photographs were published in a newspaper or magazine, as dozens of requests for the same design would arrive from women wanting to copy the style. Such requests were as likely to have been made in Shanghai as they were in New York, since Western magazines such as *Vogue* were readily available and tailors in Shanghai were known for their expertise in replicating designs from images.[27] The Nanjing Road Department stores provided the means to see the new styles in action on the dance floor in their ballrooms, and also housed tailors and a wide range of silk and goods to re-create the fashions for their customers to ensure they were up to date with the latest style. It seems, however, that the collaboration with tailors did not always go smoothly as Elsie Cormick complains bitterly about delayed appointments and ill-fitting results.[28] For women who couldn't afford tailor-made versions it was also possible to create your own Castle dresses at home as Irene endorsed patterns appearing in *The Ladies Home Journal* and *Butterick Patterns.*

The rise in popularity of the tango tea or *thé dansant* also led to a requirement for an entirely new form of dress which wasn't as sophisticated as an evening dress nor as mundane or practical as a day dress yet could be worn on afternoons and not be uncomfortably warm for dancing. The *tango-visité*, or semi-evening gown, was the result of this requirement, comprising a loose bodice and a shorter, mid-calf skirt, and like tango itself the style was thought of as extremely racy, as can be seen in the language used by *Vanity Fair* to describe the components of the dress: 'and oh! So transparent a bodice. Generally there is a deep draped waistband and long sleeves, it is true, but the rest would appear to be but a whisper, or a breath of tulle, or the finest filmiest lace.'[29] By the 1920s gowns for afternoon and evening dancing still continued to use light materials such as crepe or chiffon and have a shorter skirt (below knee to mid-calf length) with a scalloped or handkerchief edge, but they were often sleeveless and incorporated a dropped waist emphasized with a draped bow or sash and a straight cut bodice which flattened the bust.

Of course Irene Castle wasn't the only dancer to have influenced changes in attitudes towards what was acceptable to wear on a dance floor. Isadora Duncan, Ida Rubenstein and Ruth St Denis in the 1910s had begun to challenge expectations with their sheer chiffon costumes but whereas their costumes were perceived of as daring, sensuous and exotic, Castle kept her focus on simplicity of style, and her light chiffon dresses and satin-ribboned evening shoes (sold as tango slippers) became sought after and deemed *de rigueur*. Her matter of fact, didactic tone in her book and the couple's graceful and elegant manner on the dance floor did much to encourage a move away from thinking of the clothing associated with such close-couple dancing as risqué, to be feared and avoided. The couple's acceptance into polite society and Irene's position as an arbiter of good taste and style had significant ramifications on dance fashion worldwide.

It was not only outer clothing that changed as a result of women wanting to dance the tango, foxtrot and other new styles of social dance. Corsets inhibited breathing and prevented the lithe and more athletic style of movement associated with these new dances. Designers such as Lucy Duff Gordon (Lucile Ltd) and Paul Poiret, who was himself a tango enthusiast, replaced the corset with a lightweight elastic girdle and the *soutien-gorge*, the brassiere, which suited the lighter more flowing materials used in their designs.[30] As a result, many women opted to remove the corset altogether and by 1914 *Vogue* conceded that: 'the mode of the corsetless figure is an established one – for a season, at least, [it also noted that] the point has been reached where women do not have to be dictated to, as formerly, in the matter of corsets'.[31]

Elsie Cormick comments on the lack of corsets in some of the dresses worn to evening dances in Shanghai by referencing the novelist Elinor Glyn who wrote racy stories of uncorseted heroines lying on tiger skins wearing soft chiffon gowns.

> The gowns range from simple white affairs that suggest graduation frocks to shimmery, snakey draperies such as might be worn by an Elinor Glyn heroine when the misled young man decided to commit suicide at her feet. The really startling dresses are usually kept in reserve for Saturday night, which is also the evening when the largest number of bachelor tables are observable around the side-lines.[32]

The Shanghai-based *Vogue* of summer 1926 showcased a racy ball gown that perhaps fell into the category of Cormick's Saturday night 'startling dress' and is reminiscent of the description from *Vanity Fair.* The illustration shows a yellow, georgette crepe, mid-length skirt worn over a transparent petticoat, with transparent sleeves and bodice covering a sleeveless vest, a yellow ruff at the neck and transparent flounces at the cuffs of the sleeves.[33]

The memoirs of a young Crimean woman who fled to Shanghai from Moscow in 1924 highlight the importance given to appearing in public stylishly dressed. Soon after Sofia Lvovna's arrival in Shanghai and whilst staying with Russian designer Larisa Petrovna, who ran an haute couture salon on Nanjing Road,

Sofia was taken to Antoine's, a Parisian hairdressers in the French concession, to replace her long and outmoded braids with a chic bob cut. She also recalls how she was given outfits to replace her 'sensible clothes' including a day suit, several frocks and a cocktail dress so that she would fit in with the Shanghai social scene.[34] Family photographs included in the memoir give a brief insight into her life in stylish Shanghai society from excursions to nearby summer resorts to attendance at charity fashion functions and balls. One photograph of Sophia at a ball at the Majestic Hotel in 1924 (Figure 5.1) is particularly telling as it shows the international elite of Shanghai gathered together in relaxed mode. The photograph largely comprises a sea of faces with just the front line of eighteen people fully on view and showing that the men are in evening wear, whilst the women are all in the latest style of dance dress: sleeveless, straight-cut bodice, dropped waists. The dresses are of lightweight material such as crepe de chine and silk, and a few have elaborate beading. Most fall at mid-calf length (although one dress with feathered beading pattern is at a particularly daring knee length), some with flared skirts, flounces and scalloped edges to accommodate the fast-moving dances, and worn with satin, pointed toe and bar evening shoes.

Figure 5.1 Ball at the Majestic Hotel, 1924. Courtesy of Olga Hawkes.

As social dancing became more popular within the Chinese community in Shanghai, changes and developments can also be traced in the clothing worn and textiles used by Chinese women for dancing. The *qipao* shown in Figure 5.2, from the late 1920s or early 1930s, clearly demonstrates that the choice of dress style was not necessarily simply between Eastern and Western.

This dress that was designed for wearing for dancing combines a *qipao*-style bodice and a high collar with a softly pleated Western evening skirt. The strips of rainbow coloured sequins on the bodice and skirt give a colourful sheen to the design but also suggest the dynamism of a city seen in the electrical lighting and neon strips on the facades of buildings such as the Paramount in Shanghai. When dancing in this dress, any movement on the dance floor would pick up and reflect the light, ensuring that it created its own sense of energy and movement. Curator and historian Mei Mei Rado comments on the hybrid qualities of the gown as it has a 'strong European art deco flair, [and] the overall silhouette conformed to that of contemporary *qipao* in the late 1920s'.[35] She also notes that the gown bears a strong resemblance to a dress for the Yunshang Fashion Company (Yunshang shizhuang gongsi) 1928 advertisement where the

Figure 5.2 Green *qipao* with printed fabric, 1928–30. Courtesy of China National Silk Museum, Hangzhou.

black-and-white illustration shows three fashionably dressed women looking at a shop window.[36] In the advertisement, the mannequin in the window is partially covered by a block of text but it is possible to see parts of the dress: the flare of the skirt, and a coiled flower at the neckline as well as the suggestions of vertical stripes of decoration on the *qipao*. The image of three well-groomed women looking at the *qipao* signifies the garment's fashionability and by association the Yunshang Fashion Company's contemporary identity.

This hybrid style highlights the spirit of transculturalism to be found in Shanghai prompted by the search for urban sophistication:

> The fashionable Chinese woman, therefore, adapted the prevailing Parisian silhouettes with distinctive and evocative Chinese details of neckline, trim, fabric and ornament; in the West the imaginative construction of an exotic 'other' represented by sybaritic vignettes of lounging opium-smokers or seductive vamps introduced the transgressive allure of pajamas or 'Orientalized' gowns with elements though to be authentically Chinese . . . This citing of West by East, and vice-versa, resulted in designs of a surprisingly similar pastiche.[37]

The green *qipao* highlights the diversity of cultures and creativity at play in Shanghai in the Republican era. Such sartorial appropriations and cultural reflexivity were not new phenomena. Many of the tango gowns worn for parties and social events in Paris and London in the early 1900s were hybrid designs inspired by Léon Bakst's oriental designs for *Scheherazade*. Mica Nava comments that the overlap found within these tango styles of exoticized Hispanic American and oriental forms created a 'generic popular cosmopolitanism – a commercial orientalism – with a distinctive libidinal economy in which women were key players'.[38] The daring changes to dance dresses, such as shorter hemlines, lighter fabrics, special corsets and footwear, led to the fashion historian Béatrice Humbert arguing 'that tango was a true "detonator" of a new morality in France'.[39] It is clear that tango heralded cultural changes that were manifest in the developments of fashionable dancewear as well as social spaces in which to be seen, providing an opportunity for some women to begin to articulate their sense of self and their sensuality in public.

Shanghai and the 'Spectacular Modern Woman'

In her book *The Spectacular Modern Woman: Feminine Visibility in the 1920s*, Liz Connor considers the relationship between women in Western cultures and the rising visual cultures of mass media, photography and film, particularly with respect to how women exploited such images to construct their own feminine identity. Focusing on the complexities arising from women being intensively objectified through these new visual industries and yet simultaneously using these constructions to create their own modern identity, Connor argues that the modern woman was constituted by and intervened in modernity in visual or spectacular ways. The images they consumed on screen or in newspapers, for example, served to change women's perceptions of themselves and encouraged the creation of a modern woman.

> For perhaps the first time in the West, modern women understood self-display to be part of the quest for mobility, self-determination and sexual identity. This dramatic shift from inciting modesty to inciting display, from self-effacement to self-articulation, is the point where feminine visibility began to be productive of women's modern subjectivities.[40]

Connor organizes her thoughts on the modern woman through six case studies of modern female types: the city girl in the street; the screen struck girl in the cinematic scene; the mannequin in the commodity scene; the beauty contestant; the 'primitive' woman in the late colonial scene; and the flapper in the heterosexual leisure scene. Whilst focusing on an Australian context the consumerism of commodity is eminently transnational and it is possible to draw a comparison with the rise of the modern woman in Shanghai, where women were similarly objectified by, yet felt enabled and encouraged to construct their own subjectivities and spectacle drawn from, the visual culture of the city. The Chinese film industry was a fast-rising phenomenon, fashion shows and beauty contests were a regular part of the social scene, and, as already discussed, the dance halls and ballrooms were central to the leisure time of many foreign and Chinese inhabitants of Shanghai.

Whilst offering wealthy women the excitement of new experiences and broadening of cultural horizons, Shanghai and other cities with colonial enclaves also offered economic opportunities to itinerant middle- and working-class females who turned to Shanghai to find work and, where possible, freedom, owing to its commercial and recreational network of banks, offices, shops, salons, cafés, restaurants and nightclubs. Typists, clerks and shop girls from America, Europe and Australasia travelled to Shanghai looking for escape, adventure and the opportunity to make money. An article in the *Sydney Morning Herald* in March 1927 entitled 'Girl's Million Dollar Job' highlighted the financial opportunities to be had in the city as it told of a female bank clerk who had arrived in Sydney and who 'had just come from a job in Shanghai where she earned £37 a month! She did her shopping in suitcases.'[41] Cormick supports this story of a successful independent female workforce with her accounts of women who moved from one job to another, always avoiding long-term contracts so free to travel from one city to another making good use of the shipping and trading routes between Shanghai, Hong Kong, Manila, Java, Kobe and Yokohama. Moving south to avoid winter and travelling north to escape the summer, these women worked as typists or office secretaries to earn enough money to enjoy living and socializing in these cities.[42]

In the 1930s the rise in the popularity of dance halls and clubs among the Chinese in Shanghai led to a significant change in dance etiquette. In Western nightclubs men were expected to bring their own partners; by contrast, in Chinese cabarets dance hostesses (*wunü*) or taxi dancers were available to hire. Dance hostesses, most often Russian, Japanese and Chinese women, became an established element of the Shanghai dance scene. According to Frederik Wakemen, by 1936 there were as many as 5000 women from various social backgrounds working as dance hostesses in Shanghai.[43] Whilst it is not known how many taxi dancers were also supplementing their income as prostitutes, it was essential for the women to earn enough money to cover their living costs and perhaps of even greater importance that they had sufficient funds to assert their public image at the forefront of fashion trends, spending at least part of their earnings on the latest styles of hair, make-up, dresses and shoes to ensure that they were the centre of attention on the dance floor.

Whether she was an office clerk or a taxi dancer and whether she was known as a *flapper*, *garçonne*, *modeng xiaojie* or *neue frau*, the dance floor provided an ideal space for the modern woman to assert her new-found freedom and to engage and exploit her position as both object and subject of emerging femininities enjoying her sexual power and exotic presence. 'A woman who knows that she is cutting a good figure, who senses that she is drawing admiring glances when gliding across the dance floor in the arm of her dance partner gains a new sense of self.'[44]

Given that dance halls became synonymous with fashion and conspicuous consumption it is of little surprise perhaps that they became the venues for China's fashion shows, the first being held in Whitelaw's Department Store in Nanjing Road in 1926. In his autobiography Ye Qianyu recalls that he was asked to organize a fashion show to promote a British textiles company's new products, and as well as designing the collection he also signed up dancing girls from the dance halls as the models.[45] Fashion shows quickly became a part of the social calendar in Shanghai with dance halls and hotels such as the Majestic and the Yangtze providing luxurious settings for these events. Additionally, the use of dance halls for fashion shows often represented an ideal business strategy, since investors in the dance halls were frequently also involved in the silk or textiles industry in Shanghai. From the perspective of the emerging modern woman, the models represented both commodity and self to be viewed; they presented the latest fashions to the audience whilst also displaying their own bodies for consumption. In this context women were encouraged to look at the models but to also accept the notion of being looked at themselves. As Connor notes, 'Commodity displays, such as Mannequins [or live models in fashion shows] not only gave women something to look at, they also urged women not to retreat from their spectacularization, but to respond to public scrutiny by striking a pose within it.'[46]

This notion of public scrutiny was not restricted to fashion shows but extended to social life and especially the entertainment culture within the city. Whereas for the Paris of the nineteenth century the streets were the site of spectatorship, for the flâneur in Shanghai in the early twentieth century the dance floor provided rich opportunities to imagine and experience the development of the modern city. Artists and writers created a wealth of imagery and text that reflected their interests in and observations of the dance culture, its fashions and spaces for a wider audience.

In 1924 the Japanese artist Yamamura Kōka (1885–1942) produced a colour woodcut of a dance scene at the New Carlton Hotel in Shanghai (see Plate 3). In the forefront of the image two women are seated at a round table. One of the women has her back to us, her head hidden beneath a red cloche hat, while the other can be seen in profile. Beyond the women in the mid-ground are four couples in a dance embrace, with the male dancers' left and female dancers' right arms raised high. Here too the women on the dance floor lack specific details and have been reduced to bobbed hair, white arms and dresses of brightly patterned textiles. The men have been further reduced to black lines for their arms and white hands with just a hint of hair and forehead appearing above the women's bobbed hair. On the chair of the women in the left foreground is a brightly embroidered red jacket, and on the table are two cocktail glasses embellished with a red cherry in each glass. Yet despite the vivid colours and bold patterns of the dresses, jacket and hat, the flattened style of the image and lack of detail give the woodcut a melancholic air.

Whilst the women in the image lack specificity and seem generic, the cut of hair and profile of the seated women suggest that they are European rather than

Chinese. Wakeman includes a description of the Carlton Hotel which suggests that this image is of White Russian taxi dancers: 'The old Carlton closed. It opened again at once as a dancehall with Russian hostesses [and] a risqué floor show.'[47] The women at the table seem to be in polite conversation with one another but there is a languid sense of waiting in their body language and demeanour again supporting the idea that these women are taxi dancers waiting to be hired for a dance. The posture of the dancers who appear in the middle of the image also suggests the sexual availability of the taxi dancers since the man's right hand is clearly resting on the woman's buttock rather than the small of her back or in between her shoulder blades as might be expected.

The bobbed hair, fashionable dresses and the cocktails all signify the modern independent urban woman. The image also suggests that these women are the objects of desire; all but one of the women have their backs to the viewer and all are at the disposal of the viewer or voyeur. This combination of anonymous display and presentation of the women as a commodity in this woodcut by Kōka produced for a Japanese audience provides an interesting perspective on how Shanghai was thought of as an exotic city of seduction and modernity.

Zhou Shoujuan (1895–1968) provides a good example of the Shanghai flâneur. He was a prolific writer who enjoyed going to dance halls, despite being unable to dance, and commenting on the clothing and fashions he had seen at the city's dance parties. Much of his work was published as short stories, such as 'Dancing Partner and Champagne Buys a Big Smile' and often appeared in the newspaper *Shanghai huaboa* (Pictorial Shanghai) with the intention of introducing his Chinese audience to Western art and culture, and especially to the etiquette and expectations of social dancing. Alongside his stories on dancing, and information on Western paintings, the *Shanghai huabao* (Pictorial Shanghai) also reported on Chinese contemporary film and culture, sport, and published photographs of society events often featuring popular cinema stars and socialites. Zhou's approach to the city's burgeoning dance culture was as much about inspiring his reader's imagination as merely describing an event. In one of his stories, for example, he describes his evening at the Carlton Café: the Russian dancer who wore a rose pink dress and whose moves were enhanced by the colourful lights; the film stars and socialites who were present. He also describes how the room, its lighting and the music transported him to a transcendental world, and he compares the couples in the dance hall to stars around a moon, like heavenly bodies. In another story he tells of how his male friend upset a dance hostess by hiring her and then buying another hostess a bottle of Champagne. His friend has to placate her by buying Champagne for her as well.

The story ends with Zhou noting that his friend had bought tears rather than buying smiles. His Chinese readers would have understood the double meaning of his comment since 'buying smiles' was a term for being entertained by a courtesan.[48] Through this referencing Zhou was attempting to prepare his readers for the social expectations of the modern dance culture whilst reminding them that it had much in common with Chinese cultures of hospitality and entertainment.

Zhou's writing was considered by Chinese literary critics to be a part of the genre known as the Mandarin Ducks and Butterfly School (*Yuanyang hudie pai*) and is often dismissed because of its romanticized and populist content, yet his work reached a wide audience, and his stories in *Shanghai huabo* and other popular magazines did much to popularize the dancing culture to his Chinese audience who lived outside the International Settlements. His writing also played an important role in the search for a new cultural identity, reflecting the urbanization and modernization of Shanghai. The women who feature in his work provide examples of the modern woman asserting their positions within these new and complex constructions portraying both an idealized and a real identity through their sexual sophistication and cultural power.

Shanghai's entertainment industry provided many women with independent financial means and a more sophisticated grasp of their abilities and position within the emerging culture. The dance floor, fashion shows, beauty contests and film presented them with the possibilities of displaying their bodies and their abilities in public. It also provided women with the opportunity to consume new ideas on femininity and to reproduce those ideas through their own heightened visibility and their growing sense of personal identity, and as a result be able to take up their place within the modern urban environment.

Conclusion

For Western and Eastern visitors to the city, as well as for those who chose to live and work there, Shanghai offered an escape from everyday life and an opportunity to participate in a lifestyle and entertainment culture that sat outside the restraints and expectations of their homes. The leisure spaces and the fashions created to be seen in those spaces were provoked and enabled by a recognition of, or more specifically the creation of, an exotic Oriental/Occidental *other*. The cultural fluidity in pursuit of such rich exoticism facilitated the adoption and adaption of styles from the East and the West and as such highlight Shanghai's position as an alluring multi-faceted decadent metropolis. The animated dialogue between Eastern and Western styles were evidenced in the public architectural spaces created in this era such as hotels, cafés, dance halls and department stores, as well as in the imaginary spaces of emerging visual media through the printed books, calendars and film produced in the city. Dance and dance spaces gave the population in Shanghai, whether from the East or the West, the opportunity to create an imagined community on the dance floor and to build a new hybrid, idealized, fictitious cultural identity for the modernizing city. Magazines such as *Vogue*, *Vanity Fair* and *Femina* provided their readers with a wealth of advice and information on the latest dance fashions including the most up-to-date materials for dance garments such as tango-crepe, styles of shoes for dancing and what one should wear to the tango tea. New dances of the era contributed to the fantasies and desires of inhabitants and visitors to Shanghai, and facilitated the means of an escape from the realities of the everyday providing a decadent and luxurious alternative.

Women as consumers and producers of fashion held a complex position in relation to modernity in Shanghai and whilst they found ways to exert their new position they were simultaneously commodified as a representation of the city and its developing modernity. As Lee notes many of the narratives of the time present women as an embodiment of modernity, constructed in order to convey the authors' fascination with the city:

> 'Modern girl', . . . is but a narrative figure in a staged urban landscape . . . She is made to serve the larger purpose of representing the city. The fashionable woman offers an intoxicating experience of the city but at the risk of being thought of as marketable and disposable merchandize.[49]

Personal diary accounts and memoirs as well as the descriptions of Shanghai's dance scene in the 1920s by artists and writers such as Yamamura Kōka and Zhou Shoujuan all create a vivid account of the centrality of dance culture to the economic and social life of the city. Their work narrating the transition of a disparate, multinational community to an emerging cultural identity and a modern urban environment. Just how deeply embedded dance was in the Shanghai psyche is demonstrated in Cormick's belief that no matter what the political or economic situation, Shanghai would continue to pursue its decadent dance lifestyle: 'Revolutions may rise or break, exchange may go up or down, and the Far East may tie itself in knots, but throughout it all, Shanghai continues to whirl like a dancing dervish under the pink-shaded lights of its crowded cafés.'[50]

Notes

1 *North China Herald*, 5 April 1919.

2 Stella Dong, *Shanghai: The Rise and Fall of a Decadent City 1842–1949* (New York: London: HarperPerennial, 2001), 98.

3 Andrew David Field, *Shanghai's Dancing World: Cabaret Culture and Urban Politics, 1919–1954* (Hong Kong: Chinese University Press, 2010), 11–12.

4 Eduardo, Archetti, 'Masculinity, Primitivism, and Power: Gaucho, Tango, Primitivism, and Power', in William E. French and Katherine Elaine Bliss (eds), *Gender, Sexuality, and Power in Latin America since Independence* (Lanham, MD: Rowman & Littlefield, 2007), 221.

5 *North China Herald*, 1 December 1917.

6 Carrie Waara, 'Selling Goods and Promoting a New Commercial Culture in Republican Art Magazines', in Sherman Cochran (ed.), *Inventing Nanjing Road: Commercial Culture in Shanghai, 1900–1945* (New York: East Asia Program Cornell University, 1999), 61.

7 *North China Herald*, 18 June 1921.

8 Ibid.

9 Ibid., 4 June 1921.

10 Ibid., 29 December 1923.

11 Dong, *Shanghai*, 223.

12 Hugues, www.shanghailander.net (accessed March 2017).

13 Anne Sebba, *That Woman: The Life of Wallis Simpson, Duchess of Windsor* (London: Weidenfeld & Nicolson, 2012), 27.

14 Liu quoted in Field, *Shanghai's Dancing World*, 63.

15 Yang Xiliu, 'Bailemen zhi juexing' (The Construction of the Paramount), *The Chinese Architect* 14 (1934): 9–11.

16 Leo Ou-fan Lee, *Shanghai Modern: The Flowering of a New Urban Culture in China, 1930–1945* (Cambridge, MA: Harvard University Press, 1999), 11.

17 Field, *Shanghai's Dancing World*, 103.

18 Rado Mei Mei, 'Paris Fashion: Modernism and the East: Shanghai Glamour: New Women 1910s–40s', *Fashion at MOCA: Shanghai to New York* (New York: Museum of Chinese in America, 2013), 15.

19 Lu Qiguo, 2016, http://www.chinascenic.com/magazine/the-shanghai-paramount-hall-347.html (accessed September 2017).

20 James Farrer and Andrew David Field, *Shanghai Night-scapes: A Nocturnal Biography of a Global City* (Chicago: University of Chicago Press, 2015), 9.

21 Adelheid, Rasche, 'On Dance Fashion and Fashionable Bodies', in Valerie Steele (ed.), *Dance and Fashion* (New Haven, CT: Yale University Press, 2014), 184.

22 Elsie Cormick, *Audacious Angles on China, New York* (D. Appleton and Company, 1923), 41.

23 Marta E. Savigliano, *Tango and the Political Economy of Passion* (Boulder, CO: Westview Press 1995), 125–7.
24 Vernon Castle and Irene Castle, *Modern Dancing* (New York: Harper & Brothers, 1912), 146.
25 'Les Danses a la mode', *Femina*, 15 January 1913, 23
26 Castle and Castle, *Modern Dancing*, 17
27 Antonia Finnane, *Changing Clothes in China: Fashion, History, Nation* (London: Hurst, 2007), 113.
28 Cormick, *Audacious Angles on China, New York*, 92–3.
29 'The Dance Craze in Paris Creates New Types of Gowns', *Vanity Fair*, November 1913, 59.
30 Randy Ryan Bigham, 'Lucile, Her Life by Design: Sex, Style and the Fusion of Theatre and Couture', in Caroline Evans (ed.), *The Mechanical Smile: Modernism and the First Fashion Shows in France and America, 1900–1929* (New Haven, CT: Yale University Press, 2013).
31 'Corsetting the Corsetless Figure', *Vogue*, January 1914, 58.
32 Cormick, *Audacious Angles on China, New York*, 43.
33 Mei Mei Rado, 'Paris Fashion: Modernism and the East: Shanghai Glamour: New Women 1910s–40s', in *Fashion at MOCA*, 16.
34 Olga Hawkes, *Russian at Heart* (Auckland: Olga Rossi Publications, 2013), 121.
35 Rado, 'Paris Fashion', 21.
36 Ibid.
37 Harold Koda, 'Foreword: Paris Fashion: Modernism and the East, Shanghai Glamour: New Women 1910s–40s', in *Fashion at MOCA*, 3.
38 Mica Nava, *Visceral Cosmopolitanism: Gender, Culture and the Normalisation of Difference* (Oxford: Berg, 2007), 34.
39 Savigliano, *Tango and the Political Economy of Passion*, 127.
40 Liz Connor, *The Spectacular Modern Woman: Feminine Visibility in the 1920s* (Bloomington, IN: Indiana University Press, 2004), 29.
41 Sophie Loy-Wilson, *Australians in Shanghai: Race, Rights and Nation in Treaty Port China* (London: Routledge, 2017), 66.
42 Cormick, *Audacious Angles on China, New York*, 5.
43 Frederic Wakeman, *Policing Shanghai, 1927–1937* (Oakland, CA: University of California Press, 1996), 108.
44 Gerda Kerger quoted by Rasche, 'On Dance Fashion and Fashionable Bodies', 193.
45 Ye Qianyu quoted by Finnane, *Changing Clothes in China*, 131.
46 Connor, *The Spectacular Modern Woman*, 114.
47 Wakeman, *Policing Shanghai, 1927–1937*, 108.
48 Field, *Shanghai's Dancing World*, 49.
49 Lee, *Shanghai Modern*, 209.
50 Cormick, *Audacious Angles on China, New York*, 44.

6

Soong Ching-ling, Soong May-ling

Negotiating Dresses and Politics in Modern Shanghai, 1913–49

Djurdja Bartlett

Introduction

In a photograph taken in the grounds of the prestigious Wellesley College on the East Coast of America in 1913, Soong Ching-ling (Song Qingling, 1893–1981) and Soong May-ling (Song Meiling, 1898–2003), dressed in their white sailor-style tunics and long white skirts, look like typical female American college students. They are in the company of their brother T.V. Soong (Soong Tse-Ven, 1894–1971) in a Western-style suit, who himself was a Harvard student at the time.

Indeed, their father Charlie Soong (Song Jiashu, 1863–1918), a missionary turned into a successful and rich publisher, sent not only these three children but also their other three siblings to study in the Unites States. At that time, it was not unusual for the well-off Chinese to send their sons to get a university degree at a prestigious American university. Yet, when Ching-ling and May-ling left for the Wesleyan college in Macon, Georgia in 1908, following in the footsteps of their older sister Ai-ling (Song Ailing, 1888–1973), who had already been studying there for a couple of years, it was still a novelty to send one's daughters away so that they could also acquire the highest level of knowledge available at the time. But, socially progressive and American-educated himself, Charlie Soong was a Westernized Chinese. Nevertheless, Soong was also a great patriot, eager to modernize his country, by getting rid of the antiquated empire, a general social and cultural backwardness, as well as the prevailing foreign dominance over the Chinese economy, which was especially present in his native Shanghai. In this sense, providing his children with excellent education in a country known for democracy and liberal thinking could contribute towards those noble goals.

Figure 6.1 (from left to right) Soong May-ling, T.V. Soong and Soong Ching-ling. The girls are dressed in white sailor-style tunics and long white skirts, while their brother wears a Western-style suit, Wellesley College on the East American coast, 1913. Courtesy of the Soong Ching-ling Memorial Residence, Shanghai.

Such a merging of the rising national conscience and the admiration for the Western modernizing educational, cultural and economic strategies, was quite common in the upper and middle social strata in Southern China. From the mid-nineteenth century, its coastal cities developed a close relationship with the West due to a series of treaties between China and the countries such as the United Kingdom, America and France. In treaty ports, the legal arrangements favoured foreigners in all segments of life, from industry and trade to everyday lifestyles. Yet, Shanghai, the most prominent among treaty ports, eventually became a social and cultural melting pot, with its ambitious inhabitants living a hybrid existence: adopting the fast changing Western models of behaviour while not abandoning the traditional, and much slower, Confucian ideals and rhythms. As observed by the French scholar of China, Marie-Claire Bergère: 'The social rise of the nouveaux riches who, within the space of a few years or decades, made a place for themselves in the ranks of the local elites, testifies to the mobility of a society in which the law of profit was beginning to compete with Confucian values.'[1] While Bergère acknowledged that traditional Chinese society provided some basis for these innovations, she emphasized that, at the beginning of the century, 'the new social values became established chiefly through imitation; reproduction of Western ideas and practices became the most important factor in this revolution. Modernism was equated with Westernism.'[2]

Charlie Soong was one of these highly modernized members of the Shanghai entrepreneurial elite, and, due to his earlier exposure to American culture, both through his education there, and his missionary roots in the Christian Methodist religion, he had swiftly embraced Western notions of democracy, constitutionalism and pragmatism, needed to develop and run a prosperous business. Additionally, he donned a Western-style suit in his American youth, and never abandoned this dress code. But like many other members of his social group, Charlie Soong also actively engaged with the revolutionaries who wanted to bring down the empire, which, by then, had been ruled by the Manchu invaders, the Qing dynasty, for almost three centuries. Soong not only supported the republican and national programme of their leader Sun Yat-sen (Sun Zhongshan, 1866–1925) but also became one of his financial backers and his best friend.[3] As a Cantonese, raised in Hawaii and Hong Kong, Sun Yat-sen intuitively understood the aspirations of his nationally conscious, yet Westernized, compatriots, and turned their hopes, as well as their frustrations, into revolutionary programmes and actions.[4] After a number of unsuccessful attempts, the Qing Empire had fallen, and the Chinese Republic was established in Nanjing on 1 January 1912, with Sun Yat-sen as a president of its provisional national government. Under his leadership, the government had lasted only three months, and, as the political situation worsened, Sun was eventually forced into exile in Japan in 1913.

Again at home in 1917, Sun advocated the reunification of the country, but China remained politically divided and socially unstable when he died in 1925, with its various regions still controlled by the powerful warlords. Getting increasingly disappointed with the West refusing to help him to establish a modern Chinese state, Sun started to collaborate with the Soviet communists towards the end of his life. His successor Chiang Kai-shek (Jiang Jieshi, 1887–1975) turned against the communists, which resulted in the Civil War, with the nationalist forces led by Chiang, and the communists led by Mao, with both of them claiming to be Sun's legitimate heirs.[5] Consequently, Sun Yat-sen has been acknowledged and celebrated as the father of a modern Chinese state.[6]

From the early 1910s to the late 1980s, the destiny of the Soong family was closely intertwined with Sun Yat-sen, as well as with his two successors, Chiang and Mao, who, during their respective positions in power, were leading China in two politically opposite directions. Soong Ching-ling married Sun Yat-sen in 1915, while Soong May-ling wed his ideological enemy Chiang Kai-shek in 1927. Through their marriages to the two politically most powerful men in the Chinese inter-war period, Soong Ching-ling and Soong May-ling took an active part in shaping and promoting the different but equally modern narratives of China. Following Mao Zedong's (1893–1976) rise to power in 1949, Ching-ling aligned herself with the new socialist state, while May-ling fled China for Taiwan, with her husband Chiang Kai-shek. Correspondingly, their politically opposing ideologies informed their concepts of dress, gender and femininity.

This chapter investigates the sisters' respective attitudes to dress within the complex relationship between Chinese and Western culture, society, politics and fashion, while also addressing their very different practices and representational strategies in relation to the notions of gender and femininity.

Cosmopolitan Modernism

The new Republic was a modernist endeavour, with its leaders and supporters widely influenced by the Western ideal of democracy, hoping that it would eventually bring prosperity and progress for the whole country. Democracy was clad in Western clothes even when still imagined. While plotting the revolution, Sun Yat-sen travelled the world and his homeland in a Western-style suit.[7] As claimed by Henrietta Harrison in her book *The Making of the Republican Citizen*, this was indeed the required dress style:

> For some years before the revolution Western-style customs had been associated with revolutionaries. During the late Qing students who continued to wear Western clothes after returning to China did so not for aesthetic or practical reasons but because of what the clothes represented … it was the power of Europe and America that gave the new styles their prestige'[8]

Immediately after the revolution, Western dress continued to distinguish the progressive members of the new society, pointing towards the hybridity of Chinese modernism. In August 1912, the government published a law on etiquette requiring women to adopt the formal dress of Chinese women of Han ethnicity, with a long pleated skirt worn beneath an embroidered silk jacket.[9] While this dress code sartorially opposed the Manchu style, women did not accept those unpractical, uncomfortable outfits. Similar to men, they also wanted to express their republican credentials in modern Western clothes. In its fashion column published in early January 1912, only a couple of days after the founding of the Republic, the newspaper *Shenbao* (Shanghai Daily) vividly depicted the popular attitude, listing a number of items without which new born Republicans 'could not' live: a pair of sharp-toed, high-heeled leather shoes, 'violet mink' gloves and white lace for women, and a Western suit, greatcoat, and Western hat for men.[10] The China scholar Peter Carroll acknowledged the similarities between an ephemeral, modernist phenomenon such as fashion and a sudden birth of the new, modernist subject in a new, cosmopolitan-oriented Republic: 'As both sign and formative practice, the unruly transformations of fashion highlighted a plethora of anxiety-provoking possibilities regarding the constitution of the modern Republican self.'[11]

In America, clad in her modern, un-corseted clothes, consisting of ankle-length white skirts in combination with either loose white blouses or long tunics, Ching-ling was an immediate enthusiast of the Revolution. She removed the old banner of the Chinese dragon from the wall in her student room, and promptly replaced it with the new flag her father had sent her. In April 1912, Ching-ling published an article in the college newspaper *The Wesleyan*:

> Five months ago our wildest dream could not have been for a republic. To some, even the promise of an early constitutional government was received with scepticism. But deep down in the heart of every patriotic Chinese, were he a politician or a labourer, there was the anti-Manchu spirit. All the sufferings, such as famine, flood, and retrogression, in every phase of life was traced to the

> tyrannical Manchus and their court of dishonest officials. Oppression was the cause of this wonderful revolution which came as a blessing in disguise.[12]

This fierce political cry, referring in its title to the Chinese Revolution as 'the greatest event of the twentieth century', was especially remarkable considering that Ching-ling was barely nineteen at the time. Moreover, embedding the Revolution in the framework of world history fittingly matched Ching-ling's cosmopolitan Western dresses. Unlike the heavily embroidered and oppression-loaded Manchu clothes, Western clothing was modern and new, just like the newly born Republic.

Dressing à la European in Shanghai

Ching-ling returned to China at the end of the spring term of 1913, where, conveniently, many other people in her hometown of Shanghai also dressed in the Western style. Emily Hahn, a family friend turned the sisters' biographer, remarked:

> It must be remembered that the Soong girls were not exceptional in the use of American dresses. All the women of China's treaty ports during the days immediately following the Revolution had adopted foreign dress, as a part of the general protest against the Manchu-ridden past. For a while young people of China rapturously welcomed all the appearances of Western civilization, and these clothes were as important a manifestation of their spirit as were the factory machines that the new Government was ordering in quantity from America.[13]

For Ching-ling, as for her many other urbanized compatriots, the West equalled progress in all fields. Writing to an American college friend upon her return to China, she stated:

> Our life here is exactly like yours. We live and dress à la European, even to the decoration of the rooms, so you can sometimes picture me not as a friend of far-away China, soaked in oriental atmosphere, but as one of your American friends in the busy city. For Shanghai is really very modern, more so than Atlanta in many ways.[14]

Similarly cosmopolitan and still studying in America at that point, May-ling wrote to her American college friend: 'The only thing Oriental about me is my face.'[15] Indeed, she wore, like other Wellesley students, a sailor-style blouse, and sported a soft, modern hairstyle. After spending ten years in America, May-ling returned in China in 1917, also clad in Western clothes, nipped at the waist, so strikingly opposite to the straight lines of traditional Chinese dress styles, wearing hats that Chinese women never wore, jodhpurs for horse riding and tennis clothes.[16] She continued to keep up with her other American customs, such as dancing, and attending, unaccompanied, the parties within her shielded, rich and cosmopolitan circle.

In the summer of 1913, Ching-ling not only returned to her homeland but also to a radically new country, of which she only dreamed about in America. Her older sister Ai-ling was secretary to Sun Yat-sen, but when she resigned in 1914, due to her forthcoming marriage, Ching-ling took her job. Her passion for the Revolution, accompanied by her intellectual curiosity, and her knowledge of English, French and Mandarin, rapidly turned her into Sun's indispensable collaborator. Soon, their relationship blossomed into a love affair, and, defying her father's orders, Ching-ling eloped with Sun, and married him in Japan in October 1915.[17] In the photograph, presumably taken on their wedding day, Ching-ling is depicted in an elegant Western-style jacket and skirt ensemble, accompanied by a wide-brimmed hat embellished with feathers, while Sun wears a smart, three-piece Western suit.

While the Soongs contested Ching-ling marrying Sun, and thus their wedding took place in haste, her sister May-ling had a big society wedding, because her suitor Chiang Kai-shek managed to win the family over.[18] The Chiangs married on 1 December 1927, and the contemporary media described in detail the bride's long wedding gown, made of silver and white georgette, accompanied by a long white lace veil, silver shoes and silk stockings, all of which symbolized a Western-informed opulence.[19] The women of the upper and middle class, as well as those from the artistic communities, had been marrying, for some time, in white wedding gowns, with their grooms appropriately attired in formal Western wear.[20] Nevertheless, the Chiangs' wedding was different. It was certainly special due to the social standing of both the bride, who belonged to one of the most illustrious Shanghai entrepreneurial families, and the groom, who was not only a well-known military man, but also the self-proclaimed successor to Sun Yat-sen. Their marital union was celebrated with two ceremonies: the Christian, at the prestigious Majestic Hotel, and the orthodox Chinese, at the Soongs lavish house on Seymour Street, located in the smartest part of the city, the French Concession. The Majestic Hotel ceremony hosted 1300 guests, including the leading diplomats, and the media diligently reported on the names of distinguished attendees, exquisite food and fabulous flower arrangements. Moreover, taking place in 1927, when the Western-originated celebrity culture had already conquered the world, including

Figure 6.2 Soong Ching-ling and Sun Yat-sen photographed on their wedding day, Tokyo, October 1915. Ching-ling wears an elegant Western-style jacket and skirt ensemble, accompanied by a wide-brimmed hat embellished with feathers, while Sun is depicted in a smart, three-piece Western suit. Courtesy of the Soong Ching-ling Memorial Residence, Shanghai.

Figure 6.3 The official wedding photograph of Soong May-ling and Chiang Kai-shek. They married in Shanghai on 1 December 1927, with the bride wearing a long wedding gown, and the groom attired in formal Western wear. Courtesy of the National Library, Shanghai.

China, the Chiangs' wedding was carefully planned and executed, in order to achieve the maximum exposure. As observed by May-ling's biographer Laura Tyson Li: 'Every aspect of the wedding was carefully orchestrated with an eye to publicity; a film of the proceedings was made and distributed in to cinemas.'[21]

At that time, Ching-ling had already adopted Chinese-inspired dresses, first as a wife of the founder of the Republic in the years 1918–25, and as his widow from 1925 on. Yet, while she diligently wore her own minimalist Chinese sartorial style in her home country, she would resort to Western fashions when abroad. During her political exile in Moscow in the late 1920s, due to her strong opposition to Chiang's abuse of her husband's socialist programme, Ching-ling wore flapper-style dresses and fashionable cloche hats. In his autobiography *Personal History*, the American journalist Vincent Sheean, who initially met Ching-ling in Hankou in spring 1927, and, soon afterwards, again in Moscow, stated that she was wearing European-style clothes after many years, and added that she was embarrassed in her short skirts.[22] However, in the photographs from that period, Ching-ling seems relaxed in the latest Western fashions, which, after Moscow, she continued to wear during her exile in Berlin. Upon her brief return in China in 1929, Ching-ling was depicted in the picture magazine *Liang you* (The Young Companion) in a Western-style coat, sporting a cloche hat, accompanied by her fashionable friend Mme Chang Hsueh-liang (Zhang Xueliang, 1901–2001), whose bobbed hair was an equally Westernized visual statement, with both of them clutching modern pochette-style bags.[23] As, on this occasion, Ching-ling had returned to China to attend her husband's reburial from his temporary Beijing resting place to a newly built mausoleum in Nanjing, she swiftly changed into the black and solemn Chinese-style clothes during the official ceremonies. Yet, returning from Germany in the summer of 1931 to attend her mother's funeral, Ching-ling again put on a fashionable coat and cloche hat while walking on her own in the park.

The fact that, up to the early 1930s, Ching-ling slipped easily between Western dress codes and the Chinese ones, as she considered appropriate, shows that she was a cosmopolitan, or an internationalist, to borrow the term fitting the socialist worldview and its vocabulary. But, hers was a modernist, fluid type of cosmopolitanism which allowed her to inhabit both cultures, Western and Chinese. The cultural historian Bruce Robbins defines the 'actually existing cosmopolitanism' as 'a reality of (re)attachment, multiple attachments, or attachment at a distance'.[24] Both due to her privileged birth and upbringing, as well as to the precarious political situation that forced her to exile, Ching-ling practised all of these forms of the 'actually existing cosmopolitanism' in that period in her life.

Nationalist Modernism

In a Soong family portrait, taken upon the return of May-ling from America in 1917, the three sisters wore their long, white American dresses, with their father and their oldest brother T.V. in Western suits, and the mother and two youngest brothers clad in traditional Chinese clothes. However, only a year later, while still occasionally dressing in a Western style, Ching-ling chose to wear a simple ensemble, consisting of a short tunic with side fastening and high collar, and a long dark skirt, a sartorial style promoted by Chinese girl students.

While at the time Ching-ling had already been married for a couple of years, she was still only twenty-five, and had been, not so long ago, a high school pupil in China and student in America. However, as much as it suited her age, she had certainly adopted that specific Chinese style due to both its progressive message, and its modernist looks. When still in America in 1913, Ching-ling scribbled in ink the word 'The Suffragette' over her image in the photograph with her brother, T.V. Soong. But playing with that notion would not have been big news in China either, or not in the circles of young educated women. As a daughter of the prominent and well-off member of the missionary circles, Ching-ling attended Shanghai's exclusive missionary McTyeire School for Girls before leaving for America.[25] The missionaries had already promoted modernization during the late Qing dynasty, specifically opposing the binding of women's feet, and endorsing education for girls. By the time formal female education was sanctioned by the Qing imperial edict in 1907, more than 420 girls' schools were already established throughout the country.[26]

In contrast to their stay-at-home mothers, incapacitated due to their bound feet, the girls in the treaty ports marched with their unbound feet into the new world through their education, acquiring not only knowledge of literature and science, but also learning about democracy and experimenting with feminism. In the period immediately before and after the overthrow of the empire, Western-style clothes unquestionably symbolized progress, but the relation to this style became more ambivalent from the mid-1910s on. Socially and culturally, the West was still intriguing and its various achievements desired, but there was a growing opposition to its imperialist and exploiting nature that continued to greatly harm the new Republic. In her analysis on the Chinese relationship with the West, Marie-Claire Bergère emphasized that 'the merchants were by no means the only fervent nationalists. The students were often its most ardent propagandists', and further clarified that 'the modernist and nationalist ideology of the treaty ports constituted not the rejection of the West but, on

Figure 6.4 Soong Ching-ling in a simple ensemble, consisting of a short tunic with side fastening and high collar, and a long dark skirt, a sartorial style promoted by Chinese girl students, 1922. Courtesy of the Soong Ching-ling Memorial Residence, Shanghai.

the contrary, an attempt to come to terms with it both as a model and as a threat'.[27] At the same time, the intellectual elite, gathered within the New Culture movement and its new magazines, challenged traditional Confucian values and customs, and argued for a reformation of Chinese society and the liberation of women.[28]

'May Fourth' Outfit

Defying the patriarchal social structures simply by participating in a public institution, and thus in public life, the girl student became the symbol of the new times. As stated by Martha Huang: 'The transformation of traditional feminine models into the girl student represented not only the remaking of Chinese womanhood but the remaking of the Chinese society at large.'[29] While the Chinese women of Han ethnicity had traditionally worn variations of long tunics and trousers, and, on some occasions, wrapping a heavy pleated skirt over the trousers, the girl student's 'civilized new garment' consisted of a Western-style skirt with a short tunic:

> Specifications said the coat should not cover the whole hip, while the bell-mouthed sleeves should show either the wrist or the elbow, with a wrist-band usually measuring around 24 cm. This so-called '*daodaxiu*' was the most outstanding feature of Chinese women's costume of the 1920s. When the 'civilized new garment' first began to prevail, the skirt was generally black, reaching down to the ankle, until it later became shortened to the upper calf.[30]

This simple ensemble corresponded to the contemporary simplicity of Western dress, but was nevertheless Chinese due to its adoption of a side fastening and a high collar, and as such played an important role in young women becoming modern, nationally conscious subjects. When one of them ran away from home, with the help of a radical magazine, her first act was to exchange her conventional trousers and long jacket for the girl student's customary short jacket and skirt. It made her feel like 'a soldier putting on his uniform before going into battle'.[31]

Ching-ling also fought her battles for a new society in that outfit. In fact, she had already been dressed in the same combination in her 1913 'Suffragette' photograph with her brother T.V., the only difference being that her tunic now had a side fastening and a high collar. Educated in a liberal American society, the Soong sisters matured in a modernizing Chinese society, and swiftly turned not only into new women, but moreover into the nationally conscious new women. In an undated family photograph, taken once they all were back in China, thus after 1917, three of them wear the same ensembles of short tunics with wide, short sleeves, and long straight skirts, executed in a luxurious brocade fabric. As documented, Ching-ling herself was dressed in a simple white-and-black combination in the period 1918–22, when accompanying her husband in his equally simple, new style suit.[32] However, she donned a silk patterned version in

1923 when Sun Yat-sen posed in a traditional long male silk robe at their home in Shanghai. In general, the girl student's outfit had been most often made of cotton, so additionally showing the much-needed patriotic restraint in messy post-Republican times.[33]

Due to the simplicity of its cut and abandonment of any decoration, the short tunic-long skirt outfit could not have been further away from an over-decorated Manchu dress. In an essay dedicated to fashion, and published in the English-language magazine *The XXth Century* in Shanghai in 1943, the influential Chinese writer Eileen Chang captured the history of her country through the renunciation of detail in dress. By scrutinizing numerous 'astonishingly pointless' details, Chang pointed to the society closing onto itself, and rejecting any change, either from the outside world, or by furthering its own narrative in a new direction: 'This tremendous amassing of bits and bits of interest, this continual digression and reckless irrelevancy, this dissipation of energy in things which do not matter, marked the attitude towards life of the leisurely class of the most leisurely country in the world.'[34] But times were changing for the country, and the process of sartorial renunciation reached its apotheosis at the beginning of the Republican era, vividly depicted by Chang's description of the simplest of Chinese garments at that time, the girl student's ensemble: 'Clothes were never before so light and gay. The "Trumpet Sleeve", like the Western bishop sleeve, only shorter, began tight and ended a little below the elbow, large, breezy, and fluttering. The jacket reached only to the hips.'[35]

Western fashion adjusted to the new times at the beginning of the twentieth century, by promptly deflating the voluminous shapes of its dresses, and abandoning superfluous decorations. As emphasized by the fashion historian Richard Martin, fashion became modern only once it had radically changed, as the avant-garde arts had already done: 'Cubism offered in fashion, as in art, a substantive and new manner of seeing, reasoned in dynamics of time and space, rendered with the volatility of modern life.'[36] By renouncing its over-decorated clothes, and simplifying women's dress, China also embraced modernity. In this context, the flat, geometrical shape of the tunic and skirt combination was a modernist sartorial statement, the visual proof that China joined the rapidly changing modern world. Indeed, at that time, modernity had been mediated through woman and her dress, both in the West and in China.

But, the girl student's outfit was equally modernist in its capacity to blur class and social distinctions. While the so-called New Woman, both in its mediated form and in real life, had been bitterly opposed in Western conservative circles,[37] the Chinese girl student had trumpeted a much larger social change. In China, the strict rules that sanctioned the presence of women in public had been practised for centuries. As only lower-class working women and prostitutes had been walking the streets till then, the appearance of young women from good families sharing the same public space had shocked the system. In her research on female education at the beginning of the twentieth century, the American scholar Joan Judge documented that, during the late Qing period and in the early Republican era, girl students had been often, either by mistake or maliciously, perceived as prostitutes, due to their modern dress and their unconventional behaviour.[38]

On the other hand, concubines and prostitutes called singsong girls traditionally had their place in public life and its imaginary, and their influence in promoting the latest fashions only increased, due to the extreme and chaotic social upheaval brought by the sudden overthrow of the empire, as well as the rise of the picture media.[39] In 1925, the images of singsong girls, customarily clad in the girl students' ensembles, graced many pages of the *Shanghai huabao* (Shanghai Pictorial). Presented as young ambitious girls, studying acting and writing poetry, and mixing on the journal's pages with an occasional singer from the Beijing Opera or a Shanghai racy young heiress, singsong girls were among the first celebrities in the budding Chinese mass culture.[40] Equally, their up-to-date dress marked them as new women in a disoriented society in search of new role models. Georg Simmel's observation that 'the demi-monde is so frequently the pioneer of new fashion is due to its distinctively uprooted form of life' is very fitting in the situation in which not only the demimondaines but the whole society had been uprooted.[41]

By now, this specific tunic–skirt combination had been acknowledged as the prevailing national sartorial style and acquired a progressive name, 'May Fourth', honouring one of the best-known student demonstrations, held in Beijing in 1919, opposing the Versailles Peace Treaty that sanctioned German and Japanese occupation of Chinese territories.[42] Thus, in China, a simple tunic–skirt combination marked the most diversified range of the Chinese female citizens as modern women, stretching from the girl students to the re-branded singsong girls and revolutionary socialists such as Qing-ling. Yet, the modern female was so shocking that it was likened to the adventurous. Reminiscing about her early years with her close friend and confidante American journalist Edgar Snow, Qing-ling stated that she was never warmly received as Mme Sun in Christian circles: '"They called me an adventuress", she said, scornfully.'[43] On this occasion, Qing-ling referred to her secret wedding to Sun against her parents' wishes, but her peripatetic life with the revolutionary Sun up to his death in 1925 was marked with various perilous adventures. Moreover, trying to protect her husband's legacy, Ching-ling stood up against the Chiangs, i.e. her brother-in-law and her own sister, which resulted in a dramatic escape into exile in the late 1920s, living under surveillance in Shanghai in the 1930s and surviving in a wartime Chinese capital of Chongqing with her safety in constant danger.

Inventing the *Qipao*

Following her endorsement of the short tunic–skirt combination, Ching-ling's next sartorial style was equally radical. In March 1925, Qing-ling would become an unlikely fashion heroine, by launching a totally new dress style, the *qipao*, nationalist and modernist at the same time, and during a very significant national moment: the death of her husband.[44] While it was a dress, the *qipao* was a similarly minimalist outfit as her earlier minimalist two-piece ensembles. At first glance, transforming a two-piece outfit into a single one of the same shape could not seem revolutionary. Yet, the *qipao* was an authentic novelty in the Chinese context, as Chinese women exclusively wore clothes made of two pieces in the past.[45] Nevertheless, in Beijing, sitting by her husband's sickbed, mourning him in private in the garden of Iron Lion Lane house where Sun died, and standing by his coffin at the Biyun Temple (Temple of Azure Clouds) in the Western Hills outside Beijing, Qing-ling wore a long, loose dress with side closing and high collar, made of black silk.

It is quite likely that Ching-ling developed this austere yet elegant outfit herself, aesthetically drawing on her earlier minimalist two-piece ensembles, and, possibly, on her Westernized background, where dress is an ordinary women's outfit. But when and how did this radical sartorial change happen? After carefully investigating Qing-ling's peripatetic life preceding her invention of the *qipao*, the leading scholar on Chinese fashion Antonia Finnane observed that she arrived at her unique dress style not only suddenly but also by overcoming various practical obstacles, such as finding and engaging a tailor while travelling by boat and road to Beijing, and nursing her already very ill husband.[46] Yet, in the contemporary photographs, she looks calm and elegant in her black *qipao*, fully aware that the death of her husband was swiftly turning her from the widow of one man into the widow of the nation.

The Chinese references made the *qipao* an appropriate nationalist dress while its simplicity and its masculinized cut secured it the modernist credentials.[47] As precisely described by the American scholar Ellen Laing Johnston: 'The sober

Figure 6.5 Soong Ching-ling in her black *qipao*, following the death of her husband Sun Yat-sen, Beijing, 1925. Courtesy of the Soong Ching-ling Memorial Residence, Shanghai.

garment worn by Song Qingling might indeed resemble a man's robe, falling loosely from her shoulders in an A-shape entirely hiding any evidence of feminine curves.'[48] Eileen Chang had already claimed in 1943 that the *qipao*'s asexual shape was rooted in women's disappointment with their social progress in the post-revolutionary times, resulting in their rejection of femininity:

> Having cheered themselves hoarse for the Western pamphleteers who championed the cause of their equality with men, they looked around at humiliating reality and, soured and angry, were driven to reject their very womanhood. A new wave of hardened feeling prevailed over the gushing girlishness of the early Republic. The first long gowns for women were angular and puritanical.[49]

Indeed, politics had certainly been involved in the invention and promotion of the *qipao*. When in 1929 Qing-ling attended Sun's reburial, her *qipao* was a political statement, showing that she understood and embraced the symbolic importance of her role as Sun's widow in a newly emerging Chinese nationalist narrative. This narrative was now shaped by Sun's ideologically opposed successor Chiang Kai-shek, but he still needed Qing-ling there in order to legitimize his rule. Having both his wife May-ling and his sister-in-law Qing-ling by his side cemented Chiang's connection to both Sun Yat-sen and the Soongs.[50] While strongly opposing Chiang, and thus powerless, Ching-ling decided to be there, so to honour Sun's equally nationalist, yet socialist programme. She did it in her austere, but, significantly, Chinese-related dress, *qipao*. At the same time, May-ling attended the unveiling of Sun's statue in front of the Central Military Academy in Nanjing in her short, fashionable *qipao*, so sartorially announcing the new times.[51]

But the *qipao* did not turn into a national dress only because it was endorsed by a beautiful young widow with honourable political credentials. And in any case, her fashionable sister played a much more important role in the further promotion of the *qipao*. As stated by Antonia Finnane, the *qipao* was indeed initially accepted by

> the women of an emerging middle class, who lived in or were susceptible to the effects of life in the modernising cities Shanghai, Tianjin, Hankou, Guangzhou. They had some education, some financial resources, and involved or situated themselves in relation to political events of the day.[52]

The *qipao* soon turned into fashion, due to both its nationalist and its fashionable references. Conveniently, by choosing to wear the *qipao*, Chinese women could communicate their patriotism, while deflecting the suggestions that its shape and its fabrics were influenced by the West, and, moreover, snubbing the accusations that their *qipaos* were often made from imported fabrics, which had been seriously hurting the domestic silk industry.[53]

The *qipao*'s initial masculinity sparked much criticism by conservatives in China, but it corresponded to the 1920s androgynous Western styles. However, while the *qipao* retained its simple shape until the late 1920s, so still corresponding to the latest Western fashions, it was feminized with slits that revealed legs, and made with distinctly feminine textile patterns. The historian of Chinese dress Mei Mei Rado cautioned against the over-politicized interpretations of the *qipao*, and insisted on the importance of its relationship with Western fashion:

> The form and spirit of the *qipao* were essentially hybrid and cosmopolitan, resulting from China's increasing exposure to western fashion. The overall flat shape and loose silhouette of the *qipao* echoed the contemporary western fashion, which experienced a fundamental revolution from a three-dimensional to two-dimensional structure during this period.[54]

Indeed, as further claimed by Rado, 'the popularity of and evolution of the *qipao* was inseparable from a newly emerging modern fashion culture in China'[55] but that culture was nevertheless related to China's complex embrace of modernity. In semi-colonial Shanghai, the advance of fashion had to adjust to multiple temporalities, which themselves had been informed by the rhythms of the varied retrograde or progressive social agendas. In the late Qing period, and in the immediate post-revolutionary period, China indiscriminately accepted Western fashions, as well as many other Western innovations. In her 1916 travelogue on Shanghai, Mary Ninde Gamewell, a member of the missionary circles, and a perceptive observer of the rapidly changing everyday life, commented on the incomparable skills of Shanghai's tailors in copying any Western fashions. She also described a lively, Westernized fashion scene on and around Nanjing Road, with four department stores controlled by the English, and several Parisian shops offering 'the latest designs in gowns, hats and fine lingerie'.[56] Ten years later, the picture magazine *Liang you* (The Young Companion) started to present hybrid fashions on its covers in the period 1926–7, referencing both Western and Chinese iconography. The Chinese American scholar Leo Ou-fan Lee emphasized the role of this magazine in producing, through its visual imaginary, an imagined ideal of Chinese modernity.[57] Consequently, those images gradually devised both a new dress and a new body for a new woman. Indeed, The Young Companion turned to the *qipao* in 1929, and almost exclusively dedicated its covers to *qipao*-clad svelte young women from 1931 on. Inside, the magazine published the images of latest Western fashions. They still were an option, but the Chinese-related *qipao* became the national fashion.[58]

In general, due to its novel nature, modernity was a crisis- and anxiety-ridden concept. As Chiang Kai-shek's rise to power towards the end of the 1920s was accompanied by his fervently nationalistic policies, the *qipao* played an important role in addressing the contemporary national-related anxieties, especially when embraced by Chiang's wife May-ling. While Western educated and modern, just like Qing-ling, May-ling had not been interested in radical modernist projects, such as the Chinese revolution and its aftermath. Instead, upon her return in China in 1917, she threw her energies to another modernist project, leading a glamorous lifestyle, of which the phenomenon of fashion was one of the most important expressions, both in the West and in China.

In this context, May-ling became the main promotor of the fashionable *qipao*, turning it into the ultimate nationalist sartorial statement, and, moreover, making it glamorous. This type of modernism better suited both her character, and her rising ambitions to become a proper First Lady for the new age, like her sister had been in the early Republican period.[59] When May-ling joined her husband in Beijing in 1928, following the Northern Expedition, his successful military campaign that united China, her rise in a sartorial glamour started to visually accompany and support Chiang's military rise. While only a year previously she had married in a Western-style wedding gown, she charmed the guests at a 1928 Beijing reception with her *qipao*. On this occasion, the wives of the staff of the Medical College who had graduated from Wellesley invited members of the foreign community to a party honouring the new Mrs Chiang, who herself graduated from the same American college. As one of the guests observed:

> She was charm itself … beautiful, vivacious, gracious and speaking flawless English. She wore a gaily printed cheongsam with the skirt slit to the knee, displaying a very shapely leg. And she was wearing lipstick, too – new in those days. She was lovely looking, and she knew it![60]

May-ling's sophisticated looks charmed the West. When soon afterwards Chiang moved the capital from Beijing to Nanjing, the diplomatic corps followed, with the United Kingdom being among the first Western powers to recognize the new national government in the summer of 1928. In comparison with Beijing, Nanjing was a small sleepy, military town, but May-ling was determined to transform it into a capital, which would fit the Chiangs' political ambitions. At this point, to demonstrate her national feelings, May-ling exclusively wore *qipao*. Visiting shortly after the Chiangs' arrival in Nanjing, the female reporter from the New York journal *Sun* found May-ling 'dressed in a wine-coloured gown of leaf-patterned cut velvet with real-pearl buttons', and also spotted her 'diamond-and-platinum wedding band with a circle of jade, and a large jade and diamond ring'.[61] A decade later, the two British writers W.H. Auden and Christopher Isherwood found May-ling again 'exquisitely dressed … and possessed of an almost terrifying charm and poise'.[62] Meeting her in Chongqing in 1943, the left-wing American academic John Fairbank perceived May-ling as 'an actress … trying so hard to be a great lady.'[63]

During that period, May-ling's glamour did indeed increasingly acquire cinematic qualities, with her opulent *qipaos* resembling those of the actresses in both the booming Shanghai film industry, and in Hollywood films, especially those featuring the Chinese American actress Anna May Wong. During their visit to Shanghai in 1929, Hollywood stars Mary Pickford and Douglas Fairbanks stayed in the Majestic Hotel, and Fairbanks was depicted there surrounded by a group of glamorous Chinese actresses clad in luxurious *qipaos*.[64] Referring to Hollywood films, the fashion historian Harold Koda observed that 'the cinematic version of the *qipao* took on a more vampish quality'.[65] This comment could be equally applied to the *qipaos* worn by Shanghai film actresses, and indeed to May-ling, who, from the early 1930s, embraced such a dazzling, vampish look in her real life.

Under the title 'Three Sisters' the picture magazine The Young Companion published in 1931 a photograph soaked in glamour. Yue Foong-chi (Yu Fengzhi, 1897–1990), the first wife of the warlord Chang Hsueh-Liang, was in the middle, flanked by May-ling on the left and Ai-ling on the right (see Plate 4). All fabulously made-up and expensively dressed, they resembled film stars, with May-ling in a silk *qipao* with flowery pattern, just seen under her fur coat, her sister Ai-ling in a luxurious velvet *qipao* and Yue Foong-chi with a white fur stole wrapped around her silk *qipao* with a geometrical pattern. Yet, only the latter had cut her hair, while the Soong sisters had their hair pulled back in a bun, a traditional hairstyle of Chinese married women.[66] In relation to May-ling's sartorial style in the late 1930s, Emily Hahn observed:

> She likes dresses of striking pattern, large colourful flower designs like those beloved of the ancient Chinese makers of brocade and satin; the patterns and the shades set off her vivid beauty and furnish a symbolic picture of modern China, blend of two civilizations, when she makes her public appearances.[67]

In the approach of 'blending of two civilizations', May-ling competed with yet another immensely rich woman, Koo Hui-lan (Huang Huilan, also known as Madame Wellington Koo, 1899–1992), who, from the late 1920s onwards, promoted her own sophisticated, cinematic versions of the *qipao*. Madame Koo's sartorial trajectory echoed the cultural and political trajectory of China, in its struggles to move from the far-away backwater, controlled by the big foreign powers, to a country recognized as a player on the world stage. Born as the daughter of a colossally rich sugar magnate, Hui-lan charmed London high society in the late

1910s and early 1920s, clad in luxurious yet audacious Lucile dresses, shimmering Worth gowns and Cartier jewellery. While still in her early twenties, Hui-lan understood what a marginalized, yet socially ambitious, Chinese woman should wear in the West: 'clothes from the finest and most fashionable designers', and 'jewels worthy of a princess'.[68] However, upon the return to China in 1922 with her diplomat husband Wellington Koo, Hui-lan turned from a client of Western couture into a promotor of Chinese-inspired clothes.[69] Disliking the copies of Western dresses worn by fashionable Shanghai women, Madame Koo embarked on inventing her version of Chinese-influenced couture, progressing from traditional Chinese ensembles of tunics and trousers to embroidered shifts containing slits, refashioned by her own designs and executed by her tailor in Hong Kong, often from the antique Chinese fabrics that she would buy at the market.[70]

Madame Koo was depicted wearing a long embroidered *qipao* in a photograph with Edda Ciano, the daughter of the Italian dictator Benito Mussolini, in Shanghai in the early 1930s.[71] At the time, the floor-length *qipao* again resonated with contemporary Western fashions and their column-like, sleek and elongated shapes. Additionally, Western tailoring techniques such as darts were incorporated to shape the *qipao*, and to emphasize a new, curvy body shape. But the *qipao* was still a Chinese national dress, and urban women of varied social and political standing continued furthering its Chinese-ness while keeping an eye on Western fashion trends.[72] As observed by Eileen Chang, fashionable women would wear their 'floor-length gown of a sleek velveteen, with scandalously long slits up the thighs, revealing the long floppy pants of the same fabric' underneath 'the military-looking, double-breasted, belted coat of the West'. Chang ironically commented: 'A strange combination it was, symbolic of the educated women of the day, aggressive feminists in theory but rapaciously materialistic when it came to the point.'[73] Chang published her essay in 1943, at the moment May-ling paraded in such ensembles.

This style matched the Chinese politics of the day, as formulated by *Xin shenghuo yundong* (New Life Movement). Launched by Chiang Kai-shek in 1934, the New Life Movement was intended to revive traditional Confucian values, and to reform people's daily behaviour through a set of strict practical rules. As emphasized by Sandy Ng: 'Part of the reform included redefining gender roles based on a reinterpreted Confucian model. It regulated that women were to return to their traditional duties and their bodies should be concealed.'[74] May-ling actively engaged in designing the New Life Movement programme, and in applying its rules in the everyday. As the Movement's public face, she projected this contradictory image of a woman, who was strong, yet traditionally delicate. Her military coat made her look powerful, while, at the same time, her refined

Figure 6.6 Soong May-ling, wearing a floor-length *qipao* and military-looking coat, with her husband Chiang Kai-shek in his military uniform, celebrating the end of the Second World War, 1945. Source: Deng Wenyi (ed.). 1946. *The Great Chairman Chiang*, Ministry of National Defence News Agency. Courtesy of the National Library, Shanghai.

qipao, worn underneath, was supposed to both conceal and reveal her distinctive female nature. The Movement envisioned women wearing plain, simple clothes, but, during the booming mass culture of the mid-1930s, women's sartorial choices could not any longer be ideologically imposed. For them, there was no way back to the traditional concept of submissive femininity. A long curvy *qipao* was equally a fashionable and self-assured statement, there to show that they grew strong by engaging in the sports, and glamorous by mimicking the stars in the latest films.

Figure 6.7 A young Chinese woman wearing a curvy *qipao* with the geometrical pattern, *Young Companion* (Liang you), cover, no. 94, 1934. Courtesy of the Donghua University Library, Shanghai.

Both May-ling and Hui-lan Koo contributed to the *qipao*'s success in China, but their respective connections with the West in the 1930s and 1940s brought this item to the attention of Western political elites, high society and the world media. They both seduced the West precisely because, while Westernized, they abandoned the latest Western fashions, and sartorially expressed themselves in ever more sophisticated *qipao* fashions. At that time, they both started to travel to the West again, May-ling to promote Chiang's policies, and Hui-lan as the ambassador's wife.[75] In January 1943, American *Vogue* presented Hui-lan: 'Wife of an ambassador, mother of two college-age sons, Mme. Koo is the Chinese citizen of the world, an international beauty. Here she wears her own version of China's dress, and her fabulous jade.'[76] On this occasion, the famous fashion photographer Horst depicted her in one of her richly ornate *qipaos*.[77]

Promoting her country, Madame Koo wore her precious *qipaos* at diplomatic and social gatherings in Paris, London and Washington, while May-ling was clad in *qipaos* at the important political meetings with the world political leaders during the Second World War, at which table China was now invited.[78] However, her most successful political endeavour took place in America in 1943, while pleading with the American Congress to financially help China during the Sino-Japanese war.[79] There, May-ling showed her brilliant education and her oratorical skills, while also impressing the Americans with her sartorial style. In April 1943, *American Vogue* gushed: 'In a long black dress, gold-trimmed, wearing green earrings, black gloves, she looked more like next month's *Vogue* than the avenging angel of 422,000,000 people.'[80] The journalist Allene Talmey nevertheless shrewdly pointed to the performative nature of her political project:

> Madame Chiang has the same clothes understanding as a great actress. She uses them as props, for effects, and she loves them. For Congress she wore a sable coat, diamonds in her ears; for Madison Square Garden, black with gold embroideries; for Wellesley, brilliant blue velvet.[81]

Vogue's article was accompanied by a photograph of May-ling in a long, body-hugging *qipao* made of dark blue velvet. However, her biographer Laura Tyson Li observed:

> Although Mayling was showered with praise, there was also growing cynicism and resentment. . . . Her much publicized wardrobe, complete with jewels and fur coats, compounded by the reports of her silk sheets, large entourage, and royal demeanor, did not jibe with Americans' love of public figures who appeared to be homespun everymen.[82]

Figure 6.8 Soong May-ling, reading about Japan's surrender to the Allied Forces in August 1945. Source: Deng Wenyi (ed.). 1946. *The Great Chairman Chiang*, Ministry of National Defence News Agency. Courtesy of the National Library, Shanghai.

Unlike her glamorous sister, Ching-ling stayed true to her original austere *qipao* style throughout her life, as shown by a very modest 1953 version in black cotton, which is in the collection of her Memorial Residence in Shanghai.[83] Only on her diplomatic missions on behalf of Mao's government in the mid-1950s did Qing-ling venture away from her customary *qipao*, putting on, for example, a flowery patterned, silk *qipao* gown while meeting the Indonesian president Sukarno in 1956. Her modest sartorial style stayed intertwined with the socialist project, which had started with Sun and continued under Mao. Her sympathizers praised Ching-ling's integrity and purity, but also emphasized her vulnerability. When the American journalist Vincent Sheean met her in Hankou in the spring of 1927, he was surprised that this 'most celebrated woman revolutionary in the world' appeared to be 'a child-like figure of the most enchanting delicacy'.[84] Likewise, Edward Snow claimed that he 'was not prepared for her youthfulness and beauty', claiming that while in 'her mid-thirties, she looked ten years younger',[85] continuing to praise Qing-ling's 'fine, satiny skin, pale ivory in shade'.[86] High-fashion photographer Cecil Beaton arrived from a different world but similarly turned into an admirer when taking Ching-ling's portrait in the Chinese war capital of Chongqing in 1944.[87]

For Qing-ling, as well as for her admirers and followers, the idea of the revolution had to stay pure and simple. Certainly, there was a performative streak in maintaining the same image throughout the inter-war period and beyond, and Qing-ling did it masterly. But, as the project of an international socialist revolution faded away, Qing-ling was increasingly marginalized, both at home and abroad.

In the 1930s and 1940s, her dazzling sister commanded both the Chinese and the world stage. In contrast to Qing-ling's discreet and suppressed femininity, May-ling practised the varied versions of femininity. In its column dedicated to women, The Young Companion pictured her as a budding literary figure in a flowery patterned *qipao* in 1929, a calm meditating figure in traditional Chinese garb in the same year and as a virtuous, obedient wife in 1934.[88] Those depictions neatly followed her personal and political trajectory. However, in the Western accounts, May-ling was often perceived as possessing an 'exotic' Oriental femininity, dangerous and fascinating at the same time. Auden and Isherwood stated that she could be 'terrible', 'gracious', 'business-like' and 'ruthless'.[89] They claimed that her perfume was 'the most delicious either of us had ever smelt' but also added that 'it is said that she sometimes signs death-warrants with her own hand'.[90] May-ling's magnificent, sensual *qipaos* significantly contributed to the image of an Oriental dragon lady.

Figure 6.9 Soong Ching-ling's portrait, the Chinese war capital of Chongqing, 1944. Photographer Cecil Beaton. Courtesy of the Imperial War Museum, London.

There certainly was a high level of vanity in dazzling the world with clothes, but patriotism had its role in this process. Both May-ling and Hui-lan Koo entertained the complex relationship with the West. They both started their lives in the West as little, marginalized Chinese girls. Their lives considerably differed afterwards, with Hui-lan Koo, as the wife of the most prominent Chinese diplomat, never crossing the line of propriety, unlike May-ling who, together with her husband, became compromised in many ways. Nevertheless, these nationally conscious women used their respective positions of power to reclaim agency for themselves and their homeland. Assisted by the hybrid nature of *qipao*, and their own hybrid existences, they could look at themselves and let the world look at them in a historically new context. By reversing the mirror in which the Orient had been the eternal Other, the West became the Other now, conquered not by military force but instead seduced by the modernist yet nationalist sartorial statement, the *qipao*. Referring to the Asian-generated version of Orientalism in the field of Chinese literature at that time, Leo Ou-fan Lee claimed: 'It can be argued that exoticism as a phenomenon of urban culture is closely related to a search of modernity and provides a partial solution to the paradox that arises between nationalism and imperialism.'[91] Indeed, the sartorial choices of Qing-ling, May-ling and many of their urban compatriots in the Republican period point towards the interplay between Western imperialism and Chinese nationalism, in the context of advancing modernity.

Conclusion

Both sisters – Ching-ling and May-ling – carefully curated and protected their respective narratives. While those narratives shared the same roots – born in a rich, Westernized Chinese family in Shanghai, and acquiring a liberal education in America – they started to differ considerably as the sisters embarked on their personal journeys. Following Sun's death, Ching-ling led a simple, reclusive life dedicated to keep alive her husband's legacy. She shared her story only with a small number of the left leaning journalists, whose publications presented her narrative as clear and honest, corresponding to the simplicity of her secluded life in the inter-war Shanghai. In contrast, May-ling was the protagonist in a much darker narrative, tarnished by the claims of ruthlessness, corruption and nepotism during the Chiang's rule. These different narratives informed the different concepts of dress and femininity, both in the way that Qing-ling and May-ling presented themselves to the world, and in the way the world perceived them. The contemporary Western accounts drew on the concept of exotic Oriental femininity, yet informed by its two different strands, emphasizing Qing-ling's delicate body frame, while insisting on May-ling's dangerous, Far Eastern dragon-lady sex appeal.

The cosmopolitan culture of their hometown crucially shaped both sisters into the broad-minded and independent individuals who turned into equal partners in their respective marriages. While they had spent their formative years in Shanghai, their respective life trajectories took them to the other Chinese and Western cities during the inter-war period, from Beijing, Chongqing and Nanjing to Moscow, Berlin and New York. Finally, following Mao Zedong's rise to power in 1949, Ching-ling aligned herself with the new socialist state and moved to Beijing, while only occasionally visiting her Shanghai residence. Instead, being defeated by Mao, May-ling fled China for Taiwan with her husband Chiang Kai-shek.

Acknowledgements

I am grateful to Christopher Breward for inviting me to this exciting project, as well as to Professor Zhong Hong from Donghua University who was most helpful in organizing our research visits and our work in Shanghai. My gratitude also stretches to my research assistant Tian Zhiwei who facilitated my research in Shanghai with great efficiency and charm. I am also indebted to Valerie Steele, who kindly organized my visit to the Museum of Fashion Institute of Technology in New York, in order to inspect Madame Wellington Koo's *qipaos* in the Museum's Dress Collection, and to Elizabeth Way who assisted me during my visit at FIT.

Notes

1 Marie-Claire Bergère, *The Golden Age of the Chinese Bourgeoisie 1911–1937* (New York: Cambridge University Press, 1990), 43–4.
2 Marie-Claire Bergère, *Sun Yat-sen* (Stanford, CA: Stanford University Press, 2000), 48.
3 On Charlie Soong in relation to this, as well as his other activities and personal life, see: Seagrave, *The Soong Dynasty* (London: Sidgwick & Jackson, 1986).
4 On Sun Yat-sen, see Bergère, *The Golden Age of the Chinese Bourgeoisie 1911–1937.*
5 On 12 April 1927, the military forces of Chiang Kai-shek conducted the so-called Shanghai massacre attacking the communists in Shanghai, and, around that time, in their other strongholds such as the cities of Guangzhou and Changsha, killing, depending on the differing accounts, between 5000 and 10,000 communists. Aligning with the communists from that point on, Qing-ling considered Chiang the worst enemy of her husband's legacy.
6 Sun Yat-sen's Three Principles of the People – Nationalism, People's Rights, and People's Livelihood – were ideologically vague enough to be appropriated by both Chiang and Mao.
7 Like other revolutionaries and progressive Chinese men at the time, Sun Yat-sen also had cut his queue (hair braid), which the Manchus forced on the ethnic Han Chinese upon conquering their homeland.

8 Henrietta Harrison, *The Making of the Republican Citizen: Political Ceremonies and Symbols in China, 1911–1929* (Oxford: Oxford University Press, 2000), 54.

9 On the early Republican dress decrees, see ibid., 58; on the popularity of Western dress in the aftermath of the Republic see also Antonia Finnane, *Changing Clothes in China: Fashion, History, Nation* (London: Hurst & Company, 2007), 95–9.

10 Cited in Peter Carroll, 'Fashioning Suzhou: Dress, Commodification, and Modernity', *positions: east–asia cultures critique* 2 (Fall 2003): 443–5; original: Tian, 'Ziyou tan: Shimao pai' [Free talk: Fashion clique], *Shenbao*, 6 January 1912. This is an abbreviated list, with the original containing not only more, but also more extravagant accessories of Western provenance.

11 Carroll, 'Fashioning Suzhou', 447.

12 Cited in Emily Hahn, *The Soong Sisters* (Bath: Cedric Chivers Portway, 1942), 69; original: Soong Ching-ling, 'The Greatest Event of the Twentieth Century', *The Wesleyan*, April 1912.

13 Hahn, *The Soong Sisters*, 48.

14 Ibid., 76.

15 Cited in ibid., 81.

16 Hannah Pakula, *The Last Empress: Madame Chiang Kai-shek and the Birth of Modern China* (New York: Simon & Schuster, 2009), 99; Hahn, *The Soong Sisters*, 89.

17 With the age difference of twenty-six years, Charlie Soong viewed the marriage between his best friend and his young daughter as a betrayal, especially as Sun, like most Chinese men, already had a wife and three children from an arranged marriage. See also Edgar Snow, *Journey to the Beginning* (London: Victor Gollancz, 1959), 889.

18 Similar to Sun Yat-sen, Chiang had previously been in an arranged marriage, and moreover married a second wife before proposing to May-ling. The fact that he was not a Christian like the Soongs also worried May-ling's mother, but, possibly with the oldest sister Ai-ling acting as match-maker, the family approved of him.

19 The Chiangs' wedding picture was published in the picture magazine The Young Companion 21, 1927, 1. For the media reports on Chiang's wedding, see Hahn, *The Soong Sisters*, 116–19; Pakula, *The Last Empress*, 180–3.

20 For the post-Republican, so called 'civilized' wedding, which simplified the traditional Chinese wedding rituals, and comprised men in formal Western suits and women in Western white wedding gowns, see, for example, *Shanghai huabao* (Shanghai Pictorial), 52, November 1925, depicting the son of an important politician and a beautiful heiress.

21 Laura Tyson Li, *Madame Chiang Kai-shek: China's Eternal First Lady* (New York: Grove Press, 2006), 82.

22 Vincent Sheean, *Personal History* (New York: Doubleday, Doran & Company, 1935). 26–78.

23 Column 'News from North China', *Liang you* (The Young Companion), 38, May 1929, 6. Mme Chang Hsueh-liang was the first wife of one of the most powerful warlords, Chang Hsueh-liang, known as the 'young marshal'. She was one of the most fashionable women in China in the inter-war period, and friends with all three Soong sisters. Apart from her husband's name, she also used her maiden name Yue Foong-chi.

24 Bruce Robbins, 'Actually Existing Cosmopolitanism', in B. Robbins and P. Cheah (eds), *Cosmopolitics: Thinking and Feeling beyond the Nation* (Minneapolis, MN: University of Minnesota Press, 1998), 3.

25 The McTyeire School for Girls was founded in 1892 by Dr Allen and an 1864 Wesleyan alumna, Laura Haygood. The girls' schools founded by the missionaries developed the modern, Westernized syllabuses. On the girls' schools during the late Qing and early Republican period, see also Judge 2008; Gamewell 1916, pp. 116–118. As an observant contemporary writer, Gamewell described various missionary schools, but also stated that one of the girls' schools, run by the Chinese Women's Cooperative Association, was known as the 'Suffragette school'.

26 The Qing imperial edicts prohibited the binding of feet in 1902, made precise recommendations for the organization and syllabuses of the new schools in 1904 and sanctioned formal female education in 1907.

27 Bergère, *The Golden Age of the Chinese Bourgeoisie 1911–1937*, 50 and 51 respectively. On the student activism in the period from the late Qing up to 1919, see also Mary Backus Rankin, 'State and Society in Early Republican Politics, 1912–1918', in Frederic Wakeman, Jr. and Richard L. Edmonds (eds), *Reappraising Republican China* (New York: Oxford University Press, 2000), 20–2.

28 For an overview on the strikes and demonstrations, as well as the boycotts of Western goods in the early Republican period, see Bergère, *The Golden Age of the Chinese Bourgeoisie 1911–1937*; Mary Backus Rankin, 'State and Society in Early Republican Politics, 1912–1918', 6–27; on the New Culture Movement, see Louise Edwards, 'Policing the Modern Woman in Republican China', *Modern China* 26, no. 2 (2000): 115–47; Finnane, *Changing Clothes in China*, 170–3.

29 Martha Huang, '"A Woman Has So Many Parts to Her Body, Life is Very Hard Indeed"', in Valerie Steele and John S. Major (eds), *China Chic: East Meets West* (New Haven, CT: Yale University Press, 1999), 134.

30 Mingxin Bao, 'Shanghai Fashion in the 1930s', in Jo-Anne Birnie Danzker, Ken Lum and Zheng Shengtian (eds), *Shanghai Modern, 1919–1945* (exhibition catalogue, Hatje Cantz, 2004), 318.

31 Cited in Harrison, *The Making of the Republican Citizen*, 75; original: Chow Chung-cheng, *The Lotus-pool of Memory* (London: Michael Joseph, 1961), 149–50.

32 The military-style suit that Sun Yat-sen started to wear in 1920 drew on a Japanese military uniform and was probably streamlined into its pragmatic shape by Sun himself and his Shanghai tailor Wang Caiyun. Later, the suit became known as Sun

Yat-sen suit (*Zhongshan Zhuang*), and both Chiang Kai-shek and Mao Zedong donned it in their respective efforts to present themselves as true followers of the father of the Republic. In the post-Second World War period, the suit has become wildly known as Mao suit in the West. On the detailed history of this suit, see Finnane, *Changing Clothes in China*, 182–3; Verity Wilson, 'Dressing for Leadership in China: Wives and Husbands in an Age of Revolutions (1911–1976)', *Gender and History* 14, no. 3 (November 2002), 608–28.

33 See, for example, Huang, '"A Woman Has So Many Parts to Her Body, Life is Very Hard Indeed"', 136; Finnane, *Changing Clothes in China*, 143

34 Eilenn Chang, 'Chinese Life and Fashions', *The XXth Century* 4, no. 1 (January 1943), 56.

35 Ibid., 59. Eileen Chang was born to a prominent family in Shanghai with close links to the Manchu aristocracy, but developed into a new woman herself, both in her work and in her personal life.

36 Richard Martin, *Cubism and Fashion* (New York: The Metropolitan Museum of Art, 1998), 16.

37 Concerning France, see, for example, Mary Lynn Roberts, *Civilization Without Sexes: Reconstructing Gender in Postwar France, 1917–1927* (Chicago: Chicago University Press, 1994); for Germany, see Patrice Petro, *Joyless Streets: Women and Melodramatic Representation in Weimar Germany* (Princeton, NJ: Princeton University Press, 1989).

38 Joan Judge, 'The Culturally Contested Student Body *Nü Xuesheng* at the Turn of the Twentieth Century', in Doris Croissant, Catherine Vance Yeh and Joshua S. Mostow (eds), *Performing the 'Nation': Gender Politics in Literature, Theatre and the Visual Arts of China and Japan, 1880–1940* (Leiden: Brill, 2008), 115–17.

39 For an overview of the iconographic cross-overs between prostitutes and fashionable women, see Francesca Dal Lago, 'Crossed Legs in 1930s Shanghai: How Modern the Modern Woman', *East Asian History*, June (2000): 103–44; Leo Ou-fan Lee, *Shanghai Modern: The Flowering of a New Urban Culture in China, 1930–1945* (Cambridge, MA: Harvard University Press, 1999).

40 For example, in 1925 *Shanghai huabao* (Shanghai Pictorial) published such images in nos 7, 14, 20, 34, 38 and 48. One of the depicted young women, Meng Xiaodong was a Shanghai actress of Peking opera at the time, only to become a famous film actress afterwards.

41 Georg Simmel, 'Fashion, Adornment and Style', in David Frisby and Mike Featherstone (eds), *Simmel on Culture* (London: Sage, 1997), 198.

42 The demonstration was started by three thousand students at Beijing University on 4 May 1919, demanding the return to China of the German possessions and rights in Shandong that negotiators of the Versailles peace treaty intended to pass to Japan. Soon, the demonstrations spread all over the country, and included various social strata, united in the nationalist struggle.

43 Snow, *Journey to the Beginning*, 89.

44 Treated initially in the hospital, Sun Yat-sen died at the residence of the well-known diplomat Wellington Koo in Beijing on 12 March 1925. See also Hui Lan Koo, with Isabella Taves, *No Feast Lasts Forever* (New York: Quadrangle, 1975).

45 For the history of Chinese dress, see Valerie Steele and John S. Major, *China Chic: East Meets West* (New Haven, CT: Yale University Press, 1995); Wilson, "Dressing for Leadership in China'.

46 Finnane, *Changing Clothes in China*, 143–5.

47 The name *qipao* (banner gown) relates to a long coat worn by Manchu women. Qi (banner) is the name of the Manchu people, used to distinguish them from the Han Chinese. *Qipao* is also called *changshan*, *cheungsam* or *cheongsam* when spelled according to Guangdong dialect. On *qipao*, see also Finnane, *Changing Clothes in China*, Harrison, *The Making of the Republican Citizen*, 177–8; Sandy Ng, 'Gendered by Design: Qipao and Society, 1911–1949', *Costume* 49, no. 1 (2015): 55–74; Mei Mei Rado, 'Imagery of Chinese Dress', in Andrew Bolton (ed.), *China through the Looking Glass* (New Haven, CT: Yale University Press, 2015), 40–55.

48 Ellen Laing Johnston, 'Visual Evidence for the Evolution of "Politically Correct" Dress for Women in Early Twentieth Century Shanghai', *Nan nü* 5, no. 1 (2003): 102.

49 Chang, 'Chinese Life and Fashions', 60.

50 Harrison, *The Making of the Republican Citizen*, 229–33.

51 *The New Companion* 41, 1929, 3.

52 Finnane, *Changing Clothes in China*, p. 13.

53 In his study on silk production in its leading hub, the city of Suzhou, during the Republican period, Carroll, 'Fashioning Suzhou', detailed the severe economic problems caused by imported textiles. On the National Goods Movement, promoting purchase of native-made products, see Johnston, 'Visual Evidence', 86–7.

54 Rado, 'Imagery of Chinese Dress', 185.

55 Ibid.

56 Mary Gamewell Ninde, *The Gateway to China: Pictures of Shanghai* (New York: Fleming H. Revell, 1916), 57–8.

57 Lee, *Shanghai Modern*, 64–76.

58 See the precisely documented rise of the *qipao* in the mediums of the pictorial advertisement and in the advertising calendar posters (*yuefenpai*) in Johnston, 'Visual Evidence'.

59 Various biographers refer to the high level of competitiveness among the Soong siblings, and especially between May-ling and Ching-ling. The claims that, upon Sun's death, Chiang proposed to Qing-ling, and only approached May-ling after being rejected by her sister, are also often made. See, for example, Helen Foster Snow, *Women in Modern China* (The Hague: Mouton and Co. 1967); Seagrave, *The Soong Dynasty*.

60 Pakula, *The Last Empress*, 196.

61 Ibid., 208.

62 W.H. Auden, and Christopher Isherwood, *Journey to a War* (London: Faber and Faber, 1973/1939), 55.

63 John Fairbank, *Chinabound: A Fifty-Year Memoir* (New York: Harper & Row, 1982), 245.

64 Fairbanks's picture with four Chinese actresses was published in The Young Companion (42, 1929, 7). While three of them wore luxurious *qipaos*, the fourth was dressed in a traditional Chinese costume. Anna May Wong's autographed photograph was on the cover of The Young Companion in 1929 (34, January 1929).

65 Harold Koda, 'Fashioning China', in Bolton (ed.), *China Through the Looking Glass*, 38.

66 The Young Companion 54, 1931, 3. The bobbed hair had been an especially contested issue. While young women cut their hair short in the early Republican period, they were, from the late 1920s, often perceived as clandestine revolutionaries, opposing Chiang's rule, and even killed if sporting short hair.

67 Hahn, *The Soong Sisters*, 49.

68 Koo, *No Feast Lasts Forever*, 129. All other information on Madame Koo's dresses is also provided by this autobiography.

69 Hui-lan married Wellington Koo in Brussels in 1920. After ardently fighting for China's interests at the Versailles Peace Treaty in 1919, he was appointed the Chinese minister in Great Britain, but was recalled to China in 1922, in the hope that his excellent diplomatic skills could help with resolving the volatile political situation at home. Hui-lan's immensely rich father bought a compound of villas in Beijing for the young couple, which Hui-lan decorated up to the highest technological and aesthetic standards. Sun Yat-sen died there in 1925, and the Chiangs lived there in 1930, as described in Koo, *No Feast Lasts Forever*. The opulent interiors of Madame Koo and Mr Koo's respective suits are also depicted there.

70 Koo, *No Feast Lasts Forever*, 181–2.

71 The image was published in Koo, *No Feast Lasts Forever*, and dated 1929. However, Mussolini's daughter Edda only married the Italian aristocrat Gian Galeazzo Ciano in 1930. The Cianos were in China in 1931–2, and Edda had her first child in 1931 while in Shanghai.

72 For example, Wang Wenxiang, the fashionable and dance-loving wife of He Yingqin, one of Chiang's leading generals, was pictured wearing a loose white *qipao* in combination with a cloche hat and modern shoes in *Tian Peng Pictorial* in 1927. A group of 'prominent women of the Chinese capital' also opted for looser-shaped *qipaos* (The Young Companion, 47, 1930, 27). When in 1938 Edward Snow was

depicted with the prominent communist leader Zhou Enlai and his wife Deng Yingchao, the communist Deng was clad in a floor-length, geometrically patterned *qipao*, echoing the latest fashions.

73 Chang, 'Chinese Life and Fashions', 61.

74 Ng, 'Gendered by Design', 71.

75 Chiang Kai-shek did not speak English and May-ling was actively assisting him at various political functions with the West, both at home and abroad. Wellington Koo was appointed Chinese ambassador to France in 1936, to the United Kingdom in 1941, and to the United States and Mexico in 1946. The Koos formally divorced in 1956, and Madame Hui-lan Koo chose to mainly reside in America.

76 Mary Van Rensselaer, 'Mme. Wellington Koo', *Vogue*, 1 January 1943, 30.

77 This outfit is in the MET dress collection, while another richly decorated Hui-lan *qipao* is in the collection of the Museum at FIT. They were hand-crafted in China, and are dated 1932 and 1937, respectively.

78 During the summits with Roosevelt and Churchill in Cairo and Tehran in 1943, May-ling assisted Chiang not only as his translator and secretary but also as advisor, and did not shy away from using her *qipaos* with high slits to charm the members of the American delegation. See Pakula, *The Last Empress*, 469–78; Li, *Madame Chiang Kai-shek*, 238–46.

79 May-ling Chiang's visit to America and her pleas for American financial support were hugely supported by the most influential American newspaper publisher, Henry Luce, who himself was the son of missionaries. He loved the China of his childhood, and, additionally, supported the Chiangs as he himself was a political reactionary. See Pakula, *The Last Empress*, 364–5.

80 'Vogue's View', *Vogue*, 15 April 1943, 33.

81 Allene Talmey. 'May Ling Soong Chiang', *Vogue*, 15 April 1943, 34–7.

82 Li, *Madame Chiang Kai-shek*, 225. May-ling's biographers also describe the many instances of corruption, misuse of aid funds, nepotism and various other undemocratic features of Chiang's period. See, for example, Li, *Madame Chiang Kai-shek*, 216–25; Pakula, *The Last Empress*, 343–7.

83 I am grateful to Mrs Mai Lingzhi from the Soong Ching-ling Memorial Residence in Shanghai for talking to me about their collection.

84 Sheean, *Personal History*, 208.

85 Snow, *Journey to the Beginning*, 82.

86 Ibid., 91.

87 Covering the war in the Far East for the British Ministry of Information in 1944, Beaton documented Chinese everyday life and prominent figures. He praised Qing-ling's bravery: 'In a country where to be outspoken is sometimes dangerous, she does not hide her disappointment at the distance she believes the Government has travelled from the principles laid down by her husband, the father of the

Republic' (Cecil Beaton, Peter Quennell and Gail Buckland, *War Photographs 1939–45* (London: Imperial War Museum, 1981), 185).

88 The photographs were published respectively in The Young Companion 38, May 1929, 20; 42, 1929, 20; 99, 1934, 22.

89 Auden and Isherwood, *Journey to a War*, 55.

90 Ibid.

91 Lee, *Shanghai Modern*, 203.

7

Image Makers of Fashionable Shanghai, 1910–30

Chia-Ling Yang

Of the many vicissitudes that contributed to China's modernization – its conversion into an international, industrial and urban society – those in visual and consumer culture were among the most prominent. The shift in Chinese dress, especially after the defeat in the Sino-Japanese War I (1894–5), shows a relationship between fashion design and burgeoning consumerism and the nation's determination to appear modern. Although Western culture had had a visible presence in everyday life in the international settlements such as Shanghai since 1843, it was as part of this post-war reaction that Chinese educated society came to realize that the old ways, including clothing which transcended cultural inertia and traditionalism, should be reconsidered in the search for modernity. The increasing demand for new clothing styles as a signifier of a modernized nation applied to both men and women. It was first noted in a series of articles published in 1911 that changing clothing customs was a crucial matter for the nation's new identity; thereafter a polarity of opinions and social attitudes emerged commenting on institutional official uniforms, students' wear, and the new look for professional urban men and women, given that these groups were expected to represent the new society and the civilized order.

In the first decade of the twentieth century, fashion assumed mixed, versatile or somewhat confused styles. The newly established Republican government published regulations for clothing in 1912, in which both Western and traditional Chinese-style dress were included: Western-style ceremonial dress, suit and hat, and Chinese-style robe were listed as formal dress codes for men, while for women the combination of skirt and top was stipulated as formal wear.[1] The regulations abolished traditional official clothing based on an individual's social status and official ranking; the prescription of Western-style garments as correct formal dress encouraged people to dress in a mixed fashion. Building on this regulated clothing, the 'civilized costume' (*wenming xinzhuang*), a combination of upper outer garment and skirt that promoted a neat appearance and convenience, was introduced as a guideline for schoolgirls in 1913 in an authoritative publication, *Jiaoyu zazhi* (The Chinese Educational Review).[2] Marking the success of the Northern Expedition (1926–7) and the unification of China, the government published new regulations for civil servants' clothing in which formal dress for men was the Western suit with a Chinese twist in its tall-collar design; and for women the *qipao* became the sole uniform style regardless of pattern or colour, as long as the fabric and the dress were produced in China.[3] Clothing was used to mark the new political regime and national characteristics; these regulations for clothing also provoked debate and were repeatedly discussed in the popular media in Shanghai and Beijing. The fashionable way of life was affirmed in the late 1920s by the popular media publishing photographs of celebrities and glamour designs in order to suggest metropolitan styles of living. The adoption of the *qipao* as uniform largely reflected contemporary fashion in metropolitan Shanghai, as evidenced in advertising posters and photographs, which also encouraged versatile patterns and styles of the *qipao*, as a new form of urban dress for women in the Republican era.

Between 1912 and 1927 there were heated debates on correct clothing for Chinese people. The perplexities encountered in the public sphere encouraged the first generation of Chinese image makers in the fashion sector, mostly based in Shanghai, to work jointly with photographers, celebrities and the press to find solutions. The discourse on 'Chinese-ness' within an international context continued and expanded from the Republican era to the communist regime, and such confusion and pliancy has persisted even to post-Mao China.[4] As society diversifies and conforms, new tensions emerge, but what are the institutional and cultural reservoirs that foster social resilience? Are there alternative modernities? A central concern in studying the evolution of China's fashion, through visual substance and changing garments, is how individual intervention and community innovation contribute to a new urban existence. Scholars in several fields – cultural studies, art and design history, film history, business history and modern intellectual history – have explored topics linking the transformation of Chinese dress in the early twentieth century to nationalist anxiety, political transition, consumerism, industrialization, the changing social body and vernacular modernism.[5] This chapter aims to join the existing historical debates and to initiate new directions of enquiry, examining the visual culture of Shanghai's fashion system between 1910 and 1930, particularly in relation to the practice of fashion drawings for pictorials. It will focus on the first cohort of 'image makers' in Shanghai fashion who took front position in developing a *hybridity* of styles in China. This chapter poses questions as to whether there were identifiable 'image makers' for urban people. Who were they, what were their aims, and how did they collaborate with the media and custom design houses in the promotion of their ideas? What role did foreign fashion play in contributing to the internationalization of Shanghai?

Through primary research and archival work on Chinese pictorials during the period concerned, this chapter uncovers the first group of fashion illustrators, led by Zhang Guangyu (1900–65). Customarily known as a cartoonist and the father of Chinese animation, Zhang played a starring role in Shanghai's popular culture and regularly contributed fashion designs, cartoons, comments and photographs of fashionably dressed women to the daily media. Yet strikingly, in major publications on Zhang there is no discussion of his contributions to Shanghai fashion.[6] The issue of how Shanghai artists contributed to fashion design prior to 1930 has been largely ignored by current historians and art historians. This chapter first discusses the background of the development of fashion and the cultural dimension in Shanghai in relation to its image makers and media as part of the modernist movement. It argues for a broader perception of modernist aesthetics traditionally limited to movements in literature, music, theatre and painting by artists or intellectuals recognized as connecting to the extended domain of public interest, as part of the history and changing fabric of the economy and everyday life in Shanghai before 1949.[7]

Picturing Fashionable Women as the Modern Visual Style

Thanks to the introduction of the new technology of lithography, the mechanical press produced an eclectic array of newspapers and magazines. Late Qing publishing houses vigorously pursued advertising revenue to ensure their financial survival. Apart from dedicating pages to commercial use, photographs and illustrations were added to newspapers to appeal to readers through visual immediacy. Photographs of landscapes, famous monuments, works of art and reproductions of *cartes de visite* of business owners were featured in public notices and news.[8] The combination of innovative printing technology, photography, illustrations of contemporary subjects, consumerism and urbanization encouraged a greater supply of images to Shanghai's public sphere.

Traditionally, paintings of female figures would present a sitter wearing an outfit unrelated to contemporary fashion. Starting in the late nineteenth century, paintings of courtesans in fashionable clothing and contemporary hair ornaments began to appear in painting of the Shanghai School and in pictorials. In the *Album of Female Figures* by the Shanghai School painter Wu Youru (1850–93), a collection of views of a courtesan's life, in the fourth leaf he included piles of books behind a seated woman playing the Chinese lute (*pipa*), so as to indicate her high rank among prostitutes (*shuyu jinu*), a 'courtesan of the book dwelling' who could read, compose poems and play music.[9] The female figures in this album all wear a black band decorated with pearls and jewels, an ornament known as the *zhemeile* (or *lezi*), used by Shanghai women to fix their hair above the forehead.[10] In winter, the fur ornament *diaofue*, a type of head ornament made of mink's fur, was commonly used by glamorous women for comfort and decoration, especially in the Jiangnan area. And the winter coat with straight-cut design (*yikouzhong*) was fashionable among courtesans before the turn of century. The outer part of this expensive costume was normally made of silk and the inner part of fur and leather. A similar fashion in ladies' hair ornaments can be seen in photographs, and Chinese women in early photographs had to be pictured in three-quarter profile in order to display their splendid accoutrements.[11] The female sitter portrayed in Wu Youru's 1890 album is no longer wearing a two-piece garment with the airy sleeves; instead she wears a three-piece outfit: a narrow-sleeved top after the Manchu style, a three-quarter length sleeveless vest and pants, with fur underneath as well as lining the edge of the vest to suggest her celebrated status and glamorous style. Such outfits combining Manchu and Han Chinese styles were fashionable in late nineteenth-century Shanghai.[12]

'In Shanghai, prostitutes set the fashion, and upper-class ladies followed', stated Xiaoqing Yeh. These painters reflected the extravagant fashion of desirable women from the pleasure quarters, and in order to attract more readers such adaptation was also seen in Shanghai's printed media.[13] Considering the appearance of the term *Huzhuang* (Shanghai style embellishment) or *shizhuang* (contemporary beautification/embellishment), and its incorporation into the newly developed concept *Huzhuang shinü tu* (pictures of women in contemporary Shanghai-style embellishment); or *shizhuang shinü tu* (pictures of women in contemporary embellishment), it is noticeable that the new mode of female figure painting had already appeared in 1883 in an advert in *Shenbao* (Shanghai Daily) entitled 'Seeking paintings of *Women in contemporary embellishment* by Mr Zhang Zhiying (act. 1880–1900)'.[14] Images of women dressed in contemporary style gained popularity among Shanghai School painting, and later Zhang Zhiying was followed by Wu Youru, Zhou Muqiao (1868–1922) and other artists, who from 1884 onwards composed numerous images of contemporary women from China and beyond for lithographic prints in *Dianshizhai Illustrated News*. In these images, they expanded the recurring leitmotifs of Chinese drawings and introduced all modes of modern life from Shanghai and foreign countries, including theatres, museums, medicine, electricity, steamships, chemistry, men's and women's fashion, and Western restaurants. The subjects portrayed were presented in an up-to-date style suited to their nature as a supplement to the news. However, due to the tremendous popularity with general readers and to criticism from his intellectual friends, Wu decided no longer to work for illustrated news where pictures formed only an addendum to the text, with no scope for artistic freedom or personal expression. Instead, in 1890 he established a new journal, *Feiyingge huabao* (Feiyingge Pictorial), which aimed to promote new trends in Chinese visuality according to three contemporary themes: 'a hundred images of exotic animals, sensational collections from women's apartments, and women in contemporary Shanghai fashion'.[15] By 1890, the last of these, depicting fashionable women mainly high-ranking courtesans – in an exciting urban environment, enjoying domestic and outdoor gatherings and the novel entertainments offered in the treaty quarters, was already firmly established as a cutting-edge mode of expression for pictorial illustration. Wu's series of female paintings was also included as 'One Hundred Beauties of Shanghai' in the reissued 26 volumes of *Wu Youru huabao* (A Treasury of Wu Youru's Illustrations) in 1908.[16]

In 1909, Di Baoxian (1872–1941), founder of *Shibao* (The Eastern Times), one of the most successful Shanghai daily newspapers of the period, published the first photograph of a woman in contemporary dress in *Xiaoshuo shibao* (The Eastern Times Fiction Supplement), believing that alluring, attractive photographs in the new genre of *shizhuang meiren* (beauties in fashionable dress) would help sales.[17] At this time, the terms *shizhuang* (contemporary beautification/embellishment) and *Huzhuang* (Shanghai-style beautification) were replaced by the new phrases, *shizhuang* (contemporary fashionable dress) and *xinzhuangshu* (latest attire), referring specifically to the fashions within clothing, accessories and ornaments.

In one of the three photographs depicting 'The Variety of Contemporary Fashion in Shanghai' published in the third issue of 1909, two women appeared in Manchu men's costume paired with a Chinese skullcap (*guapimao*; a name derived from the shape resembling the rind of a watermelon). The other images showed female sitters wearing straight pants instead of a skirt, a close-fitting tunic with high collar (or 'ingot collar', high under the chin and low at the back of the neck) touching the ears, and narrow three-quarter length sleeves.[18] Such clothing styles and young women donning men's dress were fashionable in the early twentieth century. Women ranging from the revolutionary figure Qiu Jin (1875–1907) to Shanghai's ten top-ranking courtesans engaged in cross-dressing when posing for photographs.[19] Their intentions differed: Qiu took the concept that even women, when dressed in men's clothes, could save the nation; the courtesans expressed a popular belief in the potential for women's liberation from traditional roles in the new era, yet treated cross-dressing as a role-play game and a novel addition to their fashion. In the Republican era, *Xiaoshuo shibao* continued to publish photographs of the newest fashions worn by famous courtesans in Shanghai and Beijing. In 1912, Shi Yunlai (act. 1900–20) showed off her high-collar dress with narrow sleeves while posing for photographs in Shanghai; and in 1914, the photographs of Beijing women in Manchu dress, high-collared top and narrow pants, and in a man's Manchu gown, showed a rather hybrid style of old and new, and an intention to dismantle the gendered dress system of old China.[20]

Before the abdication of the last Qing emperor in 1911, Di Baoxian established China's first commercial women's journal, *Funü shibao* (The Women's Eastern Times). Brought to an end by the May Fourth Movement in 1917, this gender-specific journal targeted female readers and made vital contributions to continuing debates concerning women's unequal status, education and expectations. It also documented many cultural, linguistic and social shifts that defined China's modernity in the early twentieth century.[21] The women appearing in this journal aimed at female readers were no longer courtesans but rather 'Republican women and female students', the upright members of early twentieth-century society.[22] It showed greater concern for women's new roles in society and the family. Photographs and drawings of women in fashionable dress from Beijing, Shanghai, Japan and Europe were constantly published in newspapers.[23]

In the early twentieth century the advanced technology of photography was embraced wholeheartedly by newspapers and pictorials to replace painting and drawings, but photography in print could not yet achieve the bright colours and vibrant compositions that lay within easy reach of artists' drawings. For visual interest, colour paintings and drawings of women in fashionable dress continued to occupy the front cover. Cartoons, cigarette cards and calendar posters with intense colours continued to appear in all kinds of product advertising during the Republican era.[24] With high demand from Shanghai's advertising culture, the hand-drawn image industry achieved greater prominence from the late 1910s to the early 1930s, until colour reversal stock for movies and slide film was introduced by the American Eastman Kodak Company in 1935. Such technical innovations in photography and colour printing then supplanted fashion drawings in mass media.[25]

Among all the news illustrators, Shen Bochen (1889–1920) was one of the first to draw female figures in contemporary fashion for Chinese newspapers. His ball-pen drawings of contemporary women began to appear as a weekly supplement to *Da Gonghe xingqi huabao* (The Great Republicans' Weekly Illustrated News). Later those illustrations were edited and published in colour in 1913 as *Xinxin baimei tu* (New Illustrations of One Hundred Contemporary Beauties), and over ten thousand copies were sold. Due to the popularity of its subject, the author published two successive collections of contemporary beauties, *Xinxin baimei tu waiji* (Extended Collection of New Illustrations of One Hundred Contemporary Beauties) and *Xu Xinxin baimei tu* (Sustained Collection of New Illustrations of One Hundred Contemporary Beauties).[26]

In the first four issues, Shen made it clear that his female subjects were contemporary. Although they were portrayed in traditional themes, such as women performing domestic work, doing needlework, and caring for children, they were shown with unbound feet and conveyed a strong sense of physical freedom in various activities. From the tenth issue, images presented 'new women' in lavish embroidered dresses with high collar and narrow sleeves attending modern theatre (no. 11: 3), playing violin and piano (no. 15: 1, no. 20: 1), painting watercolours (no. 18: 1), or even walking a dog along the levée leading to a lighthouse (no. 11: 2). Some of those 'new Republican women' lifted heavy bowling balls with confidence (no. 20: 2), or wore fitted pants to play tennis (no. 43: 2) or sprint competitively (no. 30: 1). Shen also showed women in rather risqué poses, such as sliding down a rope from a ferry to a transit boat with legs exposed (no. 26: 1). His new beauties also suggested a novel role for 'professional women' of the formerly working class, from sculpting clay figurines (no. 21: 1), a country girl selling sweets in the city (no. 13–14), to a female tailor cutting fabric (no. 40: 1).[27] Among 108 images in the surviving 44 issues of *Da Gonghe xingqi huabao* held by Shanghai Library, apart from one woman in Western dress, one in pyjamas and a country girl in loose pants, all of the women, regardless of their class and profession, wore the fashionable tight-fitting, high-collared top with three-quarter-length sleeves and narrow pants or a long, loose skirt. Shen Bochen had worked as a clerk in the Shanghai Fabric Shop when he first came to the city in 1909. Later he studied with Pan Zhenyong (1852–1921) and Qian Hui'an (1833–1911), who were both leading Shanghai School painters famed for their female figure painting in a refined and articulated mode, *gongbi*. Perhaps as a result of this experience, the young illustrator provided the fabric patterns with great detail in elaborated brushwork.[28] While Shen's attention to contemporary fashion was apparent, there were no descriptions or detailed discussions of the fashion illustrated. The poem accompanying each image was more concerned with sentimental narratives than costume design.

By 1914, Shen Bochen's fashionable female figures in watercolours had been employed as cover images for the first three issues of *Fanhua zazhi* (Prosperity Magazine). No matter whether facing her readers and smiling, smelling fragrant flowers or gazing at her own married image, the close-up images offer an intimate experience for readers as if the latter were standing beside the subject; these young women looked confident and comfortable in their confined space. Their skin is pale and flawless, and the high-collared dress shows off their beautifully slender neckline.

Succeeding the accomplishment of Shen Bochen, Ding Song (1891–1972) also published two lithographic volumes of *Shanghai shizhuang baimei tuyong* (Illustrated Tribute of One Hundred Beauties of Shanghai in Contemporary Fashionable Costume) in 1916.[29] Resident in Shanghai since a young age, Ding studied Western painting under Zhou Xiang (1871–1933), who established the Shanghai Oil Painting Academy in 1910 and the Workshop for Painting Stage Sets in 1911.[30] Skilled in watercolour, pencil, pen and ink drawings, from 1915 onwards Ding created cover images of female figures for the weekly literary magazine *Libailiu* (The Saturday). Ding also frequently contributed satirical cartoons to *Shenzhou huabao* (China's Daily Illustrated News, 1909–16), *Xinshijie huabao* (New World Illustrated News) and *Nüzi shijie* (Women's World) between 1915 and 1918.[31] In each illustration included in his *Shanghai shizhuang baimei tuyong* collection, from babysitting to writing love letters under the electric light, the artist approached his subject using a linear drawing technique easily translated into the printed medium, and aimed to impart to his subjects a modern-day feel through fashionable hairstyles, dress and the mostly Western built environment. Women's fashion also began to move from one-piece blouse to a combination of a three-quarter-length narrow sleeved blouse underneath a tunic with rightward collar (Figure 7.1, 1916). Both Shen's and Ding's collections of one hundred beauties enjoyed commercial success, which in turn encouraged followers to produce series of one hundred beauties in modern dress.[32] It is also noteworthy that the readership for these pictorials, especially *Libailiu* and *Nüzi shijie*, shifted from just men to a mixed audience; the introduction of women's fashion was not solely offered as an object of sexual spectacle from a male perspective, but also catered to the new Republican women.[33]

Images of glamorous women were employed on the front covers of magazines, and more images of women in contemporary fashion were presented in other

Figure 7.1 Ding Song 丁悚, *Libailiu* 禮拜六 (The Saturday), no. 100 (1916), cover image.

illustrated newspapers and on calendar posters to promote commercial products in Shanghai. The women featured in popular media also shifted from courtesans to Republican women and female students: picturing fashionable women became the modern visual style, as well as offering the new look of a modern nation from 1911. These images signified the fluctuating characteristics of Chinese society; I would further argue that the social changes caused artists to drift away from picturing fashionable women, to creating fashions for women. In the following section, this chapter explores the painter Zhang Guangyu and his fellow artists as the first generation of Chinese fashion designers in Shanghai.

Graphic Artist as Fashion Designer

Scholars have considered that the first fashion drawing was published in *Guowen zhoubao* (The National News Weekly) in 1924, and it was not until the late 1920s that fashionable garment and lifestyle were established with newspaper and pictorials using new fashion designs to mark the season.[34] My research on late Qing to the Republican pictorials led to a new discovery concerning fashion sketches and their development prior to 1920: I discovered that drawings of seasonal fashion began to appear in a pictorial specifically intended for woman readers and the female students on *Qingsheng zhoukan* (Voice of the Youth Weekly) as early as in 1917.[35] Yet prior to 1918, those images were mostly published with a one-line text concerning the subject, without any detailed discussion or explanation.

In 1918, Ding Song began to make occasional drawings on the occurrence of Shanghai fashion and his imaginative design of future female fashion for the front cover of *Xinshijie huabao*. In Ding's drawing 'The Future Dress for Women 女子妝束的將來' on the cover of issue no. 7, the artist projected it with a woman wearing a long fringe that covered her eyes; her sleeves and pants were so short that her arms and legs were exposed, and she was wearing knee-high socks and high-heeled shoes of Western fashion.[36] Such drawing, forecasting the liberation of women's hairstyle and limit against the traditional social control of bodily exposure. However it was aimed at commenting on conceited women in Shanghai with an ironic tone, these drawings was not for conveying ideas of fashion design to his reader. In this respect, the first proper fashion drawing of seasonal dress that includes a comprehensive explanation of design, tailoring and material in China was actually published by Ding Song's colleague Zhang Guangyu in China's first cartoon journal, *Shanghai poke* (Shanghai Puck).

Shanghai poke was established by Shen Bochen and his brothers on 1 September 1918 and closed after four issues in December 1918. Ding Song and Zhang Guangyu were among the contributors to this journal.

In the fourth issue of this short-lived journal, Zhang Guangyu published the 'Ladies' Fashion Column'.[37] An American cape coat, sport coat of leopard with deep collar, cuffs and border of Hudson Bay seal, four wartime long dressy coats, English dressy long coat and grey Oxford with high muffler collar, European sport style in nutria, Sam Browne leather belt and Chinese attire were introduced. The texts were in both Chinese and English, which might be directly copied from European and American fashion magazines of winter 1918. In this column, Zhang first discussed the importance of fashion to European women and how fashion styles changed from 1917 to 1918. The New York-based magazine that Zhang consulted contained many references to the First World War and military-influenced women's fashion, with design that emphasized straight lines, novel buttoning front effect, fur collar and cuffs, and variation of pocket designs. But Zhang was surprised to find that even during wartime the fashions were constantly updated and seemed not to be affected at all by the hostilities. Four wartime models of women's winter fashion in America – army coat, trench coat, navy league suit and St Nicholas skating suit – were introduced with their original English texts and Zhang's own interpretations for the Chinese readers. He suggested that the one-piece dressy long coat derived from the Men's Heavy *Pom Pom* Overcoat with buckled belt and attractive pockets to show off the bodyline, and he suggested that the 'Trench Coat' of Model 2 best suited the shape of Chinese women.

Zhang considered that contemporary women's fashion in China could be divided into three categories based on fashions: students who liked to combine the Eastern and Western fashions; domestic ladies who preferred Chinese style; and courtesans with their fancy or rather vulgar dress style (the phrase Zhang used here is 'neither donkey nor horse' degenerate style, which literally means a confused, wild and uncultivated dress style). The aim of this column was to introduce the latest Western fashion to Chinese readers, in promotion of a dress revolution in China. It complained that Shanghai tailors had no sense of design, even giving them the most luxurious leather and material, they would make a long coat look like a shapeless gigantic tube. And the hat Shanghai women wore were like *shaomai* (Figure 7.2, round stuffed dumpling with a flat top), the Scottish 'Tam O'Shautter' (a misspelling of 'Tam o' Shanter') should be a better choice for Chinese women. Zhang further concluded that to change clothing in China, one must start with hairstyles. Shanghai women on average spent two to

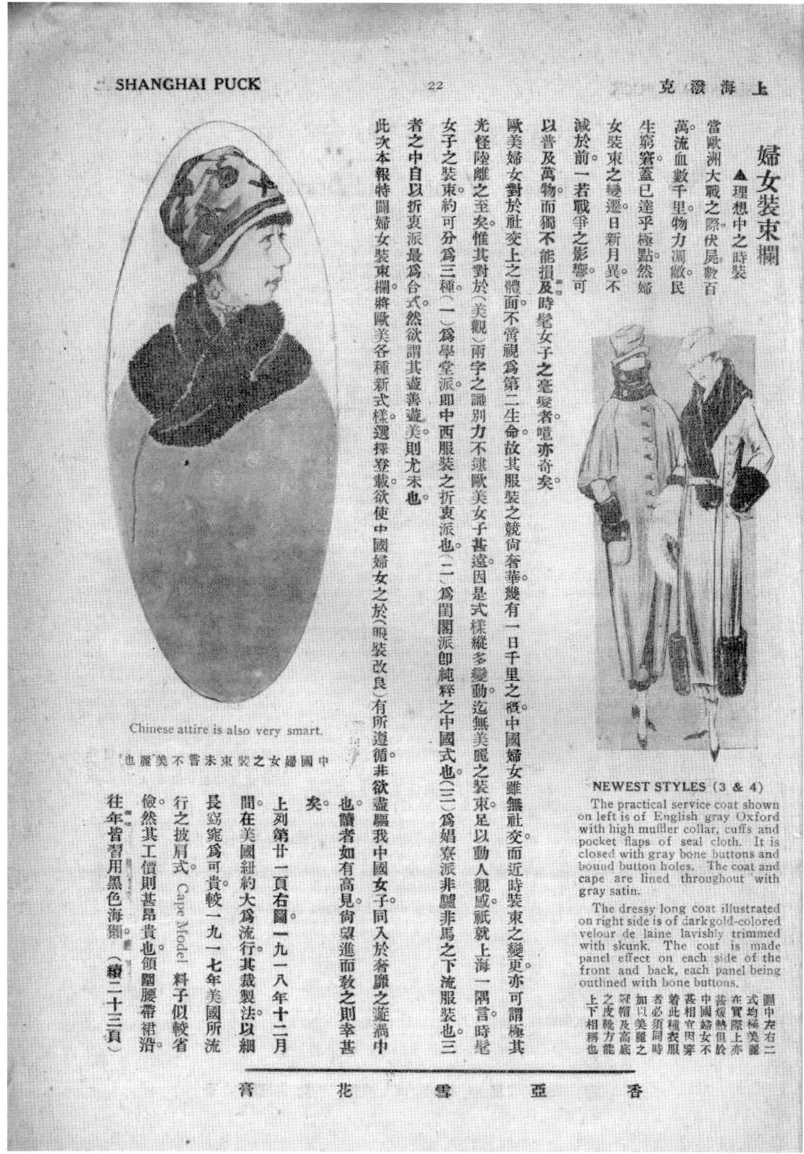

SHANGHAI PUCK 22 上海潑克

婦女裝束欄

▲理想中之時裝

當歐洲大戰之際。伏屍數百萬。流血數千里。物力凋敝。民生窮窘。蓋已達乎極點。然婦女裝束之變遷。日新月異。不減於前。一若戰爭之影響。可以普及萬物而獨不能損及時髦女子之毫髮者。噫亦奇矣。

歐美婦女對於社交上之體面。不啻視爲第二生命。故其服裝之競尚奢華。幾有一日千里之概。中國婦女雖無社交。而近時裝束之變更。亦可謂極其光怪陸離之至矣。惟其對於（美觀）兩字之識別力不逮歐美女子甚遠。因是式樣縱多變動。迄無美麗之裝束足以動人觀感。祇就上海一隅言。時髦女子之裝束約可分爲三種。（一）爲學堂派。即中西服裝之折衷派也。（二）爲閨閣派即純粹之中國式也。（三）爲娼寮派非驢非馬之下流服裝也。三者之中自以折衷派最爲合式。然欲謂其盡善盡美。則尤未也。

此次本報特闢婦女裝束欄。將歐美各種新式樣。選擇登載。欲使中國婦女之於（服裝改良）有所遵循。非欲盡驅我中國女子。同入於奢靡之漩渦中也。讀者如有高見。尙望進而教之則幸甚矣。

上列第廿一頁右圖。一九一八年十二月間。在美國紐約大爲流行。其裁製法。以細長窈窕爲可貴。較一九一七年美國所流行之披肩式。Cape Model 料子似較省儉。然其工價則甚昂貴也。領圈腰帶裙沿。往年皆習用黑色海獺。（續二十三頁）

NEWEST STYLES (3 & 4)

The practical service coat shown on left is of English gray Oxford with high muffler collar, cuffs and pocket flaps of seal cloth. It is closed with gray bone buttons and bound button holes. The coat and cape are lined throughout with gray satin.

The dressy long coat illustrated on right side is of dark gold-colored velour de laine lavishly trimmed with skunk. The coat is made panel effect on each side of the front and back, each panel being outlined with bone buttons.

圖中左右二式均極美麗在實際上亦甚煖熱但於中國婦女不甚相宜因穿着此種衣服者必須同時加以美麗之冠帽及高底之皮靴方能上下相稱也

Chinese attire is also very smart.

中國婦女之裝束未嘗不美麗也

香亞雪花膏

Figure 7.2 Zhang Guangyu 張光宇, 'Funü zhuangshu lan 婦女裝束欄' (Ladies' Fashion Column), *Shanghai poke* (Shanghai Puck), *juan 1*, no. 4 (1918): 22.

three hours tidying their hair every morning: only when hairstyles had been reformed could Chinese women achieve a new look.[38]

There is no reference provided in the text on which New York-based magazine of December 1918 Zhang sourced, and so far I have not been able to find the exact images Zhang copied. However, a similar drawing style can be found in the

Winter Fashions 1917–1918 catalogue of Bellas Hess & Co. in New York City (catalogue no. 79). Zhang's two central figures of 'War Time' Models (p. 23 – see Figure 7.3) are identical to the illustration of 'Suit of Oxford Gray Wool Mixture' (cat. IX125–IX126 – see Figure 7.4) in Bellas Hess's in terms of their gesture. The illustrator for Bellas Hess has a characteristic expression of pressing the hat low to cover the entire forehead and part of the right eye, so the model's face would be partially shadowed to enhance a sense of reality, enigmatic beauty and a three-dimensional visual effect. Zhang adapted such traits for his composition, but he did not add any shadows as for the Chinese audience, shadows on the face would be associated with ill fate and bad luck. Additionally, the woman in profile's gesture to show off the hat and the stylish fur scarf in 'Chinese attire is also very smart' (p. 22) indicated an affinity to Bellas Hess's 'scarf 29 × 208' (p. 125).[39] The mail-order catalogues contain many illustrative colour plates and finely painted covers. Originally founded as National Cloak and Suit Co. in 1888 and renamed as National Bellas Hess & Co. Inc. in 1910, Bellas Hess was a department store covering the full New York City block at Washington, Morton and Barrow streets, and claimed to be the largest building in the world in its 1917–18 catalogue. The company was also a mail-order reseller of wearing apparel, which was listed as one of the top five mail-order companies of early twentieth-century America.[40]

It is possible that Zhang copied all the English texts and edited them into this column, and the six fashion illustrations published here were drawn by Zhang Guangyu himself, with the latest fashion models and catalogues in front of him that he could learn from. The framing design for the four wartime models was an additional element added by Zhang, and the rose patterned hat and the dressy coat with full fur collar and matching pattern of the Chinese woman were Zhang's own design, since a pair of Chinese traditional satin button knots under the fur collar revealed their original identity. While the exact sources of fashion news and illustration for Zhang's early fashion drawings requires a further investigation, Zhang's column became the first fashion illustration with proper text discussing the latest women's collection of Europe and America in December 1918 for the Chinese readership. However, his achievement has not been mentioned in any publication, including Zhang's own memoirs and his writings, nor in any recent scholarship on Chinese fashion to date.

At the age of eighteen, Zhang Guangyu was already rather experienced in the publishing business as a professional illustrator and graphic designer. Born in Wuxi of Jiangsu Province to a Chinese medical doctor family on 25 August 1900, Zhang was inspired by his father Zhang Liangsheng's (act. 1880–1925) passion for painting, woodcut prints, calligraphy and art collecting.[41] Apart from

SHANGHAI PUCK 23 上海潑克

No. 1 No. 2 No. 3 No. 4

"WAR TIME" MODELS,

"ARMY COAT"
No. 1—Made in fine quality. Tan Army Coating—cut on military mannish lines, with belt—inverted plaits—high or low collar effect and pockets.

"TRENCH COAT"
No. 2—A splendid practical model—built for service ability and comfort. It is fashioned of Men's Heavy Pom Pom Overcoating. Has buckled belt and attractive pockets—Sleeves and body lined.

"NAVY LEAGUE SUIT"
No. 3—A very distinctive Suit—cut on masculine lines showing Army Collar, plaited coat effect, pockets, and belt of black Leather. Skirt very Smart—made on straight lines, two pockets and gathered back.

"ST. NICHOLAS" SKATING SUIT
No. 4—"Distinctively Russian" designed in fine quality Duvet de Laine—Showing new Slip on Coat—featuring novel pockets, buttoning front effect, belt, fur collar and cuffs. Straight skirt—showing two box plaits front and back.

上四圖皆爲美國婦女戰時之服裝也第一圖爲陸軍式二圖爲戰壕式三圖爲海軍式皆易摹倣其中尤以第二式爲最合於中國婦女之裝飾第四圖爲跑冰式黑衣白領至爲美麗此衣即名聖尼古拉跑冰衣不知是何取意

（接廿二頁）Hudson Seal 一九一八年冬季。則各種昂貴之皮料。亦皆採用。上圖左圖顯然一陸軍披肩之變相也。與從前之披肩式。雖同一名稱。而實際上則絕然相異。此式美國女子最喜採用。以其英武有鬚眉氣也。

上海婦女近來所穿之大衣。皆使一般毫無智識之成衣匠任意裁製。其式樣則儼然一巨大竹管。因是全身姿勢。喪失淨盡。雖有十分美麗之態度。亦不能表現其萬一。殊可惜也。近今婦女所穿之大衣。無不（續廿四頁）

香亞翰水

Figure 7.3 Zhang Guangyu, 'Funü zhuangshu lan 婦女裝束欄' (Ladies' Fashion Column), *Shanghai poke* (Shanghai Puck), *juan 1*, no. 4 (1918): 23.

studying, he spent most of his childhood attending Beijing opera performances in local temples, making drawings and handmade toys for himself and his two younger brothers. At the age of thirteen, Zhang's grandfather on his mother's side, a successful comprador and manager of Jiufeng Flour Manufactory's Shanghai branch, wanted him to learn about business before working for their

Figure 7.4 'Suit of Oxford Gray Wool Mixture', in *Winter Fashions 1917–1918* catalogue of Bellas Hess & Co. in New York City (catalogue no. 79), 74, Cat. IX125–IX126.

own family in the flour factory and the fabric factory. Zhang interrupted his schooling and had an apprenticeship at a local bank for a year. Soon he realized that the business did not suit him, so he was sent over to his uncle's in Shanghai to continue his learning at the Primary School Affiliated to the Second Normal College in 1914.[42]

Living close to the Xinwutai (The New Theatrical Stage), the first modern theatre in China, the young artist made friends with the theatre's lead martial art actor Zhang Delu (act. 1910–40), who allowed him backstage to make sketches of opera scenes and the faces of the actors.[43] As soon as Zhang graduated from the school in 1916, he was recommended by Zhang Delu to work in the stage set team at the New Stage under the direction of Zhang Yuguang (1885–1968). Zhang Yuguang, a famous Shanghai artist, photographer, production scenic artist, film-maker and the principal of Shanghai Academy of Fine Art (1914–19), was influential to Zhang Guangyu's learning of art and design. Zhang was taught to paint the backdrops according to the different settings of the play; he also learnt to do Western perspective painting and created works that were dramatic, eye catching and easily comprehended by the audience. After professionalizing his painting skill, the young talent was introduced by Zhang Yuguang to be the full-time illustrator for *Xinshijie huabao* (New World Illustrated News, 1918–26) in the summer of 1918.

The *Xinshijie huabao* was established by Sun Xueni (1889–1965) and published by Shanghai Shengsheng Press in August 1918.[44] Many well-known leading journal-illustrators and publishers, including Zhang Yuguang, Ding Song, Dan Duyu (1897–1972), Wan Laiming (1900–97) and Lu Shaofei (1903–95), calendar-poster artists Yang Zuotao (1897–1967), Zheng Mantuo (1888–1961) and Xie Zhiguang (1900–76), the European modern art promoters and artists Yang Qingqing (1895–1957), Yan Wenliang (1893–1988), Liu Haisu (1896–1994), Wang Jiyuan (1893–1975) and Jiang Xiaojian (1894–1939), and writers Bao Tianxiao (act. 1900–30) and Zhou Shoujuan (1895–1968), contributed their works to this new journal. Located at 243 Erma Road (today Jiujiang Road), nicknamed 'Chinese Wall Street' during the colonial period, the journal offered a meeting point for those artists to network. Among the illustrators, Zheng Mantuo, Xie Zhiguang and Yang Zuotao were celebrated for their calendar and advertising posters with female figures in contemporary fashion in an urban setting; Dan Duyu, Jiang Xiaojian, Wan Laiming and Lu Shaofei were also interested in women's fashion, and later published their illustrations of the concerned subject on Shanghai pictorials; the collaborations between them extended into the fields of graphic design, commercial publishing, film, animation, art, exhibitions and education from the late 1920s onwards.

In its first issue of *Xinshijie huabao*, pen and ink sketches of scenes from classical Beijing opera, caricatures, sketches of women in fashionable outfits and for adverts and filling images were made by Zhang Guangyu. His illustration of women wearing contemporary fashion was a new convention derived from the traditional painting of female figures. Perhaps due to his training in the New Stage where a new mode of drama with contemporary costume was played along with classical opera, the artist began to show a great interest in popular culture and changing social phenomena in the city.[45] His drawing of fashionably dressed women may have enthused his fellow illustrators Shen Bochen and Ding Song. Sharing the same passion for cartoons, contemporary fashion and politics in Shanghai, the three artists kept close contact with each other and worked as colleagues for various journals. Perhaps due to the experience working for *Xinshijie huabao* along with Ding and Shen who specialized in drawing fashionable women, Zhang was able to create the first fashion column in China in December 1918.

It is worth noting that among illustrators working for *Xinshijie huabao*, Yang Zuotao worked as the graphic designer of poster adverts for the British American Tobacco Company (BATC) at that time. The close friendship between the artists is evidenced in two portraits of Zhang Guangyu dedicated by Yang Zuotao and Ding Song in 1918.[46] Through the new contacts with those illustrators, Zhang Guangyu moved from *Xinshijie huabao* to design the advert posters for Nanyang Brothers Tobacco Company in 1921–25, and later became a full-time illustrator in the advertisement department at the BATC from 1927 to 1933.[47] During this period, Zhang not only designed calendar posters, but also continued to illustrate newspaper adverts, magazine cover images and record covers for Gaoting Record Company in Shanghai.[48] He met several cartoonists through the work in BATC and later funded the *Manhuahui* (Cartoon Association, 1926) and published journals *Sanri huabao* (Three-day Illustrated News, 1925) and *Shanghai manhua* (Shanghai Cartoons, 1928).[49] After seven years serving the BATC and having saved up some money, he decided to establish his own publishing company, *Shidai tushu gongsi* (The Modern Miscellany Publishing Company) in 1934.[50] Due to a lack of records, it is difficult to determine which Western magazines or fashion catalogues were available as sources of inspiration for the artist at this time. However, in his memoir, he recalled his experience working in a team of more than twenty Western and Chinese artists in BATC, and how much he learned from them in such an organized and stimulating environment.

Fashion Designers and Shanghai Pictorials

After the short-lived *Shanghai poke*, Zhang Guangyu brought his seasonal fashion drawings to the newly established pictorial, *Shibao tuhua zhoukan* (Weekly Illustrated Supplement to *The Eastern Times*) for the first time on 30 June 1920.[51] This weekly, established on 9 June 9 1920, was later renamed as *Tuhua shibao*

(The Illustrated Eastern Times) (issue no. 186, 17 February 1924). It signified an end of lithographic printing and the beginning of copperplate printing for the Chinese pictorials. With the new printing technology, the up-to-date photographs and illustrations were vividly presented, which significantly helped to promote *Tuhua shibao*'s sale.[52] The chief editor of *Shibao* group and the founder of *Tuhua shibao*, Ge Gongzhen (1890–1935), strategically planned this pictorial supplement with appealing photographs of female celebrities, art and news to attract the general city residents. For instance, in the first issue of 9 June 1920, two cartoons, one painting and twenty photographs were positioned densely into the four-page supplement to maximize its visual impact. With the support of the editor, in addition to Zhang Guangyu, several artists were invited to work on the journal's fashion column between 1920 and 1922. The illustrators on Shanghai fashion were Xie Zhiguang, Dan Duyu, Chen Yingxia (1896–1966), Li Xingwu (act. 1910–20s), Yin Zhiyi (1893–1985) and Sun Nansun (act. 1910–20), while Nansun and Li Xianghou (act. 1910–20s) illustrated Beijing fashion. From 1923 (no. 164) onwards, photographs gradually replaced the fashion drawings.

Apart from Xie Zhiguang, there is rather little information about these fashion illustrators. It seems that Yin Zhiyi and Li Xianghou contributed to no other journals and there are no bibliographic records for these two artists. There was only one brief biographical record of Chen Yingxia's education and art by Wang Yuren (act. 1920–40s) in 1942. It provides some useful information about the artist: Chen Yingxia, originally named Chen Yingyong, was a native of Changshou of Jiangsu province. He studied fine art at the First Business College of Jiangsu Province and continued to teach in the Fine Art Department after his graduation in 1918. Teaching in the college for more than a decade, he was then invited to teach part-time at Qingxin Secondary School for the next two decades in Changshou. The article emphasizes the achievement of Chen in traditional female figure painting with ink, that his work reflected his training in Western art and showed perspective and contrast between light and dark on the features of his subject. It also mentions that Chen was a collector of reproductions of Western painting, he had a room at home to display these works,and he was always happy to share such enthusiasm with his friends. Unfortunately, his collection was shattered by the war.[53]

There was no mention of his fashion illustrations in this article perhaps because these drawings for Shanghai journals were published in his early years in the 1920s. While Chen established himself as a specialist in female figure painting teaching in school, it might be possible that due to his interests in detailing women's clothing and bodies for his subjects, those reproductions of

Western art fed as a source of learning for his creation of female images in which East and West were blended harmoniously. Chen Yingxia's first fashion drawing appeared in issue no. 24 of *Shibao tuhua zhoukan* (14 November 1926), to which both Zhang Guangyu and Chen Yingxia contributed an illustration each. In contrast to Zhang Guangyu's pen and ink drawings, Chen Yingxia preferred using traditional Chinese brush. Chen's female sitter wore the close-fitting tunic and skirt, both the narrow sleeves and skirt are three-quarter long, showing off the delicate lines of arms and legs. Borrowing from traditional female figure painting, his sitter is depicted standing in three-quarter profile in an outdoor garden, where the spiky rocks and plants behind her echoed the radiating star pattern on her dress top. While the dress style in Chen's illustration was elegant, Zhang's fashion style was novel and bold. The sitter wore a round neck top and a patterned tightly cut ling skirt. The upper garment had no traditional collar or Chinese buttoning, and the airy sleeves were three-quarter length. The chrysanthemum was used as the hair ornament and the pattern for the dress and skirt, as well as the decorative motive in an arranged flower on the background. As suggested by Zhang Guangyu, flowers had the most brilliant and magical forms that should be employed in fashion more than they had been to convey a sense of season and colour. Since it was autumn, chrysanthemum motifs should appear in fashionable design as nature's gift that would enhance the beauty of the women. Zhang's fashion style often spoke of the urban environment, yet his patterns also borrowed elements from nature, paying attention to seasonal changes and to creating a hybrid, original and unique fashion that was often more inclined towards a Western look than the usual Chinese.

In addition to *Shibao tuhua zhoukan*, Chen Yingxia also occasionally contributed his female figure painting and fashion illustration to other journals during the 1920s, such as *Beiyang huabao* (The Pei-yang Pictorial News) in Tianjin and *Ziluolan* (The Violet Pictorial) in Shanghai. The journal *Ziluolan* was edited by Zhou Shoujuan, a close colleague of Zhang Guangyu and a famed writer who was instrumental in promoting celebrity culture, liberated love and marriage as an idealized modern lifestyle of the middle class in 1920s–30s Shanghai.[54] In Chen's '*Chudong xinzhuang*' (New Fashion for Early Winter, Figure 7.5), the outline was mostly maintained as thin and evenly controlled lines, showing his great command of the refined mode of Chinese brush and ink.[55] His drawing does not emphasize the detail of tailoring, but employs calligraphic brushwork, such as the floral design on the skirt and dripping willow leaves in front of the full moon, to evoke emotion and poetic imagery. His style of dress for women tends to be elegant and romantic. In addition to the fashion drawings

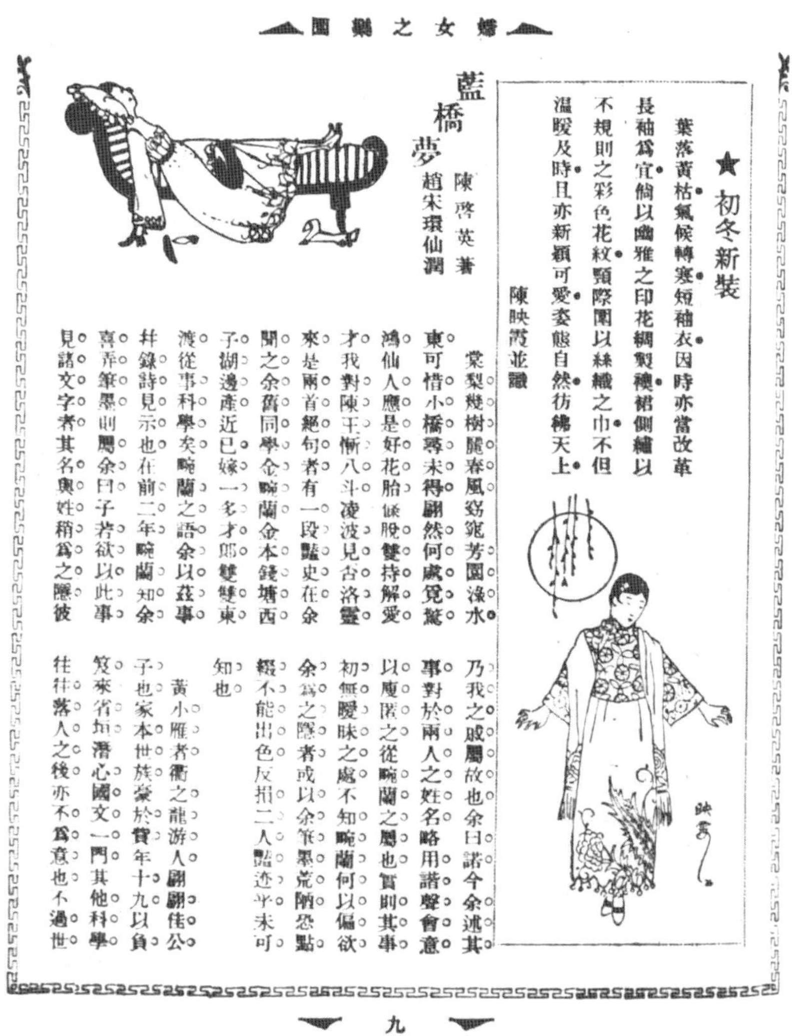

婦女之樂園

★初冬新裝

葉落黃枯。氣候轉寒。短袖衣。因時亦當改革長袖爲宜。倘以幽雅之印花綢製襖。裙側繡以不規則之彩色花紋。頸際圍以絲織之巾。不但溫暖及時。且亦新穎可愛。姿態自然。彷彿天上。

陳映霞並識

藍橋夢

陳啓英著 趙宋環仙潤

棠梨幾樹麗春風窈窕芳園淥水東可惜小橋尋未得翩然何處覓驚鴻仙人應是好花胎倏脫雙持解愛才我對陳王慚八斗凌波見否洛靈來是兩首絕句者有一段豔史在余聞之余舊同學金晚蘭金本錢塘西子湖邊產近已嫁一多才郎雙雙東渡從事科學矣晚蘭之語余以茲事并錄詩見示也在前二年晚蘭知余喜弄筆墨則屬余曰子若欲以此事見諸文字者其名與姓稍爲之隱彼乃我之戚屬故也余曰諾今余述其事對於兩人之姓名略用諧聲會意以廋隱之從晚蘭之屬也實則其事初無曖昧之處不知晚蘭何以偏欲余爲之隱者或以余筆墨荒陋恐點綴不能出色反損二人豔迹乎未可知也

黃小雁者衢之龍游人翩翩佳公子也家本世族豪於貲年十九以負笈來省垣滑心國文一門其他科學往往落人之後亦不爲意也不過世

九

Figure 7.5 Chen Yingxia 陳映霞, 'Chudong xinzhuang 初冬新裝' (New Fashion for Early Winter), *Ziluolan* 紫羅蘭 (The Violet Pictorial), *juan* 2, no. 1 (1926): 9.

published in pictorials, his best-selling *Yingxia xinzhuang baimei tu* (Illustrations of One Hundred Beauties in Modern Dress Painted by Yingxia) was edited in two volumes in 1924 showing his classical training in Chinese female figure painting.[56]

From 1925 to the early 1930s, fashion illustration began to emerge in many Shanghai pictorials, including *Shanghai shenghuo* (Shanghai Life, from no. 2,

1926), *Zhongguo shying xuehui huabao* (Illustrated News of Chinese Photography Association, from no. 34, 1926), *Ziluolan* (Violet, from *juan* 2, no. 1, 1926), *Lianyi zhiyou* (Friend of Lianyi, from no. 6, 1925), *Liangyou huabao* (The Young Companion Pictorial, from no. 13, 1927), *Jindai funü* (The Modern Lady, from no. 1, 1929), *Dianying yuebao* (Movie Monthly, from no. 3, 1928), *Yinxing* (Screen Stars, from no. 18, 1928), *Shidai huabao* (Modern Miscellany, from no. 1, 1929), *Zhongguo xuesheng* (Chinese Students, from no. 1, vol. 5, 1929), *Shanghai manhua* (from no. 1, 1928), *Baie yishu banyuekan* (White Goose Art Journal Bimonthly, from no. 1, 1930), *Linglong* (Elegance/La Petite Woman's Magazine, from no. 17, 1931), *Funü shenghuo* (Lady's Life, from *juan* 1, no. 1, 1932), and *Xin Shanghai* (New Shanghai, from *juan* 1, no. 4, 1933).

While movie stars, modern Republican women and female intellectuals were constantly featured on the covers of all sorts of periodicals throughout the 1920s, fashion illustrators were predominantly male, and it has been quite difficult to identify female fashion illustrators for want of biographical information. Archival research on Republican pictorials has to date revealed only two female illustrators who contributed to Shanghai pictorials.

Ellen J. Laing commented briefly upon her discovery of a sketch believed to be by He Zhizhen (act. 1920–30s) in *Shanghai manhua* (no. 3, December 1928), while the caption to He Zhizhen's wedding photograph in *Liangyou* (no. 83, December 1933) identified her as 'A well-known female painter Mrs He Zhizhen (C. T Ho) who was famed for her illustrations on Shanghai women's fashion'.[57] Building on these two references I found the caption to the photographs of her and her younger sister He Ai'zhen on the *Baie yishu banyuekan* (White Goose Art Journal Bimonthly, no. 2, 1930) stated her affiliation with the White Goose Painting Society.[58] She was an outgoing, celebrated figure whose photograph of dancing in traditional theatrical dress at the third anniversary masked ball held in Yingwu Musical Club was published on *Tuhua shibao* (no. 611, 1929).[59]

The White Goose Western Painting Society in Shanghai, established by Fang Xuehu (act. 1910–40), Pan Sitong (1904–80) and Chen Qiucao (1906–88) in 1924. Fang was the window designer for Xinxin Department Store on Nanjing Road whose job was to style the department store with the latest trends, new products and seasonal fashion. Fang Xuehu and Chen Qiucao published a series of illustrations of women in contemporary fashion in *Shanghai shenghuo* journal and collected them into a book with over thirty illustrations, *zhuangshumei* (Beautiful, latest attire), in 1926.[60] They also established the White Goose Institute of Western Painting in 1928, teaching mainly pencil and charcoal drawing, and watercolour, oil and pastel painting. Through the membership and training from the White Goose Painting Society, as evidenced in He Zhizhen's pencil drawing of a woman at her toilet, '*Linjing*', published along with another society member Chen Qiucao in the first issue of *Baie yishu banyuekan*, He Zhizhen was skilled and showed a keen interest in female figures in contemporary dress and self-reflection.[61]

From my archival research on early Republican pictorials, I also found that He Zhizhen not only contributed fashion sketches to many issues of the *Shanghai manhua*, but that her first fashion illustration was published in 1928 in the monthly magazine *Jindai funü* (The Modern Lady, 1928–31), published by *Liangyou* Book and Printing Company, distributed to readers in China, Hong Kong, Macau, Singapore, Taipei, Korea, Mongolia, Japan, Canada and Cuba.[62] From the available issues in the Shanghai Library and University of Heidelberg collections, I found in total five fashion drawings of the spring collection made by He Zhizhen in issue nos 7 and 9 in 1928 and 1929. There was no accompanying description for her plates apart from her signature and the year dated on the illustrations. Her design and drawing styles are identical and artistically outstanding. In the 1928 drawings for *Jindai funü*, her models wore knee-length *qipao* with high collar, but there is no Chinese buttoning system found on the garment, it might suggest that the zip often found in Western one-piece dress was introduced to her design. The lower part of the *qipao* had added dust ruffle and sliding cut from the waist to the edge, showing off the curve of the model's bodyline. All her models wore glowing make-up with a full praise on eye shadows and sculptural effect in particular. Each of them had distinctive short hair and wore earrings and a headband, as well as matching shoes.

It was apparent that He Zhizhen was acquainted with Zhang Guangyu, Ye Qianyu (1907–95) and other staff working for the *Shanghai manhua*. In 1929, He Zhizhen and Ye Qianyu also jointly published a series of five fashion drawings for early summer collection in *Zhongguo xuesheng* (Chinese Students – see Figure 7.6), in which both artists used pen and ink for their drawings and shared some similar characteristics. Both of their models are slender, dynamic and full of action, yet He Zhizhen preferred the strong contrast between light and dark on the garment, with a sliding movement of brushwork, creating a shadowing effect on the folds of the garment, so the shape of the model's body, especially the volume of breasts and leg-lines, was revealed.[63] She paid great attention to the sleeve design and hair ornament. The edges of the skirt are flared as if the model just made a movement and froze for this moment for a sketch taken, like a snapshot of the fashion in motion through the camera. In comparison with other drawings made by other male illustrators, her fashion drawings were more

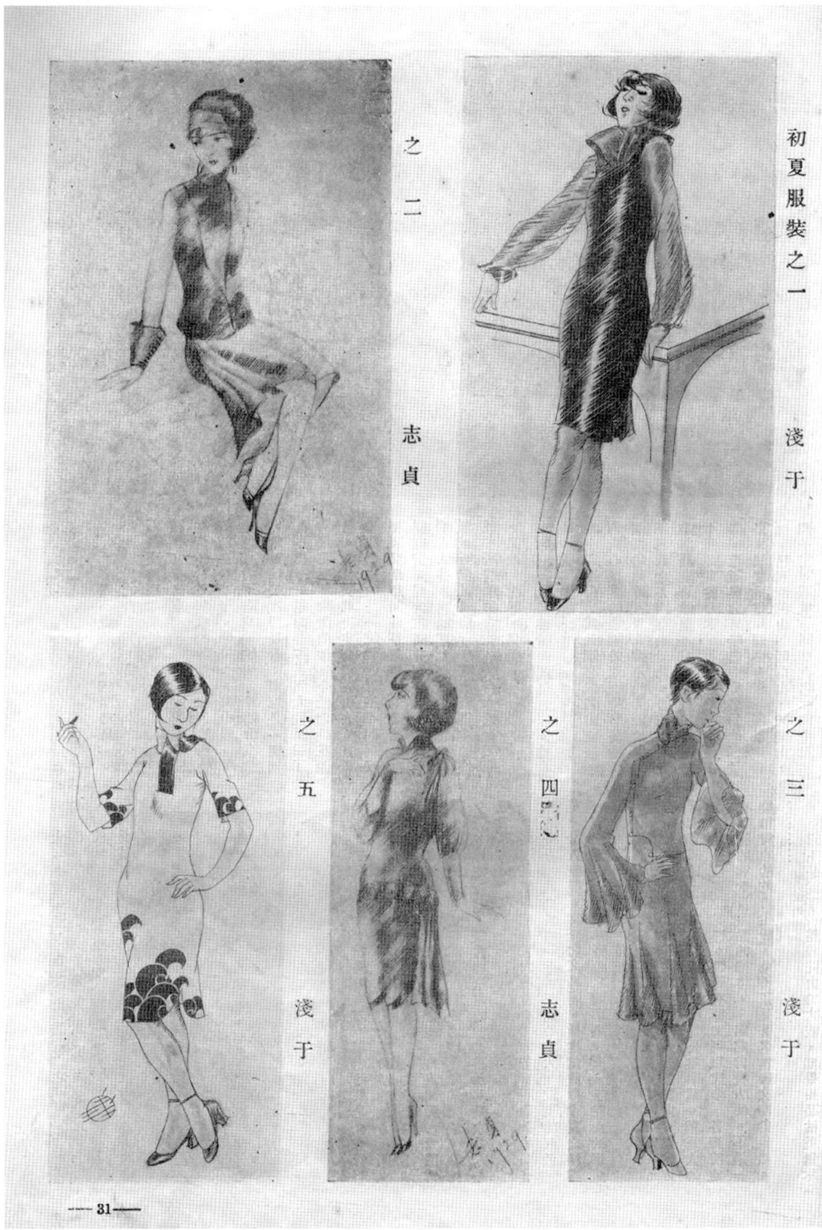

Figure 7.6 Ye Qianyu 葉淺予 and He Zhizhen 何志貞, 'Chuxia fuzhuang 初夏服裝' (Fashion of the Early Summer), *Zhongguo xuesheng* 中國學生 (Chinese Students) 1 (1929: 5): 31.

sophisticated, preferring a fusion of Western dress, hairdo, shoes, accessories and make-up in her design and representing a feel of visual entirety.

I was surprised to find another female illustrator, Kuang Wenwei (act. 1910–30), who published her fashion drawings in *Jindai funü* magazine earlier than He Zhizhen. Kuang Wenwei's work appeared in no. 4 along with the other fashion illustrations by Wan Laiming (no. 2), Ye Qianyu (no. 3), Jiang Zhaohe (1904 –86, no. 13) and Tang Tianyan (act. 1910–30, no. 13).[64] Appearing as an unspoiled natural beauty, Kuang Wenwei, a short-haired young lady in her *qipao majia* (one-piece dress using different fabrics for the sleeves and the main body of the dress), was staged as the cover girl on issue no. 4 of *Jindai funü* (Figure 7.7, 1929),

Figure 7.7 Photo of Kuang Wenwei 鄺文偉, *Jindai funü* 今代婦女 (The Modern Lady) 4 (1928: 9): cover page.

along with her four fashion illustrations (Figure 7.8) presented in the same issue. Her drawings of the 'Spring Collection' showed a mixture of styles.[65] Two knee-length *qipao* dresses with tight-cut short sleeves were represented on the lower section. The lower-right dress had traditional embroidered patterns of waves and mountains at the edge, with a flared fur ornament on the collarbone, and the

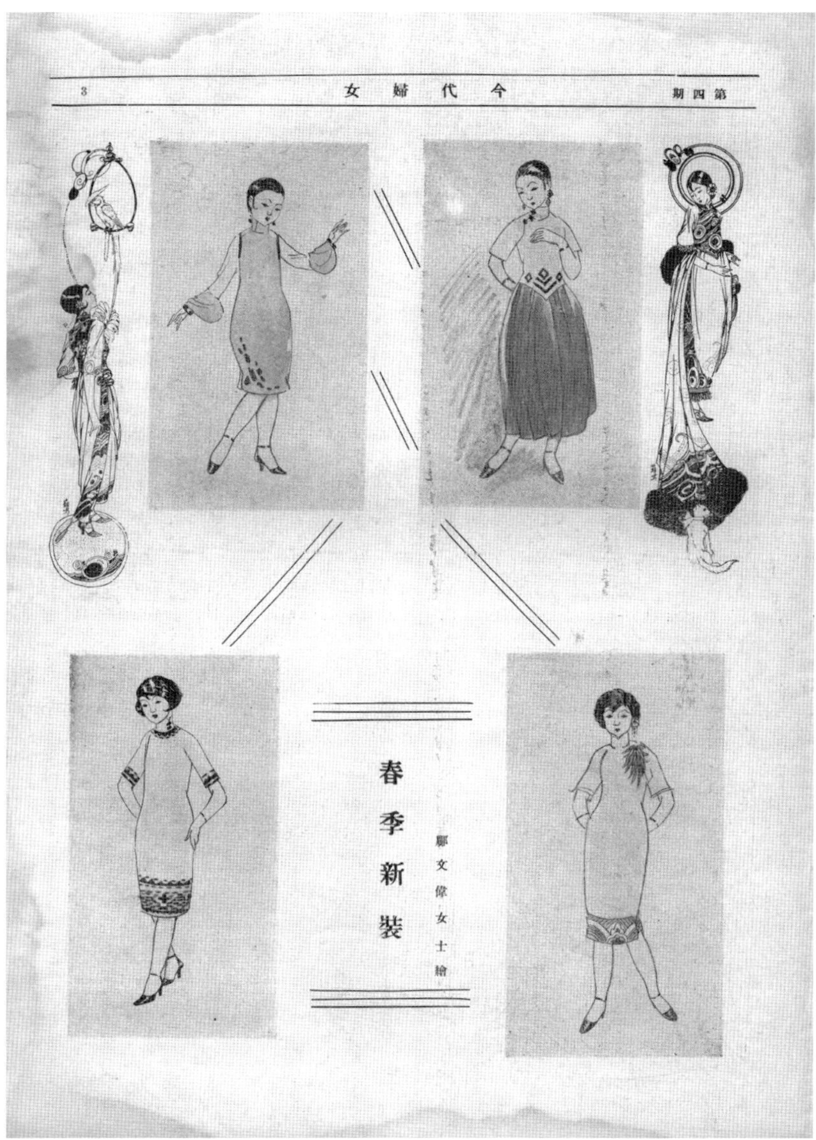

Figure 7.8 Kuang Wenwei 鄺文偉, 'Chunji xinzhuang 春季新裝' (New Fashion for the Spring), *Jindai funü* 4 (1928: 9): 3.

exaggerated large earrings were reminiscent of Art Deco style. The illustration on the lower right had the matching patterns of landscape for the neck, and fringe of sleeves and dress. Both models had their short hair permed and eyebrows thinned to meet the trend.

The dress on the upper right fused the Chinese lined short gown with the heel-length Western bubble skirt; the diamond-shaped floral pattern on the waistline echoed the tulip-shaped skirt, the buttons on the collar and the earrings. The model on the upper left wore a *qipao majia* with long sleeves fuller at the bottom and gathered into a cuff. The dramatic style of sleeves was made with two fabrics, adding flavour to the quiet fabric of the gown. In contrast to the models on the lower section, the models had slicked hairstyles, again with their fine, crescent-shaped eyebrows. Kuang's drawing style was not as artistic and imaginative as He Zhizhen's. However, these four illustrations were the only works that could be traced so far by Kuang Wenwei. Apart from *Jindai funü*, there is no further publication or news of her.

There was not much biographical information about Kuang, apart from the captions to two photographs (1929) mentioning Kuang as a fresh graduate of Zhongxi nüxue (McTyeire School) in Shanghai who was famed for her style and music sense in the issue no. 5 of *Jindai funü*.[66] In a photo that appeared in this issue, Kuang stood on the left with her classmate Wu Aizhen (act. 1910–30) amidst the sea of flowers prearranged by their relatives at their graduation from the McTyeire School. Both young ladies wore the knee-length *qipao* dresses with tall collars and tight-cut half-length sleeves. Looking confident and elegant in *qipao* and *qipaomajia* in her photos, Kuang apparently came from a privileged upbringing: it is worth noting that the McTyeire School, established in 1892 by American Jesuits, was the most elite school for women in Shanghai with an impressive list of alumnae, including Eileen Chang (1920–95) and the three Song sisters, Soong Ai-ling (1889–1973), Soong Ching-ling (1893–1981) and Soong May-ling (1898–2003).

As evidenced in Kuang Wenwei and He Zhizhen's illustrations and photographs, from 1925 to 1928, there is a notable trend of mixed styles of the old and new, the ethnic Chinese and Manchu, and the Eastern and Western, where traditional combinations of top and skirt/pants, *qipao majia* (a loose sleeve-lined top under a tight-fitting sleeveless long gown), *qipao* (tight-fitting Chinese one-piece dress; Mandarin dress) and Western one-piece dress were co-presented in Shanghai's fashion plates. It is arguably the most exciting, inventive and confusing period for women's fashion in China, before *qipao* took over the fashion plate from 1930 onwards.[67]

Due to the variable types of journals catering for diverse groups of readership, in 1928 a major change in fashion illustration became notable where the design was dictated by its function and the model's profession, such as dramatic dress for movie stars designed by Wan Guchan (1900– 95), and the splendid yet neatly cut dress for dancing, specific clothing for sport, party or degree ceremony by Hu Zhongbiao (act. 1900–40).[68] More texts were added to illustrations to explain the choice of fabric, tailoring and style. Jiang Zhaohe's two winter designs, for example, were specifically for female students, because the flowing lines and floral pattern were succinct and free-flowing which would enhance the elegant temperament of the college girls.[69] Publishers presumably found the production of fashion images a lucrative market. Most important of all for artists of sufficient talent and stature was the status of their work as inspirations and models to the readers, individual tailors and manufacturers. Some illustrators began to work closely with department stores and clothing companies, within different and more freelancing innovative business modes, as 'proper' fashion designers.

Conclusion

For most scholars and readers, Zhang Guangyu and his fellow illustrators were famous for their contributions to Chinese cartoons and calendar posters. Their fashion illustrations have been overlooked and their influence on Shanghai's lifestyle and China's fashion are much underestimated in current scholarship. In Ye Qianyu's own memoir, he clearly remembered that he would not miss any issue of *Punch*, *The New Yorker* or *Vanity Fair*, and the source of inspiration for his cartoon drawings included the *San Francisco Chronicle*, *London Illustrated News* and *Asahi shimbun* (Asahi News). In addition to cartoons, he was much enthused by the fashion illustrations in American *Vogue* that he began to make fashion drawings for *Shanghai manhua* and others.[70] It was the availability of many visual stimuli in this metropolitan city that enabled the artists to learn and to create a new form in visual culture. These illustrators reinforced an attitude of picturing fashionable women in a modern visual style, and created both commercial products and national propaganda through fashion images. This chapter has thus investigated the practice of fashion illustration in popular media and described how Shanghai painters without receiving any formal training in fashion or dress-making became influential fashion designers, and how they incorporated inspirations from various traditions and innovative sources for the art of looking modern. It has also examined the participation of women fashion designers at a time when the recognition of female talent was awakened. Whether in the hard-edged geometric mode for composition or whirling soft touch of their showy garments with the fusion of East and West, in some cases this visual inducement delivered optimism, while in others it transmitted the pleasure and sensuality of high fashion. The social and aesthetic values associated with Shanghai's metropolitan characteristics that represented China's fashion reached their summit around the mid-1930s, and deteriorated in the subsequent years owing to the rise of militarism in politics, and in graphic design by the embrace of the Russian and German styles of socialist realism and expressionism. After 1937, fashion illustrations also ceased to be creative since those graphic artists utterly shifted to work for propaganda cartoons and public art for newspapers during the Second Sino-Japanese War (1937–45).

At a basic level, why should we consider the look of the Chinese? Why was a hybridity of Eastern and Western styled clothing designed and offered to the public? Why should the trends of fashion illustrations be considered as modernist aesthetics linked to vernacular forms of modernism? These assertions expand the scope of modernist aesthetics to include the cultural manifestations of mass-mediated and mass-disseminated styles of urban life. The fluidity and diversity of such styles, which have varied dramatically by class, region and gender, suggest that a history of indigenous fashion illustrators in popular pictorials from 1910 to 1930 would complement current scholarship, adding a key element to our understanding of the history of everyday life in Shanghai through this art-historical approach.

Notes

1 'Fuzhi futu 服制附圖' (Regulations on Clothing – with illustrations), *Zhengfu gongbao* 政府公報 (Governmental Bulletin) 157 (4 October 1912): 1–8. For men, there are three types of formal wear: 1) Western ceremonial dress; 2) Western formal dress of suit and hat; and 3) Chinese-style coat and robe.

2 Unknown author, 'Qudi nuxuesheng zhi fuzhuang 取締女學生之服裝' (Banning the clothing of female students), *Jiaoyu zazhi* 教育雜誌 (The Chinese Educational Review) 5, no. 4 (10 July 1913): 30.

3 'Zhonghua minguo fuzhi tiaoli 中華民國服制條例' (Regulation on Clothing of Republic of China) was published on 16 April 1929; published in *Xihu bolanhui rikan tekan* 西湖博覽會日刊特刊 (West Lake Exposition Daily News Special Issue) 9 (13 September 1929): 4.

4 Antonia Finnane, 'What Should Chinese Women Wear? A National Problem', *Modern China* 22, no. 2 (Apr. 1996): 99–131 and 'China on the Catwalk: Between

Economic Success and Nationalist Anxiety,' *The China Quarterly* 163 (September 2005): 587–608; Christine Tsui, *China Fashion: Conversation with Designers* (Oxford: Berg, 2009).

5 Valerie Steele and John S. Major (eds), *China Chic: East Meets West* (New Haven, CT: Yale University Press, 1999); Antonia Finnane, *Changing Clothes in China: Fashion, History, Nation* (New York: Columbia University Press, 2008); Wen-Hsin Yeh, *Shanghai Spendor: Economic Sentiments and the Making of Modern China, 1843–1949* (Berkeley, CA: University of California Press, 2007); Juanjuan Wu, *Chinese Fashion: From Mao to Now* (Oxford: Berg, 2009); Jianhua Zhao, *The Chinese Fashion Industry: An Ethnographic Approach* (London: Bloomsbury Academic, 2013); Sue Thornham and Pengpeng Feng, '"Just A Slogan": Individualism, Post-Feminism, and Female Subjectivity in Consumerist China,' *Feminist Media Studies* 10, no. 2 (1 June 2010): 195–211; Christine Tsui, 'From Symbols to Spirit: Changing Conceptions of National Identity in Chinese Fashion,' *Fashion Theory: The Journal of Dress, Body & Culture* 17, no. 5 (2013): 579–604; and Rey Chow, *Women and Chinese Modernity* (Minneapolis, MN: University of Minnesota Press, 1991).

6 Tang Wei 唐薇 and Huang Dagang 黃大剛 (eds), *Zhang Guangyu nianpu* 張光宇年譜 (Chronology of Zhang Guangyu) (Beijing: SDX Joint Publishing Company, 2015); Tang Wei and Huang Dagang, *Zhuixun Zhang Guangyu* 追尋張光宇 (In Search of Zhang Guangyu) (Beijing: SDX Joint Publishing Company, 2015); Tang Wei (ed.), *Zhang Guangyu wenji* 張光宇文集 (Collected Essays of Zhang Guangyu) (Jinan: Shandong meishushe, 2011); Zhang Guangyu, *Zhang Guangyu ji* 張光宇集 (Paintings of Zhang Guangyu) (Beijing: Renmin meishu, 2015); and Ye Qianyu 葉淺予, *Xixu cangsang ji liunian* 細敘滄桑記流年 (Telling of the Changing Landscape, Remembering the Passage of the Years) (Beijing: Qunyan chubanshe, 1992); John A. Crespi, 'Beyond Satire: The Pictorial Imagination of Zhang Guangyu's 1945 Journey to the West in Cartoons,' in Carlos Rojas and Andrea Bachner (eds), *The Oxford Handbook of Modern Chinese Literatures* (Oxford: Oxford University Press, 2016), 215–44.

7 Recent scholarship began to include Shanghai silent cinema into the modernist movement or vernacular modernism, in responding to economic, political and social processes of modernization. The vernacular holds the view of specificity and routine, which can be used to address issues of democracy, organization and power. See Miram Bratu Hansen, 'Fallen Women, Rising Stars, New Horizons: Shanghai Silent Film as Vernacular Modernism,' *Film Quarterly*, 54, no. 1 (Autumn, 2000): 10–22.

8 Roberta Wue, 'Selling the Artist: Advertising, Art and Audience in Later Nineteenth Century Shanghai,' *Art Bulletin*, 91, no. 4 (December 2009): 463–80.

9 Wu Youru, *Female Figures*, 1890. Album of twelve leaves, 27.2 x 33.5 cm, ink and colour on silk, Shanghai Museum. See image in Antita Chung (ed.), *Chinese Paintings from the Shanghai Museum 1851–1911* (Edinburgh: National Museum of Scotland, 2000), 99, plate D; discussion on fashion in Shanghai School painting, see

Chia-Ling Yang, *New Wine in Old Bottles: Art of Ren Bonian in Nineteenth-Century Shanghai* (London: Saffron, 2007), 67–103.

10 Zhou Xun 周迅 and Gao Chunming 高春明, *Zhongguo lidai funü zhuangshi* 中國歷代婦女妝飾 (China Women's Fashion through Centuries) (Shanghai: Xuelin chubanshe, 1988), 112 and Figure 3.19.

11 For example, see M. Miller, 'A Shanghai Lady' (c. 1861–4), in *The Face of China 1860–1912* (Taipei: Xiongshi tushu gongsi, 1977, 1998), 55; discussion see Chia-Ling Yang, 'The Crisis of the Real – Photography and Portraiture in Late Nineteenth Shanghai', in Jennifer Purtle and Hans B. Thomsen (eds), *Looking Modern: East Asian Visual Culture from Treaty Ports to World War II* (Chicago: Art Media Resources. 2009), 20–37; and Régine Thiriez, 'Photography and Portraiture in Nineteenth-Century China', *East Asian History* 17 (1 June 1999), 77–102.

12 For example, see Ren Bonian, Three Chivalrous Travellers 風塵三俠, 1880, Hanging scroll, ink and colour on paper, 122.7 × 47 cm, Shanghai Museum and Ren Bonian, *Three Chivalrous Traveller* 風塵三俠, 1887. Hanging scroll, ink and colour on paper, 82 × 149.5 cm, Affiliate School of Central Academy of Fine Art, Beijing. Huang Nengfu 黃能復 and Chen Juanjuan 陳娟娟, *Zhongguo fuzhuang shi* 中國服裝史 (History of Chinese Clothing) (Beijing: Zhongguo luyou chubanshe, 1995), 378 and 382.

13 Xiaoqing Yeh, *The Dianshizhai Pictorial – Shanghai Urban Life 1884–1898* (Ann Arbor, MI: University of Michigan Press, 2003), 162.

14 Advert 'Requesting "Ladies in Contemporary Embellishment" by Mr Zhang Zhiying 索張君誌瀛畫'時妝仕女', *Shenbao* 申報 (Shanghai Daily) 3588 (1883.04.11): 3.

15 Advert for *Feiyingge Pictorials*, *Shenbao* 6281 (1890.10.14): 4.

16 See preface, reprinted in *Wu Youru huabao* 吳友如畫寶 (A Treasury of Wu Youru's Illustrations) (Shanghai: Shanghai guji shudian, 1983), n.p.

17 Joan Judge, 'Portraits of Republican Ladies: Materiality and Representation in Early Twentieth Century Chinese Photograph', in Christian Henriot and Wen-hsin Yeh (eds), *Visualising China, 1845–1965: Moving and Still Images in Historical Narratives* (Leiden: Brill, 2013), 135.

18 'Shanghai xianshi zhong zhong zhuangshu 上海現時種種裝束' (Current Fashion in Shanghai), *Xiaoshuo shibao* 小說時報 (The Eastern Times Fiction Supplement, 1909–17, 1922) 3 (1909): 2.

19 In one of the photographs of Qiu Jin in various guises, she wore Western men's dress and a felt cap, and carried a walking stick. See Finnane, *Changing Clothes in China: Fashion, History, Nation*, 90; Photo of 'Portrait of Ten Beauties' in which the courtesan on the right dressed in male costume. See Shanghai History Museum (ed.), *Shanghai bainian lueying* 上海百年掠影 (Survey of Shanghai 1840–1940s) (Shanghai: Renmin meishu chubanshe, 1998), 205.

20 'Two Photos of Shi Yunlai in Latest Fashion', see *Xiaoshuo shibao* (The Eastern Times Fiction Supplement) 17 (1912): 1; five photos of various fashions worn by

women in Beijing – Hong Yuanyuan, Lin Daiyu, Yin Fu and others, see *Xiaoshuo shibao* 24 (1914): 1.

21 Joan Judge, 'Sinology, Feminist History, and Everydayness in the Early Republican Periodical Press,' *Journal of Women in Culture and Society* 40, no. 3 (2015): 563–87.

22 Judge, 'Portraits of Republican Ladies,' 131 and 135.

23 For examples, see 'Riben nüzi xin zhuangshu 日本女子新裝束' (Japanese Women in Fashionable Dress), *Funü shibao* 婦女時報 (The Women's Eastern Times, 1911–17) 1 (1911): 1; for photographs of bridal dresses from Europe, Japan and China, see *Funü shibao* 3 (1911): 1–2.

24 Ellen Johnston Laing, 'The Fate of Shanghai Painting Style in Early Twentieth-Century Printed Advertising,' in Fusheng Lu (ed.), *Studies on Shanghai School Painting* (Shanghai: Shuhua chubanshe, 2001), 953–1003.

25 Nancy Martha West, *Kodak & the Lens of Nostalgia* (Charlottesville, VA: University of Virginia Press, 2000), 109–35.

26 See advert for Shen Bochen's *Xinxin baimei tu* in *Da Gonghe xingqi huabao* 19 (1913): 17; Yi Wencui 易文翠, *Yidai wenxin: wan Qing Min chu de haishang wenhua gengxu yu xinbian* 易代文心：晚清民初的海上文化賡續與新變 (Changing Literary Trends at Dynastic Transitions: Continuity and Reform of Shanghai Culture from Late Qing to Early Republican era) (Taipei: Lianjing chubanshe, 2016), 370; Wu Haoran 吳浩然, *Lao Shanghai n zi fengqinghua* 老上海女子風情畫 (Drawings of Seductive Female Figures from Old Shanghai) (Shangdong: Qi Lu chubanshe 山東齊魯出版社, 2010).

27 Issue number and page number are provided in main text. *Da Gonghe xingqi huabao*, 1912–13, Shanghai Library collection.

28 Wencui, *Yidai wenxin*, 367.

29 Ding Song, *Shanghai shizhuang baimei tuyoung* 上海時裝百美圖咏 (Illustrated Tribute of One Hundred Beauties of Shanghai in Contemporary Fashionable Costume) (Shanghai: Minguo guoxue shushi publishing 民國國學書室出版, printed by Shanghai Tianan shuju shiyin 上海天南書局石印, 1916), 2 volumes. This two-volume catalogue was sold for 4 foreign *jiao*, the size of the publication is 16.2 × 12.5 cm, each illustration is accompanied by a poem written by Mandarin Duck and Butterfly School writers of Shanghai. Discussion on the theme of 'One Hundred Beauty' and gender stereotype, see Wencui, *Yidai wenxin*, 365–442.

30 Zheng Gong 鄭工, *Yanjin yu yundong: Zhongguo meishu de xiandaihua* 演進與運動: 中國美術的現代化 1875–1976) (Evolution and Movement: the Modernization of the Fine Arts in China, 1875–1976) (Nanning: Guangxi meishu chubanshe, 2002), 88.

31 For examples, see *Libailiu* 禮拜六 (The Saturday), nos 62, 63, 65 (1915) and no. 100 (1916) cover images; *Shenzhou huabao* 神州畫報 (China's Daily Illustrated News) (1918: 1); *Xinshijie huabao* 新世界畫報 (New World Illustrated News) 21 (21 July

1918), cover; *Nüzi shijie* 女子世界 (Women's World) 5 (1915), 1–12. These Republican pictorials are in the Shanghai Library collection.

32 Examples are Lu Zichang 陸子常, *Zuixin haishang baimei tuyong* 最新海上百美圖詠 (*New Illustrations of One Hundred Beauties in Shanghai*) (Shanghai: Caiji shuju 才記書局, 1915); and Chen Yingxia, *Yingxia xinzhuang baimei tu* 映霞新妝百美圖 (*Illustrations of One Hundred Beauties in Modern Dress Painted by Yingxia*) (Shanghai: Shanghai gonghe shuju 上海共和書局, 1924).

33 Wei Xiaochang 魏紹昌, *Wokan Yuanyang hudie pai* 我看鴛鴦蝴蝶派 (My View of the Mandarin Ducks and Butterflies School) (Taipei: Commercial Press, 1992); Michel Hockx, *Questions of Style Literary Societies and Literary Journals in Modern China, 1911–1937* (Leiden: Brill, 2003); and Chen Huang-Shu 陳皇旭, 'Minchu de wenxue changyu: chungdu *Libailiu* 民初的文學場域：重讀《禮拜六》' (Literature Field of Early Republican Period: Rereading *The Saturday*) (MA diss., National Chi Nan University, 2011), accessed 12 June 2017, http://etds.library.ncnu.edu.tw/etdservice/view_metadata?etdun=U0020-3108201123475200.

34 Antonia Finnane, *Changing Clothes in China: Fashion, History, Nation* (London: Hurst & Company, 2007), 127–8.

35 Examples, see 'Nü xuesheng zhi xin zhuangshu 女學生之新裝束' (New Fashion of Female Students), *Qingsheng zhoukan* 青聲週刊 (Voice of the Youth Weekly) 3 (1917): 3; 'Chuhan zhi zhuangshu 初寒之裝束' (Early Winter Fashion), *Qingsheng zhoukan* 5 (1917): 3.

36 Ding Song, 'Nüzi zhuangshu de jianglai, qier 女子妝束的將來 (其二)' (The Future Dress for Women, Part II), *Xinshijie huabao*, 7 (13 August, 1918): cover page.

37 Zhang Guangyu, 'Funü zhuangshu lan 婦女裝束欄' (Ladies' Fashion Column), *Shanghai poke* 上海潑克 (Shanghai Puck), *juan 1*, no. 4 (1918): 22–4.

38 Ibid., 24.

39 Bellas Hess & Co. New York City, *1917–1918 Winter Fashions*, no. 79 (New York, 1918). With an introduction of its history by Lauren Stowell.

40 Ibid., 4 and 278.

41 Zhang Guangyu, 'Personal Statement in 1952', in *Zhang Guangyu nianpu*, 1.

42 The maiden name of his mother is Cao. Different from the Zhang family, the Cao family was much into modern business and manufacturing, they owned a Yongyuan Rice Shop 永源生米行 and Tongyi Fabric Manufacture 同億織布廠 in Wuxi by around 1910. Zhang Guangyu, 'Personal Statement in 1959', in *Zhang Guangyu nianpu*, 10–11. See also Wei and Huang, *Zhuixun Zhang Guangyu*, 4–7.

43 Huang Miaozi 黄苗子, *Huatan shiyou lu* 畫壇師友錄 (In Memory of Teacher and Friends from Painting World) (Taipei: Dongda tushu, 1998), 317.

44 The first issue was published on 7 August 1918 (the first day of the seventh month of *Wuwu* 戊午 year).

45 *Xinshijie huabao* 1 (7 August 1918): 1. Also see *Zhang Guangyu nianpu*, 14–15. The Chronology is confusing *Xinshijie huabao* with *Shijie huabao*, the latter was established in 1939.

46 *Zhang Guangyu nianpu*, 14.

47 Wei, *Zhang Guangyu wenji*, 3–4.

48 *Zhang Guangyu nianpu*, 22.

49 'Manhuahhui zhi chengli 漫畫會之成立' (The Establishment of Cartoon Society), *Sanri huabao* 三日畫報 (Three-day Illustrated News) 153 (8 December 1926), 1.

50 *Zhang Guangyu wenji*, 4.

51 [Zhang] Guangyu, 'Chunji zhi xin zhuangshu 春季之新裝束' (New Spring Fashion), *Shibao tuhua zhoukan* 時報圖畫週刊 (Weekly Illustrated Supplement to *The Eastern Times*) 4 (30 June 1920): 1. *Shibao tuhua zhoukan*, established on 9 June 1920, was later renamed as *Tuhua shibao* 圖畫時報 (The Illustrated Eastern Times) on 17 February 1924 (issue no. 186). Its appearance signified an end of lithographic printing and the beginning of copperplate printing for the Chinese pictorials.

52 Wang Zhixin 王治心 commented: 'The sale of *Shibao* was rather poor, after adding the pictorial supplement, it quickly boosted the business. 時報銷路，本來亦甚至微,後來添上一張畫報，居然駸駸日上了', cited in Shen Sizhuang 沈嗣莊, 'Jinggao yuezhe 敬告閱者' (To Readers), *Wenshe yuekan* 文社月刊 (The Monthly of Literature Society), *juan* 2, no. 2 (1926: 12): 1.

53 Wang Yuren 王隅人, 'Liangge guohuajia: Changdao guocui yishu de Wang Xian, Renwu huajia Chen Yingxia 兩個國畫家：倡導國粹藝術的王賢，人物畫家陳映霞' (Two Chinese Nationalist Painters), *Taipingyang zhoubao* 太平洋週報 (Pacific Weekly), *juan* 1, no. 25 (1942): 350–1.

54 So far only two fashion illustrations are found in *Violet*. Chen Yingxia 陳映霞, 'Xinzhuangshu 新裝束' (New Fashion in Clothing), *Ziluolan* 紫羅蘭 (The Violet Pictorial), *juan* 2, no. 1 (1926): 4; 'Chudong xinzhuang 初冬新裝' (New Fashion for Early Winter), *juan* 2, no. 1 (1926): 9. On Zhou Shoujuan and the *Violet*, see Pan Shaoyu, 'Fashion is No Crime: The Aesthetics of Editorship, Political Awareness and Cultural Imaginary of the Semi-Monthly Ziluolan,' *Chung Cheng Chinese Studies* 22 (2013: 2): 271–302.

55 Chen Yingxia, 'Chudong xinzhuang 初冬新裝' (New fashion for early winter), *Ziluolan*, *juan* 2, no. 1 (1926): 9.

56 Chen Yingxia, *Yingxia xinzhuang baimei tu* 映霞新妝百美圖 (*Illustrations of One Hundred Beauties in Modern Dress Painted by Yingxia*) (Shanghai: Shanghai gonghe shuju 上海共和書局, 1924).

57 He Zhizhen 何志貞, 'Sketch', *Shanghai manhua* 上海漫畫 (Shanghai Cartoons) 36 (22 December 1928): 7; 'Wedding Photo of He Zhizhen and Huang Zukang', *Liangyou* 良友畫報 (The Young Companion Pictorial) 83 (December 1933): 17. See also discussion in Ellen Johnston Laing, *Selling Happiness: Calendar Posters and*

Visual Culture in Early-Twentieth Century Shanghai (Honolulu: University of Hawai'i Press, 2004), 189. The original Chinese text is: '上海善绘妇女新装著名之女画家何志贞女士'.

58 *Baie yishu banyuekan* 白鵝藝術半月刊 (White Goose Art Journal Bimonthly) 2 (1930): 7.

59 Lang Jingshan, 'Yinwu yueshe sanzhou jinianhui 鸚鵡樂社三週紀念會' (Photo of Yingwu Musical Club Third Year Celebration Party), *Tuhua shibao* 611 (1929): 4.

60 Fang Xuehu 方雪鵠 and Chen Qiucao 陳秋草, 'Zhuangshumei erfu 裝束美二幅' (Two fashion postcards), *Shanghai shenghuo* 上海生活 (Shanghai Life, 1926) 2 (1926): 2; and *Shanghai shenghuo* 3 (1926): 2. Advert on their *Zhuangshumei* 裝束美 (Beautiful, latest attire) book, see *Shanghai shenghuo* 2 (1926): 35.

61 He Zhizhen, 'Linjing 臨鏡' (Mirroring Image), *Baie yishu banyuekan* 1 (1930): 17.

62 See the end page of each issue, *Jindai funü* 今代婦女 (The Modern Lady), 1928–1931.

63 Ye Qianyu and He Zhizhen, 'Chuxia fuzhuang 初夏服裝' (Fashion of the Early Summer), *Zhongguo xuesheng* 中國學生 (Chinese Students) 1 (1929: 5): 31.

64 Kuang Wenwei 鄺文偉, 'Chunji xinzhuang 春季新裝' (New Fashion for the Spring), *Jindai funü* 4 (1928: 9): 3.

65 Photo of Kuang Wenwei, *Jindai funü* 4 (1928: 9): cover page.

66 Two photos of Kuang Wenwei, *Jindai funü* 5 (1928: 10): 5.

67 Finnane, *Changing Clothes in China*, 151.

68 For examples, see Hu Zhongbiao 胡忠彪, 'Dancing Dress', *Dianying yuebao* 電影月報 (Movie Monthly) 3 (1928): 3; Hu Zhongbiao, 'Degree Gown,' ibid., 6 (1928): 9; and Wan Guchan 萬古蟾, 'Dress for Movie', *Yinxing* 銀星 (Screen Stars) 18 (1928): 36.

69 Jiang Zhaohe 蔣兆和, 'Dongji xinzhuang 冬季新裝' (New Winter Fashion), *Jindai funü* 13 (1930): 28.

70 Ye Qianyu 葉淺予, *Xixu cangsang ji liunian* 細敘滄桑記流年 (Telling of the Changing Landscape, Remembering the Passage of the Years) (Beijing: Qunyan chubanshe, 1992), 141.

Plate 1 Detail: a piece of roller-printed cotton fabric, 1930s, Shanghai. © University of Leeds International Textile Archives (ULITA).

Plate 2 'Shanghai Bund', large floral design, printed cotton fabric, early 1970s. Ref. No. 054, Shanghai Propaganda Poster Centre © Yang Peiming.

Plate 3 *Dancing at the New Carlton Hotel in Shanghai*, 1924. Yamamura Koka, colour woodblock print, 41.5 × 28.8 cm. © Photo SCALA, Florence, Art Institute of Chicago.

Plate 4 'Three Sisters': Yue Foong-chi, the first wife of the war lord Chang Hsueh-Liang, in the middle, flanked by Soong May-ling on the left and Soong Ai-ling on the right. *Young Companion* (Liang you), no. 54, 1931. Courtesy of the Donghua University Library, Shanghai.

Plate 5 Hongdu tailor shop in Beijing. An image in the display window (inset) shows a customer being measured up for a Western suit, the Red Group tailors' trademark product. Photograph by the author, 12 January 2018.

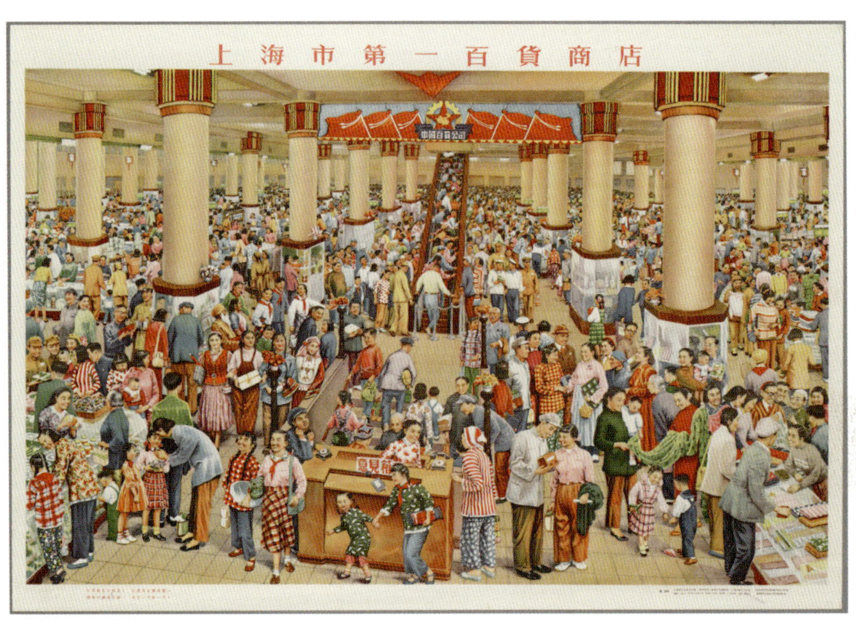

Plate 6 Shanghai No. 1 Department Store poster by Chen Fei, published by Shanghai Huapian Chubanshe, *c.* 1955. Courtesy Stefan R. Landsberger Collections. (NB: Digital copy of poster purchased from collection. No copyright on China images pre-1980s.)

Plate 7 Angel Chen in her studio. Courtesy of Anja Aronowsky Cronberg.

Plate 8 Staff only. Courtesy of Tian Zhiwei.

8

Lost in Socialist Transformation?

Shanghai Style under Mao

Antonia Finnane

The story of Shanghai fashion as told in contemporary published accounts (books, magazines, journals) generally takes the form of a tale in two parts. The first relates developments during the Republican era, represented most dramatically by the evolution of *qipao* styles, while the second recounts the achievements of the Reform Era, viewed as a time of recovery and rediscovery. For good reason, the in-between years, the Mao period, are usually bypassed.[1] The impulse towards fashion did not absolutely disappear in these years, but the fashion system that had been developing in the decades preceding the founding of the People's Republic of China (hereafter PRC) did cease to exist. Fashion needs room to move, economically and in terms of design. It requires a market, powers of discretionary spending, and capacity on the part of producers to respond sensitively and with alacrity to consumer demands. These conditions could not be met in the Mao years.

Yet the era was not long, lasting for little more than quarter of a century. Young adults of the 'liberation' years, if still alive at the beginning of the Reform Era, were by then only in late middle age. Their children, Mao's 'blank slate', had of course been shaped by socialist educational and public culture, but they had grown up among people whose values and attitudes, turns of phrase and countenance, had been formed in quite different circumstances. Even the Cultural Revolution was not likely to have completely disrupted the intergenerational transfer of sensibilities, comportment and identity, in brief the *style* of being Shanghainese. In the broad domain of clothing production, sales, consumer choices and vestimentary practices in Shanghai, the Mao period is worth examining for traces of the legacy of the Republican period and signs of the foundations of the Reform Era.

Among the many variables affecting patterns of continuity and change was Shanghai's relationship with Beijing. As capital city within a socialist system and as headquarters for the PRC's command economy, Beijing was a significant player for the country as a whole, in all aspects of life. Its manifestations of primacy since 1949 are not unlike those of Paris as described by Henry Blackburn in the preceding century, with 'people, goods, and provisions being hurried off to the capital as if there were no other place to live in or provide for,' and institutions in the provinces replicating those of the capital so that (in the words of Hippolyte Taine) 'nothing has proper roots. Everything is implanted.'[2] But the comparison between Beijing and Paris is not precise. Shanghai, despite being subdued by Beijing, continued to be a byword for style, something to which Beijing could hardly aspire. In a head-turning way, it was more like Paris than Beijing was, a fact feeding into the competition between the two cities – Shanghai/Beijing, *haipai/jingpai*. The history of the clothing industry in China during the Mao years shows that this competition entailed a series of strategic moves on Beijing's part to appropriate some elements of Shanghai style for its own use and to control or alternatively suppress other elements – namely those which continued to be fostered by the locality. The effects were both destructive and transformative, although not in entirely predictable ways.

Turning Point, 1949

On the eve of the founding of the PRC, the clothing sector in Shanghai, the country's largest city, was contracting. Factory owners packed their bags for Hong Kong, and so did many tailors.[3] A great migration was under way, impelled in the first instance by economic difficulties (post-war chaos, rampant inflation) and in the second by the advance of the communist forces from the north. In 1948 the city still had 993 registered Western clothing or fashion shops and 855 retailers of leather shoes, but, tellingly, old clothes stores also abounded – more than 100 in Stone Road alone (later Fujian Central Road). By the end of the mass movements of 1951–2, entailing fierce campaigns against bureaucrats and capitalists,[4] the number of fashion shops had dropped by two-thirds. Two hundred clothing and hat shops had gone out of business, and even the second-hand stores were in decline. Only at the bottom end of the sector was there growth. Dealers or makers of plain cotton clothing and machine-sewn clothing jumped in number from 848 to 2005.[5]

Those who hung on faced uncertain futures. Yu Yuanfang (b. 1918) typified the skilled tailor of Shanghai. A native of Fenghua, in Zhejiang province, he was one of the 'Red Group' (*hongbang*) tailors, so called because they early occupied the niche created by a need for Western clothing among the Treaty Port 'red-haired' foreigners. The Red Group tailors were mostly of Ningbo origin (the prefecture included Fenghua), in the neighbouring province of Zhejiang.[6] Their established footing in Shanghai had created a base for chain migration through apprenticeships, which in Yu's case was served at the Wang Shengtai Western Clothing Store during the period of the Japanese occupation. He worked for some years in Hong Kong before returning to take a position in the tailoring firm Bowei, established by his brother in early 1944. This history of life and work in occupied China, in combination with a specialization in making up Western suits, did not augur well for his prospects under the Chinese Communist Party (CCP), but he did unexpectedly well out of the arrival of the communist cadres in 1949. Among his more illustrious customers during the New Democracy period was the new mayor of Shanghai, Chen Yi.[7] In 1956, when India's ambassador to China, R.K. Nehru, wanted a good suit made, Zhou Enlai reportedly recommended Yu Yuanfang.[8] Subsequently, the entire Bowei firm was transferred to Beijing, there to provide outfits for high officials, foreign diplomats and members of Chinese delegations being sent abroad. Yu survived the upheavals of the sixties and seventies, and was still active during the Reform Era.[9]

This career trajectory is worth contrasting with Wang Guizhang's. Wang is also regarded as a Red Group tailor, although as a woman she is a far less typical example. A graduate in chemistry from St John's University in 1942, she had worked in this professional capacity for a few years before setting up a sewing school in the late forties, apparently for want of other employment opportunities at the time.

The sewing school appears to have been a successful enterprise. Wang's many 'how-to' publications in the domain of sewing and embroidery, including machine sewing, are still among the most readily available in the Chinese second-hand book market. In 1952, however, she fell afoul of the 'Five-Anti Campaign', which targeted capitalists across the nation. Her sewing school had to close. She was recruited instead to radio propaganda work, for which she was probably held to be qualified by the fact of being a university graduate.[10] In 1956 she returned briefly to the domain of dressmaking with the publication of two pattern books produced in the context of a 'dress beautification' (*daban piaoliang*) campaign launched by the Ministry of Culture in 1955,[11] but after that she

Figure 8.1 The site of Wang Guizhang's sewing school in 1949 (above) and now. Located on present-day Julu Road (known as Rue Batard during the French period), this was a prestigious address, and the students were probably from Shanghai's bourgeoisie. Source: Guizhang Wang 王圭璋, *Fengren nanzhen* 缝纫南针 (King Fair Instructions: Sewing and Stitching) (Shanghai: Jinghua, 1950), frontispiece. Bottom photograph taken by author, 20 January 2018.

disappears from sight. Only her publications survive to bear witness to her undertakings in those years.[12]

In the textiles and apparel industry, as these two life trajectories show, politics and patronage were significant factors. During the Mao years, Shanghai business in general suffered from the stagnation or even decline of the population. The demographic impact of the communist revolution on the city is well summarized

Figure 8.2 Pattern books compiled by Wang Guizhang between 1949 and 1956. The cover pictures on the volumes first and second from the right show designs drawn up for the dress beautification campaign run in 1955–6. Source: University of Melbourne Library, East Asian collection.

by Alan Liu: 'Before the Communist takeover, Shanghai was a cosmopolitan city with a lifestyle comparable to that of a European capital. Under the Maoist regime . . . [it] lost its old prosperity and, in 1955 alone 6 percent of its population due to migration.'[13] Some of this migration was voluntary. Foreigners continued to leave the country, along with a few Chinese who had connections or the means to make a safe exit. Other people were sent back to their home towns or villages, as part of a population readjustment policy. The outflow of people continued through to the early 1970s, so that while the population of China as a whole grew, Shanghai, between 1955 and 1973, suffered 'an average annual net loss of about 1.5 per cent.'[14] Contributing to this loss was the rustication movement, ongoing from the late fifties but intensifying in the late sixties, when young people began streaming out of the city in response to Mao Zedong's call to 'go up to the mountains and down to the villages'.

In Beijing, too, educated youth were 'sent down' (*xiafang*), but in other respects, the contrasts between Shanghai and Beijing were marked. Restored to the status of capital in 1949, Beijing gained population steadily as the government fostered its transformation from a 'parasitic' into an industrial city.[15] The focus was on heavy industry, regarded as the key to modernization. A city that in practice was to serve primarily as the seat of government and a centre of higher education acquired steel factories and machine-building plants.[16] Placed on a competitive footing with Shanghai, Beijing simultaneously leant heavily on it for fiscal support.[17] As the major provider of revenue to the central government, Shanghai stood in relationship to Beijing much as Suzhou stood to Nanjing at the beginning of the Ming dynasty in the late fourteenth century. In the latter case, as Michael Marmé has shown, a resentful central government imposed an unusually heavy tax burden on a place that had supported its rivals during the civil war at the end of the Yuan dynasty.[18] Especially as far as foreign companies in Shanghai were concerned, Beijing's policy in the early 1950s was explicitly one of 'crippling taxation'.[19]

The constraining effects on Shanghai of a shrinking population, heavy taxation and an explicitly anti-capitalist political culture were compounded by the attenuation of links with the non-Chinese world. Shanghai had acquired a name for fashion through its cosmopolitan population, international traffic, a small but powerful bourgeoisie, a modern retail sector including department stores, both foreign and Chinese-owned, and advertising and publishing industries that established a certain idea of Chinese modernity: bright, sexy and dynamic. In the 1950s, it lost most of these features. It ceased to be the main port of entry into China. Its department stores were transformed into municipal or state-owned businesses, or swallowed up in joint enterprises in which the private partner was mostly a silent partner.[20] Its cinema, once diverse and adventurous, often featuring impressive costume design, was reduced to a vehicle for party propaganda. Similarly, its graphic artists, no longer needed for designing advertisements for Shanghai-based businesses, were recruited to the task of painting political propaganda posters for a Beijing political regime.[21] Along the streets of Shanghai, as elsewhere in China, millions of citizens, old and young, could be seen making their various ways to work or school all clad in the same plain, serviceable people's suit (*renminzhuang*).

The Decline and Fall of Shanghai Fashion

What remained of Shanghai style during the Mao years? Consistently with the summary above, the account provided in the semi-official Shanghai municipal history shows a step-by-step obliteration of much that was special about the local clothing culture. Brand names established by enterprising capitalists in the Republican era were removed, often along with the bosses. Zhu Xielin's *Kangpaisi* shirts are a case in point: the brand name was registered at a time of expanding business in 1948, but was altered to *Tianping* in 1951, almost certainly because of the original brand name's associations with capitalist enterprise or a counter-revolutionary element.[22] Tailoring, once a byword for Shanghai, lost its reputation for efficiency. The turn-around for garment production extended from days to weeks to a month or more, giving rise to the phenomenon of '*zuoyinan*' (difficulty in making clothes).[23] The manufacture and marketing of Western clothes and 'fashion' (*shizhuang*) (i.e. men's suits and Western-style women's clothes) were eventually prohibited altogether, leaving the market to socialist styles: the Sun Yat-sen suit, the youth suit, army fatigues, white shirts and the dual-season top (*liangyongshan*). The main exception to this profile was provided by Chinese-style shirts and jackets, increasingly made at home or put together by street peddlers because all the 'well-known shops had disappeared: nothing distinctive was left'.[24]

Figure 8.3 Two young girls in Lu Xun Park, Hongkou. The girl in front wears a Chinese-style jacket, with an upright collar, frog-fastenings and sleeves continuous from the shoulder of the garment. Her companion's upper garment is a double-purpose coat (*liangyong shan* 两用衫). The buttoning, to the left, suggests that the photo was taken around 1975 or after, when the right-hand buttoning on women's clothes was gradually being abandoned in favour of the global standard. Author's collection.

Many of these changes can be explained by reference to macro-developments in China during the opening decades of the People's Republic, when the CCP, under the guiding hand of Mao Zedong, was endeavouring to establish a new sort of society. That this new society would be opposed in ideological and cultural respects to much that Shanghai represented in the Republican era quickly became evident. Unlike Beijing, Shanghai was not a backward, 'feudal' place in need of accelerated modernization, but its 'bourgeois customs' made it equally significant a target for mass campaigns aimed at political rectification and moral improvement.[25] During the so-called New Democracy period, i.e. the early years of the PRC, 'bourgeois elements' in Shanghai were mindful of the need to survive under the new regime and moved with some alacrity to respond to the party's call. Chemist-turned-dressmaker Wang Guizhang is a good example. In the introduction to her dressmaking primer, first published in late 1949, Wang explicitly 'responded to the party's call'.[26] The primer notably eschewed a pattern for the Western suit in favour of a pattern for the Lenin suit, introduced to Shanghai by the People's Liberation Army (PLA).

The New Democracy period gave way to the period of socialist transformation, beginning in 1953 and reaching a 'high tide' in 1956. As noted above, a dress beautification campaign was under way at this time, and Shanghai drew on its reserves of expertise in the textile and apparel industries, mounting exhibitions to popularize new prints and styles such as those drawn up by Wang Guizhang (see Figure 8.2). The campaign had only a short lifetime. Severe shortages in the Great Leap Forward beginning in 1958 led to a culture of frugality and simplicity that was only partly mitigated by the abandonment of GLF goals and a thaw in the political climate in the early 1960s. During this time, future Culture Revolution activist Huang Jinhai, then a worker in Shanghai's Shenxin Textile Factory, was labelled a 'backward element' on account of his fondness for dressing up.[27] From being the place where 'anything goes', Shanghai was being reduced to a model of submissiveness to the Yanan way. For the next twenty years, the Shanghai Municipal Clothing, Shoes and Hats Company (hereafter SMCSHC), formed at the beginning of the Great Leap Forward, presided over much of what was made, sold and worn.

Through this whole period, local government, which in a different political system might have been expected to promote local interests and help the city project a local identity, was in the hands of party members who were more likely to serve as agents of Beijing than as representatives of Shanghai. Ke Qingshi, party secretary and then mayor of Shanghai from 1954 to 1965, a veteran member of the CCP, was a close ally of Mao's and devoted mostly to upholding the banner of Mao Zedong thought. An ideologue as well as a political opportunist, he once humiliated fellow party member Chen Xiuliang by pointing to her Western-style jacket with its padded shoulders as an illustration of bourgeois dress, for the benefit of some military figures present in the room at the time.[28] He died too soon to be active during the Cultural Revolution, but he had able heirs in the persons of Zhang Chunqiao and Wang Hongwen, key allies of Mao's wife, Jiang Qing. During the Cultural Revolution, designed and guided in large part by these Shanghai radicals operating at the heart of power in Beijing, attacks on 'strange dress and outlandish garments' (*qizhuang yifu*), in other words deviant or heterodox styles of dress, reached their zenith.

The time frame indicated in this broad outline of events is structured by the recognizable mass movements of the early communist era. Maoism and the mass line had a homogenizing effect on material culture throughout China. Accordingly, 'dressed alike' is one of the most common phrases to be found in reports by visitors to the PRC during the Mao years.[29] But Shanghai was subject to more than general effects. As a source of wealth, knowledge and technological prowess, it was particularly vulnerable to appropriations of its human and cultural capital for Beijing's purposes. This was dramatically demonstrated in 1956 when a number of its well-known shops – brands, owners, equipment, staff, dependants – were moved to the capital.[30] Yu Yuanfang's Bowei Western Clothing shop was only one of a number of clothing stores affected. In one fell swoop, Nanjing West Road lost the Leimeng Western Clothing, Lantian Fashion and Hongxia Dress stores.[31] Shortages had been identified in a number of other service industries in Beijing. Hairdressing, photography, dyeing, foodstuffs and footwear shops were also relocated from Shanghai. The events even now, as spoken about in Beijing at least, are narrated with revolutionary enthusiasm ('Beijing was the capital. Who wouldn't be willing to go?');[32] but the loss to Shanghai was severe.

The official correspondence concerning these transfers reveals underlying tensions in Shanghai's relationship with Beijing. The SMCSHC was not happy at the departure of its iconic businesses. Asked for a further twenty personnel from the sector to support a forthcoming exhibition in Beijing, it complained to the Commerce Bureau that eleven of these personnel were to be retained in the north. Beijing had already asked for more than 100 men the previous month, and Shanghai was being left too short of manpower in the sector to support planned increases in production and exports.[33] Lantian, which specialized in women's shirts and pants, was particularly missed by its customers in Shanghai: 'consumers had held [the tailor] in high regard'. In March 1956, the SMCSHC reported that the removal of the business had left the premises empty, adversely affecting the streetscape.[34]

Beijing, on the other hand, profited from the transfers. Wangfujing, the capital's central shopping strip, was a major beneficiary. The restructured Leimeng (specializing in men's suits) and Lantian (specializing in women's shirts and pants) were both transplanted there. As it turned out, however, few of these relocated shops kept their identities intact even in the short term, and none survived in the long term. The twenty-one clothing firms were collapsed into a total of seven on arrival in Beijing, and most of those suffered closure over the following decade. The main legacy of the move was the metamorphosis of Yu Yuanfang's Bowei company into the 'Red Capital' (Hongdu) store, still to be seen on the site it has occupied since 1957 (see Plate 5).[35]

The entire episode is reminiscent of a story involving the Emperor Qianlong, who on a visit to Yangzhou in 1784 so admired the strange rocks in the Garden of Nine Peaks, owned by salt merchant Wang Changxing, that the hapless owner felt obliged to offer a number of them to grace the imperial pleasure grounds in Beijing. The garden was left looking forlorn.[36]

Strange Clothing and Outlandish Garments: The Counter-Narrative

This narrative of decline and fall of the fashion industry in Shanghai invites consideration of a possible counter-narrative. Tales of what was lost by or erased in Shanghai simultaneously reveal what was very much present and, despite all, retained or re-grown. The testimony of Huang Jinhai is illustrative. Huang may have been accused of dandyism and declared a backward element, but his confession shows that he was dressing up in an environment that fuelled his sartorial interests. He bought a necktie, evidently still available in some Shanghai shop, and also a second-hand Western suit, the latter at 'a shop that sold exotica'. He wanted to be seen wearing these clothes, and would don them for an excursion downtown. He paid more than 40 yuan, close to a month's salary, to purchase a leather jacket, again obviously available in some Shanghai shop. Apparently, other young men in Shanghai were wearing leather jackets, because Huang confessed to having been inspired by seeing them. It takes an effort of imagination to visualize the beat generation on the streets of Shanghai in the early 1960s, but Huang Jinhai was doing his best to make that possible. He sported a beard. On weekends, instead of 'engaging in proper duties' (cleaning his room, mending his clothes, attending meetings), he would slouch off to the outskirts of Shanghai and while away the time with a fishing line in the muddy waters of the Huangpu.[37]

What or where were the shops that 'sold exotica' in Shanghai? Far from having disappeared, the number of shops dealing in 'old goods' (*jiuhuo shangdian*) more than doubled after 1949. Causative factors were unemployment turning people to petty trade, and the quantity of abandoned or unwanted goods in the city. Of the latter, there were so many, and they were cumulatively so valuable, that the government established a huge warehouse to store them, and a security detail to protect them.[38] Those stored by the government can only have been a fraction of all that was available, for in 1951 the number of dealers in old goods stood at 1060, a majority of whom were independent traders.[39] The number soon dropped, helped along by the 'Five-Anti Campaign' which led to the closure of many businesses in Shanghai and elsewhere; but that same campaign increased the stock of confiscated or relinquished goods. These included jewellery, furs, and other items of definitively bourgeois character.

In 1958, nearly a decade after the revolution and well into the period of socialist transformation, Shanghai had 580 dealers in old clothes. They were mainly located in 'nationally famous' market places such as at Jinjiafang in the old city and Huaihai East Rd, in the former French Concession, and otherwise scattered through sites at Jiangyin Street, Mengzi Street, Datong Road in Zhabei, and Dawang Temple. Around 30 per cent of the trade was run by 'black elements' (*heifenzi*), the sort of people who had few reasonable employment prospects in 1950s China: former members of the police and armed forces in the puppet administration during the Japanese occupation, and former rich peasants. The stock, sourced both locally and from elsewhere in the country, included metal-ware and bric-à-brac, but a large proportion was second-hand clothes and fabric items: made-over Sun Yat-sen suits, Western trousers, overcoats (short and long), stage costumes and carpets. Often the clothes had been reprocessed and repurposed: cut down, dyed, mended, and reshaped to extend their usefulness. The report, prepared by the Municipal Industry and Trade Administrative Bureau, was critical of the capitalist practices in this sector: prices were unregulated, and some traders did no more than buy and sell, not processing the goods in any way so as to add value to them. Importantly, from the perspective of Shanghai's sustained reputation as a centre of fashion, these second-hand markets attracted buyers from other parts of the country.[40]

This rambunctious trade did not survive the Great Leap Forward. Following the above report, the traders were brought together under one roof, at the Yiletian Teahouse in Nanjing Road (near to Wing On and Sincere Department Stores), in a spectacularly unsuccessful attempt to organize and regulate the trade. By February 1961, less than three years after the reform, price approvals had dropped 90 per cent from 200 to 20 per day, and the nine personnel employed by the municipality to manage the market had been left with little to do. The teahouse was by then doing no more than serving as a drawcard for unruly elements who hung around at the doorway engaging in illegal activities.[41] But second-hand clothes had other outlets. 1962 registrations of 'old goods' shops, including co-operatives, joint ventures (state–private), and even state-owned enterprises, show that this was a thriving, or at least a very busy area of commerce, with many shops employing large numbers of employees Wu Yongkang's joint-venture second-hand clothes store in Fujian Middle Road, in operation since 1932, had business premises of 250 square metres, employed sixteen staff and in the first three-quarters of 1963 had a turnover of 285,200 yuan.[42] This was a medium-sized enterprise. In the same street, Yao Yongkan's store, established in 1919, was still going strong in 1963, with twenty-seven employees and a business turnover of 314,700 for the same period, not including business for goods sold on consignment.[43]

It is difficult to follow the history of these shops through the period of the Cultural Revolution: on the face of things, left-over capitalists such as the two Yongkans, both of whom had lived through the Kuomintang (KMT) and Japanese periods, are unlikely to have survived the sustained attack on the 'four olds'. On the other hand, the state-owned Huaihai Road Old Products store, with its double-storey building and triple-width street frontage, continued business well into the Reform Era. In the 1970s it was crammed with goods from households that had been turned over by the Red Guards. Items of redwood furniture – tables, chairs, wardrobes – were among the stock. According to former employees, thieves were known to conceal themselves in wardrobes and chests during the day, emerging at night after the store's closure to take their pickings from among smaller items that they could easily carry away.[44] Such petty criminals may have been among the 'hooligans [and] dandies' (*liumang afei*) whom Wang Hongwen roundly condemned in an address to a crowd of Mao Zedong Thought activists in Shanghai's Nanshi district in March 1968.[45] Their activities anyway point to the continued existence and circulation in Shanghai of the products of capitalist society, whether made in pre-1949 China, or imported from overseas for use in the homes of Shanghai's disappearing bourgeoisie.

The use of the term 'dandy' (*afei*) in the context of the Cultural Revolution deserves closer enquiry, especially in light of Christopher Breward's exploration of the phenomenon of the Shanghai dandy in longer historical perspective. *Afei* is usually combined with the term *liumang* (hooligans, vagrants, layabouts), as in the speech by Wang Hongwen mentioned above; alternatively, an anti-social, counter-revolutionary element might be described as 'either a hooligan or a dandy' (*bushi liumang ershi afei*). But this Shanghai dialect word has a clear connection with dress style and comportment. Its repeated appearance in documents from the Cultural Revolution period, combined with reports of Red Guards attacking people on the streets on the grounds of how they were dressed, tells us that at the height of the terror individualized dress practices were still evident on the Shanghai streets; and if the Red Guards managed for a while to whip people into line, the period of conformity was short-lived.

Second-hand clothes stores were one source of 'strange clothes and outlandish garments'. There were others. Edgar Snow, visiting China in 1971, was surprised to see women in one house he visited poring over a Japanese pattern book.[46] Such materials typically included well-scaled patterns. At a time of expanding sewing-machine ownership, women could make the clothes themselves, for wear at home or among friends. Foreign films, especially from Albania in this period, were capable of setting off minor fashion trends.[47] Foreigners themselves, few as they were in China at this time, were a source of inspiration. Investigations by the Shanghai Municipal Clothing, Hats and Shoes Company in the summer of 1975 attributed decadent clothing practices among the young to the influence of magazines, films, and actual clothes worn by foreigners and overseas Chinese in Shanghai.[48]

What constituted the category of 'strange clothing and outlandish garments' in 1970s Shanghai? In 1975, the revolutionary committee of the No. 1 Bureau of Trade in Shanghai itemized them as follows: 1) short skirts; 2) large pointy collars ('like pigs' ears'); 3) flares, with cuffs up to a foot wide; 4) trousers cut too close to the buttocks; 5) patterns embroidered onto collars, lapels, or the cuffs of garments; 6) young men wearing clothes in girls' colours (e.g. checks, or jade green), or else sporting dark-coloured singlets under their white shirts. The characteristics of such clothing were diametrically opposed to the new styles being proposed that year for the socialist market, which were 'plain, uncomplicated, generous in cut, and possessed of national characteristics . . . satisfying the needs of the workers, peasants, and soldiers'.[49]

Deviant dress was not only trotted out at night, but worn to work. At the Luwang Clothing and Accessories Company, an investigation in June 1975 found that six out of 278 workers were found to be wearing short-waisted collarless blouses and flares, all home-made. Six is a small proportion of the total workforce, but a larger one of young women workers at the factory, among whom these six must have been rather daring trend-setters. In their endeavour to counter the trends, the authorities emphasized the role of the clothing industry as the first line of defence.

Shanghai was undoubtedly a weak point in the country's defences against the outside world. It was a port of trade, exporting ready-made clothing to Hong Kong and Southeast Asia and importing technological equipment and materials. Personnel in the clothing industry had to be especially vigilant not to let 'strange clothing and outlandish garments' slip into Shanghai 'through the road of socialist commerce'. But this was an impossible charge. As Peidong Sun has shown, the shortage of fabrics in the market at this time meant that in rural areas even packaging materials were used for clothing, leading to very bizarre effects indeed.[50]

It seems probable that the limited production of ready-made clothes, and the export focus of the garment manufacturing in Shanghai had the unanticipated effect of creating space for departure from norms in dressmaking. The main commercial model for garment production was *lailiao jiagong*: making up garments from cloth brought into the store by the customer. From 1970 onward, the SMCSHC used a published guide to clothing styles and standard measurements explicitly as a means of 'controlling clothing styles and combatting strange clothing and outlandish garments'.[51]

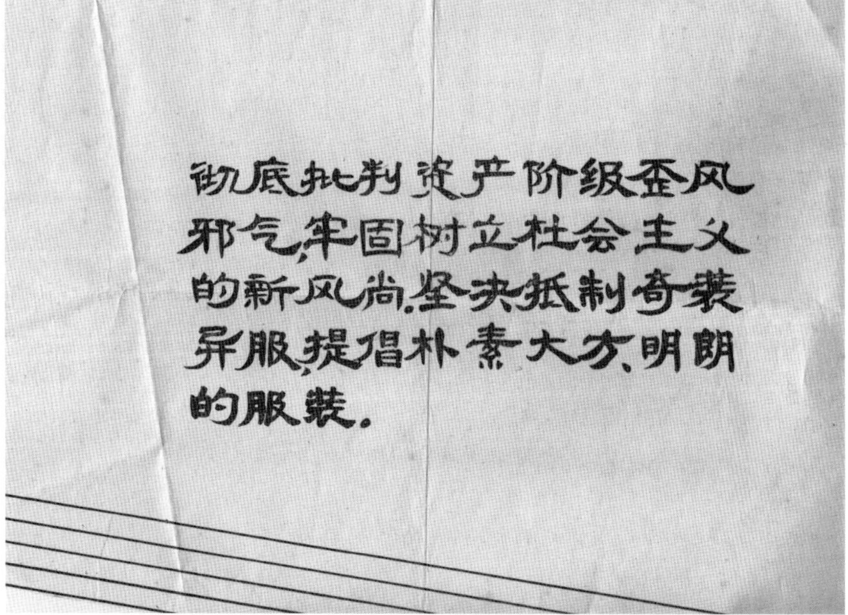

Figure 8.4 Fragment from a 1970s garment pattern, carrying propaganda aimed at 'strange clothing and outlandish garments' (*qizhuangyifu* 奇装异服): 'Thoroughly criticize bourgeois unhealthy trends and evil practices; securely establish the new customs of socialism; firmly resist strange clothing and outlandish garments; promote clothing that is simple, of generous cut, and unadorned.' Author's collection.

The identification of deviant dress was often made by reference to these standards. Cuffed trousers, for instance, had a standard of 1.2 centimetres for the cuffs. Trousers with cuffs of 2.2 centimetres breached the standards and were criticized as 'strange' and wasteful. On the other hand, clothes were sometimes cut rather too economically: skirts were too short and pants were too tight. In Jingan district in the summer of 1975, an inspection of seventy co-ops found that of the 122 lengths of material cut for trousers, the cut was too narrow by 3 centimetres or more. The spokesman for the Jiancheng Clothing Co-operative Store in Jingan District stated openly: 'Skinny pants and flares are being worn on the street. Why can't our shop make them? Why are the authorities placing such values on trouser legs?' Bare legs were even more of a problem. In the main streets, it was calculated that around 16 per cent of girls wearing skirts were wearing skirts short enough to expose the thighs; while as many as 55 per cent were wearing them at least above the knee. Not only co-ops were guilty of producing such garments: SOEs (state-owned enterprises), too, were failing to adhere to standards. In Nanjing West Road, the SOE Eastern Clothing Shop was at this time found to be producing skirts with too little material.

The main source of deviant dress was acknowledged to be the independent peddler or hawker stratum (*geti tanfan*). These street traders were a perennial source of anxiety to the authorities. In 1963, Shanghai had an estimated 90,000 unregistered manual (handicraft) workers and peddlers, covering around 100 lines of trade. A registration drive at that time, and subsequent culls in 1964–5, was thought to have reduced the number to just over 20,000 by the beginning of the Cultural Revolution. Most were over fifty years of age with no labour experience or qualifications and many had no other possible means of earning a living because they were former 'landlords, wealthy peasants, counter-revolutionaries, or bad elements'. In 1965, they had been coaxed into attending training classes to 'develop political consciousness and advance their service ethic'. Ten years later, they still had capitalist tendencies. They were resistant to guidance, and even to investigation. Apart from referring them to the relevant Peddler Governance Committee Small Group for investigation, criticism and help, the authorities had few ideas about how to bring them to heel. Recommendations for combatting unwelcome tendencies in the manufacture and wear of clothing had ideological work in the lead: 'All relevant companies should study the theory of the dictatorship of the proletariat, [work to] change outlooks, advance socialist fashions, investigate all employees' dress, use education [to reform], and monitor finished goods and the lengths of cloth [brought along by customers for making up].'[52]

Ubiquitous, often unregistered, and resistant to authority, the sewing peddlers (*fengren tanfan*) set up sewing machines by the side of the road and mended and made clothes to order. Investigations of 107 independent peddlers in the central Shanghai districts of Huangpu, Jingan, Luwan and Xuhui, again in 1975, identified problems in the cutting and sewing practices in more than a third of cases.[53] In Jingan district, eleven garments of the forty-eight inspected fitted into the deviant category; in Xujiahui, the figure was fifty-one out of seventy, or around 80 per cent. The existence and practices of this sizeable group of independent garment manufacturers undoubtedly placed pressure on the co-op and SOE stores. To quote again the spokesman of the Jiancheng Clothing Co-operative Store: if the Co-op workers cut according to regulations, 'no one wants to buy; business just goes elsewhere'. While the textile and apparel sector in Shanghai was far from being a free market, consumer choices were clearly driving modest changes in style; and unlike during the high tide of revolutionary fervour in the late sixties, when a genuine PLA uniform was the last word in fashion, these choices were informed by world trends.

Almost uniquely in the annals of China's modern vestimentary history, a sustained attempt was under way around this time to popularize a particular dress style. The 'Jiang Qing dress', as it has come to be known, was one of the 'newborn things' (*xinsheng shiwu*) that defined the cultural landscape of China after its makeover during the Cultural Revolution. Unlike other characteristic garments of the Mao era, it has known beginnings, and a documented history of design, manufacture and distribution. In the opening decades of the PRC, regulations for dress were limited to workplace or occupational clothing. The cadre suit (*ganbu zhifu*) became popular in the 1950s because it was a status garment, and also a symbol of the exciting, progressive times. The fashion persisted despite industry attempts to persuade young women in particular to diversify their dress habits. The craze for wearing PLA uniforms swept through the younger generation in the sixties for much the same reasons. In the 1970s, judging by the campaign against deviant dress, young people in Shanghai were in search of a new fashion, one that spoke meaningfully to their times. The one foisted on them from Beijing and Tianjin in 1975 clearly did not satisfy their needs.

The Jiang Qing Dress in Shanghai

The Jiang Qing dress has taken a while to re-emerge from the ashes of the Cultural Revolution. Despite some early published accounts, a mention of the dress by fashion historian Valerie Steele in 2005 was dismissed out of hand by Jiang Qing's biographer Roxanne Witke and subsequently treated with caution by costume historian Verity Wilson.[54] In Chinese mainland sources, the technical name of the garment, *kaijinling qunyi* (or in Shanghai, *kaijinling lianyiqun*), appears in official industry histories in the 1990s, but not in costume or fashion histories. It is only in the last decade, with the opening of archives of the Cultural Revolution period, that more detailed accounts have become possible, and knowledge of the garment more general. An internet search of the term *kaijinling qunyi* now yields a plethora of results.

The dress reportedly had its origins in Jiang Qing's desire for a formal dress for Chinese women, one that matched the Sun Yat-sen suit for men. Jiang Qing had some experience in costume design and construction from her early days as costume seamstress and then as an actress in Shanghai. As it happened, such a background was not untypical for dress designers in the PRC. There were no fashion designers as such. In the 1950s, designers for the dress beautification campaign were drawn from the fine and performing arts areas. There is a certain congruence between this fact and the character of the clothing produced, whether in the 1950s under then Minister of Culture Zhou Yang or later under Jiang Qing. The garments were more costume rather than fashion, and the potential wearers were unsure of what part they might be meant to play in these costumes.

Jiang Qing drew on the talents of arts and culture personnel from key Beijing cultural organizations for help in designing the new national dress. It was to incorporate elements of Chinese historical costume while also being new and fresh, as befitting a 'newborn item' (*xinsheng shiwu*) in the assemblage of cultural products of the New China. The result was a one-piece dress with cuffed sleeves, a gathered or pleated skirt, and a surplice neckline with inset. The draft design was handed over to the Tianjin Clothing Factory for development. On 15 July, exhibitions of the garment were opened at Tianjin Municipal Department Store, People's Market, and the Worker, Soldier, Peasant Market, and people flocked in to have a look:

> There was a steady flow of expressions of appreciation. People were saying that at present, in the middle of *pi Lin pi Kong* ('criticise Lin Biao, criticise Confucius'), this clothing innovation fully encapsulated the party's concern for the broad masses of women in politics and in life, and the way in which the garment was made in every respect reflected beauty, generosity, and our nation's national characteristics.[55]

Mention of *pi Lin pi Kong* is a reminder of the particular political moment at which the Jiang Qing dress was launched. Launched in January 1974, this was the last mass movement of the Mao era, sweeping up the exhausted masses in meetings and demonstrations that were directed overtly at the former Minister of Defence Lin Biao, and covertly at Premier Zhou Enlai, Mao's beleaguered second-in-command. In the spring of 1975 'the daring and militant garment workers of Shanghai' were busy preparing for the biannual clothing exports exhibition – an exhibition that included samples of the Jiang Qing dress – and were simultaneously participating in 'the movement to criticize Lin Piao [sic] and Confucius'. This involved 'studying the history of the struggle between the Confucian and the legalist Schools, and of class struggle as a whole, using the Marxist stand, viewpoint and method'.[56]

During this period, as Mao Zedong became increasingly frail, Jiang Qing was waging a campaign within the party leadership to ensure her own succession prospects. Simultaneously she embarked on the task of re-crafting her own public image in the international arena, not least through interviews with American writer Roxane Witke in 1972.[57] In September 1973, she appeared at a state occasion wearing a dress in honour of the visit of Georges Pompidou, whose arrival in Beijing marked the first state-level visit from a Western power in the history of the PRC.[58] The following year, she allegedly had some gowns made up for her in anticipation of a visit from Ferdinand and Imelda Marcos. According to Mao's physician Li Zhisui, these were inspired by Empress Wu of the Tang dynasty.[59] In the context of these times, Jiang's search for a national dress for Chinese women seems inextricably entwined with her search for a distinctive presence for herself in a very masculine political landscape.

Two further developments in 1974 suggest that Jiang, and perhaps everyone else as well, was becoming self-conscious about the appearance of Chinese people on the world stage in ways that directly influenced thoughts about what they were wearing. One is a furious controversy over Michelangelo Antonioni's *Chung Kuo*, a documentary film attacked by Jiang Qing as unfriendly to China. The controversy is widely viewed as having been stirred up by Jiang Qing to further her campaign to destabilize Zhou Enlai, but for those who actually saw the documentary, there was surely much to cause concern if it was to define China's international image. A segment of the film focused on Shanghai, where Antonioni spent a long time on major streets – Jinling Road, the Bund – with the camera panning over the crowd. It was a hot summer day, and people appear on screen lightly dressed in pants and shirts with not too many differences in clothing observable between one person and the next. Street urchins scamper around in their underwear. The sartorial spectacle is dreary: people look poor and not very happy. In criticizing the film, Jiang Qing homed in on a particular shot of the Yangtze River Bridge, the engineering masterpiece of the Cultural Revolutionary period;[60] but her move within months to create a national costume for Chinese women suggests that she took note of the appearance of women in Antonioni's film.

The second development was the Asian Games, due to be held in Tehran in September with the PRC participating for the first time. Hitherto, the Chinese team at these games, as at the Olympics, had been represented by the Republic of China (Taiwan). Iran's recognition of the PRC in 1971, the PRC's entry into the UN in 1972, and the establishment of the first Iranian embassy in Beijing in late 1973 paved the way for a change in the status quo at the Asian Games. China's sporting prowess would now be on show, and so, en masse, would the actual athletes. At the opening ceremony for the games, the male athletes would be wearing the Sun Yat-sen suit. The problem of what the women would wear must surely have been a factor in the development of the new national costume for women. The result is visible in photos of China's women athletes at the Tehran games, which are among the few readily available images of the Jiang Qing dress actually being worn. Blazers and high-heeled shoes completed the athletes' outfits.[61]

The Shanghai clothing industry became involved in Jiang Qing's project in the summer of 1974. In July, the revolutionary committee of the management bureau for handicrafts in Shanghai sent a representative to Tianjin to attend a meeting focused on the production and marketing of this 'newborn thing'. The report from this meeting shows that the project entailed a suite of garments developed under the direction of 'central leaders' (here signifying Jiang Qing), and 'warmly welcomed by the broad masses of women'. Apart from the frock (which itself came in slightly different forms), this included a front-fastening jacket (to match the frock), a long 'skirt of one hundred pleats', and a short 'skirt of one hundred pleats'. The ready-to-wear open-neck frock appears, however, to have been the only garment to have undergone mass production, the others remaining at sample stage. By 10 August, 80,000 dresses had been rolled out from factories in Tianjin.[62]

The correspondence surrounding the introduction of the Jiang Qing dress to Shanghai encapsulates the complexities of the relationship between Shanghai and Beijing (and in this case its proxy, Tianjin) against the backdrop of shifting political positions and alliances within the party leadership. In Shanghai, as in Tianjin, the response of the masses to the appearance of the open-neck frock in stores was reportedly positive: Some said: 'We should design a few more plain, simple and generous women's styles.' Some said: 'This garment has all the structural features of our nation's ancient clothing, while in manifesting a modern form, it is also a forceful means of grasping ideological class struggle in respect of dress.' Such responses were used to 'demonstrate that the workers, peasants and soldiers are admiring of the open-necked frock, and support it'.[63] Not surprisingly, what the masses were reported as saying was consistent with the official position on clothing, which was that it reflected class outlook: 'since liberation, the problem of clothing had consistently featured a fierce struggle between two classes, two roads, two lines'.[64] Those two classes were the proletariat and the bourgeoisie. The SMCSHC was naturally committed to following the proletarian road and advocating the proletarian line.[65]

In the detailed planning for production and distribution of the frock, however, can be detected a range of concerns and problems to be solved if the launch was to be a success. Whether a successful launch was ultimately desired seems doubtful, and at the very least highly dependent on political developments in Beijing; but in the short term the logistics of manufacture and distribution required close attention. As opposed to the relatively unmediated market in deviant dress conducted on the streets, the structure of the market for this approved dress was highly organized: oversight and directives were provided by the relevant municipal bodies, distribution via the main state-owned, or municipal, retail outlets and responses from the masses of the people. Putting politics in command, the SMCSHC declared itself ready to learn from Beijing and Tianjin, and work hard to launch the open-neck frock in Shanghai. Under the oversight of the No. 1 Municipal Bureau of Commerce, seventeen stores in eight districts were charged with the production of 900 garments. The three big department stores served as outlets but not sites for the production of the garment. Worth noting is the explicit exclusion of street peddlers or neighbourhood service centres from production and marketing.[66]

Behind the careful mapping out of sites of production and consumption were party members and industry bureaucrats making a series of careful decisions designed to ensure visible compliance with directives from Beijing and avoid complications arising from undertaking a non-routine task. Possible complications included pressures on the supply of cloth in Shanghai, consumers' unwillingness to waste their precious cotton coupons on the dress, and breaches of acceptable clothing norms through the use of inappropriate materials for the dress. Guidelines addressed these various concerns:

> The materials used should in the main be of low to medium grade. The technique should be to simplify and renew while retaining the specific characteristics of

> the open-necked [garment] and without adding too much fussy detail. Cotton coupons need to calibrated closely. In economising on materials, take the utmost care to lighten the burden on the masses. As for the colour and finish of the fabric, in the case of dresses for children and young girls the cloth can be a bit prettier, but it would not be appropriate for it to be too brightly coloured.[67]

Importantly, there were a number of features of the original design that Shanghai designers did not like: the exposed lining of the surplice collar and the sleeves was in white; they thought it should be the same colour as the dress. They wanted to replace cloth belts with plastic or canvas (definitely more up to date). There should be variations in the cuffs (turned-up or flat), and in the rows of buttons along and down the surplice collar (single or double). Pleats should be added at the bust so that the top of the frock sat more comfortably. Note was taken of the different dimensions of the frock as constructed in Beijing and Tianjin respectively, and a decision made to offer a variety of skirt styles, including gathers, knife pleats, box pleats, and fine pleats. Skirt and blouse variations on the original frock should be offered.[68] All these variations, and probably more that did not make it onto the list of recommendations, suggest a general dissatisfaction with the garment rather than particular dissatisfactions with any single element; and also point to a sense within the industry that in skills and understanding of clothing design and production, Shanghai ruled.

Finally, there was a problem in the plans for manufacture that take us back to the narrative of loss, in this case a loss of skills. The problem was probably particularly severe in the suburbs, where many workers in the industry were young and inexperienced. In one district, more than 800 workers in thirteen factories had reportedly lifted production by 54.23 per cent between 1973 and 1974, but the expansion was not supported by technical training: 'in the [clothing] processing plants, there are basically no professionals at all'. In one state-owned store in the district, 'the only one with experience in the clothing industry is 64 and he is going to retire. There's no experienced person to take his place … [Thus] we don't really have the capacity to make the open-necked frock.' The manager went on to ask, plaintively, whether they couldn't be allocated some experienced personnel to help with the task.[69] In a revealing statement on attitudes towards remuneration and work, this same correspondent drew attention to the remnant of autonomy possessed by workers in the command economy. The clothing factories in the district were all part of the collective economy: if a task was complex and the remuneration low, they might simply refuse to take it on.[70] For this among other reasons, manufacture of the garment fell well short of plans. By June 1975, 346,000 metres of cloth in new patterns had been allocated for the manufacture of 115,000 dresses, but nearly half that amount of cloth was left over and had to be diverted to other uses.[71]

As indicated above, it seems doubtful whether the SMCSHC was very enthusiastic about this project. One sign of its moving slowly was that a new edition of *Dressmaking* (*Fuzhuang caijian*) had been proposed for 1975. The first edition had come out in 1970 and was reputed to have been warmly welcomed by the masses. The new one was to incorporate new styles of the 1970s, including the open-neck frock. Planning for this edition reached an advanced stage: a revised forward had been composed, promising that with victory over Liu Shaoqi and Lin Biao, a new socialist style was now in full development. Whether or not clothing really appropriate to the needs of the workers, soldiers and peasants could be designed was certainly 'a sensitive problem, a problem of standpoint, a problem of world view', but it was a problem that tailors, cadres and technicians had worked together to resolve, making possible the new edition of *Dressmaking*.[72] The 1975 edition, it appears, never went into print; or if it went into print, was never distributed. Not until 1979 was a new edition available in the shops. In fact, it is difficult to find published (and therefore disseminated) patterns for the dress anywhere. Perhaps only Changchun municipality, in the northeast, was sufficiently courageous (or naïve) to forge ahead. A sketch and pattern for the dress appears in its 1975 *Introduction to Sewing*.[73] In Shanghai, a 1975 brochure of designs for the export market shows a very tiny image of the dress, in plain blue and floral apricot shades. The dress was hung on the rear wall of the exhibition room. For readers of the brochure it would be easy to miss if the text did not clearly identify it.[74]

In the end, the problem with the Jiang Qing dress was that people did not buy it. This was not because consumers were loath to purchase and wear anything new-fangled. Polyester fabric, for instance, quickly proved a sensation when it appeared in Shanghai's stores in the late sixties,[75] and by the mid-seventies, as we have seen, flares and short skirts were worn in the face of frank social disapproval. But even in the socialist marketplace, the open-neck frock had no traction. Perhaps the workers, peasants and soldiers sniffed the political winds and sensed that change was in the air. Left hanging on racks for want of buyers, the Jiang Qing dress was finally removed from the public eye after the fall of the Gang of Four. The much-vaunted 'newborn item' of 1974 was denounced in 1977 as 'fawning on the West, and antiquarian'. It turned out to be, after all, just one more example of deviant dress: 'after smashing the gang of four, the revolutionary masses and the personnel of the clothing industry, with class struggle as the key, denounced the front-opening frock along with all strange clothing and outlandish garments, promoting a new proletarian fashion'.[76]

Conclusion

Marie-Claire Bergère has remarked of Shanghai in the Republican era that it prospered to the extent that it could operate with a high degree of local autonomy.[77] The international concessions had naturally helped facilitate the city's independence from Beijing and, later, Nanjing, helping it operate at the level of a world city rather than a provincial one. With the establishment of the People's Republic of China, Shanghai was yoked firmly to Beijing. During the Mao years, it continued to be China's economic powerhouse, but was in thrall to metropolitan interests. Its political energies, as if denied natural outlet, were turned inward. The Cultural Revolution was launched from a Shanghai power base, and largely run by a Shanghai clique. To Antonioni, it seemed that the transformation wrought by socialism was more obvious in Shanghai than anywhere else in China.

On ascension to power in 1949, the Chinese Communist Party aimed to wipe the national slate clean of feudal, bourgeois and foreign practices and influences, replacing these with a blueprint for socialism, to follow a period of 'New Democracy'. There were productive outcomes from this undertaking: territorial reunification with some marginal exceptions; strengthened national defences; enhanced industrial capacity; close to nationwide literacy. Along with the benefits came costs: local violence in the course of 'class struggle', loss of life on a large scale through famine and political conflicts, exceeding total losses from the Second World War; and the destruction of property and cultural forms. Shanghai felt these costs and benefits in different ways.

It is a testament to the strong foundations of this city's cultural capital that it continued to be a byword for what was advanced and desirable among the few consumer goods that China had on offer during these years.[78] It was a resilient city. The depth and breadth of its pre-1949 industrial and commercial capacity long continued to be evident in the survival of small businesses and street trade. To emphasize the continuities instead of the profound changes would be romantic, but the changes themselves were unpredictable and diverse. From archival records in Shanghai, derived largely from government offices, it would be possible to reconstruct an official history of clothing production during the Mao years, and to illustrate it with designs from pattern books approved or even produced by the Shanghai Municipal Clothing, Shoes and Hats Company. But these same archives, with their mentions of 'strange clothing and outlandish garments', hint at a domain beyond the reach of the SMCSHC. This domain, of which we know so little, was evidently inhabited by members of a generation who had been raised under the shining red sun of Mao Zedong thought. It is consistent with their Shanghai heritage that in wearing flares or skinny pants, shirt skirts or over-long shirts they showed an instinct for responding to world trends.

Notes

This chapter has drawn extensively on documents from the Shanghai Municipal Archives (SMA), referenced below by the file or document number with the date if supplied. In some cases, however, the full title of the document is particularly informative, and has been supplied in the notes.

1 See inter alia Calvin Hui, 'Mao's Children are Wearing Fashion!' in Alison Hulme (ed.), *The Changing Landscape of China's Consumerism*, pp. 23–56 (Oxford: Chandos, 2014); Juanjuan Wu, *Chinese Fashion from Mao to Now* (Oxford: Berg, 2009). Note that the term fashion is sometimes used uncritically of the Mao years, e.g. Xurong Kong, 'Military Uniform as a Fashion during the Cultural Revolution', *Intercultural Communication Studies* XVII, 2 (2008): 287–303; Hung-yok Ip, 'Fashioning Appearances: Feminine Beauty in Chinese Communist Revolutionary Culture', *Modern China* 19, no. 3 (July, 2003): 329–61. For a sociological approach that eschews this question, see Shan Ren, 任珊, 2013, '1949–1965 nian Shanghai fuzhuangye fazhan yanjiu 1949–1965 年 上海服装也发展研究' (The development of the Shanghai's clothing industry, 1949–1965), MA thesis, Donghua University.

2 Gavin Murray-Miller, *The Cult of the Modern: Trans-Mediterranean France and the Construction of French Modernity* (Lincoln, NE: University of Nebraska Press, 2017), 50.

3 Ji Xueyuan 季学源 et al., *Hongbang fuzhuangshi* 红帮服装史 History of Red Group clothing (Ningbo: 宁波出版社, 2003). On Shanghai industry in Hong Kong, see Carles Brasó Broggi, *Trade and Technology Networks in the Chinese Textile Industry: Opening Up Before the Reform* (Basingstoke: Palgrave Macmillan, 2016).

4 See June Teufel Dreyer, *China's Political System: Modernization and Tradition* (Basingstoke: Macmillan, 1996), 86–7.

5 'Fuzhuang, xie, mao hangye 服装鞋冒行业' (Clothing, shoes and hat trades), in *Shanghai tongzhi* 上海通志 (Complete Gazetteer of Shanghai), Vol. 5, Ch. 7, Pt 5 (2008). Retrieved from http://www.shtong.gov.cn,8/6/2017.

6 See Ji Xueyuan 季学源, 'Hongbang fazhanshi gangyao 红帮发展史纲要' (Outline History of the Development of the Red Group), in *Hongbang caifeng pingzhuan*

红榜裁缝评传 *(Biographies of Red Group Tailors)*, ed. Ji Xueyuan 季学源, Zhu Xiaoen 竺小恩, and Feng Yingzhi 冯盈之 (Hangzhou: Zhejiang daxue chubanshe, 2011), 3–88.

7 Ji Xueyuan 季学源 and Zhong Zhengyang 钟正扬, 'Zhongguo Fuzhuangjie de "Guojiadui" – Beijing Hongdu Fuzhuang Gongsi 中国服装界的 '国家队'：北京红都服装公司' (The 'National Team' in the World of Chinese Tailoring – the Bejing Red Capital Clothing Company)', *Journal of Zhejiang Textile & Fashion Vocational College* , 2011, no. 1 (2011): 40–5.

8 Ibid.

9 Ji, Zhu and Feng, *Hongbang Caifeng Pingzhuan*, 212.

10 SMA C42-1-86-2. The 'Five-Anti Campaign' was against bribery, theft of state property, tax evasion, cheating on government contracts and theft of state economic information.

11 Wang Guizhang 王圭璋, *Funü fuzhuang caizhifa* 妇女服装裁制法 (Cutting methods for women's dress) (Shanghai: Shanghai wenhua chubanshe, 1956); Guizhang Wang 王圭璋, *Funü chunzhuang* 妇女春装 (Spring Clothing for Women) (Shanghai: Shanghai wenhua chubanshe, 1956).

12 Further on Wang Guizhang, see Antonia Finnane, 'Cold War Sewing Machines: Production and Consumption in 1950s China and Japan', *Journal of Asian Studies* 75, no. 3 (August 2016): 765–68, https://doi.org/10.1017/S0021911816000607. It is speculated in this article that Wang had been educated in Japan. A recently discovered document in the Shanghai Municipal Archives has shown otherwise.

13 Alan P.L. Liu, 'Communications and Development in Post-Mao Mainland China', in Bih-jaw Lin and James T. Myers (eds), *Forces for Change in Contemporary China* (Columbia, SC: University of South Carolina Press, 1993), 148.

14 Liu, 'Communications and Development in Post-Mao Mainland China', 148.

15 Jie Fan and Dong Chen, 'Technological Advantage of Beijing and Its Effect on Urban Development', in Ingo Liefner and Yehua Dennis Wei (eds), *Innovation and Regional Development in China* (Abingdon: Routledge, 2014).

16 Sen-dou Chang, 'Peking: The Growing Metropolis of Communist China', *Ekistics* 20, no. 120 (November 1965): 293–7.

17 Peter T.Y. Cheung, 'The Political Context of China's Economic Development', in Yue-man Yeung and Yun-Wing Sung (eds), *Shanghai: Transformation and Modernization Under China's Open Policy* (Hong Kong: Chinese University Press, 1996), 49–92.

18 Michael Marmé, *Suzhou: Where the Goods of All the Provinces Converge* (Stanford, CA: Stanford University Press, 2005).

19 Jonathan J. Howlett, 'Accelerated Transition: British Enterprises in Shanghai and the Transition to Socialism', *European Journal of East Asian Studies* 13 (2014): 177, https://doi.org/10.1163/15700615-01302003.

20 Lynn T. White III, 'Low Power: Small Enterprises in Shanghai, 1949-67', *The China Quarterly* no. 73 (Mar., 1978):45–76.

21 Ellen Johnston Laing, *Selling Happiness: Calendar Posters and Visual Culture in Early-Twentieth-Century Shanghai* (Honolulu: University of Hawaii Press, 2004), 225–6.

22 'Fuzhuang, xie, mao hangye'.

23 See Shangyebu, Qinggongyebu, Shanghai diyi shangyeju, fuzhuanggongsi guanyu fuzhuang biaozhun diaoyan he jiejue zuoyinan wenti de tongzhi, baogao 商业部，轻工业部，上海市第一商业局，服装公司关于服装标准调研和解决做衣难问题的通知，报告 (Ministry of Commerce, Ministry of Light Industry, Shanghai No 1 Bureau of Commerce, the Clothing Company: notification and report on surveying clothing specifications and solving the problem of difficulties in having clothes made. SMA B123-10-905.

24 'Fuzhuang, xie, mao hangye'.

25 Neil J. Diamant, *Revolutionizing the Family: Politics, Love, and Divorce in Urban and Rural China, 1949–1968* (Berkeley, CA: University of California Press, 2002), 46.

26 Wang Guizhang 王圭璋, *Fengren Nanzhen 缝纫南针* (King Fair Instructions: Sewing and Stitching) (Shanghai: Jinghua, 1950).

27 Elizabeth J. Perry and Nara Dillon, '"Little Brothers" in the Cultural Revolution: The Worker Rebels of Shanghai', in Susan Brownell and Jeffrey N. Wasserstrom (eds), *Chinese Femininities, Chinese Masculinities: A Reader* (Berkeley, CA: University of California Press, 2002), 269–86.

28 Cheng Xiuliang 陈修良, *Jujue Nuxing--Zhong-Gong Mimi Nanjing Shiwei Shuji Chen Xiuliang Zhuan 拒絕奴性--中共秘密南京市委書記陳修良傳* (Rejecting Servility: Biography of Chen Xiuliang, Nanjing Underground Party Secretary) (Hong Kong: Hong Kong Open Page Publishing Co., 2012), 287.

29 For a critical discussion of this impression, see Ai Hua 艾华 (Harriet Evans) and Li Yinhe 李银河, 'Guanyu Nüxingzhuyi de Duihua 关于女性主义的对话' (In Dialogue about Feminism)', *Shehuixue yanjiu* 2001, no. 4 (July): 118–25.

30 Ji Xueyuan 季学源 and Zhong Zhengyang 钟正扬, 'Zhongguo Fuzhuangjie de "Guojiadui" – Beijing Hongdu Fuzhuang Gongsi 中国服装界的‘国家队’：北京红都服装公司' (The 'National Team' in the World of Chinese Tailoring – the Bejing Red Capital Clothing Company)', *Journal of Zhejiang Textile & Fashion Vocational College* 1 (2011): 40–5.

31 For individual business files of these firms, see SMA B123-2-1398-84; B123-2-1394-108; B123-2-1422-107.

32 Xiao Ting 萧婷, '1956: Beijing laile Shanghai shifu 1956：北京来了上海师傅' (1956: Shanghai tradespeople come to Beijing), 73.

33 SMA B123-3-179-10 (5/5/1956).

34 SMA, B123-3-785-1 (30/3/1956).

35 Ji and Zhong, 'Zhongguo Fuzhuangjie de "Guojiadui"'; Li Zhi 李治， 'Hongdu de gushi 洪都的故事' (The story of Hongdu) *Shoudu jianshe bao* 5 (30/5/2008), 2. [1–6]

36 Gao Xiang 高翔, *Qianlong xia Jiangnan* 乾隆下江南 (Qianlong goes down to Jiangnan) (Beijing: Zhongguo Renmindaxue Chubanshe, 1989), 19.

37 Huang's 1977 testimony is held in the Shanghai Municipal Archives. The description here is based on a partial translation in Perry and Dillon, '"Little Brothers" in the Cultural Revolution: The Worker Rebels of Shanghai', 274.

38 Shao Daxing 邵大星, 'Hui Wang "Huai Guo Jiu" 回望 '淮国旧' (Recalling the Huaihuai State-Owned Old Goods Store), *Memories and Archives* 2014, no. 1 (2014): 46–48.

39 Chen Chunfang 陈春舫, *Shanghai Riyong Gongyepin Shangyezhi* 上海日用工业品商业志 (Commercial Gazetteer for Industry Products in Daily Life) (Shanghai: Shanghai Academy of Social Sciences Press, 1999), 322.

40 Shanghaishi gongshang xingzheng guanliju guanyu Shanghaishi guyi jiaoyicheng chengli hou de qingkuang baogao 上海市工商行政管理局关于上海市估衣交易市场成立后的情况报告 (Report from the Shanghai Municipal Trade and Commerce administrative bureau on circumstances since the establishment of the old clothes exchange market), 5/9/1958. SMA B182-1-1057-19.

41 SMA B182-1-1171-1.

42 SMA B123-5-1736-164.

43 SMA B123-5-1736-166.

44 Shao, 'Hui Wang "Huai Guo Jiu"', 48.

45 Wang Hongwen 王洪文, Wang Hongwen zai Shanghai Nanshiqu huoxue huoyong Mao Zedong sixiang jiji fenzi daibiao dahui shang de jianghua (tiyao) 王洪文在上海南市区活学活用毛泽东思想积极分子代表大会上的讲话 （提要） 'Summary of Wang Hongwen's talk at the meeting of representatives of the Study and Practices Mao Zedong Thought activists in Nanshi district, Shanghai', in Yuehan Xixifosi 約翰•西西弗斯, *Qunzhong baozheng yu zhengzhi touji: Wang Hongwen yu 'Wenge' (shang)* 群眾暴政與政治投機: 王洪文與「文革」(上) (The dictatorship of the masses and political speculation: Wang Hongwen and the Cultural Revolution, Vol. 1), 216th edn (Xinbei: Xixifosi chubanshe, 2016) , 51.

46 Edgar Snow, *The Long Revolution* (New York: Vintage Books, 1973), 24.

47 Simon Shen and Cho-kiu Li, 'The Cultural Side-Effects of the Sino-Soviet Split: The Influence of Albanian Movies in China in the 1960s', *Modern China Studies* 22, no. 1 (January 2015): 229.

48 Shanghaishi diyi Shangyeju geming weiyuanhui : guanyu dangqian zuohao dizhi qizhuang yifu gongzuo de qingshi baogao 上海市第一商业局革命委员会： 关于当前做好抵制奇装异服工作的请示报告 (Revolutionary committee of the Shanghai Municipal No 1 Commerce bureau: report for advice on combatting strange clothing and outlandish garments), 2/8/1975. SMA B123-8-1400.

49 SMA B123-8-1400-12 (28/6/1975).

50 Peidong Sun, 'The Collar Revolution: Everyday Clothing in Guangdong as Resistance in the Cultural Revolution', *The China Quarterly* 227 (September 2016): 773–95, doi:10.1017/S0305741016000692.

51 SMA B123-8-1400/76 (17/6/1975).

52 SMA B123-8-1400.

53 Ibid.

54 For early accounts, see Jiaqi Yan and Gao Gao, *Turbulent Decade: A History of the Cultural Revolution* (University of Hawaii Press, 1996), 445; Ross Terrill, *Madame Mao: The White Boned Demon* (Stanford, CA: Stanford University Press, 1999), 294–6. On Witke's response to Steele's claim, see Antonia Finnane, 'In Search of the Jiang Qing Dress', *Fashion Theory* 9, no. 1 (2005): 3–22.

55 Shanghaishi shougongye guanliju geming weiyuanhui: guanyu sheji zhanxiao kaijinling qunyi de qingshi baogao 上海市手工业管理局革命委员会：关于设计展销开襟领裙衣的请示报告 (Revolutionary committee of the Shanghai Municipal handicrafts industry administrative bureau: report for advice on design, exhibition and sale of the open-neck frock), 24/8/1974. SMA, B123-8-1400.

56 Shanghaishi fuzhuang gongye gongsi (ed.), *Shanghai fuzhuang gongye zai qianjin* 上海服装工业在前进 (Shanghai Garment Industry Is Advancing) (Shanghai: Shanghaishi fuzhuang gongye gongsi, 1975), [4].

57 See Witke, *Comrade Chiang Ch'ing.*

58 See Bruno Barbey's photographic portrait of the occasion, in Beverley Hooper, *Foreigners under Mao: Western Lives in China, 1949–1976* (Hong Kong: Hong Kong University Press, 2016), 111.

59 See Finnane, 'In Search of the Jiang Qing Dress', 14.

60 John H. Holdridge, *Crossing the Divide: An Insider's Account of Normalization of U.S. –China Relations* (Lanham, MD: Rowman & Littlefield, 1997), 149.

61 See photos in Xu Zhongyou 徐忠友, 'Xin Zhongguo Tiyu Daibiaotuan Shouci Canjia Yayunhui de Muhou Gushi 新中国体育代表团首次参加亚运会的幕后故事' (Stories from behind the Scenes of the First Participation in the Asian Games by a Delegation of Athletes from New China), *Dangshi Zonglan 党史纵览* 2014, no. 12 (2014); and Zhongyou Xu 徐忠友, 'Zhongguo Shouci Canjia Deheilan Yayunhui de Taiqianmuhou 中国首次参加德黑兰亚运会的台前幕后' (Front Stage and behind the Scenes at China's First Participation in the Asian Games, Tehran), *Shihai Gouchen 史海钩沉* (2015): 81.

62 'Tianjin tuiguang kaijinling qunyi shoudao guangda funüde huanying 天津推广开襟领裙衣收到广大妇女的欢迎' (The open-neck frock promoted in Tianjin is warmly welcomed by the broad masses of women), 24/8/1974. SMA B123-8-1400.

63 SMA, B123-8-1063-23.

64 SMA, B123-8-1400.

65 Ibid.

66 Ibid.

67 Ibid.

68 Ibid.

69 Ibid.

70 Ibid.

71 Ibid.

72 Ibid.

73 *Fuzhuang caijian jieshao* 服装裁剪介绍 (Introduction to Garment Cutting) (Changchun: 1975).

74 Shanghaishi fuzhuang gongye gongsi, *Shanghai fuzhuang gongye zai qianjin,* [7].

75 See Antonia Finnane and Pei-dong Sun, 'Textiles and Apparel in the Mao Years: Uniformity, Variety, and the Limits of Autarchy', in Wessie Ling and Simona Segre Reinach (eds), *Making Fashion in Multiple Chinas* (London: I.B. Tauris, 2018).

76 SMA, B248-2-1032-1.

77 Marie-Claire Bergère, *The Golden Age of the Chinese Bourgeoisie 1911–1937* (Cambridge: Cambridge University Press, 2009), 240.

78 A point made in Jos Gamble, *Shanghai in Transition: Changing Perspectives and Social Contours of a Chinese Metropolis* (London: Routledge, 2005), 78.

9

'新三年，旧三年，缝缝补补又三年'

'New for three years, old for three years, fix for another three years'

Anthony Bednall

Clothing Frugality and the Narrative of the Ordinary, 1960–76

Against the context of a century or more of economic, social and political developments in China, fashion or clothing has acted as a representational and symbolic illustration of a culture trying to clarify its own existential questions.

Its urban populations, with Shanghai being historically the most vibrant, negotiated unparalleled turmoil and seismic societal and economic volatility, which contributed to changes in individual and collective dress codes and represented the birth and rebirth of a series of distinctive cultural and sartorial norms. Shanghai pre-1949 has been described as 'a beautiful young woman' and by foreign inhabitants during the 1930s as the 'Paris of the Far East' but its continuation as a fashion capital and a consumer city with a multinational imperial heritage was always going to be ideologically at odds post-1949, when the city was 'liberated' by the forces of the New Republic.[1]

Undoubtedly for Shanghai, the powerful historical narrative of the new state replacing and eclipsing any previous localized societal cultures and expunging its 'imperialist' past would come to mean a loss of relevance and its former status as a key metropolis would become overshadowed by the success of the newly established Chinese Communist Party (CCP) regime.[2] It is, however, inconceivable that the population instantaneously dismissed previous social models, lifestyle and aesthetic sentiments which had their roots within a previously well-developed capitalist and bourgeois ethos.[3] Ultimately it is this 'red narrative' of regime change, which dissects not only China's, but Shanghai's, history, into a pre-1949 era and a post-1949 era.[4] There has been a significant amount written around this juxtaposition between the 'new society' post-1949, which often makes assumptions of limited linkage or continuity between the two eras.[5] The city's existing commercial environments and retail spaces continued to trade alongside its mature, light and textile industries, all of which existed within a well-conceived modern infrastructure.

The influences on the city's population and on how ordinary Shanghai residents procured, adapted and constructed clothing for themselves and their families could not have been a simple or singular transformation. Garments that were not only functional, economically viable and responded positively to new visual codes and social dogma were also not the direct effect of a series of political campaigns or directives, but would, like the majority of the country be a response to broader narratives of political alliances, global aspirations, revolutionary doctrine heavily reinforced by powerful visual imagery, and in some cases misguided or unsuccessful socio-political policies.

This chapter explores some of these broader narratives during the first decade of the new republic, from 1949 to 1959, and their direct contribution to the cultural and sartorial landscape of China in general terms and Shanghai specifically, whereby clothing loses its aesthetic significance to be replaced predominantly by functionality, gender neutrality and asexuality. It also reflects, through personal narratives, how ordinary Shanghainese residents, during the period 1960 to 1976, pragmatically responded to the conditions within this new landscape by navigating situations and ideologies as best they could and resourcefully clothed themselves through a variety of methods and opportunities.

External and Internal Influences on Dress, 1949–59

There were touchpoints within the first decade of the new regime when there were opportunities and an appetite from the new government to consider how the urban populations of China, such as Shanghai, could develop a stronger sense of dress and style to reflect a positive socio-cultural landscape. However, the complex nature of a fledgling government formulating a new modern China based on socialist, Marxist and Maoist theories meant that conditions were such that by 1960 Chinese urbanites and the population as a whole had no choice but to consider clothing purely through a functional and utilitarian lens.

In Shanghai, like other cities, this functionality was reflected through resourcefulness, shared community, adaption, economic viability and an individual response to the expectations of egalitarian positioning and social norms.[6] Information with reference to clothing and its relationship to the local population during this period was somewhat limited, as like the majority of China conditions, initially rooted within a heavy Soviet influence and latterly through centralized strategic domestic and international policies, were such that fashion or clothing was not deemed a priority or a subject worthy of much documentation.

Even if the subject was not high on the political agenda the growing population still required clothing and there was continued and sustained influence, guidance and recommendations, often in the form of posters, from central government as it responded, to internal and external socio-political pressures.

Externally the Soviet influence on China as a political and economic ally, post-1949, was somewhat predictable. China had no real choice but to form an international united front with the Soviet Union and other socialist nations against the United States and Japan.

Mao himself said in 1949 in his famous 'lean-to-one-side statement' that China must:

> Externally, unite in a common struggle with those nations of the world which treat us as equal and unite with the peoples of all countries. That is, ally ourselves with the Soviet Union, with the People's Democratic countries, and with the proletariat and the broad masses of the people in all other countries, and form an international united front. . . . We must lean to one side.[7]

By committing to the 1950 Sino-Soviet Treaty of Friendship, Alliance and Mutual Assistance, China's new leaders, who had no previous experience of running a country, sought to position China globally by consolidating economic and cultural ties with the Soviet Union, and garner its experience of organizing and delivering a socialist society as part of a new world order.[8]

This new alliance, which was intended to substantially support China in achieving its aims, also gave the Soviet Union certain rights. These included land and finance, in return for military support, weapons, and large amounts of economic and technological assistance, including technical advisers and machinery. As an existing manufacturing hub, Shanghai could have been a key area to support the new regime's first five-year plan of industrialization to heavy industry and the move to a Soviet influenced totalitarian narrative of self-reliance and modernization.[9] This did not, however, transpire as the new government focused away from the city ports embracing a collaborative Soviet designed centralized system which supported new and heavy mechanization.

Cultural Relativism and Stylistic Adoption

Through the Sino-Soviet collaboration there was significant population mobility between the countries with an estimated 80,000 Chinese being allowed to either train or study in the Soviet Union and 20,000 Russians travelling to China as foreign experts to support economic and cultural growth.[10] Scholarship on the historical timeline, and the economic and ideological relationship forged within the Sino-Soviet Treaty of Friendship, Alliance and Mutual Assistance has been well documented. However, where there is less investigation is into the cultural dynamics and social environments of urban populations that were symbiotically influenced by a newly organized, Soviet influenced and politically positioned ruling party.

As part of this agreement, between 1950 and 1956 the Soviet Union exerted a strong influence not only on Chinese economics and industry but also on art, education and significantly culture. Russian experts were invited into universities and colleges to teach students. Russian language, Marxism and Leninism were compulsory Chinese school subjects and Russian language skills enhanced individuals' social standing.

There is little evidence of what motivated or influenced dress from a population perspective and certainly the CCP did not issues edicts regarding acceptable notions of dress as the nationalists had done previously.[11] The party did, however, reiterate the use of the phrase '*pusu*' embedded within directives and slogans to convey a sense of simplicity across all forms of revolutionary idioms and the new government taking its lead from established Soviet art propaganda methods of visual representation of muscular state heroes and radiant heroines, used the power of imagery, across a range of media, to reinforce not only political doctrines but acceptable modes of dress.[12] Ultimately political ideologies were embedded and reinforced across all areas of society through visual communication which supported and redefined the cultural landscape from the individual to the collective.

For men, the transition to the collective is well documented and defined by hierarchical visual association, the abandonment of Western styles and an appetite to associate with and stylistically align with newly embraced cultural heroes. The modified *Zhongshanzhuang* and its less formal version the *zhifu* (uniform) (Figure 9.1), both of which shared similarities with the military uniform and the visual codes relating to the cadre, worker, peasant and soldier, were clearly sanctioned through all propaganda outlets and were defined enough to position the wearer succinctly within the new ruling party.

Figure 9.1 Zhifu Jacket, factory manufactured in Shanghai, *c.* 1971. Author's archive.

Women's clothing was somewhat more complex to redefine, as most forms of adornment and outward hints of sexuality did not sit well with revolutionary doctrine. Posters, one of the key methods of distributing ideologies, showed hyper-realistic, ageless workers, soldiers and peasants with strong and healthy bodies which over time erased gender distinctions.[13] Initially women appropriated what became known as the Lenin suit as a form of status dress; this not only reflected what the early female revolutionary leaders had worn in the early 1940s but also aligned individuals with the new CCP regime outwardly displaying their political allegiance. They also adopted the 'people's dress', a basic shirt and trousers, which again symbolically imbued the wearer with empathy for the spirit of revolution. Stylistically these garments led women to abandon traditional attributes of femininity whilst assuming anonymity and through both dystopian and normative scenarios the population in general had an appetite to associate with, and stylistically align itself with influential cultural and political icons. This may have been particularly challenging for Shanghai's urban female population as it transformed itself from the Paris of the East, but commentators at the time illustrate how powerful and quickly the transition to a new visual dynamic occurred. A.C. Scott, in his 1958 study of the development of Chinese dress in Shanghai, Beijing and Hong Kong, observed this rapid transition at first hand: 'almost overnight as it seemed, the nation was garbed in a dress whose sexless regimentation of style and shapelessness symbolized the liberation of a new national spirit according to Marxist theory, although to less politically perceptive eyes it appeared, however utilitarian, unnecessarily drab'.[14] Whilst Noel Barber a long-term resident and cultural commentator of Shanghai pre-1949, notes on his return to the city in the early 1950s that, 'its satellite suburbs depressingly reflect the Soviet architectural influence, and its people in identical uniforms pad the street like sexless ghosts'.[15]

Inevitably with a pro-Soviet political landscape, the influx of soviet cultural media, which quickly displaced banned Western counterparts, and the cross-cultural movement of peoples came a filtration of cultural styles and imagery that began to influence the female urban populations of China. As they did previously with the speedy acceptance of the *qipao*, Chinese women would begin to admire and desire a gender-specific item and the Bulaji dress started to appear as a common female garment.[16] This style of dress had originally become popular as the daily wear of Soviet Union women.[17] Although a simple garment it became iconic when an eighteen-year-old Soviet heroine, Zoya Kosmodemyanskaya, was executed in 1941 for championing her cause against the Nazis, in just such a dress, defining the garment as a symbol of revolution and progress.[18]

Fashion as Cultural Capital

If the Sino-Soviet Alliance was the foundation of a gradual osmotic adoption of Russian styles of dress in the early 1950s then it could be argued that the events of 1953 propelled this influence forward at a much greater pace and opened up a broader debate around the significance of clothing in relation to global representation and the recognition of a successful socio-political environment. Stalin's death in 1953 as well as the end of the Korean War led to a shift in political visioning and influence.[19] Whereas Stalin advocated cultural imperialism, the new premier, Khrushchev, was not as opposed to cultural discourse and exchange, opening up a broader dialogue around a more liberal and dynamic future for the

USSR developed though socialist internationalism. This view in turn signalled the re-opening of the Glavny Univesalny Magazin or GUM department store in Moscow's Red Square.

The store was built as a commercial arcade in the late nineteenth century and comprised more than a thousand shops.[20] It closed in 1917 as part of the Bolshevik Revolution, was re-opened in 1921 by Lenin and closed with plans for demolition by Stalin in 1930.[21] For unknown reasons, it was not demolished and re-opened on 23 December 1953. There are clear parallels of the influence, both positively and negatively, of political environments, on notions of commerce and of the role of commercial outlets that had previous existences under differing political parameters. The existing Shanghai department stores such as the Yongan store and the Shanghai No. 1 Department Store are prime examples, both of which operated with great success in a pre-revolutionary commercial environment and both of which, like the GUM store, ironically survive today as beacons of designer-focused experiences albeit within communist controlled environments.

The opening of an 'exemplary' department store in Moscow in 1953 that would offer the best possible goods and commodities was a global statement that GUM, by its location to the east of Red Square, would not only become a major attraction but be significant proof of the achievements of Soviet power in the field of trade and of serving the population. In the spring of 1954 the Fashion Atelier opened within the store and positioned itself in the category of 'Lux', the highest end possible.[22]

Also in 1954 the Department of Fashion Design was established and although officially a trade organization it had a broader remit, which included the design of clothes as well as the propagation of fashion and good taste among the populace. This was enabled through the publishing of fashion magazines and booklets and by organizing regular fashion shows within the demonstration hall at GUM.

There was a team of designers who not only designed menswear, womenswear and accessories but also started to create seasonal collections and 'Lux' as GUM took on the role as the sartorial leader for Russian style. Anastas Mikoyan, who was Khrushchev's right-hand man, fully supported the workings of the Department of Fashion as he understood that fashion, like culture in general, was an international phenomenon. He promoted international co-operation in fashion to such an extent that in 1956 a delegation from the Russian ministry of trade including fashion designers from GUM went to Paris for twenty days to study the Paris fashion houses.[23]

The USSR's propaganda machine had become well honed at sparring with the United States in terms of identifying the cultural richness of the communist ideal through posters, periodicals and films, all of which, as already stated, were prominent in China and became further reference points for political posters and media that reinforced doctrine as well as expectations of clothing. A popular Soviet magazine entitled *Rabotnitsa* (The Woman Worker), which featured fashion amongst its content, declared that: 'With the growth of the material well-being of the Soviet people the demand for clothes has also grown [and] the soviet person has become more beautiful, both in mind and soul, so his clothes must also be beautiful.'[24]

Whether this was at odds with Mao's vision of China is unclear, but the Chinese leaders were certainly unsettled by Khrushchev's stance towards de-Stalinization and a peaceful co-existence with the West. As the fifties unfolded there was a series of conflicts between the Communist Parties of China and the Soviet Union, particularly around Khrushchev's open criticism of key policies and initiatives. He disparaged the Hundred Flowers Movement, which was a programme designed in 1957 to give intellectuals an arena to submit different ideas opinions and suggestions, often contrary to China Communist Party philosophy. He also denounced the Great Leap Forward which aimed in 1958 to meet China's industrial and agricultural problems by the mass mobilization of the population into communes. These communes typically numbered around 20,000 people and were tasked with producing food and industrial goods to generate surpluses for use and benefit by the state.[25] Khrushchev's and Mao's differing views consequently evolved into open debates and conflicts of inter-party relations, and led to the deterioration of state relations and ultimately the end of the Sino-Soviet Alliance in 1960.[26]

Nonetheless the huge political, economic and cultural influence from Russia demonstrated the significance of a population's appearance. The Soviet Union developed a surprisingly sophisticated image of its population, during the mid-1950s, through fashion magazines, film and media. The popularity of Russian visual information therefore further illustrated the gap in style represented by individual socialist regimes.

The Chinese government was also keenly aware from their Soviet experiences that the outward global image of China as a newly formed political and cultural nation was significant in establishing itself as a serious and contemporary addition to the world's political and cultural community. In reality the Soviet Union had already been through the process of serious debate around clothing as representation, as appropriate for a newly formed modern nation and suitably desirable for happy and fulfilled citizens of a socialist country. As the discussion around style and appearance seems to have gathered momentum there seems to be a deliberate and considered shift in the mid-fifties to re-imagine how the population of China's urban population should also represent itself by encouraging more variety in the type of garments worn. It could be argued that taking a lead from what had developed in Moscow with the re-opening of GUM and other stores like it across major cities, the development of the Atelier and the Department of Design within GUM and other official fashion organizations such as the All Union House of Clothes Fashion Design (known as ODMO), the Chinese leaders decided to respond in a similar manner and effectively cultivate and develop a broader visual identity for its population. The population itself had already been raising concerns about how it looked and was perceived through forums that were reported in the media whilst the observations of outside visitors supported these concerns:[27] 'practically every foreign visitor who came to China whether for or against the regime, agreed on one point, the dress of the Chinese people was colourless and drab'.[28]

To that end in April 1955 the Ministry of Culture, through a forum of leading artists and journalists and in conjunction with the New Observer, launched the Dress Reform Campaign led by Yu Feng.[29] This set out to encourage the population to 'dress up nicely' (*daban piaoliang*) and to identify a range of styles that might be considered appropriate stylistically within the context of new China. Like the Soviets this was manifested through publication, the development and production of new fabrics including print and the creation of new styles, which were shown in exhibitions and fashion shows across urban China. *The People's Daily* consequently reported on Shanghai's and Beijing's upcoming events to both advertise the exhibitions and reflect the CCP's positive endorsement; 'Shanghai will hold a women and children's clothing exhibition in March. The clothing exhibits will be divided into sections for admiring and for practical use.' It also notes that some of the styles will be going to an exhibition in Beijing.[30]

> Fashion Exhibition opens today, there will be 535 pieces of clothing exhibited for men, women's and children and for Spring, Summer and Autumn seasons. There will also be a variety of new design of flower (printed) cotton fabric, silk and wool. Already 83,000 people have registered to visit the show.[31]

If the purpose of the Dress Reform Campaign and the fashion exhibitions was to enhance the appearance of the population and to challenge international perceptions of style under the Chinese Communist Party, then it could be argued that this was relatively successful. The international press certainly took note and a dedicated article entitled 'Shanghai Is Revived as a Fashion Capital' appeared in the *New York Times* on 11 May 1956, noting that: 'Shanghai, thwarted for some time as the supressed Paris of China, apparently is outdoing Peiping [Beijing] now that its tailors are being officially encouraged to relieve the grim sartorial picture on the mainland.' This flirtation with dress as cultural capital, whereby fashion shows were officially organized and publications that sat alongside the production of new styles were sanctioned by senior officials, does seem to have captured the imagination of the public and given them an appetite to engage with 'fashion' and clothing beyond pure functionality. *The People's Daily* noted that by the end of the Beijing exhibition some 290,000 persons had visited it.[32]

In reality economic conditions were unfavourable to support dress reform and the drive from the government for rapid industrialization meant that textile output was held down to the minimum necessary to clothe the population in a serviceable fashion.[33] Demand for grain and cotton, therefore, outstripped supply as early as 1953 and 1954, as poor harvests and increased urban populations forced the government to instigate grain rationing in 1953 and the rationing of cotton and cotton cloth in September 1954.[34]

Allocation of coupons for cotton cloth were issued yearly and could be used for goods such as readymade clothing, fabric, bedding and sometimes underwear and socks.[35] Individual allocations varied minimally dependent on region and urban or rural location but initial provisions were 12 to 16 Chi per person, 1 Chi being equivalent to 0.33 metres.[36] This significantly reduced by 1960 and 1961 as the failure of the Great Leap Forward due to well-documented mismanagement and drought meant individual allocations came down to as little as 1.6 to 3 Chi per person.[37] The practice of rationing cotton continued until 1983 and, as conditions and technologies improved during the 1970s, there was some lifting of allocations. In Shanghai queueing up for sugar reportedly began around the same time as the first issuing of cotton coupons and it is conceivable that, against this background and as a response to a failure to expand textile production, the propaganda of frugality became a common message even before the instigation of the Dress Reform Campaign and was probably the true driver of the diversification of styles. Articles from 1954 had already introduced the population to a more conservative approach to using fabric as well as advising and encouraging them to use a range of existing garments including *qipao* and skirts in relation to womenswear as a move away from the blue cloth uniforms habitually worn by all ages and genders.

Positive propaganda broadcasts through Beijing radio, announcing that Chinese women would be wearing brightly coloured flowered print frocks by the spring of 1956 and that 54,000 bales of printed calico had been turned out by Shanghai manufacturers, although illustrating an upturn in production, seem at odds with the broader realities of the times.[38] Hence as the Dress Reform Campaign petered out in late 1956 and early 1957, and as a prelude to the beginning of the Great Leap Forward in 1958, real concerns around supply and demand and usage of fabrics for clothing emerged.

Economy, Practicality and Looking Good

In October 1957, the Shanghai Cultural Department in conjunction with the Shanghai Government Group (Apparel) produced a pattern-making, clothing construction book showing practical examples of how to re-work and re-model existing garments. *New Clothes from Old Clothes* sets the true temper of the times in part of its introductory statement: 'Lessening resources and raw materials, significant volumes of historic pre-worn and waste garments and inefficient and ineffective ways to recycle garments and fabrics on a commercial scale.'[39]

Whether the Cultural Department was under pressure to work with textile companies to produce more fabrics as part of government targets or whether they took the lead in considering the re-appropriation of old garments is difficult to verify. The Shanghai Government Group (Apparel) had 'acquired' most of the fashion firms built pre-liberation in Shanghai, making it one of the largest state-owned garment enterprises in China, and significantly the formal introduction of the publication roots itself clearly in a contextual position relating to the broader issues of the period.[40]

It states:

> After 1949 our production of fabrics and silks increased considerably as did the quality of life and expectations of the people. Increased production of fabric however is not enough alone to meet the people's needs. We should therefore not just increase production to meet demand but look at how we can use and save fabric. One of the important and practical ways to increase fabric saving is to change old clothes into new clothes. It seems such a waste that there are so many large mountains of old clothes that are stored in cases and homes so if we could change old clothes into new clothes we could meaningfully save large amounts of goods (raw materials) for the country and also save spending on fabric.[41]

This certainly seems to contradict some of the values of the dress reform campaign as well as the remit of fashion shows in the spring of 1956. The book also recognized that there would be a differentiation in skill levels and that the makers/tailors would need an exact design and pattern to convert clothing accurately in terms of the correct fit and appropriate styling.

Within the introduction there is also a short description of two fashion events held in Shanghai in the spring and summer of 1957, both of which are noted as being very popular and introduced the public to how to change old clothes to new clothes and the best ways to save fabric. The book's authors also refer to the 1957 exhibitions as being pivotal in collating information which inspired and informed the final ninety designs included within the publication. They concluded that the individual pieces may not yet have been perfect in terms of technique due to the authors' own lack of experience in the development of re-working garments, but hope the public at large would find the publication of use in producing garments that supported the country's values and individuals' responsibilities.

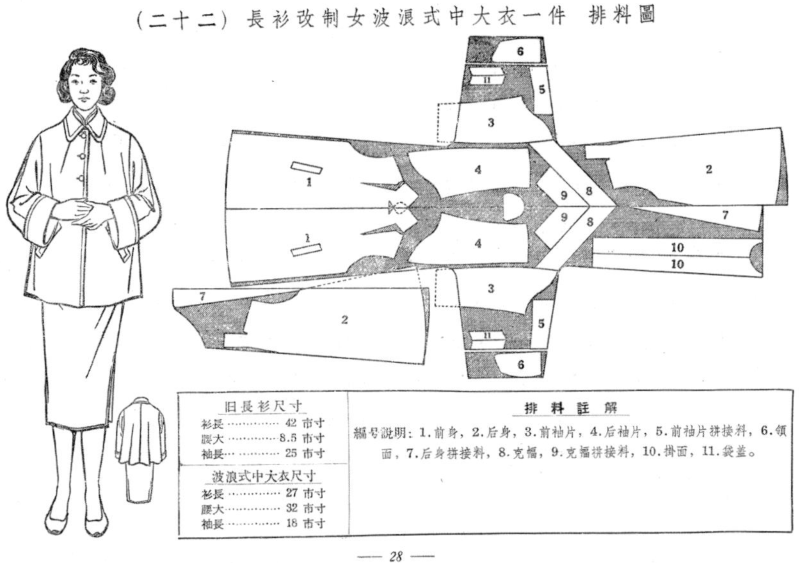

Figure 9.2 Women's coat pattern from traditional men's Changpao garment. *New Clothes from Old Clothes* published by the Shanghai Government Group (Apparel), *c.* 1957. Author's archive.

The pattern book seemed to be identifying styles that the public suggested it wanted to wear and reinforced the notion of frugality whilst contextualizing the broader political issues of sustaining a large population with its basic needs, clothing being one of them. It is probable that the 1957 Shanghai exhibitions were inspired by the popularity of the 1956 fashion shows and that this popularity inspired a format for communicating ideas and engaging the local population in a new debate around clothing which supported a sustainable future, both for the manufacturers and in line with government policy.

What is notable is the question as to whether this was purely a pragmatic exercise in using existing garments, due to a lack of basic resources, or a clear response to the fact that the government were subtly influencing and encouraging a more varied wardrobe from the mid-fifties. Skirts, for example, use less fabric than trousers, a *qipao* less than shirt and trousers. Whatever the reasoning the designs within the publication do hint at a cosmopolitan influence, all be it one tempered with Chinese characteristics.

Indeed the characters visualized illustratively throughout the publication depict urbanized educated women, which in turn suggests a powerful and deliberate message around the acceptance of 'style' within the accepted political paradigms. The men's styles such as the *Zhongshanzhuang*, remodelled from Western suits, is consistent with the period. However, the women's styles seem particularly at odds with perceptions of the period, including the *qipao*, two piece suits and even swing-back three-quarter-length coats, seemingly styled on Dior's new look, albeit within moderation.

As noted, the dress reform campaign had disappeared by this point, the Sino-Soviet alliance had started to dissolve, and one wonders whether there is a specific cultural attempt to re-affirm styles that confirm and contribute to a modernist Chinese vision. Certainly, for women, the Lenin suit had become less popular and was replaced by cadre clothes, the female version of the man's *Zhongshanzhuang* jacket with a turned-down collar and the two chest pockets removed to make it more suitable for women. The Bulaji dress was also less popular and the *qipao* appears to be more or less redundant.

A tailor from the Western District Clothing Co-operative from the period stated:

> From the early 1950s we had a lot of requests to remodel suits. Back then materials were expensive but labour was cheap, and it only cost a few Yuan to re-fashion a suit. We would advertise this with a sign reading Reconditioning of Western Suits (*fanxiu xifu*). Uniforms were recognised as the mark of state

employees, to wear one was to be progressive. If you wore a western style suit people thought, you were a capitalist.[42]

A second publication entitled *How to Use Less Fabric when Cutting Clothing*, produced in Shanghai in early 1958 by the same government office and group, reinforced the message further but this time rather than the re-modelling of old clothes to new, the book looked at the most efficient ways to develop a pattern and lay plan for optimum savings.[43] Just a few months on from the first publication, the message in the introduction of this publication is positioned with much more specificity:

> The three principles of the role of clothing is economy, practicality and looking good. All of the fabrics whether silk, cotton or suiting are all precious goods of the country and we should not waste them. Since we have developed the idea of managing the country in a saving way and not wasting anything, the problem of how to use the fabric wisely becomes an important consideration for everyone. It is an honour for anyone working with cloth to have the spirit of saving and to use all fabric wisely. In the design of clothes, we should try not to use unnecessary cut or stitch and try the best to use every piece of the fabric, by a pattern lay that reduces fabric usage and waste.[44]

The authors refer back to the previous fabric exhibitions held in Shanghai in April and October 1957 identifying that the most popular element of the exhibition with the public was the new designs which saved fabric through pattern and cut. It is a fair assumption that both books relate to the same exhibitions of 1957 and that this particular area of pattern and lay-plan development, as they note themselves, did not, at the time of the shows have enough designs developed in either quantity or quality to constitute the full development of a publication.

This required further development for the publication to be completed with a total of seventy-seven designs featured, identified as being for men, women and children and suitable for all seasons. Once again they stated the book was not perfect and that they were still working on new designs that fulfil the key principles noted originally. It is difficult to say whether this type of publication could be a solution to the problem of clothing as practical necessity or cultural compliance. Certainly, the agenda for frugality had been set both nationally and locally for a number of years. The Soviet influence through cultural relativism, expertise and knowledge exchange had ended and China's own strategic policies had become prominent societal drivers which in turn reflected stylistically on dress throughout the population. The view from external viewers remains somewhat disdainful, irrespective of the positive attempts to engage communities such as Shanghai with a discourse around sustaining resources. The British Consulate-General in Shanghai, for example, commented thus on the fashion events of 1957:

> A ladies' fashion show was opened on April 1. The dresses exhibited showed a sad falling away from the standard that at one time earned for Shanghai the title of the 'Paris of the Far East'. Still, they were certainly better than the sort of thing that is generally worn around the streets these days.[45]

In hindsight China was probably not fully prepared to exist independently post-1949. For a fledging government to oversee a vast and diverse country as it embarked on a philosophical doctrine and series of initiatives aimed to transform China economically in record time was inevitably going to prove problematic. One of the main initiatives, the development of communes to operationalize the Great Leap Forward of 1958 with its twin slogans of 'Politics in charge' and 'Walking on two legs' meant a shift of emphasis to a rural and agricultural system. As the decade ended Beijing released a design and pattern-making book that is in stark contrast to the ones produced two years previously in Shanghai. *Entitled New Design of Labour Clothes and Kids Wear Cutting Book* and produced by the Beijing Light Industry Apparel Institute, it is a celebration of the labourer, the farmer and the worker.[46] Embracing powerful visual imagery of contented people working for the good of the nation, it was beautifully illustrated (Figure 9.3), printed in colour, and whilst still ensuring that consideration of economy of resource was reinforced there was a positive and uplifting sense of a common identity. It is no coincidence, of course, that by early 1959, 700 million people had been placed into 26,578 communes and were struggling to meet production targets. The styles are utilitarian, stripped back even from the Shanghai designs, with no skirts or *qipao*, and with a huge number of the population working in communes the focus shifted to appropriate clothing for rural and working environments as opposed to purely urban environments. The cover itself was the antithesis of the relatively stylish, educated urbanite on the cover of *New Clothes from Old Clothes*, with any reference to styles appropriate to a contemporary landscape replaced by a seemingly contented farm girl and a lay plan identifying an efficient use of fabric.

Ironically and in an alternative socialist setting, over five nights in 1959 the GUM store in Red Square hosted a Christian Dior fashion show exhibiting Yves St Laurent's functional reimagining of the original Dior 'new' look.

Figure 9.3 Garment illustration from *New Design of Labour Clothes and Children's Wear Cutting Book*, published by the Beijing Light Industry Apparel Institute, *c.* 1959. Author's archive.

Shanghai in Context 1960

Without doubt by 1960 and after the Great Leap Forward conditions across China were incredibly harsh. A C.I.A. report in 1961 drew a number of conclusions:

> Although firm information is lacking, non-food crops also experienced a poor year in 1960. The important cotton crop is estimated to have been less than in

> 1959, temporarily halting growth in the textile industry and bringing on even stricter rationing of cotton cloth. And: the Chinese communist regime is now facing the most serious economic difficulties it has confronted since it consolidated its power over mainland China. As a result of mismanagement and especially of two years of unfavourable weather, food production in 1960 was little if any larger than in 1957 at which time there were about 50 million fewer Chinese to feed. The dislocation caused by the Leap Forward and the removal of Soviet technicians have disrupted China's industrial programme. If Soviet technicians in large numbers do not return, industrial production is likely to increase about 12% annually as compared with 33% in 1959 and 16% in 1960.[47]

As an American report, there may well have been some bias; however, it is a clear observation that agriculture had been given a higher priority with a dropping of the Great Leap Forward approach to industry in response to severe shortages in resources. This combined with the implementation of extensive rationing, including ration coupons for all textile products, even lengths of sewing thread, clothing, although essential, was not of significant importance on the social or political agenda in the early years of the 1960s. All across China garments were referred to as 'New for three years, old for three years, fix for another three years', and the propaganda of frugality became a common message. In turn the population had no other choice but to repair, re use and re-make not only from existing garments but through a resourceful and pragmatic approach to the system of rations and fabric availability.

Irrespective of how a government perceives a nation should represent itself to the outside world, there is a compelling argument to say that the population themselves made the final choices in what to wear during the first years of 'New China'. The semiotics of status, a sense of belonging and a visual affiliation to a political ideology are powerful narratives which the population embraced. Clothes were modified, personalized, made and re-made and there is some evidence from individual interviews and personal memoirs of the development of individuality in response to even the harshest of conditions. The invention of small tokens of decoration, the slight changing of details in cut and shape, although modest and barely noticeable to an outside viewer, convey a sense that even within a powerful regime there were nonetheless emotions and desirability attached to clothing and lifestyle accessories albeit on an extremely modest scale. Shanghai's history as a metropolis might have been disabled and eclipsed historically by the powerful notion of 'the state' but the metropolitan experience continued through the initial years of the newly founded republic.

From 1949 to 1978, with 1 per cent of the population in China, Shanghai contributed 16.7 per cent of the national fiscal income and 10 per cent of industrial output. By 1960, however, the city, like many others in China, was low on resources, suffering from a lack of investment and in an environment of overt, often positively framed propaganda. It is only through the population's individual recollections that the impact of the previously noted centralized policies and the resulting effect of limited resources on daily life can be graphically illustrated.

With this in mind a number of interviews of present Shanghai residents who could recall everyday life between 1960 and 1976 were undertaken to directly inform this section of the chapter. Accepting that the experience of wearing specific items of clothing is central to the formation of an understanding of the self within both the wider world and the local community, these oral testimonies and memories enable an appreciation of the nuance of garments and individual environments outside of the traditional fashion related historical methodologies.[48] They also illustrate individual and contextual responses to the issues surrounding clothing and lifestyle whilst evoking social experiences and a privileged glimpse into the 'ordinariness' of the day. The emphasis on first-hand experiences, particularly in relation to emotive objects such as clothing, can be problematic due to the accuracy of memories; they do, however, reflect the way lives are remembered and made meaningful. In this particular situation, during a period of extreme propaganda and fluctuating political agendas, individual oral narratives supply a powerful reflection of daily routines and encounters. The Shanghai residents who recount their narratives offered similar but nuanced experiences that articulate a personalized representation of the time.

Jie Li's detailed account of family life in Shanghai over a number of decades during this period barely touches on her family's relationship with clothing, but she does recognize that a generation of women her grandmother's age 'imprinted their needlework on every piece of fabric worn by their families, as most people wore handmade clothes and shoes from the 1950s to the late 1970s, often treating them with greater care than their own bodies'.[49]

The following interviews, therefore, present a description of the period, the context of the conditions, the relationship and importance of clothing across differing ages and maturities and the pragmatism employed to ensure individual and family needs were met as lack of resources meant the continued rationing of cloth and thread.

Haircuts, School and a Three-Pocket Jacket

Yuming Lu, born in 1947, was not uncommonly from a large group of siblings, of which he was the eldest of six brothers.[50] Residing in Tilanqiao Street in the Hongque district of Shanghai he recalls attending school during the early 1960s with a powerful memory of what he referred to as 'The Great Disaster'.

> In my school lunch hour we went home from school and all the family had to eat was rice with a lot of water. There was so much water that we wanted to go to the toilet very soon so all the kids tried desperately to hold it in as long as possible so that they would not feel hungry at school in the afternoon.
>
> None of my school friends wore clothes without patches we all had one outfit which we wore every day. Even our school bags were covered in patched fixings but in primary school in the late fifties my friend had a leather school bag. It was an old bag maybe from his father or grandfather but I remember it very clearly, it was like looking at gold and all of my classmates were really jealous of that leather bag.
>
> When I was in senior school I managed to get a bicycle, and travelled 2km to school every day. This daily journey on my bicycle was very special to me, it was like I was flying a plane, I felt speed and independence and I could see that people looked at me, admiringly, and that were very jealous of my bicycle as there were just not many bicycles around at the time.[51]

As a schoolboy, it is clear that he placed little importance on clothing, as food was the highest issue on his agenda, something he kept reiterating throughout the discussions. He was convinced that the reason why there was nothing to buy in Shanghai was directly as a result of the split with the USSR which he felt impacted significantly on the supply of even basic produce and materials. Intriguingly, human emotions such as jealousy and admiration seemingly continue to have a place even within an egalitarian society. He, like all the residents interviewed, commented on the aspiration to own 'three rounds and sound' (*Sansheng yixiang*), a wristwatch, bicycle, sewing machine and radio, symbols of modernization and to a certain extent success.[52]

He describes going to the local barber shops to get his hair cut. There was one style for men and boys, irrespective of age, and one price, 8 Fen, which equates to around 8 pence in the UK or 11 cents in the US. He does, however, remember just before the Cultural Revolution some fashionable young men in Shanghai had a quiff-style haircut rather than the tidy short style of the majority but they were considered 'bad people', basically hanging around on street corners, maybe cheating people and with no education. He recalls these types of characters quickly disappeared as the political climate changed during the Cultural Revolution. For women's clothing and styling at the time he was very specific, noting that he could not recall young girls wearing bright prints and that this was, in his view, pure party propaganda. In terms of styling he recalled that no women wore any make-up, as this represented capitalism, and no women curled their hair as, if they did, they were considered to be prostitutes.

After attending a good secondary school, at the age of sixteen he faced three choices: he could go to work, or go on to high school, or go to a training school. At the time, only the best students went to a training school and he managed to get a place at a school that supported the training of engineers, which was his dream. Disappointingly he did not achieve his dream and in 1968 started work in a factory, making electrical adapters and valves. As a worker, however, he had significant kudos and would stay in Shanghai rather than being sent to the countryside.

> When I started my first job my Aunty was a skilled seamstress and she made me a new outfit which was a three-pocket jacket called a *qingnianzhuang* (youth jacket). This was made of an open weave cotton called Labour Fabric (*laodong*) and people felt this was a slightly younger looking version than other styles.[53] I was issued with a worker's outfit of blue overalls but I was only allowed to wear them at work and not for daily life. It was so rare to get new clothes that I was very precious of the clothes I had and looked after them very well. Since the workers' overalls was never cleaned I protected my own clothes by changing at work and managed to keep a shirt in reasonably good condition for 5 years.[54]

His opinion about clothes is consistently pragmatic throughout the period with limited demand for style, just a requirement for warmth. He maintains that most clothes were handmade with many people making copy uniforms and adding cachet to the clothing by acquiring original military buttons to use on them.

When asked about the decisions around clothing and whether there were pressures to conform stylistically he pointedly stated that everyone (male) wanted to be the same as everybody else – they did not want to stand out or be different from other people.

So, for him personally he did not really care what he looked like as long as he looked as similar as possible to everybody else and that way he would get no trouble.

Escalators, Knitting and a Sense of Community

Another resident, Shuzhen Zhang, born in Shanghai in 1954, the eldest girl and the second eldest of seven siblings of five boys and two girls, lived on Henan Middle Road *linong* 3. The *linong* were neighbourhoods of lanes populated by housing in differing styles that had developed from the mid-nineteenth century. This particular *linong* is located in the centre of Shanghai close to Nanjing Road and members of Mrs Wang's family still live there. She has strong recollections of Nanjing Road which was and still is the busiest commercial high street in Shanghai.

> There were large department stores in Nanjing Road that had been there for many years including the Yongan Department Store and the Shanghai No. 1 Department Store. All the stores had the same products and all were the same price, in general there were limited items. I remember when I was young going into the Shanghai No. 1 Department store not to buy anything but just to ride the escalator for fun.[55]
>
> It was like being in a spaceship to us, like a playground ride. There were also famous fabric stores in Nanjing Road, one was called Baodaxiang and the other Xiedaxing.
>
> There you could get common fabrics and very rarely more higher quality (fancy) fabrics. There was also some slightly better quality fabrics where the officials would go to get garments made that were more formal. Of course all the fabrics were purchased using your individual coupon allowance.[56]

A poster created by Chen Fei in July 1955 (see Plate 6) of the ground floor of the Shanghai No. 1 Department Store clearly shows the escalator located in a central position within the ground floor. It is a powerful view of consumers engaging with purchasing. Western styles are still prevalent as are the people's dress and Bulaji garments which co-exist in a warm and vibrant environment of colour and community. This may well have been representative, notwithstanding the exaggeration of the early years of the new republic in Shanghai, when production was up, but some years later the oral narratives of the residents clearly define a much more understated and less visually flamboyant environment. It was populated only by local customers, with limited goods, all of which were sold in similar retail outlets and priced the same with insufficient ration coupons to support needs.

Shuzhen Zhang says:

> For fabric, you could get 4.5 feet per person per year, this fabric was for clothes, curtains, bedding, sheets, pillows everything. In reality no family had enough

> fabric so all the neighbours worked together and shared the coupons. One year the families would pull together so that one family could get enough fabric for winter coats. The next year coupons would be shared so a family could get bedding and curtains and so on and so on. We knew resources were limited and we were all in the same situation with the same incomes so local sharing and responding to families who needed added to our sense of comradeship and community.

As in common with other interviewees she recalls that the majority of clothes throughout this period were handmade and this included shoes, underwear and socks. Within the *linong* community she remembers there were workers/tailors who could not find jobs who would make small amounts of money making garments for residents within the community. There were also hairdressers and local embroiderers who sometimes took on factory work helping to complete orders for pillow cases and table cloths. She talked fondly about knitting:

> People knitted for themselves a lot it was popular amongst the communities and we learnt from each other. Some people were more inventive than others and they shared and inspired us with different techniques. I would unpick the yarn from old jumpers and then mix this with the cotton thread that we used for stitching shoes together to remake a new double yarn to knit with. I would also construct yarn from old fabrics by tearing them into fine strips then twist them together to make new yarns for knitting.[57]

The image of her wearing a knitted top (Figure 9.4) made this way was taken in 1974 and is a picture of her on her first day at work. Not only had she knitted the jumper, but she had also made the shirt, obtaining some small lace from the community embroidery workers, which she then added to the edge of the shirt collar. She has strong recollections of her manager (*lingdao*) telling her to remove the lace as it was far too fancy and not revolutionary enough. As a young woman starting at work this minor modification of clothing and personalization is put into perspective by the works manager, who would have been the local official representative ensuring adherence to centralized codes of practice.

Zhang recalls it being extremely rare for anyone to buy new clothes and she recollects with fondness being given a new bright red, Western-style coat for her tenth birthday by her aunty. This would have been in 1964 just at the point when there was a brief respite from severe hardship. From 1962, when production increased and the party leaders took a more pragmatic and somewhat commercial approach to the overarching communist philosophies, rationing was relaxed and urban areas such as Shanghai started producing and trading in greater volumes adding to the choices available in fabrics and products.[58]

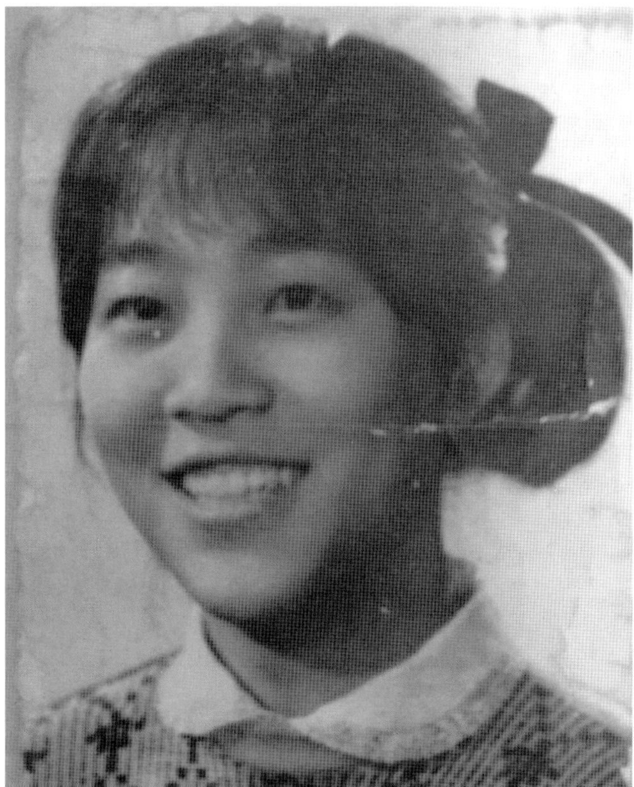

Figure 9.4 Image of Shuzhen Zhang on her first day at work, *c.* 1974. Courtesy Shuzhen Wang.

The Story of the Shoe

All of the Shanghai residents interviewed commented on the making, buying, wearing and owning of shoes. Leather shoes were really rare; families could only buy one pair of shoes a year through the coupon ration system. They all described the most popular leather shoe of the time which was called the 765 shoe.[59] This was due to its price which was 7.65 RMB: no matter whether it was women's or men's shoes the price was the same. This was a cheaper version of the 18 RMB ox/cow-leather shoe; it was the same style but made of pig leather. The 765 was more popular and resilient because it had a rubber sole as opposed to leather, making it cheaper and more hard wearing. Normally the majority of people made shoes themselves: they could buy the soles, the fabric and the thread, and stitch up the shoes themselves.

Another resident, Meijuan Wang, recalls going to a shop next to Zhongshan Park in Shanghai where you could buy paper patterns for shoes. Whilst, Shuzhen Zhang recalls, the patterns for shoes were lent and drawn around. There was a shoemaker who carried their tools around the street. You could stop him and ask him to make complete shoes, or to sole the ones you had made yourself with rubber. His technique was more professional than the homemade shoes, with expertise in hiding the stitching inside and under the shoe as opposed to externally visible stitching. He also carried a range of shoe lasts for different foot-size fittings as well as slight stylistic variations, a strap across for women's shoes and some elastic to pull in the top and front. Again, there were minor variations which allowed for a selection process to take place and the option, however minimal, to take individual ownership. Hence shoes seem to have taken on a key role and a sense of importance within the fashion systems of the time.

Shuzhen Zhang recalls going on a day trip with her family:

> My father took all of us children to the park for a day. He had worked out how much the bus prices were and how far the family could travel by bus and how far we then had to walk to get to the park. My brothers and sisters cared very much about our shoes so we took them off and walked barefoot until we got to the park to protect them.

She has strong recollections throughout this period that every piece of clothing had to last as long as possible. For the younger children, the clothes were passed down, then added to, either lengthened through the sleeve and the hem. If any new clothes were made they already had longer hems built into the structure of the garments in order to prolong usage. In line with other interviewees she doesn't remember seeing any children without patches on their clothes or hem extensions in different fabrics. She doesn't recall ever wearing her own brand new garments until she bought some for her first day at work, and vividly recalls knitting and fixing socks continually as part of her ensemble.

She also has no recollection of anyone wearing make-up. Many young girls had plaited hair and elder women had short hair bobbed either with a fringe or not. During the Chinese New Year celebrations, as a minor concession young girls and students were allowed to make a red bow out of plastic string as decoration for the New Year on the end of their plaits, but this was allowed only for young girls and not adults. Shuzhen Zhang describes a second-hand outdoor market in Nanjing Lu. She recalls her two brothers going there to buy some better-quality shoes. Like many young men of the time they were sent to the countryside to work, not knowing when they would be returning to Shanghai.[60]

> We went to the outdoor second-hand market in Nanjing Road to get some shoes for my brothers. Unlike the stores there was no quotas and you could buy a much broader range of products. My brothers bought a pair of ex-military plimsolls. I remember they were 8 Mao a pair, less than 1RMB.

Meijuan Wang was once again from a large family: one of six sisters and brothers, she was the third in line. This is consistent with the population growth and political encouragement to do so, which in turn imposed further demands on a range of issues around resourcing. She was born in 1954 and lived on Changning Street in the 396 *linong* within the Changning District of Shanghai. Her narrative around clothing is somewhat nuanced as she recalls the family having their clothes both made and bought from shops. She remembers the children all getting new clothes every year on the Chinese New Year and how excited they were at this prospect. This seemed to be at odds with other versions of the accounts of children's clothing acquisitioning and she elaborated on how the siblings all received new clothes every year.[61]

> My mother worked in a shoe factory in Shanghai before the revolution (1949). She moved from the countryside to the city becoming a factory worker. Not long after she secured work my father went to join her in Shanghai also taking on a role in a factory. After 1949 they continued working in the factory and gained greater status as workers which meant they both had salaries allowing them to buy new clothes for us every year.[62] Most of the clothes we had through the early 1960s were made by tailors. My mother would buy fabrics then the tailors would stay in our house for a few days and make clothes for us all. This sounds like it would be expensive but it was not as we offered the tailors food and a place to live for a short time. Also, we never used our fabric allowance for curtains, only for clothes.

Significant garments are clearly retained in early memories, not only as desirable objects but also as powerful visual statements. Wang recalls a particular pink top made of corduroy, which was in a Western style, that she wore at nursery for spring and autumn. She also distinctly remembers, as a nine-year-old in 1963, queuing with her mother to buy her very first pair of nylon socks at a store in Caojiadu Road, which was another local high street with smaller shops than Nanjing Road. These socks were a new innovation as they had stretch as opposed to a fixed cotton non-stretch fabric.

When she was seventeen she got her first job in a factory making parts for textile machines. She wore dungarees which were provided but had to wear her own shirt. She received an apprentice wage of 17.83 RMB per month for the first year, then in the second year the salary increased to 19.83 RMB per month and finally after three years she was on a full salary of 36 RMB per month, which she remembers having for at least the next four years. She notes this salary was not unusual as most of the 'working classes', including office workers, doctors and accountants, received the same salary with only extraordinary workers getting 41 or 43 RMB per month.

> Your first day at work was always an event and you planned what to do with your first salary. In 1971 when I first started work I still needed coupons but I remember buying a pair of ox leather shoes and some fabric for my mother to make a short sleeve shirt. This was very important to me as it was the first gift I had ever given to her.

She recalls buying fabric from the fabric store, where the tailors would work out how much fabric you needed for your size. They would then cut the pattern out for you and you would take it away and sew it yourself, which made the process more economical. She still has some fabric cut but not made into garments.

The Narratives in Context

Shanghai's character changed from a cosmopolitan consumer based city of the 1930s to a socialist producer city defined by a centralized devised economy in the 1950s. Its population had no choice but to respond to the external and internal factors that came to define the second and third decade of the People's Republic of China, with the 1960s represented by, first, severe economic hardship and, second, by violent upheaval in the form of the Cultural Revolution.[63] The 1970s saw the revolution normalized and routine processes involving political study, demonstrations of revolutionary faith and vigilance against counter-revolutionary influence combined with the relative ordinariness of work and school.[64] The oral narratives of the residents identify similar approaches to the environments that they lived in, as well as subtle changes in the making and acquisition of clothing. There is a consistent sense of excitement, as often occurs with young children when they are given gifts that are representative of a special occasion. The natural human instincts of minor jealousies and of the emotions of personal possessions and aspirations still occur as the population moves into the teenage years and a sense of the pragmatic with minor individual nuances prevails with the interviewees as they prepare or begin to engage with work. Ultimately this complex and commodity-poor economic period in Shanghai illustrated through these selected memoirs will be recognized by many who lived through the period. However, it might be an opportunity to further bring into question the perceived dreariness of the clothing of the time and the generalizations of commentators whose initial view is of a homogeneous sartorial landscape.[65]

What becomes apparent through conversation with the Shanghai residents who lived through this period is that they managed to successfully procure and adapt clothing for themselves and their families in a difficult economic and political environment. They also maintained a response to the expectations of visual codes and, by modification and personalization, individuality, no matter how discreet, managed to find its role even in the harshest of conditions.

Meijuan Wang, reflecting on her and her peers' relationship to clothing in the early 1970s, illustrates this beautifully:

> Us young girls would learn how to make things so we could make minor alterations to customize the clothes. Maybe just a little lower on the neckline or the collar a little longer or shorter, but of course within acceptable parameters. We would wear coloured shirts in summer, normally one colour, light blue or pale pink. Occasionally flowered pattern shirts but only with very small and discreet flower patterning.
>
> There was a definite line not to cross, but this was not prescribed or written down anywhere, but we all knew what it was.

Notes

1 Leo Ou-fan Lee, *Shanghai Modern: The Flowering of a New Urban Culture in China, 1930–1945* (Cambridge, MA: Harvard University Press, 1999), 331–2. The full quote is: 'Shanghai changed from 1949 to 1979 as a vision from a beautiful young lady into a middle-aged, coarse woman.'

2 Kerrie MacPherson, 'Shanghai History: Back to the Future', *Harvard Asia Pacific Review* (Harvard University, Department of East Asian Languages and Civilizations, 2002), 39.

3 Jishun Zhang, 'Shanghai around 1949: Continuity or Rupture?', *Journal of Modern Chinese History* 10, no. 1 (2016): 100–5.

4 Ibid.

5 Jishun Zhang, 'Cultural Consumption and Popular Reception of the West in Shanghai 1950–1966', *The Chinese Historical Review* 12, 1 (2005): 122.

6 Jie Li, *Shanghai Homes: Palimpsests of Private Life* (New York: Columbia University Press, 2015). Jie Li discusses at length the local changes in the residents of the *linongs* as part of a community in new collective spaces.

7 Mao Zedong, 'On the People's Democratic Dictatorship', 30 June 1949, *Mao Zedong xuanji* (Selected Works on Mao Zedong) (Beijing: The People's Press, 1965), 1477.
8 *The Treaty of Friendship, Alliance and Mutual Assistance between the Peoples Republic of China and the Soviet Union, February 1950* (C.I.A. Report and translation, approved for release 30/08/2000).
9 Xu Jianguo, *Shanghai Industries* (Boston: Cengage, 2008), 3–6.
10 Chen Jian, 'The Sino-Soviet Alliance and Chinas Entry into the Korean War' (Working Paper No. 1, Cold War International History Project, Washington, 1992).
11 Liao Jun, Xu Xing. *100 Years of Chinese Costume* (Shanghai: Shanghai Cultural Publications, 2009), 80.
12 Verity Wilson, 'Dress and the Cultural Revolution' in V. Steele and J.S. Major, *China Chic: East Meets West* (Ithaca, NY: Yale University Press, 1999), 172, 178.
13 Stefan Landsberger, *The Rise and Fall of the Chinese Propaganda Poster* (Chinese Propaganda Posters, Taschen, 2003), 19.
14 A.C. Scott, *Chinese Costume in Transition* (Singapore: Donald Moore, 1958), 92.
15 Noel Barber, *The Fall of Shanghai* (London: Macmillan, 1979), 223.
16 Antonia Finnane, *Changing Clothes in China* (London: Hurst, 2007), 151. Cheng Fangwu, in an article on Shanghai fashion in 1926, commented: 'Even in Hunan province slender young women were sweeping up and down the streets wearing *qipao*, a style that had spread more quickly than any intellectual trend.'
17 Mark Gamsa, 'The Cultural and the Social in Chinese–Russian Relations', *Cultural and Social History* 9, no. 3 (2012): 398.
18 Yan Li, *In Search of a Socialist Modernity: the Chinese Introduction of Soviet Culture* (Boston: Northeastern University, 2012), 148. The image of Russian heroine Zoya Kosmodemyanskaya, an eighteen-year-old martyr whose story was recorded in books and made into the 1944 film *Zoya*, in a flowery bulaji made the dress a symbol of revolution and political progressiveness in China.
19 Xiaoming Zhang, 'China, the Soviet Union, and the Korean War: From an Abortive Air War Plan to a Wartime Relationship', *The Journal of Conflict Studies*, 22, 1 (August 2002), https://journals.lib.unb.ca/index.php/JCS/article/view/368/582.
20 Olga Vainshtein, 'Mapping Moscow Fashion: Spaces and Spectacles of Consumption', in Christopher Breward and David Gilbert (eds), *Fashion's World Cities* (Oxford: Berg, 2006), 145.
21 Natalya Lomykina, 'Mysteries of GUM: Stalin's Tears, Secret Chanel Suits and Gagarin's Pass', *RBK Daily*, 1 August 2015.
22 V.J. Gronow and S. Zhuravlev, *Fashion Meets Socialism*: Fashion industry in the Soviet Union after the Second World *War* (Helsinki: Suomen Kirjallisuuden Seura, 2015), 135.
23 Ibid., 141.
24 Lynne Atwood, *Creating the New Soviet Woman: Woman's Magazines as Engineers of Female Identity 1922–1953* (Basingstoke: Macmillan, 1999), 164.

25 Geoff Stewart, *China 1900–1976* (Harlow: Heinemann, 2006), 114–18.

26 Shen Zhihua, *The Great Leap Forward, The People's Communes and the Rupture of the Sino-Soviet Alliance* (Parallel History Project on NATO the Warsaw Pact and the Cold War History of Sino-Soviet Relations), June 2005.

27 'New Democracy Youth League Central Committee and All-China Women's Federation Hold a Forum: Discussing Some Questions on Improving Clothing Styles and Colours', *People's Daily*, 2 February 1956.

28 A.C. Scott, *Chinese Costume in Transition* (Singapore: Donald Moore, 1958), 97.

29 Finnane, *Changing Clothes in China*, 210–23.

30 'Shanghai shi jiang zaisan yue jian ju xing yi ge fu nv er tong fu Zhuang zhan lan hui' (Shanghai will hold a women's and children's exhibition in March), *People's Daily*, 25 February 1956.

31 'Fu Zhuang zhan lan hui jin tian kai mu' (The Clothing Exhibition Opens Today), *People's Daily*, 31 March 1956.

32 'Shou du fu zhuang zhao lan hui bi mu' (The clothing exhibition closes today), *People's Daily*, 21 May 1956. By the end of the 'clothing exhibition' on 20 May 1956, around 290,000 persons had attended it, while the China Cotton, Yarn and Cloth Company reported that it had sold around 54,000 metres of clothing material.

33 C.I.A Intelligence Document, *Communist China: Threadbare Outlook for Cotton Textiles* (C.I.A. report no. 46, 1971).

34 Ralph Huenemann, 'Urban Rationing in China', *The China Quarterly* 26 (April–June 1966), 47–9.

35 Ibid.

36 Nai-Ruenn Chen and Walter Galenson, *The Chinese Economy under Maoism: The Early Years 1949–69* (London: Routledge, 2011), 181–3.

37 Ibid.

38 A.C. Scott, *Chinese Costume in Transition* (Singapore: Donald Moore, 1958), 100.

39 *New Clothes from Old Clothes* (Shanghai Cultural Department & the Shanghai Apparel Company, 1 October 1957). Translation of overarching introductory statement.

40 Christine Tsui, *China Fashion: Conversations with Designers* (Oxford: Berg, 2009), 18.

41 *New Clothes from Old Clothes.*

42 Claire Roberts, *Evolution & Revolution: Chinese Dress 1700s–1990* (New York: powerHouse, 1998), 46.

43 Lay plan is the term used in fashion for placing patterns on fabric to cut the most efficiently and cost effective way. Contemporary factories who manufacture a large number of garments often use digital CAD/CAM systems to provide accurate lays.

44 *How to Use Less Fabric when Cutting Clothing* (Shanghai Cultural Department & the Shanghai Apparel Group, 1 February 1958). Translation of the introductory statement.

45 British Consulate-General, Shanghai, 'Shanghai Political Summary', 23 March–5 April, No. 5/56, 13/04/1956, in Robert L. Jarman (ed.), *China Political Reports, 1911–1960*, vols I–XI (Cambridge: Archive Editions, 2001), 224.

46 *New Design of Labour Clothes and Kids Wear Cutting Book* (Beijing Light Industry Apparel Institute, 1 June 1959).

47 Central Intelligence Agency (C.I.A.), The Economic Situation in Communist China, Special National Intelligence Estimate 13-61 (SNIE 13-61, 04/04/1961 released June 2004), 1.3.

48 Jo Turney, *Textiles and Texts: Re-establishing the Links between Archival and Object Based Research* (London: Archetype Publications, 2005), 58–60.

49 Jie Li, *Shanghai Homes, Palimpsests of Private Life* (New York: Columbia University Press, 2015), 140.

50 United Nations, Department of Social and Economic Affairs, Population Division: *World Population Prospects, the 2010 Revision New York 2011* (www.unpopulation.org). China's women on average had more than six children in the early 1950s. The total fertility rate (TFR) briefly dropped in the late 1950s and early 1960s as China went through the disaster of the Great Leap Forward, one of the largest man-made famines in recorded history.

51 J. Yifu Lin and D. Tao Yang, 'On the Causes of China's Agricultural Crisis and the Great Leap Famine', *China Economic Review* 9, no. 2 (1998): 125–40.

52 J. Inch, *China's Economic Supertrends* (Victoria, BC: InChina, 2012), 47.

53 *Apparel Cutting Handbook* (Beijing: Beijing Apparel, Shoes and Hats Industry Group, 1971), 27.

54 Extracts from the author's interviews with Yuming Lu, July–September 2017.

55 Porter Erisman, *The Six Billion Shoppers: The Companies Winning the Global E-Commerce Boom* (New York: St. Martin's Press, 2017), 33.

56 Author's interview with Mrs Shuzhen Zhang, translated and edited from three separate interviews, 5 August–30 September 2017.

57 Ibid.

58 Anton Cheremukhin, Mikhail Golosov, Sergei Guriev and Aleh Tsyvinski, *The Economy of People's Republic of China from 1953* (New Haven, CT: Yale University Press, 2015), 22, 23, 32. The period of 1962–6 was a time of recovery from the disaster of the Great Leap Forward. In 1962, the government backtracked by reducing the size of communes to 'production teams' of about 20–30 households per team and 20 million workers were sent back from cities to the countryside.

59 Wang Zhiqi, 'Have You Ever Owned a Pair of 765 Leather Shoes?' (Shangguan, *Shanghai Observer*, 2017).

60 Thomas P. Bernstein, *Up to the Mountains and Down to the Villages: The Transfer of Youth from Urban to Rural China* (New Haven, CT: Yale University Press, 1978). The brothers would have been sent from Shanghai as part of this government policy

which began in a limited manner during the Great Leap Forward but accelerated during the Cultural Revolution from 1966.

61 Author interviews with Meijuan Wang, September–October 2017.

62 Satya J. Gabriel, 'The Structure of a Post-Revolutionary Economic Transformation: The Chinese Economy from the 1949 Revolution to the Great Leap Forward', China Essay Series, 1998. State-owned and privately owned capitalist firms operated together within the Chinese industrial sector. The workers continued to work as wage labour employees of these firms often with matched pre-1949 salaries.

63 Nien Cheng, *Life and Death in Shanghai* (London: Grafton, 1987), 64–84.

64 Finnane, *Changing Clothes in China,* 244.

65 Tina Mai Chen, 'Dressing for the Party: Clothing, Citizenship, and Gender-formation in Mao's China', *Fashion Theory: The Journal of Dress, Body & Culture* 5, 2001: 143–71.

10

The Shanghai Dandy

Men in the City

Christopher Breward

In reviewing the fortunes of Hong Kong based luxury brand Shanghai Tang in the spring of 2014, the *China Economic Review* confronted its new chief executive officer (CEO), Raphael le Maine De Chermont, with the fundamental tensions between invented and real traditions, modernity and consumer aspirations that lay at the heart of his brand's identity, and the contemporary construction of fashionable masculinities, in China generally and Shanghai in particular. De Chermont acknowledged that

> luxury fashion is about gaining acceptance; what you wear and how you wear it is a projection of who you are as a person and how you want to be seen ... Getting a professional office worker in Shanghai to sport a mandarin collar instead of a necktie is no easy task – no matter how premium the product on offer.[1]

He went on to assert that the romantic version of orientalism that the company had been promoting internationally since the mid-1990s held little appeal to local markets, noting that: 'as it bids for the attention of wealthy consumers who disdain dragons on their jackets, the brand is remaking its image with a far lighter Chinese touch, [but] the change in ideology is not without its challenges'.[2] Indeed, the CEO carried the challenge right through into his own dress style. As the interviewer explained: 'the mandarin collar is low, unfolded and can be buttoned to fit snugly around the neck, conjuring the image of a Qing dynasty scholar. For less conspicuous wear, it can be unfastened into a V neck.'[3] It was in the latter, more market-friendly fashion that De Chermont chose to appear.

For the past five years I have visited Shanghai every spring and autumn, engaging in teaching and research activities in the fast-moving context of one of its most dynamic art and design schools. My colleagues at the Shanghai College of Fashion, Donghua University (formerly the China Textile University), have provided me with privileged access both to the city's proactive fashion industry and to the energizing cultural ecology of the metropolis. I like to think I am an experienced historian of masculinities, urbanism and menswear in Europe and North America, but am acutely aware of my novice status in terms of the exploration of parallel sartorial histories in China. Yet even after a relatively short immersion in Shanghai's distinctively layered fashion cultures, I can see that the nuanced negotiation of past and future, 'East' and 'West', which Shanghai-Tang faces is a challenge fundamental to any proper understanding of masculinity and fashion in China's premier style city. The presence or not of adapted mandarin collars is only a surface symptom of more complex histories. It is this challenge that this chapter will attempt to address through a reading of the codes of clothing on men's bodies and in men's literatures in Shanghai through the last century and a half.

In setting out to describe the material and representational expression of what we might call 'Shanghai Dandyism', the fashion writer is both blessed and frustrated by his primary sources. On the streets of contemporary Shanghai evidence of an enthusiastic local engagement with all forms of fashion knowledge is easy to come by. High-end international menswear brands are profusely represented in the many luxury malls that pepper Shanghai's central zone; and tourist-focused though they may be, the traditional tailors and shirt-makers of the garment district's markets appear to enjoy a healthy trade in made-to-measure suits and accessories. At the corner of many streets magazine kiosks purvey a wide range of glossy periodicals serving the lifestyle interests of young men that easily outstrip in quantity the variety available in London or New York. On local and national Chinese television the well-groomed male celebrity is ubiquitous and his cinematic counterpart is similarly ever-present on advertising hoardings and in online promotions. And the male population itself (or at least the affluent portion of it) disports in the cafes, bars, shops and parks, on public transport and in the glimpsed interior spaces of offices and homes in well-cut suits or modish sportswear.

In many ways Shanghai's sartorial landscape appears as fecund for analysis as any other world city's, but its generic qualities, described above, also betray a certain studied 'reticence' that provokes further interpretation. On the surface, an engagement with the 'everyday practice' of clothing the body in fashionable, globally influenced dress appears to be a normalized habit, but I suspect that underneath such quotidian expression more complex historical, economic, political and sociological forces are at play.

This can also be seen in those absences that mark the more spectacular constructions of design discourse that drive innovation in Shanghai's fashion industry. At succeeding Shanghai Fashion Week shows, for example, it is notable that menswear collections are rare. Similarly the concept of Men's Fashion Weeks, familiar in Milan or London, is an alien one. And while the promotion of high-fashion Chinese-designed brands for women has become a familiar journalistic and curatorial conceit in recent years, discussion of 'Made for China' menswear lines is muted. In some aspects, then, the discourse of Chinese dandyism is a silent or 'invisible' one that requires further investigation (though as I will go on to describe, its iteration in Shanghai is a little more sharply defined than in some other Chinese cities).

Between Wen and Wu: Locating Fashionable Masculinities

Arguably this apparent lack of direct or overt engagement with the question of masculine appearances by local actors (and the inability of scholars trained in Western cultural paradigms to fully understand them) has theoretical and historiographical roots, as does the solution for addressing any perceived 'lack' of proactive analysis. Thomas Lacquer in his Foreword to Susan Brownell and Jeffery Wasserstrom's edited collection of essays on Chinese gender formations, lays out the binary and shared historical approaches to understanding materialist expressions of gender in the West and China that have fostered such appropriations and disconnects, and made them seem natural:

> For better or for worse the development of [Western] capitalism – and with it economic and military advances – seemed linked to individualism and liberty in all realms, including that of gender: freedom from the extended family was a key element of freedom more generally, as was the ability . . . to dress, wear one's hair, or make up one's face as one pleased. The private, again and again, was rendered public and political even as its distinctiveness was maintained. Beginning in the middle of the nineteenth-century, Chinese political reformers . . . took these intellectual imports on board. Thus the Chinese past, present and future came to be articulated through what was taken to be a sort of universal history of gender. The prostitution or seclusion of women, a life of leisured, refined literary learning for men: all came to have different meanings – and called for new political responses – when regarded by Chinese thinkers through the lens of Western historicism.[4]

As I have argued elsewhere, there is no garment more adapted to expressing some of these socio-political complexities than the tailored suit, and as the particular case of Shanghai reveals, its communicative power as a marker of cultural change was, and continues to be, prevalent here as well.[5] In tracing such a history I echo Laquer's assertion 'that no political or economic or social history is possible without a cultural history: a history of the meanings of things, actions, events, movements, gestures, clothes and accomplishments [and] there can be no cultural history without a history of gender'. And as Laquer continues,

> these claims are internal to the history of China: twentieth-century male bandits and rebel workers recapitulate older, elite tensions between the ideal of the warrior male and the ideal of the man of cultivation and learning . . . thus the nature and organization of Shanghai politics are in some immediate sense comprehensible only in a specific historicist context of traditions of masculinity.[6]

Laquer's observations clearly carry implications for a better understanding of contemporary sartorial practices as well, particularly in the predictive context that Brownell and Wasserstrom sketched out in their Afterword to the same volume. Writing in 2002 they observed that 'as China enters the twenty-first century, one narrative has just begun to unfold: the story of the market reforms and the growth of consumerism'. Alongside and linked to this they suggested that 'for better and also for worse, Chinese masculinity may be recovering its potency after a century of feelings of emasculation'.[7] Over a decade later, though ostentatious consumption has been politically checked as unpatriotic, the ghosts of earlier debates around the potency or otherwise of Chinese manhood continue to cast shadows. It is perhaps within these that we can find a means to decode persistent but fugitive versions of the Shanghai dandy.

In their more recent study of masculinities in contemporary China, Geng Song and Derek Hird question the very constitution of 'masculinity' as a coherent concept in the current Chinese context, which may account for the ghost-like semi-presence of anything approaching a precise local definition of male fashionability on Shanghai's streets. At the heart of this resistance towards classification, argue Song and Hird, lies an ambivalence towards Western cultural hegemony, the disorientating effects of modernity and globalization, and the spectre of China's twentieth-century past. Thus 'notions and practices of masculinities in contemporary China are constituted through "assemblages" of masculinity composed of transnationally circulating images and practices, and locally situated identities, practices and locales' and are so intimately connected to the self-construction of the nation that both teeter on the edge of semantic cohesion. In this sense 'the ever transforming assemblages of myriad elements that construct the "effect" named China is no more a coherent, unitary entity than is the subjectivity or selfhood of an individual Chinese man or woman'.[8]

Nevertheless, certain irrefutable historical and present contexts and definitions do offer a loose framework in which we can understand Shanghai's shadowy dandy to have emerged as a discrete concept. Song, Hird and other historians have pointed to the importance of the *wen* (literary)/*wu* (martial) dyad in setting parameters for appropriate models of masculine behaviour in imperial and post-imperial China. Of these, the tendency amongst elites towards a preference for wen qualities also informed the relative prominence given to the image of the scholar (*caizi*) in literary and artistic productions extolling model male virtues. As Song has argued, the internal balance between literary and martial characteristics in the construction of *caizi* manliness was also an important expression of yin yang harmony and a more socially affective dichotomous model than that pertaining to binary gender construction. In this respect he suggests that questions of effeminacy or homosexuality carry far less weight in Chinese discourse on gendered identity than in the West, because hegemonic models of masculinity defined against femininity or the 'other' were absent.

That is not to say, however, that *wu* characteristics were never overplayed. Indeed, Antonia Finnane, in her ground-breaking work on Chinese clothing, offers an astute reminder that the complex political conditions of the late nineteenth and early twentieth centuries fostered a counter-intuitive suppression of *wen* qualities by those very elites whose own culture had always favoured and relied on *caizi* prestige. In their anxiety to promote martial attributes in order to combat external and internal threats, the ruling Manchus suffered from a double-bind. Their 'own military weakness relative to the foreign powers … excited a military response in Chinese Society' and so in the end emasculated rather than enhanced their authority.[9] These important homosocial debates on the constitution of idealized Chinese manhood, which were so significant in informing national events in the past, have then bequeathed an enduring and particular legacy for considering the ways in which Chinese men dress and behave in the present.[10]

Since the early 1990s China's transformation into an economic, political and military global powerhouse, alongside its integration into international cultural and media flows, has set the background against which older models of masculinity can be rejected, adapted and played out. In Song and Hird's words, 'these changes have swept away both Confucian and Maoist models of manhood.

As productivist and consumerist values … gradually … replaced the Maoist legacy of class struggle in the official ideology, the selfless and asexual revolutionary hero lost his audience allure.'[11] The dominance of capitalist measures of personal success has also provided the script for enacting new social stereotypes that play on divisions between rich and poor, urban and rural, old and new wealth. In this fraught terrain of unfamiliar rules the discerning projection of taste, or *pinwei*, that might once have been associated with the *caizi* takes on a heightened relevance.

Modern Men in Republican Shanghai: Accommodating Western Style

These concerns of the twenty-first century were, as we have seen, debates that also arose at the turn of the twentieth as Chinese society transitioned in line with reformist calls for modernization along Western lines. Accelerated by defeat in the Sino-Japanese War of 1894, social and sartorial change was swiftly imposed, much of it via the militarization of the population and of public institutions. The material consequences, inspired by Prussian and Japanese precedent, saw the increasing prevalence of the modern uniform and an emphasis on physical and moral strength in Chinese daily life, ensuring that 'the armed forces were at the vanguard of vestimentary change'.[12] But it is also significant that much popular discussion on the implications of reform focused on the introduction of the civilian three-piece European suit on China's streets, particularly in Shanghai where the proximity of European and American fashionable styles was ever-present. Indeed, the appropriate fashioning of male bodies became a discursive terrain at the frontier of political transformation in both military and civic contexts simultaneously. As Robert E. Harris, Verity Wilson and others have noted, a familiarity with and interest in foreign clothing was well established in China, but its deliberate mobilization as a tool of social change was something new and radical, evoking strong feelings.[13]

Chinese elites had enjoyed dressing up in 'barbarian' styles since the Tang dynasty, and following the increasing incursions of Jesuit missionaries and traders from the sixteenth and seventeenth centuries the identification of synergies and differences between fashion styles and systems lead to a sophisticated understanding of sartorial semiotics. However, the impact of European imperialism and the economic effects of colonialism sharpened divisions between Chinese and Western habits and meanings of dress from the mid-nineteenth-century to its end. In the eyes of reformers, the overtly modern suits of the British, French, German, American and Japanese businessmen, adventurers and diplomats who flooded into the concessions of Shanghai offered a contrasting model of progress to the elegant historicism of *caizi* historicism, one worthy of emulation. Harris quotes the words of reformer Kang Youwei in 1908:

> Today in the intercourse of the ten thousand nations, all are inclining toward a greater unity. It is only our nation whose dress is different, and they do not feel close to us, and friendly relations with them have not been secured … Today's is a mechanized world. With many machines, there is strength; with a few machines, there is weakness … But to be bound by the thousands of years of the Chinese large-sleeved and broad sashed Confucian scholar's robe, and with a long robe and elegant gait to enter the world of competition with the ten thousand nations, this would be like wearing tinkling jade pendants to put out a fire, and truly is not appropriate.[14]

The arising debates about dressing for modern life were passionate and often self-contradictory. Chinese commentators recognized something novel and virile in bifurcated Western styles, but also cleaved to historical and spiritual precedent in favouring traditional robes, more suited to Chinese attitudes to the body. At the same time, such robes appeared to emphasize all the problems endemic in Chinese society. Compared to the suit, their forms appeared effeminate and retrograde. The difference was an essentialist one, summed up by the critic and novelist Lin Yutang: 'Now the philosophy behind Chinese and Western dress is that the latter tries to reveal the human form, while the former tries to conceal it. But as the human body is essentially like the monkey's, usually the less of it revealed the better.'[15]

Harris demonstrates the ways in which this uncomfortable meeting of cloth, body and cultures produced both material anomalies and representational anxieties in Shanghai's streets and press. The physical affect and unaccustomed freedom of wearing tailored trousers like those of the 'straight long leg' foreigners appeared to change the posture of those Chinese men who dared adopt them, propelling them with literal speed into the twentieth century.[16] Indeed, Mao Zedong himself fell back on a critique of the grace of the robed scholar in an essay promoting physical culture of 1917. He 'argued that one reason Chinese men avoided … exercise was because Society honoured those who wore cumbersome long gowns and walked with a leisurely air. For such men … "to stick out their arms and expose their feet, to extend their limbs and bend their bodies" would be shameful.'[17] Yet the kinetic confusions of 'cross-dressing' brought on by the introduction of the suit were also disorientating, and Shanghai's status as an international entrepôt magnified them. Finnane has described the fluidity of meaning that attached itself to the new cosmetic fashions and items of clothing that were introduced into the Chinese wardrobe in the Republican era, such that essentialist signifiers of race, social caste, age and gender were for some commentators becoming unacceptably blurred, and for some social actors (particularly those women who also adopted Western-style men's suits and hairstyles in defiance of convention) challenged in provocative and exciting ways.[18] In 1912 the *Shenbao* newspaper lamented:

> Chinese people are wearing foreign clothes, foreigners are wearing Chinese clothes, men are wearing female adornments, women are wearing male adornments, prostitutes are imitating schoolgirls, schoolgirls are imitating prostitutes, common people are dressing like officials, officials are dressing like commoners.[19]

History tells us that, despite such confusion, the modernity and commercial potential of the suit triumphed over fear. Lin Yutang's nostalgia and internalization of perceived Western superiority were already beginning to sound quaint by 1937, when he published his essay 'The Inhumanity of Western Dress' in New York:

> No Shanghai kidnapper would think of kidnapping a Chinese in foreign clothes, for the simple reason that he is not worth the candle. Who are the people wearing foreign clothes today in China? The college students, the clerks earning a hundred a month, the political busybodies who are always on the point of landing a job, the dangbu young men, the nouveaux riches, the nincompoops, the feeble-minded.[20]

Suited for Shanghai: Local Tailoring Traditions and their Legacies

Rail as Lin Yutang might, glamorous images of the suit prevailed in Shanghai's thriving film and advertising industry during the 1920s and 1930s, and its figure-fitting lines increasingly graced the lithe bodies of Chinese movie stars, singers and athletes in the pages of glamour magazines.[21] Such was the demand for clothes capturing the modern spirit that Shanghai soon became associated with a particular expertise in modern tailoring techniques. In common with many other Chinese towns and cities, and indeed with cities in the rest of the world, tailoring formed an important occupation, supplying a basic need to the local population, and straddling traditional forms of itinerant hand-wrought production that had remained unchanged for centuries, alongside newer practices enabled by revolutions in technology (the sewing machine), retail (the department store), and promotion (advertising). The same was true for tailors in London, New York, Vienna and Paris, and like them Shanghai also benefitted from a large, cosmopolitan population supplying both skilled artisans and eager and enlightened consumers.

Finanne describes forms of local tailoring history familiar from the wider historiography of tailoring, where individual 'pioneer' tailors and long-standing tailoring districts and traditions inform entrenched mythologies that themselves go on to fuel the success of dynastic enterprises and the expansion of profitable industrial sectors. Regardless of the veracity of their creation myths, Savile Row and Naples have benefitted from very similar reputational phenomena. In Shanghai, the founding father was Zhao Chunlan, who established the 'first' Western-style tailor's shop in the early 1850s following a visit to the United States. By the early twentieth century:

Figure 10.1 Louis-Philippe Messelier, 'At the Race Course', Shanghai, *c.* 1930s. Copyright Louis-Philippe Messelier, courtesy of Photography of China.

> tens of thousands of tailors served the vestimentary needs of a portion of the three million or more people living . . . in Shanghai. Tailors sat behind some of the best known shopfronts: the Hongxiang fashion store, established in 1917 . . . Rongchangxiang tailors in Nanjing Road, the most famous place for men's Western suits; and the Yunshang Fashion Company near Jing'an Temple Road.[22]

A cursory surf of online resources relating to the history and culture of tailoring in Shanghai will reveal that out of these beginnings the city supported a flourishing regional practice, alternatively termed the Ningbo or Red Gang (Hongbang) style (red referring to the hair and complexions of European clients), which in turn spread Shanghai tailoring trends to other parts of South East Asia and the world via the Shanghainese diaspora, particularly in Hong Kong, after 1946. The majority of men working in the Shanghai menswear business were migrants from Ningbo, a smaller, poorer port city to the south which traditionally provided skilled artisans for many of Shanghai's luxury trades. According to legend, some of these had first migrated to Dongbei in the very north of China where their knowledge of Western styles and fit was informed by Russian influences. But a more likely source of training in cutting methods alien to Chinese craftsmen would have been the opportunities presented by enterprising British tailoring companies operating out of the concessions, many of whom employed Ningbo workers. Whatever the origins of their approach, the resulting form was distinctive. Mark Cho, founder of the celebrated Drake's and Armoury luxury menswear stores in New York and London, describes it clearly:

> Shanghai tailoring, being based on British and Russian techniques, made jackets with a full, shaped chest, requiring time and skill with steam and pressing techniques to create curvature, and was particularly suited to a Caucasian build. Cantonese tailoring did not use the same techniques as it was more geared towards a Chinese physique thus requiring less work in shaping the chest. This type of tailoring was known as the 'Guang Dong Gang'.[23]

In a recent interview with Qi Baijun, a contemporary Red Gang tailor descended from seven generations in the industry and still based in Ningbo, Ruby Gao of the *Shanghai Daily* newspaper elaborates on the attention to detail that characterizes the approach:

> The core of Hongbang tailoring . . . is to shape the wearer and the cloth as one. To achieve that, measurements should be precise and complete. Hongbang has around 40 body measurements, 30 more than normal tailoring. 'The more precisely you measure, the better you know the wearer's curved shape. Italian

> tailors very likely benefitted from their country's prolific body sculpture art' says Qi. As well as the customer's body, character and personality are also built into the measurement process.[24]

By 1941, building on its reputation for such fine craftsmanship, the city had cemented its status as a centre for exquisite men's tailoring, bolstering its claims with the creation of the Shanghai Cutting and Tailoring College, but subsequent political and economic turmoil through the 1940s led to the migration of most Ningbo tailors out of China and a rejection of European sartorial values. Those who remained found work re-modelling suits into revolutionary uniforms. One retired tailor, who worked in Fenghua in Zhejian Province and was interviewed for an exhibition on Chinese dress in the Powerhouse Museum, Sydney in 1997, describes a process that must have been familiar in cities across the nation during the 1950s and 1960s:

> When you work with clothes, you can do just about anything with them. Western suits, for example, can be transformed … The tailors where I worked did just that. From the early 1950s we had a lot of requests to remodel suits. Back then materials were expensive but labour was cheap … So lots of tailors provided this particular service. They'd advertise it with a sign on the counter or hanging outside which said 'Reconditioning of Western Suits'. … If you wore a suit people thought you were a capitalist, an interpreter or someone who'd returned from overseas. … For the first few years after Liberation no one changed, and although people didn't wear suits to work, you would see them on Sundays or when people visited each other. If you had money you just put them away and wore something else. All that changed after the Great Leap Forward (1957–1958). That's when rationing was introduced. Rationing was the great equalizer. The rich had no choice but to remodel their suits.[25]

When Western-style suits finally reappeared in public life during the early 1980s their presence marked an acceptance of fundamental political and social change by reformist members of the Central Committee of the Communist Party. Tellingly the Fenghua tailor viewed the shift with a degree of nostalgia and a cause for some regret, noting that

> Chairman Mao never wore a western suit. Foreigners like talking about 'Mao Suits' but for us that uniform was national dress. … the first time I saw [Hu Yaobang] on TV in a [Western] suit, I was stunned. I thought it was the end of the Revolution.[26]

For the expatriate Ningbo tailors, the resurgence of Western-style sartorialism represented an opportunity. As Mark Cho records:

> although young tailors are rare in Hong Kong, they do exist and continue to develop a style descended from their Shanghainese and Cantonese predecessors. Hong Kong tailors have also made inroads into China, developing workrooms . . . catering to the modern Chinese consumer and for some, coming full circle from their exodus in the '40s.[27]

To all appearances, by the 1990s the Shanghai dandy was back.

Twenty-First-Century Pinwei: Negotiating Fashion Now

The social and cultural changes that have accompanied political and economic reform since Hu Yaobang appeared on television in October 1984 wearing a dark blue Western suit have been profound, and in the vestimentary realm such change has clearly registered most starkly on the bodies of young men and via the manner of their representation in the media. In the first-tier cities of Shanghai, Guangzhou and Beijing, an initial racing after the cultural capital of Western luxury brands has subsided in favour of a more subtle, sophisticated approach to

Figure 10.2 Magazine Covers, purchased by the author in Shanghai, summer 2015. Copyright James Brook.

fashionable consumption, while in second-tier cities including Chongquing, Chengdu and Harbin 'luxury sales . . . are booming' (or they were in a McKinsey report issued in 2014).[28] The confusing and multi-layered discourse of fashion that has fostered, guided and reflected these changes is perhaps best considered through a reading of the many fashion and lifestyle magazines that have directed their values towards Chinese readers since the late 1990s.

In a study of the business practices and reception of the Chinese version of the US copyrighted *Esquire* magazine since its launch as the first male fashion magazine produced under an international copyright co-operation in January 1997, Cao Jin offers a critical view of the ways in which foreign models of commodification have aimed to manipulate and reconstruct 'the traditional gender order' in order to fuel 'western capitalism's global expansion'.[29] In this approach the construction of aggressively aspirational forms of fashionable masculinity, appealing to an educated and wealthy young readership, open to the acquisition of those luxury global goods (sports and designer clothing, watches, luggage and accessories, cosmetics and perfume, cars and high tech commodities) that account for 28 per cent of magazine content and drive the financial profits of the publisher, has encouraged a radical re-fashioning of masculine moral attributes described through a deliberate editorial strategy:

> Esquire constructs a version of masculinity [that] emphasizes . . . professional reputation, social influence, business competence and consumption capacity, which combine together to give prominence to the dignity of civilized gentlemen. The new chief editor of Esquire has summarized the magazine's goals . . . as 'three represents'. First, Esquire represents the advanced productive forces – humans are the most powerful productive forces, therefore the figures in Esquire must be the most powerful, influential and up flowing group of this era. Second, it also represents the advanced culture, which not only embraces openness, vigor, innovation, harmony, luxury and classics but also reflects masculinity and power. Finally, the magazine represents the life aspirations of [the] Chinese new wealthy class by [offering] a comprehensive guide to the latest . . . products and activities both in and outside China, as well as the broadest horizons of international consumption.[30]

For Cao Jin, the corrosive effects of this objectifying strategy has distorted values and 'successfully veiled the serious issues of class differentiation and inequality caused by the globalization of the market economy'. In China, where the state 'once promised urban workers job security and superior status through stable employment and welfare . . . [guaranteeing] peasants scared identity and political trust', now:

> only those gentlemen with economic competence can possess the status . . . and prestige of a modern man. . . . As a result, such hegemonic masculinity depreciates the social status of those men and women who do not have competence in [the] market economy and consumption, and excludes their voice from [the media].[31]

In a replay of some of the concerns and tensions raised by the introduction of the suit into Chinese, and particularly Shanghainese life a century earlier, the proliferation of style magazine culture in the early twenty-first century has also led to a questioning of moral and aesthetic values in the face of a collision between local and international social and sartorial trends. But such values have perhaps been subject to a more nuanced process of negotiation than the pure Marxist analysis of Cao Jin might allow. Song and Hird, for example, draw attention to the ways in which particular registers of taste have emerged to accommodate conflicting styles of consumption. These have produced a form of Chinese dandyism distinct from Western versions of the rather generic 'metrosexual', one based on the concept of *pinwei*, roughly translatable as 'taste for fine things':

> The overwhelming emphasis on pinwei distinguishes Chinese men's magazines from those in other parts of the World. However, although pinwei is often translated as 'good taste', the English phrase fails to convey the word's connotation of hierarchy and elitism . . . The cult of pinwei is in keeping with the ubiquitous discourse of quality in post-socialist China, which . . . 'articulates the boundaries of China's newly differentiating social strata' and 'produces subject positions necessary for capitalist accumulation'.[32]

There is something in the concept that enables Chinese producers and consumers of 'style' to forge a form of cosmopolitanism fitted to China's place in a contemporary world of globalized commodification, whilst also remaining respectful of historical precedent and political contradiction. The pursuit of dandyism in twenty-first-century Shanghai is an art demanding all the skills that an understanding of *pinwei* can bestow. Song and Hird demonstrate how pervasive this approach has become through reference to the publication of Wang Yingbo's popular self-help book *Men Absolutely Must Earn Money: The Successful Man's Path to Riches* of 2009. Drawing on the repertoire of style signifiers set out in the new men's lifestyle magazines, Wang's book, aimed at white-collar workers, offered a *pinwei* take on sartorial, corporeal, professional, social, sexual and emotional matters. Reviving the Qing ideal of Shenshi masculinity (a form of refined 'gentlemanliness' associated with men of letters and influential civil servants), Wang's six-step regime for success provides an extraordinary echo of the advice manuals read by aspiring young English gentlemen in the early nineteenth century – Brumellian dandyism with Chinese characteristics:

> If your body has a 'peculiar smell' you must clean yourself often. Keep your hair neat and stay clean-shaven to look young. Wash your face often with facial cleanser to prevent it from becoming oily. Don't be effeminate, which means not applying powder or paint or overly strong perfume, not wearing garish clothing, or acting or speaking affectedly. Your clothing shouldn't be too casual or unappealing. You need to maintain a cheerful, optimistic mental outlook.[33]

In almost two centuries then, since the advent of American and European interests in the port of Shanghai, writers, tailors, retailers, designers and consumers themselves have been grappling with the registers of masculine style in this most worldly of cities. It is perhaps no surprise that the tenets of English dandyism and Shenshi etiquette have found common ground in addressing the material pressures of political turmoil, globalization and market reforms. Such philosophies, in their love of rhetoric, knowingness and game play are ideally suited to dressing bodies in flux. Like the apocryphal Ningbo tailor fitting a suit for a candidate of the Imperial civil service examinations in the early 1900s, the skill lies in adapting form to context:

> If you are qualified to be a candidate when you are young, you should be proud and slightly arrogant, so you are used to sticking out your chest. I will then make the suit long in the front and short in the back. If you are qualified to be a candidate when you are old, you might be humble and used to bowing. Then I will make the suit short in front and long in the back.[34]

Notes

1 'China's First Luxury Brand Battles to Shed Cultural Cliches', www.chinaeconomicreview.com/shanghai-tang-struggle-heritage-history-chinese-consumer-luxury, 3 April 2014 (accessed September 2016).
2 Ibid.
3 Ibid.
4 T. Laquer, 'Foreword', in S. Brownell and J. Wasserstrom (eds), *Chinese Femininities: Chinese Masculinities: A Reader* (Berkeley, CA: University of California Press, 2002), xiii.
5 C. Breward, *The Suit: Form, Function, Style* (London: Reaktion Books, 2016).
6 Laquer, 'Foreword', xiii.
7 Brownell and Wasserstrom, *Chinese Femininities*, 442.

8 Geng Song and Derek Hird, *Men and Masculinities in Contemporary China* (Leiden: Brill, 2014), 6–7.
9 A. Finnane, *Changing Clothes in China: Fashion, History, Nation* (London: Hurst, 2007), 71.
10 Ibid., 4–5.
11 Ibid., 8.
12 Finnane, *Changing Clothes in China*, 71.
13 R.E. Harris, 'Clothes Make the Man: Dress, Modernity and Masculinity in China 1912–1937', in Wu Hing and K.R. Tsiang (eds), *Body and Face in Chinese Visual Culture* (Cambridge, MA: Harvard University Press, 2005); V. Wilson, 'Western Modes and Asian Clothing', in G. Riello and P. McNeil (eds), *The Fashion History Reader: Global Perspectives* (London: Routledge, 2010).
14 Harris, 'Clothes Make the Man', 180.
15 Ibid., 175.
16 Ibid., 177–9.
17 Ibid., 181.
18 Finnane, 177–200.
19 Harris, 'Clothes Make the Man', 188.
20 Ibid., 191.
21 Ibid., 184–6.
22 Finnane, 111.
23 www.markcho.com/abridged-history-of-tailoring-in-hong-kong/, 18 March 2015 (accessed September 2016).
24 www.shanghaidaily.com/feature/ideal/Hongbang-tailoring-tradition-a-snug-fit-for-master-craftsmen/shd, 26 May 2016 (accessed September 2016).
25 C. Roberts (ed.), *Evolution and Revolution: Chinese Dress 1700s–1900s* (Sydney: Powerhouse Publishing, 1997), 46–7.
26 Ibid., 47.
27 www.markcho.com/abridged-history-of-tailoring-in-hong-kong/.
28 www.chinaeconomicreview.com/shanghai-tang-struggle-heritage-history-chinese-consumer-luxury.
29 Cao Jin, 'Male Fashion Magazines and Western Capitalist Expansion in a Post-Colonial State', Harvard-Yenching Institute Working Papers (Shanghai: Fudan University, 2012), 2.
30 Ibid., 24–5.
31 Ibid., 28–9.
32 Song and Hird, *Men and Masculinities in Contemporary China*, 61.
33 Ibid., 153–4.
34 www.shanghaidaily.com/feature/ideal/Hongbang-tailoring-tradition-a-snug-fit-for-master-craftsmen/shd.

11

The Luxury Malling of Shanghai

Successes and Dissonances in the Chinese City

Agnès Rocamora

Introduction

This chapter looks at the role of one particular type of urban formation in the redefinition of Shanghai: the luxury shopping mall. In the 1990s and following China's post-Cultural Revolution opening to the West as well as the party-state's adoption of a socialist market economy, the city saw the emergence and rapid proliferation of luxury shopping malls. Multi-storey buildings hosting international brands such as Fendi, Chanel, Louis Vuitton or Coach are recurring sights, with Plaza 66, CITIC and Westgate Mall (known as the Golden Triangle of luxury malls) only a few among the still rising list of luxury shopping malls. These malls are part of a wider phenomenon of urban redevelopment in Shanghai. Indeed throughout the 1990s the city experienced an unprecedented programme of urban renewal, economic restructuring and growth.[1] Shanghai shifted from a manufacturing economy to one focused on finance, real estate and the service sector.[2] This urban and economic shift was reflected in the restructuring of the spatial organization of the city, with skyscrapers, avenues and newly constructed roads central to its reshaping and globalizing.[3]

Informed by a series of visits to Shanghai in the course of 2014–16[4] and in dialogue with some of the extant literature on Shanghai and China, the chapter shows that to understand the presence of luxury malls in Shanghai one needs to look at the wider context of China's embrace of both shopping malls and luxury, as well as at the city's history as a cosmopolitan consumerist centre (first section). Shanghai's history has long been tied to the fortunes of global capital and its reputations. The rise and success of both malls and the luxury market is predicated on the specifics of the nation's adoption of capitalism, concurrent with the city's intense pace of urban regeneration (second section). It is a rise dependent on a logic of exclusion and the formation of an urban semioscape of Western brands deterritorialized from the material realities of much of the local population (third section).

The Proliferation of Shopping Malls

In 2015, luxury fashion brand Louis Vuitton published a guidebook on Shanghai, as part of the brand's city guides series. The publication draws attention to two related dimensions of the Chinese metropolis: the definition of Shanghai as a fashionable city, a city whose geography hosts multiple fashionable spots including retail spaces; the role of luxury brands in its making both in terms of the work of discursive construction undertaken by guides such as Louis Vuitton's, but also in term of their visibility in the city's landscape. Shanghai abounds with luxury retail spaces such as flagship stores, designer boutiques and concept stores, which all participate in the city's fashioning as a glamorous, wealthy metropolis. Such retail spaces are a part only of Shanghai's wider fashion map for the city has become a thriving 'landscape of consumption', to borrow Benjamin's words.[5] Department stores, international fashion chains and knock-off stores as well as market stalls are also part of Shanghai's fashion make-up, which extends online too with e-commerce and social commerce, and platforms such as Taobao, Weibo and QQ. Another significant sight in this landscape of consumption is the shopping mall, and in particular luxury shopping malls, which, in mainland China, emerged in the 1990s.

The first shopping mall was built in the US in Seattle in 1947. In the shape of a dumbbell, a format that came to characterize many shopping malls, it featured, at street level, an anchoring department store, another recurring feature of malls, ample adjoining parking spaces being another one.[6] It is in the 1950s, however, with the building of Southdale, designed by Victor Gruen, that the mall as an enclosed space with a regulated temperature and cut off from its surrounding as if looking inward appeared, in the suburb of Edina, Minnesota.[7] This 'introverted'[8] ensemble brought together shops, cafes and public art around a central courtyard[9] sealing the future of malls as 'escapist cocoon[s]'.[10] The years 1960 to 1980 saw the 'golden years' of malls in the US.[11] By the end of the 1990s, though, 'the malling of America' was reaching saturation and, in the 2000s, in the face of proliferating 'ghost malls', questions were being raised about the relevance of such large shopping environments.[12]

However, the shopping mall concept has spread throughout the world, with Latin America, Asia and Eastern Europe seen as 'the new frontiers' for the development of malls.[13] In Hong Kong they appeared in the 1980s,[14] but it is in the 1990s that the malling of mainland China starting taking place, led, mostly, by investors from Southeast Asia.[15] In 2016 there were about 4,000 malls in China, and in spite of an economic slowdown the figure is expected to reach 10,000 by 2025.[16] As Jewell puts it, the nation has become 'the leader of the international mall arms race'.[17]

The first shopping mall to open in Shanghai was Shanghai Square, in 1993, on Huaihai Road, followed, in 1998, by Westgate Mall, on West Nanjing Road.[18] Since then malls have proliferated, and in 2015 the city was constructing 'more malls than any other city in the world'.[19] Among them are luxury shopping malls – ICC, Westgate, Citic, iapm (2014), K11, Kerry, Réel and Plaza 66, for instance – retail spaces devoted to high fashion brands such as Chanel, Fendi, Coach, Saint Laurent and other big brands born out of the Western fashion system.

In Shanghai, two streets in particular are hosts to luxury shopping malls. They are Huaihai Road and Nanjing Road, both centrally located and nearby each other. Huaihui Road has been described as 'the city's chicest shopping artery'.[20] It hosts Shanghai Times Square, Hong Kong Plaza and IAPM. The latter, for instance, opened in 2013 and covers 1.3 million square feet. It is nested in ICC Shanghai, a complex of two towers for both offices and residence owned by Hong Kong property group SHKP.[21] Before the construction of the complex and its mall, the SHKP site was already a well-known consumer spot as it is where Xiangyang Market was located, a destination for cheap fashion and counterfeits.[22] This transformation from a low-cost fashion shopping destination to a luxury one captures the gentrification of central Shanghai that is currently taking place there, at the expense, like gentrification across the world more generally,[23] of less affluent residents, an issue I return to in the second and third sections of this essay.

Nanjing Lu, 'historic Shanghai's premier axis of consumption',[24] has been called the city's '5th Avenue'.[25] Although it has opened up to mass fashion brands such as Gap and Uniqlo it is still a key destination for luxury shopping, including malls such as Jing An Kerry Centre, Réel and Plaza 66, which are a few minutes' walk away from each other, Plaza 66 on 1266 Nanjing Road, Jing An Kerry on 1515 Nanjing Road and, next to it on 1601 Nanjing road, Réel, the trendiest and most avant-garde of all three. Plaza 66, 'home to luxury' as the website states, features brands such as Bulgari, Cartier, Céline, Chanel and Dior; Jing An Kerry's many boutiques include Burberry, Boss, Etro, Michael Kors, Loewe and Armani;

while at Réel one can find Balenciaga, Acne, Givenchy, Helmut Lang, Isabel Marant, Marni, Y-3 and many others. All three malls are spotless and exude an atmosphere of luxury.

Whereas malls in other parts of the world such as the US tend to be located in the suburbs, in China they are often centrally located, although in recent years they have started to open in the suburbs too due to urban congestion.[26] Suburban malls are dependent on access by car, but the centrally located Chinese malls are accessible by metro and are indeed often linked to the subway network and public transport.[27] The subway line 7, for instance, is connected to Jing An Kerry Centre.

The malls are also pedestrian shortcuts across the city. Doors often feature at various sides of the buildings along the east–west and north–south streets that border them. During the many hours I spent in the Nanjing Road luxury malls, for instance, observing its stores and occupants, I often witnessed pedestrians entering from one side and exiting from another, clearly using the retail spaces as a way of cutting through the city. In that respect luxury malls recall the Parisian arcades Benjamin[28] commented upon: like arcades they form arteries across the city, like arcades they are spaces of exhibition of luxury items, passageways devoted to the ideal of consumption, thereby further inscribed in the make-up of the city.

The high concentration, in Shanghai, of luxury shopping malls is an instance of the city's embrace of luxury – and indeed of China's more generally. Indeed, although the Chinese economy has slowed down in recent years the nation has become a prominent luxury market. In 2012 President Xi Jinping (b. 1953) implemented measures to fight officials' corruption and ostentatious consumption by prohibiting the buying of luxury goods with public funds and by investigating those officials denounced by the public as possessors of luxury items.[29] The measure led to a drop in their sales.[30] However, luxury remains a strong sector, with a 'new momentum' being reported in 2016.[31] In 2013 there were more than 300 billionaires in China, a number second to that of the US only, while Shanghai households had the highest per household consumer expenditure: US$16,605.[32] China was the second largest luxury market in the world in 2016, after the US,[33] and while in 2016 China represented 7 per cent of the global luxury market, Chinese consumers accounted for one-third of all luxury consumers.[34] Chinese consumers may well be 'moving away from "bling" and towards more understated' brands but they are still drawn towards high-end products and still buy more luxury items than consumers in most developed countries.[35] Indeed, it was estimated that in 2015 they had bought '46% of luxury goods globally'.[36]

To understand the presence of luxury malls in Shanghai it is necessary to look at the wider context of the nation's embrace of capitalism and the boom in property development since the 1990s. As mentioned earlier, malls appeared in China in the 1990s, and their arrival on the Chinese urban landscape is tightly linked to the nation's adoption of a 'socialist market economy'.

Capitalism Chinese Way and Urban Redevelopment

After having been closed to Western business partners since 1949, the date of the constitution of the People's Republic of China, in 1978 China adopted an open-door policy,[37] and in the 1980s the nation's leaders embraced the slogan 'bringing China into the world's orbit'.[38] The country adopted a series of measures aimed at allowing it to move away from a centrally planned economy to market-based privatization, also giving local authorities a greater role in the conduct of economic and urban growth.[39] China became the fastest growing economy in the world during the 1990s,[40] and in 2001 it joined the World Trade Organization.

The year 1992 represents a particularly important year in China's turn to a market economy. It is when the Southern Excursion Tour of Premier Deng Xiaoping 鄧小平 (1904–97) took place in cities such as Guangzhou, Shenzhen, Zhuhai and Shanghai.[41] A series of 'special economic zones' were established on the eastern coast to boost foreign investment,[42] and the trip is now understood as 'a watershed moment in the development of Shanghai and the south as the country's economic hubs'.[43]

The 1990s is also when Deng Xiaoping coined the term 'commodity economy with Chinese characteristics',[44] a variant of which is also known as 'socialism with Chinese characteristics'.[45] It is characterized by the co-existence of a powerful and influential state with the adoption of radical market forces, privatization and the promotion of consumption.[46] Indeed since 1979, the Chinese state 'has implemented policies to encourage the development of consumerism, viewing it as an engine for both economic growth and social stability'.[47] Knight notes that the expanded use of the term *guangchang*, meaning 'plaza', captures the importance of the value of consumption in contemporary China.[48] Where *guangchang* used to refer to public squares used for political assemblies it now commonly refers to shopping centres. Brooks also captures this overtaking of the political by consumerism when she observes: 'The only place the people can congregate in the renovated People's Square is in its underground shopping mall.'[49]

In China consumption has become both an important leisure activity and a national policy, with the government actively promoting spending.[50] In 2011, for instance, the newly enacted Twelfth Five-Year Plan comprised three key components: 'a greater focus on jobs, urbanization to boost wages, and financing a social safety net that encouraged families to spend rather than save'.[51] Compared with the Mao years the state's influence has diminished to give way to 'new ideologies of cosmopolitanism and luxury which the global brands embody'.[52] The presence of luxury shopping malls across China, and in Shanghai in particular, crystallizes this new orientation.

The transformation of cities from places of production to places of consumption has been supported by industrial restructuring and the shifting of factories outside of city centres, which are experiencing tertiarization.[53] At the same time, values such as individualism, self-worth and materialism are spreading (especially among the younger generation), which contrast with the anti-consumerist collectivism of Mao's years.[54] Jewell draws attention to the ideological and spatial manifestations of China's 'socialism with Chinese characteristics' when he notes that:

> In effect the discourse of the collective subject has shifted from the valorization of the proletariat to its erasure in order to position the idea of a consuming middle class in its place. Similarly the spatialization of this ideological shift has transferred from the collective space of the parade ground and work unit to the realm of consumption.[55]

But what about the position of Shanghai in this new China, a 'desiring China' as Rofel[56] puts it?

Before China, and with it Shanghai, turned away from Western influence under Mao, the city had been a thriving commercial hub. In 1842 the Nanjing treaty had declared Shanghai one of five ports open to international commerce, and in the late nineteenth and early twentieth centuries the city turned into a buoyant commercial and intellectual cosmopolitan centre, the legendary 'Paris of the East'.[57] Lee has richly documented the dynamism of Shanghai at the time, its consumerism, cosmopolitanism and modernity, culminating in the city's golden era of 1920s–30s, when the city became the fifth largest city in the world.[58] In the Chinese imagination Shanghai became synonymous with the modern, fashion and style its expression.[59] In the 1930s, Shanghai also saw intensified urban development and the construction of high-rise buildings and theatres, as well as new department stores,[60] all key in consolidating the city's definition as a modern centre.[61]

However, with the Sino-Japanese war and following Mao's accession to power, until his death in 1976, Shanghai was neglected by the central government and 'condemned to immobilism',[62] while across the nation private commerce was eliminated and replaced by nationalized businesses.[63] Once a thriving shopping and financial core, Shanghai's inner city became a manufacturing hub and the site of residence of its workers.[64] When Deng Xiaoping came to power in 1978 he did not trust the local Shanghai power, which still partly consisted of followers of Mao and was resistant to Deng's reform.[65] Shanghai was outside of the national political scene until the nomination, in 1985, of Shanghai's mayor Jiang Zemin (b. 1926), followed in 1988 by that of Zhu Rongji (b. 1928). Changes remained slow, however, and in the late 1980s Shanghai was still relatively behind in terms of reform. Foreign investors could not benefit from the same advantages as in other cities such as Guangdong, where foreign investments were much superior to that in Shanghai.[66]

However, things changed in the 1990s, during which Shanghai was selected to become the 'dragon head' of the reform undertaken by Xiaoping, and the symbol of the Chinese economy more generally.[67] The official policy has been to turn Shanghai into a global city defined by a strong tertiary sector; the manufacturing industries declined and the city's government promoted banking, finances and real estate.[68] As a result 'Shanghai has experienced the fastest economic growth of any megacity from the early 1990s, averaging 12 percent annually'.[69] Bao singled out 1998 to 2000 as particularly significant years for the everyday life of Shanghainese people.[70] During that time leisure and entertainment places proliferated, encouraged by the local government and supported by an enthusiastic press.[71]

The positioning of Shanghai as a global city and the 'dragon head' of China has gone hand in hand with a staggering pace and scale of urban redevelopment since the 1990s.[72] As He and Wu note: 'Prosperous property development and large-scale urban (re)development . . . have become elements of Shanghai's grand scheme of recasting itself as a world city'.[73] Since the 1990s a large programme of construction of new infrastructures has been taking place that has seen the building of bridges, elevated roads, subways (new line 1) and high rises.[74] In the space of three years, between 1992 and 1995, as many office buildings were constructed in Shanghai as in Hong Kong in four decades,[75] while, writing in 2009, Chen notes that over the last ten years more than 4,000 high rises have been built, which is twice as many buildings as in New York.[76]

A noticeable part of the reconstruction Shanghai has been undergoing for the last two decades includes the development of retail spaces: 'more than half of the world's retail development is in China, with 3.3 million square metres currently under construction in Shanghai alone',[77] and in 2006 Wang et al. observed that Shanghai, now acknowledged as 'the business capital of China', was leading the nation in terms of the development of shopping malls.[78] Their proliferation is an instance of 'the commodification of urban space' that has informed many cities across the world.[79]

At the same time as malls have been proliferating they are often striking for their lack of tenants, or, as was often the case with the luxury malls I visited in Shanghai, their very small numbers of customers. This phenomenon is known as 'ghost malls'.[80] The ghost-like quality of luxury shopping malls can be explained by a series of factors, starting with the shopping habits of luxury customers in China. Due to high import taxes luxury goods are comparatively more expensive in China than in Europe, and mainland China accounts for only 20 per cent of Chinese shoppers' purchase of luxury goods.[81] 'The same luxury handbag can often cost 40 per cent more in Beijing than in Paris, for example'.[82] Shoppers who can afford luxury goods therefore travel to Europe to buy them at a lower cost. 'The average Chinese traveller to Europe spends US$15,000 on each trip.'[83] Similarly, Hong Kong is a cheaper destination for luxury shopping.[84]

The *daigu* system also encourages the acquisition of high-end items outside of mainland China. It is a grey market whereby agents based abroad buy luxury goods there for China-bound buyers, and illegally avoid import duties while making a profit, although the Chinese government has recently tried to curb this practice by tightening custom controls.[85] In a similar bid to dissuade Chinese shoppers from buying luxury goods abroad rather than in mainland China, in 2015 brands such as Chanel, Cartier and Gucci raised their prices in Europe while lowering them in China.[86]

In China, the luxury sector is also becoming more dynamic online, which is 'now the world's third largest luxury market',[87] and takes trade away from bricks and mortar stores. On the internet consumers can both buy, and learn about, luxury brands,[88] and luxury brands are increasingly embracing Chinese social media such as WeChat and e-commerce platforms such as Mei.com.[89]

The malls' visible lack of costumers is not synonymous with lack of success. Indeed, as Jewell also observes, though Plaza 66, for instance, may well look empty, it is nevertheless one of China's most successful malls.[90] Built in 2006 by Hong Kong's Hang Lung Properties it is 130,000 square metres and 288 metres tall. There, Jewell notes, customers are not absent, they have been made invisible: 'the real business of selling happens behind closes doors: Plaza 66 is served by a network of concealed rooms that represent the domain of its intended "public". … Drive into the mall basement and a concierge will escort you to a private room. Here the mall's wares are presented by a personal shopper for delectation'.[91] In late 2017 some transformations were brought to the mall to enhance its luxurious appearance such as warm lighting to complement its bronze, gold and marble elements, and Louis Vuitton opening a private lounge, accessible by invitation only.'[92]

Brands can profit from being present in a mall simply by virtue of being there. Commenting on their ghost-like appearance, Greenspan mentions a discussion she had with a branding expert, who informed her that on Nanjing Road the cost of a large banner advertisement is nearly identical to that of running a store: 'The empty store, therefore, make sense purely from an advertising perspective.'[93]

The cost international brands may encounter when setting up base in a mall may also be lowered by advantageous rents, for 'In order to attract international retailers, some malls offer zero base rent and charge only percentage rent geared towards sales'.[94] Hang Lung Properties, for instance, the company behind the development of Plaza 66, 'was granted favourable land use rights by the Shanghai Municipal Government in late 1993 to construct two luxury shopping centres, Grand Gateway Plaza and Plaza 66'.[95]

Thus, even if luxury malls dot not have customers they can be profitable, and to a broad range of players. As Dávila notes in her study of shopping malls in Latin America: 'There are countless ways to make a profit in and from shopping malls, all of which go beyond the point of purchase and are mostly invisible.'[96] Among the many players that can profit from malls, she mentions architects, designers, security companies and marketing companies. 'At the heart of it all', she argues, 'is the purchase, development, and leasing of land, or in industry terms, the acquisition of "footprint" – the core and most profitable activity and the most invisible.'[97] This is true of Shanghai, where one of the beneficiaries of mall construction include local governments. Indeed, the city's urban redevelopment and the concurrent hike of shopping mall openings has been supported by China's adoption of a market economy and its governmental decentralization, which have given local authorities more power and financial autonomy to promote, and benefit from, urban growth.[98] City governments are some of its key beneficiaries. Municipal and district governments own the land, which they lease against fees that account for their main source of local income.[99] There is thus a strong incentive for municipalities to promote urban development, which has changed from being supported by the government to being property-led.[100] The reconstruction of Pudong and Xintiandi are cases in point, and has attracted much scholarly attention.[101]

Malls have also been instrumental to the property-led redevelopment of the city, and Shanghai's government has even acknowledged their contribution to the city in that they create employment, generate property tax revenue and stimulate the real-estate development of the neighbourhood.[102] In China as in the Latin American countries Dávila discusses, urban policies have supported the development of shopping malls, which 'have become a feature of "worlding" practices and the quest for recognition as world-class cities'.[103] Thus the Shanghai municipality added malls to its Tenth (2001 to 2005) and Eleventh Five-Year Plans for Commercial Activity Development, stipulating that they would serve as anchors to commercial nodes (Tenth Plan) as well as to Suburban Business Districts (Eleventh Plan).[104] This approach informed the revitalization of Huihai Road and Nanjing Road,[105] both hosts, as mentioned earlier, to luxury shopping malls.

This refashioning of central Shanghai via luxury malls is not without its drawbacks though, and this includes the process of social exclusion that the reconfiguration of the city has been concurrent with.

Dissonances

Exclusion is the logic of both luxury and capitalism, and nowhere is this more visible maybe than in the spatial and material configuration of a city. As Bourdieu[106] notes, geographical space is social space reified; the redefinition of central Shanghai through the construction of luxury malls is also a redefinition of its social make-up. Indeed the luxury malling of the Chinese city is part and parcel of the gentrification that has been taking place there since the 1990s. It is an outcome of the rebranding of Shanghai as a world city in the context of China's adoption of neoliberalism.

As with most instances of gentrification across the world[107] this reimagining of Shanghai has gone hand in hand with the rise of new types of inequalities such as the bourgeoisification of central Shanghai at the expense of poorer local communities.[108] As Yu puts it, 'after several decades of living under a strict socialist ideology in which wealth and signs of class difference were stamped out, inequality has come back with a vengeance, as the difference between the wealthy and the poor becomes exacerbated each year'.[109] This also means that practices of social distinctions have re-emerged.[110] These are practices of dress through the display of luxury branded items, as the success of luxury in China intimates, but also spatial practices as articulated through luxury malls. Indeed various forms of socio-spatial distinctions and segregation have been embedded in Shanghai's geography of malls, which can be seen as manifesting themselves in three different ways: in the internal practice of the malls; in their immediate surroundings; and in a centre–periphery reconfiguration.

With regards to the first form of spatial distinction, the internal dynamic of the malls, luxury shopping malls, as mentioned earlier, are often void of customers. Bar the occasional shopper and the few pedestrians who use them to walk across the city in a sheltered environment, their relative emptiness is conspicuously at odds with the busyness of adjacent streets. Many passers-by no doubt self-exclude from these luxury spaces, a process that can only be reinforced by the intimidating presence of porters at the entrance of the malls, reminding visitors that, like malls more generally,[111] they are private enclaves subject to a tight control. Indeed, while developers across the world have often promoted, and idealized, malls as community environments, spaces of togetherness and sociability, this neglects the fact that they actually are 'purified' controlled spaces and often exclude various portions of the population.[112] This is true of luxury malls in Shanghai; designed as exclusive retail environments they are simultaneously spaces of exclusion. Brook[113] notes that a broad constituency of individuals walk through Nanjing Road. They include rural migrant workers who have moved to Shanghai in the hope of finding work. For them the goods on offer in luxury malls are out of reach:

> Called out by their leathery skin and ill-fitting, raggedy sport coats, they are the great human contradiction of the new Shanghai. Surrounded by the modern world, the migrants are in the city but not of it, second-class citizens too poor to enjoy many of the city's amenities.[114]

Those migrants from China are also the workers who operate neighbourhood stores selling everyday goods such as groceries, cigarettes, and clothing affordable to ordinary Shanghainese.[115] The stores' simple, functional appearance sharply contrasts with the splendour of adjacent luxury shopping malls.

During lunchtime the malls fill with people. These are not shoppers, however, but office workers, who, keeping to the escalators, head straight to the upper floors, where eateries are located. They do not often diverge from their up-and-down journey and the luxury boutiques remain largely devoid of buying and selling activities. Lingering outside of the shops and in the passageways to rest and socialize is not encouraged as luxury malls rarely offer sitting places except at coffee shops.[116] Indeed, in shopping malls resting is designed to equate with consuming.[117] At Plaza 66, for instance, seating is available at Cova Pasticceria-Confetteria, where, in April 2015, a cappuccino was 74.80 RMB (approx. £8).

The splendour of Shangai's luxury malls contrasts with the shabby yet lively streets and alleyways that can be found in their vicinities. Next to Nanjing Road streets and stores that appear comparatively rundown are brimming with activities. On Nanyang Road, for instance, parallel to Nanjin Road and two streets behind Plaza 66, convenience stores, cheap eateries and outlets selling other affordable goods co-exist with accommodation outside of which can been seen laundry drying on wires (see Figures 11.1 and 11.2). A short walk away from Réel and Kerry is Fumin Road. There a series of run-down local shops have closed down and seem abandoned, a sign, probably, of the further commercial gentrification of the street (Figure 11.3). Low-income housing still stands, in stark contrast with the luxury and (hyper)modernity of the nearby malls (see Figures 11.4 and 11.5). As Jewell observes, such streets 'maintain a seemingly parallel existence with the macro-consumptionist agenda of the mall complexes that loom over them. Although separated by little more than tens of metres, the disparity in relative wealth could not be more evident.'[118]

However, the central streets and shops of low-income residents are being replaced by trendy bars and boutiques catering to wealthy Chinese and expatriates.[119] For the redesigning of Shanghai by way of its luxury malling, like

Figure 11.1 Nanyang Road, near Plaza 66. Courtesy of Agnès Rocamora.

Figure 11.2 Nanyang Road, near Plaza 66. Courtesy of Agnès Rocamora.

Figure 11.3 Fumin Road, near Réel and Kerry. Courtesy of Agnès Rocamora.

Figure 11.4 Fengxian Road, near Plaza 66. Courtesy of Agnès Rocamora.

Figure 11.5 Plaza 66. Courtesy of Agnès Rocamora.

much of the real estate redevelopment that has refashioned the city into a consumerist urban centre, has been premised on the destruction of existing low-income neighbourhoods – 'Deemed messy, unsightly and uncivilised'[120] – that have been replaced with high-end housing and commercial estates aimed at the emerging middle class.[121] A 'destructive construction' is operating in Shanghai whereby the city's 'organic street culture' is being swept away.[122] Unable to afford the new housing, low- and middle-income families have been forced outside of central Shanghai and to its outskirts,[123] which draws attention to a third social-spatial imbalance: a centre-periphery reconfiguration along the lines of class. As He observes: 'In parallel to gentrification in Western cities, housing redevelopment in Shanghai predominantly involves a process of "class transformation," that is, displacement of low-income residents and its inherent negative social impacts.'[124]

Throughout the 1990s one-tenth of Shanghai households were moved to the suburbs.[125] Writing in 2007 He notes that the number of relocations constantly increased from 1999 onwards, with 820,458 households having been relocated since 1997 and 41.88 million square metres of housing destroyed to pave the way for new developments and a reimagined city.[126] According to Brook: 'Overall, one million families were moved in the effort to remake Shanghai.'[127] Baudrillard warned against the system of extreme security, control and dissuasion that inform malls such as Paris's Beaubourg. Such malls, he wrote, are 'emptying machines'.[128] So are Shanghai's luxury malls in that they are emptying the areas in which they appear of unwanted citizens, those who cannot consume the luxury goods on offer in the new retail landscape and can no longer afford to live in their old neighbourhood.

From 1999 to 2001, Xintiandi, for instance, formerly a neighbourhood of middle- to low-income residents, was turned into a consumer spot of expatriates and other high-spenders able to enjoy the smart eateries and bars that now exist alongside the old Shikumen, whose façades have been preserved for the 'tourist gaze'.[129] Within six months 1,950 households were excluded from Xintiandi and resettled and 'more than 3,800 households and 156 work units in the [nearby] Taipingqiao Park were relocated in only 43 days. This was a record for the fastest residential relocation in Shanghai.'[130] The redevelopment of Pudong, which now hosts several luxury shopping malls, was facilitated by the action of armed police, who used force to evict those residents unwilling to leave their home: 'Oftentimes, the authorities would cut off water and electricity to neighborhoods they were clearing to convince the hesitant', although in 2005 the Shanghai government banned this practice.[131]

Thus, the refashioning of Shanghai has gone hand in hand with the expansion of its periphery: 'ten years ago, 5 km away from the Inner Ring Line would have been peripheral enough; now, this boundary is pushed further by another 5 or even 10 km'.[132] Although resettled in accommodation that might be a material improvement from their old housing, low-income residents have seen their neighbourhoods destroyed while they have suffered from a lack of local amenities as well as unemployment not least due to exorbitant commuting costs.[133] As Chen et al. observe, the redevelopment of Shanghai has taken place 'with little concern for the urban poor';[134] belonging and inclusion have been sacrificed to the imperative of turning Shanghai into a world-class city.[135]

Exclusion, Madanipoor writes, 'should be regarded as a socio-spatial phenomenon'.[136] Reminding us that shopping malls are private spaces with 'controlled access and boundaries', he notes how 'a socio-spatial geometry of difference and segregation' born out of land and property development as well as spatial planning becomes 'the foundation of exclusion'.[137] This logic is visibly at play in the redevelopment of Shanghai.

However, clear boundaries are not only material but also symbolic: they are the walls and guarded doors that enable the controlled access Madanipoor talks about, but they are also made of the system of signs luxury malls are the bearers of. Cartier notes that the 'globalizing iconicity' malls in large cities often display is 'consonant with the interests of the transnational capitalist class'.[138] Included in this iconicity are the luxury brand names and attendant advertisements and windows that luxury malls feature, and that pave one's walk along streets such as Nanjing Road or Huaihai Road. There, Fendi, Balenciaga, Chanel, Coach are signs that occupy Shanghai's 'brandscape'[139] and participate in its staging as a cosmopolitan city.

As Yu observes, 'China's city centers have transformed from sites of manufacturing and production, under Chairman Mao, to sites of consumption and imagination'; they are 'not just spaces where money and goods are exchanged, but also spaces of representation'.[140] Embedded in the centre of the city, Shanghai's luxury mall are visions of 'a good life',[141] a life of plenty that intimates success and Shanghai's position as a world city. As Crawford puts it 'malls lend glamour and success to their urban setting, suggesting that the city is important, exciting and prosperous'.[142] When such malls are luxury malls they bring an added aura of distinction and exclusivity to the urban geography they are part of.

In his description of the Shanghai Museum, opened in 1996, Abbas notes its exceeding cleanliness:

> There always seems to be some workers polishing the brass on the railings or the marble on the floor. Even the toilets are kept meticulously clean. The dirtier the streets around it, the cleaner the museum. And suddenly you realize that the museum does not think itself as being part of a local space at all, but as part of a virtual global cultural network. The Shanghai Museum is not just where artworks are being shown in Shanghai; it is also where Shanghai *shows itself off* in the museum, with its image cleaned up and in hope that the world is looking.[143]

Here Abbas could well be talking about the city's luxury malls. Like the museum they are sparklingly clean. There too workers are permanently walking around wiping every surface and ensuring the environment remains as glossy as the goods on display in the stores. In fact cleaning personnel, along with security staff, are often the main presence in the malls' empty plazas and corridors. Like the Shanghai Museum, the malls' sanitized luxury sharply contrasts with the messiness of surrounding streets, and like it 'it is also where Shanghai shows itself off'.

Shanghai's brandscape of luxury fashion logos and the malls and boutiques on which they float also somehow tears the city apart from its local fabric by displaying faces and words (often English) that look and sound foreign to Chinese local residents. Those are the words and faces of a still poorly diversified Western fashion system, where the field of luxury remains dominated by European and American brands. Inside the malls and on their outside walls the large advertising billboards for the luxury brands available there – such as, during my visits, Armani, Jill Sander, Dior, Fendi, Coach and many others – featured Caucasian faces (see Figure 11.6).

As Ermann observes, 'branding is usually connected with de-teritorialization'.[144] The English words that hover on the walls and windows of the malls further de-territorialize them from their locale. At IAPM, a sign on the floor, for instance, indicates that following the arrow are 'more shops' (see Figure 11.7), and at Super Brands Mall a wall reads 'Lots of Choices, Full of Joyce' (see Figure 11.8). Klingman notes that today's brandscapes, made of 'signature buildings, shopping centers, expositions, and planned residential developments', often 'fail to establish sensitive connections to particular contexts by imposing standardized forms and formulas on the urban or suburban landscape'. Luxury malls and the luxury fashion industry they feed on participate in this 'severing' of 'identity from the complexity of the social fabric' that Klingman argues characterizes contemporary brandscapes.[145]

Deterritorialization goes hand in hand with reterritorialization,[146] here that of Shanghai's urban landscape with the signs and values of the West. As Askegaard

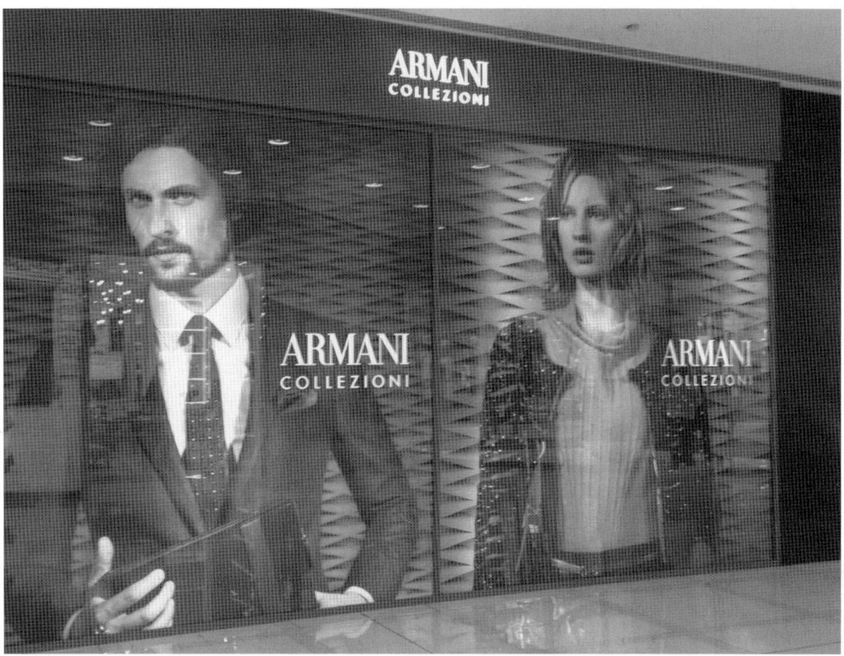

Figure 11.6 IMG, West Nanjing Road. Courtesy of Agnès Rocamora.

Figure 11.7 IAPM. Courtesy of Agnès Rocamora.

Figure 11.8 Super Brand Mall. Courtesy of Agnès Rocamora.

notes: 'brands are among the most significant ideoscapes in the globalization processes'.[147] This is an ideoscape in the service of Western interests and, in China, of a still influential Western ideal[148] that further reinforces Western hegemony.

Conclusion

In this chapter, I have argued that the fashioning of Shanghai by way of its luxury-malling must be looked at in the context of two concurrent phenomenon: China's embrace of luxury, itself linked to the nation's adoption of capitalism; and the rapid and intense urban regeneration of the city. This has gone hand in hand with a process of exclusion of large numbers of urban residents, which draws attention to one of the many human costs that can be associated with the fashioning of cities. Exclusion and expropriation also take a semiotic form through the inscription of Shanghai's urban landscape with the logos and brand names of European and American luxury fashion companies. Writing the city into a global network of fashionable metropoles, such logos and names have taken over local signs, and deterritorialized the local socio-geographical map. The redefinition and rebranding of cities by way of fashion is a multi-dimensional process that sits across symbolic and material forces and realities, as I have shown in this chapter. Understanding this process means understanding the formation of both cities and fashion across the world and the network of signs, systems, materials and human beings that are caught in it, as well as in its tensions and inequalities.

Notes

1 J. Gamble, *Shanghai in Transition* (London: RoutledgeCurzon, 2003); A. Go Yeh, F.F. Yang and J. Wang, 'Economic Transition and Urban Transformation of China: The Interplay of the State and the Market', *Urban Studies*, 52, no. 15 (2015): 2822–48.

2 X. Chen, 'A Globalising City on the Rise: Shanghai's Transformation in Comparative Perspective', in Xiangming Chen (ed.), *Rising Shanghai: State Power and Local Transformations in a Global City* (Minneapolis, MN: University of Minnesota Press, 2009).

3 S. Sassen, 'The Global City Perspective: Theoretical Implications for Shanghai', in Chen (ed.), *Rising Shanghai*; Tingwei Zhang, 'Striving to be a Global City from Below' in Chen (ed.), *Rising Shanghai*.

4 The visits took place over six trips of one to two weeks each. Informed by an ethnographic approach, each visit involved systematic lengthy observations of luxury shopping malls in central Shanghai, the exploration of adjacent streets, and of the city's 'fashion map' (Steele) more generally. The data was collected in the form of extensive written notes and photographic diaries.

5 W. Benjamin, *The Arcades Project*, ed. Rolf Tiedemann, trans. Howard Eiland and Kevin McLaughlin (New York: Belknap Press, 2002).

6 M. Crawford, 'The World in a Shopping Mall', in Michael Sorkin (ed.), *Variations on a Theme Park* (New York: Hill and Wang, 1992), 20.

7 Ibid.; C. Marshall, Southdale Center: America's First Shopping Mall – A History of Cities in 50 Buildings, Day 30', *Guardian*, 6 May 2015. Available online: https://www.theguardian.com/cities/2015/may/06/southdale-center-america-first-shopping-mall-history-cities-50-buildings (accessed 10 September 2017).

8 Gruen, cited in Marshall, *Southdale Center*.

9 Marshall, *Southdale Center*.

10 Crawford, 'The World in a Shopping Mall', 22.

11 Ibid., 8.

12 Ibid., 8, 10; Arlene Dávila, *El Mall: The Spatial and Class Politics of Shopping Malls in Latin America* (Oakland, CA: University of California Press, 2016).

13 Dávila, *El Mall*.

14 Crawford, 'The World in a Shopping Mall', 11.

15 S. Wang, Yongchang Zhang and Yuanfei Wang, 'Opportunities and Challenges of Shopping Centre Development in China: A Case Study of Shanghai', *Journal of Shopping Centre Research* 20 (2006): 19–55.

16 Zhen, 'Mainland China Shopping Malls and Department Stores Struggling as Economy Slows', *South China Morning Post*, 7 March 2016. Available online: http://www.scmp.com/property/hong-kong-china/article/1921878/mainland-china-shopping-malls-and-department-stores (accessed 10 January 2016).

17 Nicholas Jewell, *Shopping Malls and Public Space in Modern China* (Farnham: Ashgate, 2015), 111.

18 Wang et al., 'Opportunities and Challenges of Shopping Centre Development in China', 27; J. Wu, 'Globalization and Emerging Office and Commercial Landscapes in Shanghai', *Urban Geography* 32 no. 4 (2011): 512, DOI: 10.2747/0272-3638.32.4.511.

19 H. Roxburgh, 'Does Shanghai Need This Many Shopping Malls?', *Time Out Shanghai*, 3 February 2015. Available online: http://www.timeoutshanghai.com/features/Shopping_Style-Shopping_features/25063/Does-Shanghai-need-this-many-shopping-malls.html (accessed 7 August 2016).

20 C. Cartier, 'Model Hong Kong Malls and their Development in Mainland China: Consumer Iconicity and the Trans/national Capitalist Class', *Global Networks*, 2016, 14. DOI: 10.1111/glob.12121.

21 https://www.shkp.com/Pages/shanghai-detail-2#sales_tab=/en-US/Pages/shanghai-detail-2-resident.

22 Cartier, 'Model Hong Kong Malls', 14.

23 See, e.g., S. Zukin, P. Kasinits and X. Chen, *Global Cities, Local Streets: Everyday Diversity from New York to Shanghai* (New York: Routledge, 2016).

24 Jewell, *Shopping Malls and Public Space in Modern China*, 139.

25 Cartier, 'Model Hong Kong Malls', 14.

26 Jewell, *Shopping Malls and Public Space in Modern China*; Roxburgh, 'Does Shanghai Need This Many Shopping Malls?'; Wang et al., 'Opportunities and Challenges of Shopping Centre Development in China'.

27 Ibid., 22.

28 Benjamin, *The Arcades Project*.

29 F. Roberts, 'What is Really Happening in China's Luxury Market?', Luxury Society, 2014. Available online: http://luxurysociety.com/articles/2014/10/what-is-really-happening-in-chinas-luxury-market (accessed 12 October 2014).

30 Ibid.

31 Bloomberg, 2016; K. Chitrakorn, 'Can China End the Illicit "Daigou" Trade?' (Business of Fashion, 2016). Available online: https://www.businessoffashion.com/

articles/global-currents/can-china-put-an-end-to-the-illicit-daigou-trade (accessed 10 February 2016).

32 Roberts, 'What Is Really Happening'; L. Yu, *Consumption in China* (Cambridge: Polity, 2014), 63, drawing on *Business Insider*, 2013.

33 Dehua Chi, 'China Becomes World's Second Largest Luxury Market', *Global Times*, 12 December 2017. Available online: https://gbtimes.com/china-becomes-worlds-second-largest-luxury-market (accessed 27 January 2018).

34 J. Rapp, 2017, 'China's "Wannabe Consumers" Will Grow the Fastest by 2020, Says Bain Report', *Jing Daily*, 25 September 2017. Available online: https://jingdaily.com/chinas-wannabe-consumers-will-see-fastest-growth-bain/ (accessed 2 October 2017).

35 Yu, *Consumption in China*, 64, 71.

36 'Report: Chinese Shoppers Bought Almost Half the World's Luxury Goods in 2015', *Jing Daily*, 25 September 2016. Available online: https://jingdaily.com/report-chinese-shoppers-bought-almost-half-the-worlds-luxury-goods-in-2015/ (accessed 18 February 2016).

37 See, e.g., S. He, 'State-sponsored Gentrification Under Market Transition: The Case of Shanghai', *Urban Affairs Review*, November 43, no. 2 (2007), 10.1177/1078087407305175.

38 Y. Bao, 'Shanghai Weekly: Globalization, Consumerism, and Shanghai Popular Culture', *Inter-Asia Cultural Studies* 9, no. 4 (2008): 557.

39 He, 'State-sponsored Gentrification Under Market Transition', 175; Lisa Rofel, *Desiring China: Experiments in Neoliberalism, Sexuality, and Public Culture* (Durham, NC: Duke University Press, 2007).

40 Rofel, *Desiring China*, 6.

41 Rofel, *Desiring China*; Yu, *Consumption in China*.

42 Rofel, *Desiring China*.

43 Yu, *Consumption in China*, 12.

44 M. Keane, 'Creative Industries in China: Four Perspectives on Social Transformation', *International Journal of Cultural Policy* 15, no. 4 (2009): 433.

45 Rofel, *Desiring China*.

46 S. He and C.S. Lin George, 'Producing and Consuming China's New Urban Space: State, Market and Society', *Urban Studies* 52 no. 15 (2015): 2761; Rofel, *Desiring China*.

47 Yu, *Consumption in China*, 13.

48 D.S. Knight, 'Shanghai Cosmopolitan: Class, Gender and Cultural Citizenship in Weihui's Shanghai Babe', *Journal of Contemporary China* 12, no. 37 (2003): 639–53, drawing on Stevenson.

49 D. Brook, 'Head of the Dragon: The Rise of New Shanghai', *Places*, February 2013, 15. Available online: https://placesjournal.org/article/head-of-the-dragon-the-rise-of-new-shanghai/ (accessed 5 November 2016).

50 Bao, 'Shanghai Weekly', 559; Cartier, 'Model Hong Kong Malls and their Development in Mainland China', 2.

51 Yu, *Consumption in China*, 13.

52 Ibid., 20.

53 S. He and F. Wu, 'Property-led Redevelopment in Post-reform China: A Case Study of Xintiandi Redevelopment Project in Shanghai', *Journal of Urban Affairs* 27 no. 1 (2005): 3.

54 X. Chen and R. Yuan, 'Modernity and Globalization: The Local and Global Sources of Individualistic and Materialistic Values in Shanghai', *Globalizations* 13, no. 1 (2016): 22; Yu, *Consumption in China*.

55 Jewell, *Shopping Malls and Public Space in Modern China*, 115.

56 Rofel, *Desiring China*.

57 M.-C. Bergère, *Histoire de Shanghai* (Paris: Fayard, 2002); Lee Leo Ou-Fan, *Shanghai Modern: The Flowering of a New Urban Culture in China, 1930–1945* (London: Harvard University Press, 1999).

58 Lee, *Shanghai Modern*.

59 Ibid., 5, 73.

60 Xianshi (Sincere, opened in 1917), Yong'an (Wing On, opened in 1918), Xinxin (Sun Sun, opened in 1926) and Daxin (Sun Company), 'all built with investments from overseas Chinese businessmen' (Lee, *Shanghai Modern*, 13). They were all near or on the Nanking Road, 'the main thoroughfare of the International Settlement' and a commercial street akin to Oxford Circus (Lee, *Shanghai Modern*, 15).

61 Ibid., 5, 73, 312.

62 Bergère, *Histoire de Shanghai*, 388.

63 H. Yu, X. Chen and X. Zhong, 'Commercial Development from Below: The Resilience of Local Shops in Shanghai', in S. Zukin, P. Kasinitz and X. Chen (eds), *Global Cities, Local Streets: Everyday Life from New York to Shanghai* (New York: Routledge, 58–88).

64 Y. Ning and Z. Yan, 'The Changing Industrial and Spatial Structure in Shanghai', *Urban Geography* 16, no. 7 (1995): 577–94.

65 Bergère, *Histoire de Shanghai*.

66 Ibid.

67 Ibid.; He and Wu, 'Property-led Redevelopment in Post-reform China'.

68 Chen, 'A Globalising City on the Rise'.

69 Ibid., xv.

70 Bao, 'Shanghai Weekly', 559.

71 Ibid.

72 See, e.g., He and Lin, 'Producing and Consuming China's New Urban Space'; Sun X. and Huang Ronggui, 'Extension of State-Led Growth Coalition and Grassroots Management: A Case Study of Shanghai', *Urban Affairs Review* 1, no. 27 (2015):

1–27; F. Wu, 'The Global and Local Dimensions of Place-making: Remaking Shanghai as a World City', *Urban Studies* 37, no. 8 (2000); J. Wu, 'Globalization and Emerging Office and Commercial Landscapes in Shanghai' *Urban Geography* 32, no. 4 (2011), DOI: 10.2747/0272-3638.32.4.511.

73 'Producing and Consuming China's New Urban Space', 7–8.

74 See, e.g., F. Wu, 'The Global and Local Dimensions of Place-making'.

75 Bergère, *Histoire de Shanghai*, 441.

76 Chen, 'A Globalising City on the Rise', xv.

77 Roxburgh, 'Does Shanghai Need This Many Shopping Malls?'

78 Wang et al., 'Opportunities and Challenges of Shopping Centre Development in China', 22.

79 See A. Klingmann, *Brandscapes: Architecture in the Experience Economy* (Cambridge, MA: MIT Press, 2007).

80 See also Anna Greenspan, *Shanghai Future: Modernity Remade* (London: Hurst & Company, 2014), 53; Jewell, *Shopping Malls and Public Space in Modern China*, 130.

81 C. D'Arpizio, Federica Levato, Daniele Zito and Joelle de Montgolfier, *Luxury Goods Worldwide Market Study* (Fall–Winter 2015), Bain & Company. http://ikusmer.blog.euskadi.eus/wp-content/uploads/2016/11/Luxury-goods-worldwide-market-study.pdf (accessed August 2016).

82 Roberts, 'What Is Really Happening in China's Luxury Market?'

83 Yu, *Consumption in China*, 11.

84 Ibid.

85 K. Chitrakorn, 'Can China End the Illicit "Daigou" Trade?'

86 Ibid.

87 Ibid.; Y. Pan, 'More Luxury Stores Closed in China Over the Last Year Than in Any Other Country', *Jing Daily*, 28 September 2017. Available online: https://jingdaily.com/luxury-brands-close-most-stores-in-china/ (accessed 29 September 2017).

88 Yu, *Consumption in China*, 70.

89 L. Flora, 'Tmall Kicks Off Mei.com-Backed Luxury Channel with Star-Studded Launch in Shanghai', *Jing Daily*, 31 March 2016. Available online: https://jingdaily.com/tmall-kicks-off-mei-com-backed-luxury-channel-star-studded-launch-shanghai/ (accessed 2 June 2016); C. Hall, 'China's Social Media Celebs Turn E-Commerce Moguls', WWD, 10 October. Available online: https://wwd.com/fashion-news/designer-luxury/chinas-social-media-celebs-turn-e-commerce-moguls-10523851 (accessed December 2016); Liz Flora, 'Report: Chinese Shoppers Bought Almost Half the World's Luxury Goods in 2015', *Jing Daily*, 16 February 2016. Available online: https://jingdaily.com/report-chinese-shoppers-bought-almost-half-the-worlds-luxury-goods-in-2015/ (accessed 18 February 2016).

90 Jewell, *Shopping Malls and Public Space in Modern China*, 130; see also S. Li, 'Hang Lung Says Luxury Brands at its Mall in Shanghai Double Retail Space', *South China Morning Post*, 30 July 2015. Available online: http://www.scmp.com/business/china-business/article/1845250/hang-lung-says-luxury-brands-its-mall-shanghai-double-retail (accessed 3 August 2016).

91 Jewell, *Shopping Malls and Public Space in Modern China*, 135.

92 MarketWire, 2017; Quintessentially, 2017.

93 Greenspan, *Shanghai Future*, 220.

94 Wang et al., 'Opportunities and Challenges of Shopping Centre Development in China', 47.

95 Ibid., 32.

96 Dávila, *El Mall*.

97 Ibid.

98 He and Wu, 'Property-led Redevelopment in Post-reform China:'; Sun and Huang, 'Extension of State-Led Growth Coalition and Grassroots Management'; F. Wu, 'The Global and Local Dimensions of Place-making: Remaking Shanghai as a World City', *Urban Studies* 37, no. 8 (2000): 1359–77.

99 Sun and Huang, 'Extension of State-Led Growth Coalition and Grassroots Management'; Wu, 'The Global and Local Dimensions of Place-making'.

100 He and Wu, 'Property-led Redevelopment in Post-reform China'; Sun and Huang, Extension of State-Led Growth Coalition and Grassroots Management'.

101 On the former see, for instance, Brook, 'Head of the Dragon'; Greenspan, *Shanghai Future*; Wu, 'The Global and Local Dimensions of Place-making'. On the latter, see He and Wu, 'Property-led Redevelopment in Post-reform China'.

102 Wang et al., 'Opportunities and Challenges of Shopping Centre Development in China', 48.

103 Dávila, *El Mall*: 12.

104 Ibid.

105 Ibid.

106 P. Bourdieu, *La Misère du Monde* (Paris: Points, 1993).

107 Yu et al., 'Commercial Development from Below'.

108 Rofel, *Desiring China*, 111.

109 Yu, *Consumption in China*, 6; see also X. Chen, L. Wang and R. Kundu, 'Localizing the Production of Global Cities: A Comparison of New Town Developments Around Shanghai and Kolkata', *City & Community* 8 no. 4 (2009): 459.

110 Yu, *Consumption in China*, 63.

111 J. Goss, 'The "Magic of the Mall": An Analysis of Form, Function, and Meaning in the Contemporary Retail Built Environment', *Annals of the Association of American Geographers* 83, no. 1 (March 1993): 18–47.

112 Goss, 'The "Magic of the Mall": An Analysis of Form, Function, and Meaning in the Contemporary Retail Built Environment', 26.

113 Brook, 'Head of the Dragon', 24.

114 Ibid.

115 Yu et al., 'Commercial Development from Below'.

116 See also Wang et al., 'Opportunities and Challenges of Shopping Centre Development in China', 36–7.

117 Goss 'The "Magic of the Mall"', 34.

118 Jewell, *Shopping Malls and Public Space in Modern China*, 186; see also Greenspan, *Shanghai Future*, 60.

119 X. Wang, 'From Architecture to Advertising – the Changes in Shanghai's Urban Space Over the Last 15 Years', *Inter-Asia Cultural Studies* 11, no. 1 (2010): 25.

120 Greenspan, *Shanghai Future*, 60.

121 He, 'State-sponsored Gentrification Under Market Transition'.

122 Greenspan, *Shanghai Future*, 53, 60.

123 Wu, 'The Global and Local Dimensions of Place-making', 1364.

124 He, 'State-sponsored Gentrification Under Market Transition', 173; see also T.R. Samara, 'Politics and the Social in World-class Cities: Building a Shanghai Model', *Urban Studies* 52, no. 15 (2015): 2906–21.

125 Bergère, *Histoire de Shanghai*, 441.

126 He, 'State-sponsored Gentrification Under Market Transition', 177.

127 Brook, 'Head of the Dragon', 10–11.

128 Jean Baudrillard, 'Machines à faire le vide', *Simulacres et Simulations* (Paris: Editions Galilée, 1981), 93–4.

129 J. Urry, *The Tourist Gaze* (London: Sage, 1990); He and Wu, 'Property-led Redevelopment in Post-reform China', 9.

130 He, 'State-sponsored Gentrification Under Market Transition: The Case of Shanghai', 181.

131 Brook, 'Head of the Dragon', 10–11.

132 Wang, 'From Architecture to Advertising', 33.

133 Brook, 'Head of the Dragon', 10–11; He, 'State-sponsored Gentrification Under Market Transition', 181; He and Wu, 'Property-led Redevelopment in Post-reform China', 15.

134 Chen et al., 'Localizing the Production of Global Cities', 446.

135 He and Lin, 'Producing and Consuming China's New Urban Space', 2767.

136 A. Madanipoor, 'Social Exclusion and Space', in Richard T. LeGates and Frederic Stout (eds), *The City Reader* (Abingdon: Routledge, 2011), 188.

137 Madanipoor, 'Social Exclusion and Space', 192.

138 Cartier, 'Model Hong Kong Malls', 27.

139 Klingmann, *Brandscapes*.

140 Yu, *Consumption in China*, 34.

141 Jewell, *Shopping Malls and Public Space in Modern China*, 135.

142 Crawford, 'The World in a Shopping Mall', 27.

143 Ackbar Abbas, 'Cosmopolitan De-scriptions: Shanghai and Hong Kong', *Public Culture* 12, no. 3 (Fall 2000): 782

144 Ulrich Ermann, 'Consumer Capitalism and Brand Fetishism: The Case of Fashion Brands in Bulgaria', in Andy Pike (ed.), *Brands and Branding Geographies* (Cheltenham: Edward Elgar, 2011), 117.

145 Klingmann, *Brandscapes*, 3.

146 Gilles Deleuze and Felix Guattari, *Mille Plateaux* (Paris: Les Editions de Minuit, 1980).

147 S. Askegaard, 'Brands as a Global Ideoscape', in Jonathan E. Schroeder and Miriam Salzer-Morling (eds), *Brand Culture* (London: Routledge, 2006), 94, drawing on Appadurai.

148 Yu, *Consumption in China*, 117.

12

'There will never be a Chinese fashion'

Staking a Claim for Shanghai as a Fashion City

Anja Aronowsky Cronberg

Prologue

I first thought of 'Chinese fashion' as a concept a few years ago when I interviewed a portentous gentleman who at the time held a very important position in the French fashion industry. He spoke disparagingly of Chinese designers coming to Paris to showcase their work during fashion week: 'We've had a number of established Chinese designers showing in Paris by now, but after a while we realised that they had no talent and that no press was interested.'[1] Being many decades younger, and perhaps because of it subject to a different notion of the importance of both diversity and political correctness, I was quietly scandalized. But at the same time, the man's sneering off-the-cuff remark made me reflect on my own attitude towards Chinese fashion. Was the fact that I hadn't even considered it not a sign of the same prejudice?

Afterwards, I became curious about what could be classified as 'Chinese fashion', and how it might manifest itself on the international high fashion scene. Were there Chinese designers showing in New York, London or Milan? Or, in fact, in Paris? How come I'd never heard of any? Why was 'no press interested'? Was it because the designers had 'no talent' or because other journalists and editors had as muddy a grasp of the phenomenon as I did? Was it particularly hard for a Chinese designer to establish himself or herself in one of the four fashion capitals, and if so, why?

When, in 2014, I began to research contemporary Chinese fashion in Shanghai in earnest, these were some of the questions I brought with me on my first journey. Some rudimentary research proved that only a handful of designers had representation on the main fashion websites (at the time these were Style.com, now Vogue.com, Nowfashion.com and Businessoffashion.com), and that few, if any, got their shows reviewed in the main newspapers during fashion week (*The New York Times, The Washington Post, New York Magazine*). I counted only a few Chinese names on the official calendars in Paris, New York, Milan and London – commonly held to be the main cities for showcasing fashion – and those who did tended to have bad scheduling slots (typically early in the morning or on the day before the majority of editors and buyers arrive in town). Perhaps predictably, the Chinese-sounding names in mainstream high fashion belonged to Chinese Americans – Anna Sui, Alexander Wang, Vera Wang.

In light of all this I have spent three years travelling to Shanghai hoping to better understand how young Chinese designers regard the Western-dominated fashion industry, and how this fashion system sees them in return. Considering the resistance mounted by people like my notable interviewee, and the fact that mainland Chinese designers don't 'need' either international press or buyers to mount a sustainable business, is making it abroad still considered an important part of a successful career?[2]

Scene 1: 1436 × Uma Wang S/S 2017 Presentation, Yuanmingyuan Road, Huangpu District

I am standing somewhere out of the light, observing, as the most fashionable editors, buyers, bloggers and media stars file into what I've been told is the most anticipated show of the season. It's running late, of course – some things don't change, regardless of whether the stage is set in Paris, in New York or in Shanghai. This being Shanghai, though, the wait is made bearable by plenty of champagne. Cliques coalesce quickly; everybody seems to know each other. I spy the designer from afar: she appears remarkably calm as assistants and well-wishers buzz around her. I see a young man in a hooded sweatshirt, shaped as if tailor-made for Quasimodo – it's Vetements, an expensive and hard-to-find fashion brand from Paris: the latest for those in the know. Someone tells me he's a famous blogger on WeChat. I see another man wearing sunglasses though we are inside; he's apparently an editor from *GQ China*, the men's magazine. I see a young girl with bright pink hair wearing bunny ears, and another with a buzz cut and huge dangling earrings. So far, so familiar. It's curious really, to have travelled so far to find a scene so similar to the one I've left behind.

Compared to Paris though, whose earliest incarnation of fashion week arose in 1945, Shanghai is in fashion kindergarten. Fashion week here started in 2001, as an initiative hosted by the Shanghai Municipal Government and supported by the Ministry of Commerce. In 2012, China's then president Hu Jintao announced a strategy to 'build a great nation of culture',[3] which created a noticeable upswing in the attention and budget lavished on the Chinese fashion industry. Today, Shanghai Fashion Week is organized by the Shanghai Textile Group, and its main venue has for the past years been a huge tent in Xintiandi, Shanghai's most exclusive shopping district. Ticket scalpers, fashion professionals and students jostle for space outside the main entrance, but lately many designers have complained about the uniformity of the tent, and the difficulty of making it 'yours', so for the past two seasons a 'pioneer fashion and arts festival' called 'Labelhood' has also received funding to put on exhibitions and shows by up-and-coming Chinese designers. I've been told that the Labelhood shows are the only ones worth attending now – the others are 'boring, too mainstream. Nobody goes there anymore.'[4]

I'm here to find some answers to my many earlier questions, but also to better understand what makes a 'Shanghai fashion designer' today as opposed to a 'Chinese fashion designer' or just a 'fashion designer', and though this is my third visit to the city I'm still having trouble with my classifications. Is it someone born here? Or someone who studied here? Someone with a studio in the city, and employees? Or perhaps it's someone who sets up shop here twice a year to take advantage of the rapidly growing fashion scene? The designers whose shows and showrooms I have become familiar with over the past few years all fall into one of these categories, though usually not two. The designer Yang Li is an interesting case in point. Born in Beijing, he left China as a ten-year-old to spend the next decade of his life in Melbourne. At twenty he moved to London to study at Central Saint Martins, the fabled fashion school that has become a prerequisite for success in China. Since 2013 he has shown his eponymous womenswear line at Paris Fashion Week twice a year, and now he is in Shanghai to promote it. We meet at a cocktail party held in his honour at Dong Liang, a store in the city's French Concession that has made it their mission to promote Chinese designers to the Chinese customer. I'm reminded of a headline in *The Washington Post* a few years ago, hailing Li as a 'designer putting China on fashion's biggest stage',[5] but also of something an editor told me, about how Yang Li who at first didn't want to be seen as a Chinese designer now has realized that it makes good business sense to identify with China in order to sell more here.[6] After the prerequisite air kissing (the transcontinental greeting for fashion people) and small talk about the weather (rain) I ask him about what he makes of being described as a 'Chinese designer' in the West, considering that he has spent most of his life abroad. He tells me that he has begun thinking of himself as Chinese again, that he's interested in coming here more often.[7] Later, Tasha Liu, one of the proprietors of the store as well as the instigator of Labelhood, tells me that Li's clothes are among their bestsellers, but that she never considered Li a Chinese designer, until she asked him and he replied: 'Tasha, I am. I am *Yang Li*. I was born in China so I am kind of like a spy. I am living in London, in a Western country, and I spy on their habits, their culture and experience and I want to bring them back [to China] to share them with the young generation.'[8]

But back to the fashion show, which is about to begin. Uma Wang, the designer, is the greatest pride of the Chinese fashion editors who travel unfailingly to Europe and America for the fashion weeks. With a sophisticated aesthetic and a refined image, she has been showing at Milan fashion week since 2014 and has recently been taken on as a client by Michèle Montagne, one of Paris's most revered PR agents, and for autumn/winter 2017 she will hold her first show in Paris. Later, over hot ginger tea on another rainy day, she tells me that she divides her time between a small village in Italy, where her factory is, and Shanghai, where she keeps a studio, and that though her collections are stocked worldwide it's still in China that she makes the most money.[9] Today she is showing a new initiative, a collaboration with Erdos, one of the largest cashmere manufacturers in China who are keen to be magnified by the aura that currently surrounds Uma Wang. 1436 is their most exclusive cashmere line, and Wang has made asymmetrical dresses, cardigans with trailing frills and dainty milkmaid bonnets from it. After a short promo film that shows the designer looking poetically melancholic among goats, the models file out in a semi-choreographed constellation, slowly circling the stage before eventually lining up so that the audience can get close in order to touch a fabric, check the detailing or just take a selfie.

When did Chinese shoppers, otherwise known for spending lavishly on Western luxury brands, start favouring Chinese designers? Uma Wang tells me that she was curious herself, so she started asking her clients why they were buying her clothes rather than the more well-established European brands. The answer was quite clear: once Louis Vuitton, Dior, Gucci, Hermès and other French-owned corporations started opening stores all over Shanghai and Beijing, as well as in second- and third-tier cities across the country, their exclusivity evaporated. An omnipresent brand has little appeal to the fashion jet set: now a Chinese designer with a high-fashion pedigree is proof not just of wealth, but of good taste and sophistication – a mark of distinction.[10]

Figure 12.1 1436 × Uma Wang. Courtesy of Tian Zhiwei.

Scene 2: Tube Showroom S/S 2017 Presentations, Yuyuan Road, Changning District

Zemira Hu and Echo Zhuang, the owners of Dia Creative Communications and, since 2015, Tube Showroom, are, like all good sales agents, brisk in their manner and brimming with enthusiasm when speaking about the designers they represent. They tell me that most of them are 'sea turtles' – designers who have studied abroad only to return to China to set up shop. They are graduates from London mostly: Central Saint Martins as well as London College of Fashion and the Royal College of Art. Some come from Parsons in New York.

The showroom is brimming with activity, and unlike similar spaces in Paris the designers are all here themselves, schmoozing with potential clients and selling their collections. Zhuang explains that Chinese designers 'want to know everything. They want to know all the people; they want to know all the connections. They want to know how an order works. They really care about their product.'[11] Tube Showroom broke away from the official trade show Mode Shanghai earlier this year, and work only with Chinese designers, all of them in their early to mid-twenties with labels only a few years old. Their focus is mainly on the domestic market, though Hu and Zhuang tell me that all their designers want to be known internationally. Zhuang explains.

> They are two-way. They either start domestic and want to go overseas, or start overseas and want to go domestic. Frankly, it's about money. The buyers from second and third tier cities all come with big budgets [and] stores in China are loyal to designers. The buyers want to be in the fashion circle. They come and buy almost every piece from the designer they like; they have *large* budgets. Even Dong Liang don't usually drop designers.[12]

Zhuang continues:

> We approach designers after they've presented one season at another trade show. I apply a Corso Como[13] standard to whether their work falls in to the category for 'good design'. I ask myself, 'Would this sell in Corso Como?' When I worked there I would sometimes get the question, 'How do you know if something will work at Corso Como?' And I would answer, 'It's very difficult to explain: when you see it, you know it.'

Zhuang and Hu make contracts with the designers they represent on a season-by-season basis, extending them as they notice an ongoing and stable interest from buyers. They teach them about manufacturing and logistics in the China market, and encourage designers who are still based in Europe or America to move their production to China, as high import taxes otherwise make for prohibitively hefty wholesale prices. As we walk around the showroom, I am introduced to Steven Tai, a Chinese-Canadian designer. Hu is quick to tell me that Tai shows in London, *on schedule*. And, indeed, the first thing Tai himself tells me after we say hello is also that he shows at London Fashion Week. Later, Zhuang confirms that showing in either London, Milan, New York or Paris is part of the appeal of a Chinese designer for a Chinese buyer, as is having studied in either London or New York.

Une Yea, who has run her menswear label Staffonly since 2015 with her partner Shimo Zhou, tells me that she is keen to get a Paris showroom, though for a show she would 'definitely' go for London, where she and Zhou recently graduated from the Royal College of Art and London College of Fashion respectively. 'I've heard that in Europe it's quite hard to survive your first or second season, but in China they are really into trying new things.'[14] Yea tells me that she decided to return to China because 'production is easier here', and because she knew she would have practical and financial support from her family, were she to start her brand here.

Family support is a common thread among the young designers I encounter at Tube. Momo Wang, the founder of Museum of Childhood, a brand defined by its childlike aesthetic (frills, straw hats, knee-high socks, pink and lilac bralettes and lots of embroidery) readily tells me about deciding to come back home to start her company after graduating with a BA in Fashion Design from Central Saint Martins (Figure 12.2). There is less competition in China, and it is both cheaper and easier to hire a team and organize production. And then there's the family factor. 'Chinese [designers] are rich people's kids. Our parents were encouraged in the seventies and eighties to have their own business; they worked very hard. They grew up poor, but now they have money, and they want to make their children's dreams come true.'[15]

Figure 12.2 Museum of Friendship. Courtesy of David Myron.

Scene 3: Angel Chen Studio, Changan Road, Zhabei District

> The Chinese want to become better, they want to learn, they want to have a more mature culture. Many years ago there was only the Chinese copycat, but now [customers] don't just want 'made in China', they want 'designed in China'. People's minds are changing. They're growing. They're eager to see what Chinese designers are doing outside of China.[16]

This is what Angel Chen, a twenty-five-year-old designer from Shengzhen, tells me while fiddling with her iPad. We're in her studio, in a high-rise near the Shanghai Railway Station (see Plate 7). Her clothes are colourful and a little zany, the sort of thing a club kid might wear to attract the attention of a street-style photographer during London Fashion Week. There are silver-spangled trousers, pink and turquoise frilly dresses, plenty of orange jackets and her bestseller – an oversized version of the coat a *bōsōzoku*, or Japanese motorcycle gangster, might wear but with heavy embroidery of Chinese characters spelling out either 'dragon', or 'I am on top of the universe'. Chen is one of the designers supported by Labelhood and Dong Liang – she has garnered a huge following of self-described 'bad kids' who religiously follow her social media feeds and buy her clothes. In fact, I saw one in action a few days earlier at Dong Liang: a young man with exaggeratedly effeminate manners in Chen's *tokkō fuku* coat and two friends in tow who spent the better part of an afternoon trying on the new deliveries of Chen's line. 'He comes here every week to buy something of Angel's', Tasha Liu told me at the time. I was surprised because he looked so young, and Chen's clothes are expensive. 'What does he do?' I asked. 'He's a student.'

Chen explains that she often looks to Japanese culture for inspiration, but that she's been looking at Chinese culture lately as well: the classic text *Shanhaijing* (Guideways through Mountains and Seas) about mountain and sea myths was an inspiration for her most recent collection. When it comes to how her brand is perceived, she echoes what I have heard repeated many times by young Chinese designers of her generation – she cares more about what the Western press say than she does the Chinese. 'The international press are much more intelligent than the Chinese. The Chinese press don't really care – there are so many fashion wannabes, and all the fashion press started about five years ago.' She continues, 'Chinese people always look forward, they look at what's happening in the UK, at what's happening in Europe, that's how they are.'

Scene 4: Fédération Française de la Couture, Rue Faubourg Saint-Honoré, 8ème Arrondissement

> There will never be a Chinese fashion. There are no fashion designers in China; they are all in Paris. We were very surprised when we started having some Chinese participants actually. We've had a number of established Chinese designers showing in Paris by now, but after a while we realised that they had no talent and that no press was interested. But still, their fame in China was such that they were totally upset when I told them that there was no purpose for them to go on showing in Paris, as it didn't bring any interest from the visitors. I feel strongly about the fact that a brand has to be relevant to the European and American press to merit being on the fashion week schedule in Paris. If the interest only comes from China or India, or wherever they come from, I think our role is to tell the brand, 'Okay, you've had your fun, but it's enough now.'[17]

This is what Didier Grumbach, affectionately and respectfully known in the fashion industry as Monsieur Grumbach, tells me one winter day in his office. At the time, Grumbach was the president of the Fédération Française de la Couture, du Prêt-à-Porter des Couturiers et des Créateurs de Mode, the governing body for the French fashion industry, and though he has since retired, his presence loomed large over Paris Fashion Week for the sixteen years he spent at its helm, and still makes itself felt. His views on Chinese fashion are telling. Insinuations or outright assertions of Chinese designers as less sophisticated are recurring when discussing the topic with French fashion professionals – that is, if they know anything at all about it. Simona Segre Reinach has written about the two 'fashion stereotypes' that afflict China in relation to Italy: 'Italy as the creator, designer, and then exporter of Italian brands to China, and China as predominately the manufacturing base and consumer outlet for Western brands.'[18] The same point could plainly be made about France and Paris, or indeed any Western fashion capital. I noticed it when speaking to Western press in Shanghai, invited either to cover the proceedings, or lend an aura of internationality to them. The august fashion writer Colin McDowell, for instance, complained about Chinese design looking just like European and American fashion, 'only worse'.

That France has a lot to lose in accepting the ability of China to generate its own high fashion designers is clear – after all there is a vested interest for all players on the Paris fashion stage in keeping the city's reputation as a byword for fashion intact. With this in mind, it's interesting to observe that, with the notable exception of Shanghai-based Masha Ma and Uma Wang, the only Chinese designers on

Paris's high-profile womenswear prêt-a-porter schedule are Yang Li and Yinqing Yin, who both left China as children to grow up in Australia and France respectively. Repealing the negative connotations associated with 'made in China' is a slow process, and one that requires the development of a high-fashion aesthetic that is at once unifying enough to be marketable, but simultaneously unique enough to allow for the individual creative expression so important in fashion today. The international set of Chinese fashion editors, buyers and other industry professionals recognize the difficulty of this balancing act, and as a general rule, though proud of home-grown talent like Uma Wang, ('Uma Wang is far higher than the other designers. We are really proud of her, so we don't say bad things about her'[19]) tend to speak derogatively about Chinese designers in general. This could, perhaps, be seen as a case of self-Orientalizing – the internalization of the stereotypes associated with the Eastern 'Other'. When the Monsieur Grumbach quote above, after being published in *Vestoj*, was translated into Chinese by a number of fashion bloggers, it unsurprisingly caused a bit of a stir on WeChat and Weibo, China's two most prominent social media outlets. Many were offended and upset by his remarks, but equally as many seemed gripped by a sort of *mea culpa*, as if the remarks of this Parisian fashion authority were highlighting the shame that China has been unable to produce an international fashion star in the few years since fashion has been a cultural priority.

This brings to mind Ann Marie Leshkowich and Carla Jones's definition of Edward Said's notion of Orientalism, 'which held that colonised groups could not recognise the value of their own cultural, historical, and natural resources and therefore needed Western archaeologists, ethnographers, historians, and connoisseurs to discover and preserve this value'.[20] Though the historical relationship between China and the West is more complex than what a straightforward reading of colonialism would suggest, the cultural colonialism that is still perpetrated by the West in general, and Paris in particular, when it comes to fashionable taste and know-how is an important factor when looking at not just how the Paris cognoscenti view the Chinese fashion industry, but also how they view themselves.[21]

Scene 5: Uma Wang A/W 2017 Show, Musée de l'Armée, Rue de Grenelle, 7ème Arrondisement

It's a beautiful crisp winter day in early March, and Uma Wang is staging her first Paris show, after four years on the official schedule in Milan. She has told me about her ambivalence about changing cities, but that she has finally succumbed to her French PR agent's arguments: Paris after all remains the world stage for fashion.

The show is held at the Army Museum in Les Invalides (which also houses Napoleon's gilded tomb), and the fashionable guests are trying to navigate the cobblestones in their high heels as best they can, while tourists look bemusedly on. The venue is impressive, as most Parisian venues tend to be: stone floors, high ceilings and gold-plated detailing. The audience are seated on simple wooden benches, in two long rows. I am whisked to the front by a genial PR lackey – how nice!

I look around and notice familiar faces. Many of the press and buyers I've got to know these past few years in Shanghai are present. But, perhaps not surprisingly, few of their high-status European and American equivalents are here. It takes time to be accepted in Paris.

The show itself is a vision in nineteenth-century Romanticism: pyjama silhouettes and cocoon shapes, long flowing robes, dusty floral prints and ruffled necklines (see Plate 8). Elizabeth Siddal and Jane Morris would have been pleased. The models file down the long catwalk; they are mostly white, with two or three light-skinned black models thrown in for good measure. There are no Asian models. Uma Wang comes out afterwards to take a bow, also wearing a long velvet robe; she is smiling broadly. The show over, we all file out and I notice some fashion bloggers dressed in Uma Wang, twirling around the courtyard while street-style photographers snap away.

Afterwards I check the reviews online: Uma Wang is conspicuously absent from Businessoffashion.com and Vogue.com where most of the fashion industry go to read show reviews and watch the shows, after they happened. She does, however, get favourable reviews in *Women's Wear Daily* and *The Washington Post*, where the well-respected fashion critic Robin Givhan writes: '[Wang] is among a new generation of designers who are transforming China's reputation from the home of low-quality manufacturers to a place of dynamic creativity fueled by entrepreneurs ready to compete on fashion's global stage.'[22]

I speak to a friend afterwards, a Chinese editor, one of the few who sits front row at every fashion show in Paris. I ask him about the absence of Chinese models on Uma Wang's catwalk – what's his take? He argues that the models on a designer's catwalk should be allowed to be the creator's fantasy woman, an ideal that matches the clothes and mood of the season. But, I argue, doesn't a Chinese designer on the Paris catwalk have a stake in making 'Chineseness' more appealing? To broaden the acceptable beauty ideal? But why, he argues back. Why does a Chinese designer have to make a political statement, or any kind of statement for that matter? We discuss back and forth while our sub-par French espresso grows cold. I'm left wondering again, what makes a 'Chinese fashion designer' as opposed to just a 'fashion designer'? Is it fair to expect the few who are beginning to take steps towards respectability and status abroad to operate under some kind of politically aware banner? Do they have to advertise their Chineseness? And what is 'Chineseness' anyway?

Scene 6: Mr Willis, Anfu Road, Xuhui District

We go back in time now, to November 2015. I'm meeting Tim Lim, the fashion director of Modern Media, China's main independent publishing group, listed in Hong Kong. The publishing situation in China is as complex for fashion magazines as it is for any other type of periodical. Here no one can publish without a state-issued publication number, a *kanhao*, which is given only to government-affiliated agencies. This means that, in theory, private business is locked out, though in practice many agencies rent their *kanhaos* out. *Kanhao*-sharing is therefore a common, though intricate, affair, which, combined with the franchising of foreign media brands, makes up the bulk of Modern Media's titles. Lim has been overseeing all the fashion content of the group's thirteen lifestyle-focused titles since 2006, and is a stalwart presence on both the Shanghai and international fashion scene.

I wait for Lim, who has warned me that he's coming directly from his pilates class. The sofas at Mr Willis, a genial though somewhat conspicuous Australian restaurant, are deep and soft and I don't mind waiting. Soon though Lim hurries in, a little flustered and apologising for being late. We order coffee, and I turn my recorder on. I want to hear about Lim's experience working for Chinese titles that mainly feature Western luxury brands. How has he been welcomed (or not) into the fold? And I want to know how he has seen the industry change in Shanghai, in the decade that has passed since he moved here from Hong Kong. Lim tells me that when he started no one from China was invited to shows in Europe or in the States. 'No one cared about Asia, no one cared about China,' he tells me. 'I had to deal with PRs who were absolutely, totally racist. I would receive invitations to 'Tim Lim, Hong Kong, *Japan*. There was just a lot of ignorance. There were no Chinese models, no Chinese editors, no visible Asian designers, apart from Anna Sui and the Japanese.'[23]

Slowly things began to change, and about eight years ago, Lim became part of the first wave of Chinese editors travelling to the main fashion capitals in the world to see high fashion. The rise of China had happened, and suddenly 'there was a real shift: people started acknowledging you in a real way, to know who you were.'[24] Lim goes on to describe how the Chinese adapted to a more outward-facing approach too. 'Before people just were not professional. They didn't know how to dress, they didn't know how to act. So much in this job is about decorum and protocol, and you just didn't know what to expect from a Chinese editor or media partner. People have become so much more sophisticated; they are educated now. You have to remember what a young industry [fashion] is in China. The learning curve has been very quick and very steep.'[25]

This sentiment is one I have heard echoed often among my interviewees, all of whom are part of the 'sophisticated, educated' clique that Lim has identified. One evening, buying cookies at a street stall I meet an older, elegant woman who introduces herself to me as Grace Han. Seemingly pleased to meet a foreigner, she invites me to tea at the Ritz. Intrigued and curious I accept. We walk together and she tells me about her work; over the past three decades she has taught Chinese models, beauty queens and young girls how to become more acceptable to Westerners. 'I started travelling very young and I noticed that foreigners look down on Chinese. The Chinese make noises when they eat, they don't know how to act when they're abroad. I knew all those things, and I realised I could make money out of teaching others.'[26] In the 1990s, Han tells me, she got her first clients, one of whom would go on to become the most famous Chinese model of her day. Business boomed. Today she gives her lessons to wealthy young women from the very table we are sitting at: the decorum and protocol that Lim stressed the importance of, Han is dispensing at a price. And the families who can afford it are lining up; they know how important it is for their young daughters (and a smattering of sons) to fit neatly into this globalised world. If you want to become someone outside of China today, you have to know how to dress and act in a way that's acceptable to us in the West.

The sea turtles know this. They go to school in London and in New York and learn, not just how to make patterns, cut fabric and put a collection together, but how to dress and act. Angel Chen, the young designer from Shenzhen, told me about her struggle to fit in when first arriving in London as a seventeen-year-old, and then going from hanging out only with other Asian students to gradually befriending Westerners, and adopting a style more palatable to her peers. ('Gradually when I was in the U.K., I started to dress in vintage; I dressed myself like a Christmas tree.'[27])

But perhaps I digress a little. I would like to return to Tim Lim, seated comfortably in the plush sofa at Mr Willis on Anfu Lu in Shanghai's Western-friendly French

Concession. We will end this scene here, with something else that Lim told me, something that has come to play a major role in the recent rise of Chinese fashion:

> People are very patriotic here. They like to support Chinese designers and wear Chinese-inspired clothing, so long as they feel that [the brand] is legitimised in a certain way. Not cheap or common. Yes, Louis Vuitton continues to be popular here, but there are always people who want to celebrate their Chineseness, and traditional Chinese values.[28]

Scene 7: Xintiandi Style, Madang Road, Huangpu District

I've just been looking at the Ziggy Chen store, located on the second floor in Xintiandi Style, one of Shanghai's most exclusive shopping malls. The clothes are dark and moody, and quite a bit Rick Owensy in style. The décor is minimal and sophisticated, and everything both looks, and is, expensive. In Ziggy Chen you find only menswear. One door down is the Uma Wang store and it's easy to imagine that while she shops at Uma's, he goes to Ziggy's next door.

After my store visit is over, Ziggy and Hiroki, his Japanese right-hand man, take me for a coffee on the plaza. Hiroki translates for Ziggy; it's obvious they have this double act down pat. Ziggy, via Hiroki, tells me that he began in fashion by starting the brand Decoster in 1999 with his wife. At the time it was one of the first Chinese designer brands, and it did well. Eventually his wife decided to retire and Ziggy too was ready to do something new. Decoster, his 'family business', was looking after itself, and Ziggy had begun travelling to Paris for inspiration. He discovered the Clignancourt flea market, and the vintage clothing and antique furniture on sale had him mesmerized. 'That was the very first time I realized what I was really into.'[29] In 2011, his new brand was born. The beginning was difficult. 'When we started, everybody was wearing Western luxury brands, and they didn't understand how a Chinese brand could be this expensive. We had some customers who came to our store, saw the price tag, and just got pissed.' He laughs. 'They started throwing stuff around, like, "What are you doing?"'[30]

But Ziggy continued, undeterred. He got an international agent and tried to establish himself in Europe and in the States, where his flea-market inspired aesthetic is more familiar. The first advice his new agent gave him was to change his brand name. In China in 2011, using an individual's name for a fashion brand was still uncommon and Ziggy had opted to call his new brand 'The Concept'. But for a company aiming to do well abroad, following the current convention of enhancing brand aura by direct association with its designer is a safe bet. As his agent pointed out, 'Chen' is unmistakably Chinese, and 'Ziggy' easy to remember. And soon the fortunes of Ziggy Chen began to change. The brand was taken up by L'Éclaireur, one of the most exclusive stores in Paris, known for its dark and moody aesthetic. In typical status-oriented fashion, buyers look to what other buyers pick, and inclusion in one of the world's most prestigious stores can alter the trajectory of a brand. Add to this that the mood in China was shifting too.

> [Chinese people] used to love logos, but suddenly they changed. The economy went down, and people started thinking differently about value. At the same time the media was pushing for less recognizable brands. Chinese designers profited from this too; it became trendy to give attention to home grown talent. The perception of value was changing. We felt the change in customers. We stopped having customers yelling at us about the price, and started getting customers who believed in what we were doing. They're proud, like, 'Oh, China can do something different, we can create something valuable.'[31]

Scene 8: Labelhood Pioneer Fashion & Arts Festival, Yuanmingyuan Road, Huangpu District

Spending time at Labelhood is like taking the temperature of the hippest segment of Shanghai fashion. It's *hot*. It's October 2016, and for four days the next generation of Shanghai fashion is everywhere on Yuanmingyuan Road. A whole building, along with two adjacent gallery spaces, have been taken over by Labelhood's designers and cohorts. Uma Wang's show with 1436, on Labelhood's last day, is the big draw, but many of the designers I've encountered while familiarizing myself with the Shanghai fashion scene these past years have become natural components of Tasha Liu's initiative. Museum of Friendship is showcasing their nymphets on opening day, Angel Chen's bad kids flood the building on the second and Staffonly bring their heavily detailed and streetwear-inspired menswear to the catwalk on the third.

Numéro China, one of the titles Tim Lim works with, is exhibiting fashion films in one of the adjacent galleries. Sankuanz, along with Uma Wang, one of the most respected Chinese designers, who, like her, now shows in Paris, albeit on the menswear schedule, is another participant. Journalists, buyers, students and other hangers-on mill around the space all day, every day. Street-style photographers abound. It's clear why the shows in the conventional tent pale in comparison: this is where the creativity and eccentricity of Shanghai fashion is concentrated.

Considering that this is Labelhood's first season, what Liu and her partners have amassed is impressive, though perhaps not surprising. Someone had to do it. The amount of young designers who have returned home to start their brands in the past couple of years is remarkable, and they are full of determination to show what they have learned. Not willing, or, perhaps, able to fit into the rather more staid format of the official schedule, they want to make their mark on something new. There is a certain clannishness to the fashionistas here: they are all young (none seem over thirty) and they dress for attention in urban, cool kid outfits. The Dalston/Lower East Side influence is palpable. Interestingly, the shows here have no tickets or seating plan: you queue up, show the bracelet you received at registration, and in you go. First come, first serve. I hypothesize that perhaps this lack of hierarchy is due to the fledgling nature of the Chinese fashion scene; the industry is too intimate and too young to have developed a very strict pecking order. That said, here, as everywhere, the fashion week participants find ways to signal their status – there are the brands worn for one (Vetements is very popular, as is Supreme and Balenciaga, while of the locals Sankuanz is a favourite), but also the lucky few who get whisked past the queue to gain access to the show space before everyone else. This is my third Shanghai Fashion Week, and whereas no one paid me much heed at the beginning, thanks to some local press about *Vestoj*, a few articles in translation that have gone WeChat viral, a handful of talks at several small and one large venue alongside dogged interviewing with the who's who of Shanghai fashion, I find that my own status has risen. More than once I'm being whisked past the queue at Labelhood, only to awkwardly inhabit the show space, trying to look unaffected – much like I would back home in Paris. Two years after my first visit, I have become both observer and participant.

Scene 9: Labelhood Pioneer Fashion & Arts Festival, Suzhou Road, Huangpu District

Six months have passed since I was last in Shanghai, and it's time for fashion week again. For its second offering Labelhood have taken over the Bailian Fashion Center, an old disused factory building on the Suzhou Creek where you might otherwise see a stream of joggers headed towards the Bund. For four days this April, however, the quiet residential street is instead taken over by Shanghai's most pre-eminent fashion-lovers, pros and fans alike. The concrete building has three floors and countless rooms, and something seems to be going on in every one of them. There is a coffee-shop on the ground floor, making espresso and macchiato – still a relatively new fad here. Nike has set up shop, exhibiting a collaboration with a young British designer, and Lipton Tea has taken over one room and decorated it with plastic cherry blossoms and a candy-coloured bar that serves artificially flavoured teas all day long. Converse has their corner too, set up like a makeshift photo studio, where visitors can try on sneakers and have their pictures taken against a logoed backdrop.

Alongside the sponsors, Yang Li, the Australian/Chinese designer, is visiting from London for two days, to put on a pop-up shop for his new initiative 'Samizdat' to go alongside the concert night he is also hosting, and Angel Chen is DJing another evening. Like last season, the set-up is a mixture of small-scale fashion shows, static exhibitions and performances. The designers with shows have been chosen via a panel of judges, mostly Chinese along with a smattering of foreigners. This year I have been asked to be one of them. I have also been asked to play a more active role in Labelhood; together with the editor of *Numéro China*, Karchun Leung, who has become a friend over these past years, I am hosting what we are, tongue-in-cheek, calling 'The Serious Talks Series'. This means that we, for three mornings, are a more or less improvised duet, attempting to bring some 'seriousness' or at least some refection to proceedings with the help of a selection of designer guests. On the first day we speak to designers Steven Tai, Xu Zhi and Momo Wang about 'The Siren Call of the West: Why do Chinese designers continue to court the attention of the Western fashion establishment?'

The conversation goes along what is, by now, to me, familiar lines. All three designers studied in England, at Central Saint Martins. All three make a point of being 'London-based', and they have all experienced being part of London Fashion Week at some point: Museum of Friendship showed in 2015, Steven Tai has been showing since 2015 and Xu Zhi is with the London Showrooms, an initiative that promotes London-based designers abroad. As the designers tell it, London is typically the first port of call for a Chinese designer wanting to show during one of the four main fashion weeks (New York, London, Milan, Paris), and there are currently six Chinese designers showing on schedule. Paris, by contrast, is where you aim to go – being accepted here is a mark of distinction. At the time of writing only four Chinese designers show on the ready-to-wear menswear or womenswear schedule in Paris – Uma Wang, Yang Li, Masha Ma and Sankuanz – though many more have a showroom presence with one of the myriad international showrooms that flock to Paris every fashion week (including the three on our panel).

During our conversation, Tai, Xu and Wang agree that though they are able to support themselves via the local market, having strong connections to one of the fashion capitals in the West helps elevate their brands in the eyes of domestic customers. Interestingly, having a presence abroad also helps the Chinese designers' reputation at home in another way: being a part of the select group of industry people who are able to travel – to see shows and showrooms for editors and buyers, and to present your work for the designers – is proof of your ambition as well as your economic and social status. The most important Chinese editors and buyers support their home-grown talent by coming to see their work, and designers, who often share the same showrooms, network with one another and share tips about who to work with. Informal dinners add to the feeling of being one of the 'chosen few', and, unsurprisingly, a lot of deals get made this way.

Being able 'to show' former teachers, friends and peers in Europe or the US how far you've come is also a reason why so many sea turtles are keen to present their work in the West. This is a sentiment echoed by Une Yea, of Staffonly. During our interview she told me that building a brand in China is 'easy' now – the production is cheaper and more straightforward, and the support system is already in place. But once you have a good thing going, you want to show it off. 'We really want a presentation abroad, because I studied there so I want to show how I've grown to my teachers and friends and also to the market.'[32]

Epilogue

During the three years I have spent travelling regularly to Shanghai something curious has happened – I've gone from being a bystander to being a contributor. Arriving for the first time in October 2014, I had countless questions and no answers. Today some of those questions have been answered, though many others have arisen in their place.

That the designers I've encountered in Shanghai see Paris as the pinnacle of success is clear – the city represents history and tradition and, in the eyes of young Chinese designers, remains the citadel of high fashion. Every season those who can afford it, and some who can't, travel to the city to showcase their wares and rub shoulders with peers. As of yet these are mainly other Chinese designers, though little by little a few of the more established designers are making inroads into the French fashion establishment. Becoming a recognized part of the fashion system in Paris is a slow and costly process, however. Masha Ma, one of the more well-known Shanghai-based designers, has, for example, elected to establish her company in Paris, with which comes hiring French staff and paying taxes in the country. In return she, for the time being, has a guaranteed slot during fashion week. Uma Wang, as mentioned earlier, has a formidable French PR agent – one she shares with Yang Li. Nevertheless, becoming accepted is a circuitous process. The Chinese designers who show during Paris Fashion Week are typically saddled with bad scheduling slots, either on the first day of the week before most press and buyers have arrived in the city, or early in the morning when the fashion glitterati are disinclined to rise.

Interviews and casual enquiries with Paris-based fashion industry participants, from PR and sales agents to press and designers, confirm what I already suspect: few have any grasp of what Chinese fashion is. When pressed, the designer typically mentioned is Yang Li, though most consider him either Australian or 'London-based'. Another designer sometimes mentioned is Guo Pei, who has a studio in Beijing and who recently rose to prominence in the West due to a dress worn by the singer Rihanna to the Met Ball in 2015, organized to celebrate the museum's high-profile exhibition *China: Through the Looking Glass*. Guo Pei now shows on the Paris *haute couture* schedule, though her shows suffer from the same dearth of a high-profile Western fashion industry audience.

The Western fashion industry is loath to move on from the perception of China as fashion's 'bad guy', whether the 'bad' in question concerns production methods or aesthetic sophistication. As long as China remains inferior, Western fashion brands can compare themselves favourably, and in the process add value to high prices and an exclusive stance.

As for me, the ignorance I arrived with has, at least partially, subsided. My first visits to Shanghai were dominated by self-consciousness and self-reproach; why had I never bothered to find out what fashion in China was like? Is there such a thing as 'Chinese style'? And how should I judge the work I encountered? This last question plagued me the most, and still does. Arriving as an observer, scholar spectacles perched on nose, I know better than to judge. But unwittingly I still do. I compare the designers I encounter in Shanghai with the designers I know back home, and I find them wanting. I get frustrated and rebuke myself; why compare this nascent industry to the one in Paris, going as it has been for more than half a century? But then again, if these Shanghai-based designers are aiming for international recognition and to show during Paris Fashion Week, why not hold them to the same standards? Though if I do, I find I end up with the same prejudiced stance that I reject when expressed by a Didier Grumbach or a Colin McDowell.

Becoming an, albeit peripheral, part of the Shanghai fashion scene has added another layer to this conundrum because as you become a part of the phenomenon you're ostensibly researching your perspective shifts. I've been asked my opinion about Shanghai designers, on and off the record, more times than I care to remember. I've been invited to judge, and to partake. A memorably illustrious moment occurred on my last trip, April 2017. Travelling as a guest of the Shanghai Fashion Week Organization, I am to host my 'Serious Talks Series' on three consecutive days, then another talk about *Vestoj* a few days later at Mode, the official tradeshow. Courtesy of Shanghai Fashion Week I am staying at the Langham, a five-star hotel with an endless breakfast buffet that has me greedily getting up much earlier than I otherwise would. In between talks, shows and showroom visits, I am invited to lunch with Lv Xiaolei, or Madame Lu as she is affectionately called. Madame Lu is vice secretary general of Shanghai Fashion Week Organization, and has done more than anyone else to raise the profile of Shanghai Fashion Week and establish the city as China's foremost stage for fashion. An amiable, not very fashionable-looking woman in late middle age she speaks no English. Nevertheless she asks many questions and is keen to converse with the help of Landon Du, the US-educated press representative of Shanghai Fashion Week, and Tasha Liu, proprietor of Dong Liang and Labelhood's initiator. 'What do you think of Shanghai Fashion Week?' 'What can we do better?' I try to answer in a way that lies somewhere between diplomacy and sincerity, and Madame Lu seems pleased.

Little by little I have noticed attitudes changing in Paris vis à vis Chinese designers, though unsurprisingly for the acceptance the designers I encountered crave, there is a long way to go. An interesting tension is that the Western fashion industry still appears to expect Chinese designers to, in some way, address their cultural heritage in their work – to conform to a Western notion of 'Chineseness' – whereas the designers I encountered in Shanghai are all reluctant for their aesthetic to be pegged as 'Chinese'. As they see it, they are 'designers' above all – to be seen as a 'Chinese designer' would be reductive and anyway wouldn't reflect the range of influences drawn on, or the complexity of Chinese cultural history. In these diverging expectations lies an important clue that goes at least some way to explain the difficulty I have had in knowing what lens to apply when judging what I have encountered on the contemporary Shanghai fashion scene, and the vague grasp that many of my peers have of Chinese fashion designers in Paris.

That Paris continues to exert allure for young Chinese designers is clear. Not surprisingly this allure has less to do with financial necessity than it does the symbolic capital that international recognition has for any designer. Paris continues to be the world's premier stage for fashion, and the air of exclusiveness that the Fédération Française de la Couture carries on honing is vital in preserving this function. As Chinese designers continue to make inroads in the bastion that is Paris Fashion Week, an intricate negotiation is taking place on behalf of both the designers themselves and their desired audience. The 'Chinese fashion' that Monsieur Grumbach doubted the presence of already exists. But how can fashion designers in Shanghai and elsewhere in China exert the influence they hanker after, while rebuffing the preconceived (Western) idea of Chineseness? And by refusing to conform, are they shooting themselves in the foot?

Notes

1 A. Aronowsky Cronberg, interview with Didier Grumbach, 5 February 2013 as published in 'On Power', *Vestoj*, 2013, xxv.
2 For further reading, see Juanjuan Wu, *Chinese Fashion: From Mao to Now* (London: Bloomsbury, 2009); Zhang Hongxing and Lauren Parker (eds), *China Design Now* (London: V&A, 2008); A. Bolton, *China: Through the Looking Glass* (New Haven, CT: Yale University Press, 2015).
3 Jianyang Fan, 'The Emperor's New Museum', *The New Yorker*, 7 November 2016, 31.
4 Interview with Kian Zhang, proprietor of Old Lyric and Autumn Sonata, 17 November 2015.
5 Robin Givhan, 'Meet Yang Li, a Designer Putting China on Fashion's Biggest Stage', *The Washington Post*, 26 October 2014. https://www.washingtonpost.com/lifestyle/style/designer-yang-li-is-putting-china-on-fashions-biggest-stage/2014/10/26/637f6f62-4ff7-11e4-babe-e91da079cb8a_story.html?utm_term=.7b15ef4fb7d.
6 Interview with Queennie Yang, editor of *Business of Fashion* China edition, 20 November 2015.
7 Interview with subject, 14 October 2016.
8 Interview with subject, 25 October 2016.
9 Interview with subject, 15 November 2015.
10 Interview with subject, 22 October 2016.
11 Interview with subject, 14 October 2016.
12 Interview with subject, 14 October 2016.
13 10 Corso Como is a renowned fashion store with a flagship on Milan's Corso Como, run by former *Vogue Italia* editor Franca Sozzani since 1991. In 2013 Sozzani partnered with Trendy International Group and Samsung Cheil to open an outpost in Shanghai.
14 Interview with subject, 14 October 2016.
15 Interview with subject, 14 October 2016.
16 Interview with subject, 24 October 2016.
17 Interview with subject, 5 February 2013 as published in 'On Power', *Vestoj*, 2013, xxv.

18 Simona Segre Reinach, 'The Identity of Fashion in Contemporary China and the New Relationships with the West', *Fashion Practice* (Oxford: Berg, 2012), 65.

19 Danielle Hu in interview with author, 26 October 2016.

20 Ann Marie Leshkowich and Carla Jones, 'What Happens When Asian Chic Becomes Chic in Asia?', *Fashion Theory* 7, no. 3/4 (2003): 281–300.

21 For further reading, see Peter McNeil and Giorgio Riello (eds), *The Fashion History Reader: Global Perspectives* (London: Routledge, 2010).

22 Robin Givhan, 'This Designer Wants to Swaddle You in So Many Yards of Sensual Velvet this Fall', *The Washington Post*, 5 March 2017. https://www.washingtonpost.com/news/arts-and-entertainment/wp/2017/03/05/uma-wang-will-swaddle-you-in-so-much-velvet-youll-feel-like-a-dickens-novel/?utm_term=.50c27ba68951.

23 Interview with subject, 22 November 2015.

24 Ibid.

25 Ibid.

26 Interview with subject, 23 October 2016.

27 Interview with subject, 24 October 2016.

28 Interview with subject, 22 November 2015.

29 Interview with subject, 18 November, 2015.

30 Ibid.

31 Ibid.

32 Interview with subject, 14 October 2016.

Glossary

afei 阿飞 (dandies)
Anfu Road 安福路
aoqun 袄裙 (coat-and-skirt)
Asahi shimbun 朝日新闻 (Asahi News)
Baie yishu banyuekan 白鹅艺术半月刊 (White Goose Art Journal Bimonthly)
baizhequn 百褶裙 (a skirt that has all-round small pleats)
Bao Tianxiao 包天笑 (act. 1900–130)
Baodaxiang 宝大祥
bazijin 八字襟 (character-eight-openings)
Beiyang huabao 北洋画报 (The Pei-yang Pictorial News)
Beiyang tongshang dachen 北洋通商大臣 (Beiyang trade minister)
Biyun Temple 碧云寺 (Temple of Azure Clouds)
Bowei 波纬 (tailor firm)
bushi liumang ershi afei 不是流氓而是阿飞 (either a hooligan or a dandy)
caizi 才子 (scholar)
Caojiadu Road 曹家渡路
Chang Hsueh-liang 张学良 (Zhang Xueliang, 1901–2001)
Chang, Eileen 张爱玲 (1920–95); see also Zhang Ailing
Changan Road 长安路
Changning District 长宁区
Changshou 常熟
Charlie Soong 宋嘉树 (Song Jiashu, 1863–1918)
Chen Qiucao 陈秋草 (1906–88)
Chen Weiji 陈维稷 (1906–83)
Chen Xiuliang 陈修良 (1907–98)
Chen Yi 陈毅 (Shanghai mayor, 1901–72)
Chen Yingxia 陈映霞 (1896–1966); see also Chen Yingyong
Chen Yingyong 陈应镛; see also Chen Yingxia
Chen Zhifo 陈之佛 (1896–1962)
Chiang Kai-shek 蒋介石 (Jiang Jieshi, 1887–1975)
Chudong xinzhuang 初冬新装 (New Fashion for Early Winter)
Chung Kuo 中国 (China)
Chunji xinzhuang 春季新装 (New Fashion for the Spring)
Cixi 慈溪
cun 寸 (one-third of a decimetre)

Da Gonghe xingqi huabao 大共和星期画报 (The Great Republicans' Weekly Illustrated News)
daban piaoliang 打扮漂亮 (dress beautification)
dahua beimian 大花被面 (large floral designs for quilt covers)
Damalu 大马路 (the Great Road)
Dan Duyu 但杜宇 (1897–1972)
daodaxiu 倒大袖 (inversed big sleeves)
Datong Road 大统路
Deng Xiaoping 邓小平 (1904–97)
Di Baoxian 狄葆贤 (1872–1941)
Dianshizhai 点石斋
Dianying yuebao 电影月报 (Movie Monthly)
diaofue 貂覆额 (a type of head ornament made of mink's fur); see also *lezi* 勒子 and *zhemeile* 遮眉勒
Ding Song 丁悚 (1891–1972)
Dongbei 东北 (Northeast China)
doujiaoling 豆角领 (a style of collar shaped like string bean)
Eileen Chang 张爱玲 (1920–1995) see also Zhang Ailing
Emperor Qianlong 乾隆皇帝
Erma Road 二马路 (today Jiujiang Road 九江路)
Fang Junbi 方君璧 (1898–1986)
Fang Xuehu 方雪鹄 (act. 1910–40)
Fanhua zazhi 繁华杂志 (Prosperity Magazine)
fanxiu xifu 翻修西服 (reconditioning of Western suits)
Feiyingge huabao 飞影阁画报 (Feiyingge Pictorial)
Fenghua 奉化
fengren tanfan 缝纫摊贩 (sewing peddlers)
fenpei 分配 (allocation)
First Business College of Jiangsu Province 江苏省立第一商业学校
Funü fuzhuang zhi jingguo 妇女服装之经过 (Development of Women's Fashion)
Funü shenghuo 妇女生活 (Lady's Life)
Funü shibao 妇女时报 (The Women's Eastern Times)
Funü zazhi 妇女杂志 (The Ladies' Journal)
Funü zhuangshu lan 妇女装束栏 (Ladies' Fashion Column)
futai 富态 (a positive description for noble and slightly overweight women in Chinese tradition)
Fuzhi tiaoli 服制条例 (Regulation on Clothing)
Fuzhuang caijian 服装裁剪 (Dressmaking)
ganbu zhifu 干部制服 (cadre suit)
Gang of Four 四人帮
Gaoting Record Company 高亭唱片公司
Ge Gongzhen 戈公振 (1890–1935)

Ge Luxi 葛璐茜
Gengyi ji 更衣记 (Chronicle of Changing Clothes or Chinese Life and Fashion)
geti tanfan 个体摊贩 (independent peddler, hawker stratum)
gongbi 工笔
guangchang 广场 (plaza)
Guangdongbang 广东帮 (Guangdong Gang)
guanggaose 广告色 (poster colour)
Guangzhou 广州
guapimao 瓜皮帽 (Chinese skullcap: a name derived from the shape resembling the rind of a watermelon)
Guowen zhoubao 国闻周报 (The National News Weekly)
Haipai 海派 (Shanghai style)
Han 汉
Hangzhou 杭州
Hankou 汉口
Harbin 哈尔滨
He Ai'zhen 何爱贞 (sister of He Zhizhen)
He Zhizhen 何志贞 (act. 1920–30s)
heifenzi 黑分子 (black elements)
Henan Middle Road 河南中路
Hongbang 红帮 (Red Group)
Hongdu store 红都 (Red Capital store)
Hongkou 虹口
Hongxia Dress store 红霞服装店
Hongxian zhizhan 洪宪之战 (The War of Anti-Yuan Shikai)
Hu Die 胡蝶 (1908–1989)
Hu Huaichen 胡怀琛 (1886–1938)
Hu Lancheng 胡兰成 (1906–81)
Hu Yaobang 胡耀邦 (1915–89)
Hu Zhongbiao 胡忠彪 (act. 1900–40)
Huaihai East Rd 淮海东路
Huaihai Road 淮海路
Huang Jinhai 黄金海 (1935–)
Huangpu District 黄浦区
Huangpu River 黄埔江
Huzhuang shinü tu 沪妆仕女图 (pictures of women in contemporary Shanghai-style embellishment)
Huzhuang 沪妆 (Shanghai-style embellishment)
Jiang Hailian 江海莲
Jiang Qing dress 江青服
Jiang Xiaojian 江小鹣 (1894–1939)
Jiang Yuanlin 姜长麟 (1899–1987)

Jiang Zemin 江泽民 (b. 1926)
Jiangsu Province 江苏省
Jiangyin Street 江阴街
Jiaoyu zazhi 教育杂志 (The Chinese Educational Review)
Jindai funü 今代妇女 (The Modern Lady)
Jingan District 静安区
Jingan Kerry Centre 静安嘉里中心
Jingpai 京派
Jinjiafang 金家坊
Jinmen guibin 津门贵宾 (Honoured Guests in Tianjin)
Jiufeng Flour Manufactory 九丰面粉厂
jiuhuo shangdian 旧货商店 (old goods shop)
kaijinling lianyiqun 开襟领连衣裙; see also Jiang Qing dress
kaijinling qunyi 开襟领裙衣; see also Jiang Qing dress
Kang Youwei 康有为 (1858–1927)
Kangpaisi 康派司 (Compass)
kanhao 刊号 (a state-issued publication number)
Ke Qingshi 柯庆施 (1902–65)
Koo Hui-lan 黄慧兰 (Huang Huilan, also known as Madame Wellington Koo, 1899–1992)
Kuang Wenwei 邝文伟 (act. 1910–30)
lailiao jiagong 来料加工 (making up garments from cloth brought into the store by the customer)
Lang Hua Film Company 朗华电影公司
Lantian 蓝天 (clothing company)
laodong 劳动 (labour)
laoshi 老师 (tutors or senior designers in the factory studio)
Lei Guiyuan (1906–89) 雷圭元
Leimeng Western Clothing 雷蒙西服店
lezi 勒子(a type of head ornament made of mink's fur); see also *diaofue* 貂覆额 and *zhemeile* 遮眉勒
Li Hongzhang 李鸿章 (1823–1901)
Li Minghui 黎明晖 (1909–2003)
Li Xianghou 李襄侯 (act. 1910–20s)
Li Xiaqing 李霞卿 (1912–98)
Li Xingwu 李星五 (act. 1910–20s)
liangyongshan 两用衫 (dual-season top)
Liangyou huabao 良友画报 (The Young Companion Pictorial)
Liangyou 良友 (The Young Companion)
Lianyi zhiyou 联益之友 (Friend of Lianyi)
Libailiu 礼拜六 (The Saturday)
Lin Biao 林彪 (1907–71)

Lin Huilü 林慧吕
Lin Yutang 林语堂 (1895–1976)
Ling Boyuan 凌伯元
lingdao 领导 (leader, government officials in leading positions)
Linglong 玲珑 (Elegance; La Petite Woman's Magazine)
Linjing 临镜
linong 里弄 (neighbourhoods of lanes populated by housing in differing styles that had developed from the mid-nineteenth century)
Liu Haisu 刘海粟 (1896–1994)
Liu Shaoqi 刘少奇 (1898–1969)
liumang 流氓 (hooligans, vagrants, layabouts)
Lu Shaofei 鲁少飞 (1903–95)
Lu Xiangting 卢香亭 (1880–1948)
Madam Fang Yu 方于 (1903–2002)
Madam Su Mei 苏梅
Madang Road 马当路
majia 马甲 (waistcoat)
mamian 马面 (skirt panel, the flat surface with no pleat); see also *qunmen*
Man Ying 曼英
Manchu 满洲
Manhuahui 漫画会 (Cartoon Association, 1926)
Mao Zedong 毛泽东 (1893–1976)
Mengzi Street 蒙自路
modeng xiaojie 摩登小姐 (modern girl)
Nanjing Road 南京路
Nanshi District 南市區
Nanyang Brothers Tobacco Company 南洋兄弟烟草公司
Ningbo 宁波
nuanpao 暖袍 (a dress with straight bodice, loose waist, wide cuffs and long length)
Nüxuesheng de fuzhuang wenti 女学生的服装问题 (Female Students' Clothing Problem)
Nüzi dangchu zhuangshi 女子当除装饰 (Women Should Abolish Fashion)
Nüzi fuzhuang de gailiang 女子服装的改良 (Improvement on Women's Fashion)
Nüzi shijie 女子世界 (Women's World)
Nüzi zhuanshu de jianglai 女子妆束的将来 (The future dress for women)
Pan Sitong 潘思同 (1904–80)
Pan Zhenyong 潘振镛 (1851–1921)
Peiping 北平 (now Beijing)
Peng Rucong 彭汝琮
pi Lin pi Kong 批林批孔 (criticize Lin Biao, criticize Confucius)
pinwei 品味 (taste)
pipa 琵琶 (Chinese lute)
Primary School Affiliated to the Second Normal College 上海第[illegible]师范学校附属小学

Pudong 浦东
pusu 朴素 (simple and unadorned)
Qi 旗 (Bannerman)
Qian Hui'an 钱慧安 (1833–1911)
Qing dynasty 清朝 (1644–1912)
qingnianzhuang 青年装 (youth jacket)
Qingsheng zhoukan 青声周刊 (Voice of the Youth Weekly)
Qingxin Secondary School 清心中学
Qinyingzhai 钦英斋
Qipao de xuanlü 旗袍的旋律 (The Melody of *Qipao*)
qipao majia 旗袍马甲 (one-piece dress using different fabrics for the sleeves and the main body of the dress)
qipao 旗袍 (tight-fitting Chinese one-piece dress; Mandarin dress)
Qiren 旗人 (Manchu people)
Qiu Jin 秋瑾 (1875–1907)
qizhuang yifu 奇装异服 (strange dress and outlandish garments)
qizhuang 旗装 (the female robes of the Banner style)
qunmen 裙门 (skirt panel, the flat surface with no pleat); see also *mamian*
ranzhi sheji 染织设计 (textile design)
renminzhuang 人民装 (People's Suit)
Sanri huabao 三日画报 (Three-day Illustrated News)
Sansheng yixiang 三声一响 (three rounds and sound)
Shanghai Academy of Fine Art 上海美术专科学校 (1914–19)
Shanghai Chiao-tung University 上海交通大学 (Shanghai Jiao Tong University)
Shanghai funüzhi bianzhuan weiyuanhui 上海妇女志编纂委员会 (Complication Committee of the Recordation of Shanghai Women)
Shanghai gongshangye meishujia xiehui 上海工商业美术家协会 (Shanghai Association of Industrial and Commercial Artists)
Shanghai huabao 上海画报 (Pictorial Shanghai)
Shanghai Huadong fangguanjü 上海华东纺管局 (Shanghai Eastern China Bureau for Textiles)
Shanghai jiqi zhibu jü 上海机器织布局 (Shanghai Bureau of Machine-Woven Textiles)
Shanghai manhua 上海漫画 (Shanghai Cartoons)
Shanghai Oil Painting Academy 上海油画院
Shanghai poke 上海泼克 (Shanghai Puck)
Shanghai shenghuo 上海生活 (Shanghai Life)
Shanghai Shengsheng Press 上海生生出版社
Shanghai shizhuang baimei tuyong 上海时装百美图咏 (Illustrated Tribute of One Hundred Beauties of Shanghai in Contemporary Fashionable Costume)
Shanghai 上海
Shanghaizhuang 上海装 (Shanghai-style clothes)
Shangmei Studio 尚美图案馆

Shanhaijing 山海经 (Guideways through Mountains and Seas)
Shanhe suiyue 山河岁月 (China through Time)
shaomai 烧卖 (round stuffed dumpling with a flat top)
sheji 设计 (design)
Shen Bochen 沈泊尘 (1889–1920)
Shen Wenying 沈文英
Shenbao 申报 (Shanghai Daily)
Shengzhen 深圳
shenshi 绅士 (gentlemen)
Shenzhou huabao 神州画报 (China's Daily Illustrated News)
Shi Yunlai 时韵籁 (act. 1900–20)
Shibao tuhua zhoukan 时报图画周刊 (Weekly Illustrated Supplement to *The Eastern Times*)
Shibao 时报 (The Eastern Times)
Shidai huabao 时代画报 (The Modern Miscellany)
Shidai tushu gongsi 时代图书公司 (The Modern Miscellany Publishing Company)
shifu 师傅 (technical masters in engraving, printing, finishing, etc.)
shimao 时髦 (modern)
Shishang pinglun gaizhuang 时尚评论概状 (General Survey of the Fashion Criticism)
shizhuang meiren 时装美人 (beauties in fashionable dress)
shizhuang shinü tu 时妆仕女图 (pictures of women in contemporary embellishment)
shizhuang 时装 (contemporary beautification/embellishment)
shuyu jinu 书寓妓女 (a high-ranking courtesan; courtesan of the book dwelling)
Song dynasty 宋朝 (960–1279)
Songjiang district 松江区
Soong Ai-ling 宋蔼玲 (Song Ailing, 1888–1973)
Soong Ching-ling 宋庆龄 (Song Qingling; Soong May-ling's older sister; 1893–1981)
Soong May-ling 宋美龄 (Song Meiling, also known as Madame Chiang, 1898–2003)
Sun Chuanfang 孙传芳 (1885–1935)
Sun Nansun 孙南荪 (act. 1910–20)
Sun Qifang 孙琪芳
Sun Xueni 孙雪泥 (1889–1965)
Sun Yat-sen 孙中山 (Sun Zhongshan, 1866–1925)
Suzhou Road 苏州路
Suzhou 苏州
T.V. Soong 宋子文 (Soong Tse-Ven; Song Ziwen, 1894–1971)
Taipingqiao Park 太平桥公园
Tang dynasty 唐朝 (618–907)
Tang Tianyan 汤天雁 (act. 1910–30)
Tianjin 天津
Tianping 天平, see also *Kangpeisi* (Compass)
Tilanqiao Street 提篮桥街

tongxiu 通袖 (the sleeves continuous with the shoulder of the dress)
Tu Shipin 屠诗聘 (act. 1940s)
tu'an 图案 (pattern)
Tuhua shibao 图画时报 (The Illustrated Eastern Times)
tuodi qipao 拖地旗袍 (sweeping *qipao* dress)
Wan Guchan 万古蟾 (1900–95)
Wan Laiming 万籁铭 (1900–97)
Wang Changxing 汪长馨 (act. 1750s–80s)
Wang Guizhang 王圭璋 (*c.* 1920–)
Wang Hongwen 王洪文 (1935–92)
Wang Jiyuan 王济远 (1893–1975)
Wang Shengtai 王升泰 (tailor firm)
Wang Yuren 王隅人 (act. 1920–40s)
Wangfujing 王府井
wen 文 (literary)
wenming xinzhuang 文明新装 (civilized costume)
wenyang 纹样 (motif)
White Goose Institute of Western Painting 白鹅西画研究所
White Goose Painting Society 白鹅画会
Workshop for Painting Stage Sets 背景画传习所
Wu Aizhen 吴霭真 (act. 1910–1930)
Wu Yongkang 邬永康
Wu Youru huabao 吴友如画宝 (A Treasury of Wu Youru's Illustrations)
Wu Youru 吴友如 (1850–1893)
wu 武 (martial)
Wujuan guilai 舞倦归来 (Exhausted after Dance)
wunü 舞女 (cabaret dance hostesses)
Wusi yishi 五四遗事 (Stale Mates: A Short Story Set in the Time When True Love Came to China)
Wuxi 无锡
Xi Jinping 习近平 (b. 1953)
xiafang 下放 (sent down)
Xiaoshuo shibao 小说时报 (The Eastern Times Fiction Supplement)
xiaoyuanbao 小元宝 (little shoe-shaped gold ingot)
Xie Zhiguang 谢之光 (1900–76)
Xin Shanghai 新上海 (New Shanghai)
Xin shenghuo yundong 新生活运动 (New Life Movement, 1934–49)
Xinhuase 新花色 (New Patterns)
xinsheng shiwu 新生事物 (new-born things)
Xinshijie huabao 新世界画报 (New World Illustrated News)
Xintiandi 新天地 (New World)
Xinwutai 新舞台 (The New Theatrical Stage)

Xinxin baimei tu waiji 新新百美图外集 (Extended Collection of New Illustrations of One Hundred Contemporary Beauties)
Xinxin baimei tu 新新百美图 (New Illustrations of One Hundred Contemporary Beauties)
xinzhuangshu 新装束 (latest attire)
Xu Dishan 许地山 (1894–1941)
Xu Kuangdi 徐匡迪 (b. 1937, mayor of Shanghai 1995–2001)
Xu Xinxin baimei tu 续新新百美图 (Sustained Collection of New Illustrations of One Hundred Contemporary Beauties)
Xuhui District 徐汇区
Yamamura Kōka 山村耕花 (1885–1942)
Yan Wenliang 颜文梁 (1893–1988)
Yan'an xilu 延安西路 (Bubbling Well Road; Yan'an West Road)
Yang Naimei 杨耐梅 (1904–60)
Yang Qingqing 杨清磬 (1895–1957)
Yang Ximiu 杨锡缪 (S.J. Young, 1899–1978)
Yang Zuotao 杨左匋 (1897–1967)
Yangzhou 扬州
Yao Yongkang 姚永康
Ye Qianyu 叶浅予 (1907–95)
yi shi zhu xing 衣食住行 (Wearing, Eating, Living, Transportation)
yikouzhong 一口钟 (the winter coat with straight-cut design)
Yiletian Teahouse 一乐天茶楼
Yin Zhiyi 殷志怡 (1893–1985)
Yingwu Musical Club 鹦鹉乐社
Yingxia xinzhuang baimei tu 映霞新妆百美图 (Illustrations of One Hundred Beauties in Modern Dress Painted by Yingxia)
Yinxing 银星 (Screen Stars)
yishang 衣裳 (a typical clothing style consisting of an upper garment called *yi*, which was also known as tops, and a lower garment called *shang*, which was also known as bottoms and could be either skirt or trousers)
yizijin 一字襟 (pull-on style with the horizontal opening recalling character-one-openings)
Yongan Department Store 永安百货
Yu Yuanfang 余元芳 (b. 1918)
Yuan dynasty 元朝
Yuan Shikai 袁世凯 (1859–1916)
yuanbaoling 元宝领 (a style of collar in the shape of the traditional Chinese shoe-shaped ingots)
Yuanmingyuan Road 圆明园路
Yuanyang hudie pai 鸳鸯蝴蝶派 (Mandarin Ducks and Butterfly School)
Yue Foong-chi 于凤至 (Yu Fengzhi, 1897–1990)

yunqi 云起 (whirling clouds and air motif)
Yunshang shizhuang gongsi 云裳时装公司 (Yunshang Fashion Company)
Yuyuan Road 愚园路
Zhabei 闸北区
Zhang Ailing 张爱玲 (1920–95)
Zhang Chunqiao 张春桥 (1917–2005)
Zhang Delu 张德禄 (act. 1910–40)
Zhang Guangyu 张光宇 (1900–65)
Zhang Liangsheng 张亮生 (act. 1880–1925; Zhang Guangyu's father)
Zhang Yuguang 张聿光 (1885–1968)
Zhang Zhiying 张志瀛 (act. 1880–1900)
Zhang Zhiyu 张至煜 (1913–2000)
Zhang Zhiyun 张织云 (1904–?)
zhemeile 遮眉勒 (a type of head ornament made of mink's fur); see also *lezi* 勒子; *diaofue* 貂覆额
Zheng Mantuo 郑曼陀 (1888–1961)
Zheng Yimei 郑逸梅
zhifu 制服 (uniform)
Zhongguo fangzhi jianshe gongsi 中国纺织建设公司 (China Textile Development Corporation)
Zhongguo jianzhu 中国建筑 (Building in China)
Zhongguo shying xuehui huabao 中国摄影学会画报 (Illustrated News of Chinese Photography Association)
Zhongguo tu'an zuofa chutan 中国图案作法初谈 (Exploring the Methods in Chinese Patterns)
Zhongguo xuesheng 中国学生 (Chinese Students)
Zhongshanzhuang 中山装 (Chinese tunic suit, less formal uniform)
Zhongxi nüxue 中西女学 (McTyeire School)
Zhou Enlai 周恩来 (1898–1976)
Zhou Muqiao 周慕桥 (1868–1922)
Zhou Shoujuan 周瘦鹃 (1895–1968)
Zhou Xiang 周湘 (1871–1933)
Zhou Xibao 周锡保
Zhu Rongji 朱镕基 (b. 1928)
Zhu Xielin 朱燮林 (act. 1940s)
Zhuang Kaibo 庄开伯 (act. 1910–20s)
Zhuangshi 装饰 (Decoration)
zhuangshumei 装束美 (Beautiful, latest attire)
Ziluolan 紫罗兰 (The Violet Pictorial)
Zuoyinan 作衣难 (Difficulty in making clothes)

Index

Page numbers in **bold** indicate a Figure.